ETHNIC STUDIES
An Introduction

FOURTH EDITION

Edited by

Gregory Yee Mark ■ Boatamo Mosupyoe ■ Brian Baker
■ Julie López Figueroa

California State University—Sacramento

Kendall Hunt
publishing company

Kendall Hunt
publishing company

www.kendallhunt.com
Send all inquiries to:
4050 Westmark Drive
Dubuque, IA 52004-1840

ISBN 978-1-7924-5838-5

Published in the United States of America

Contents

RACE, CLASS AND GENDER

IDENTITY AND INSTITUTIONS

RESPONSE AND RESPONSIBILITY

About the Authors

Gregory Yee Mark

Gregory Yee Mark is a professor of Ethnic Studies at California State University, Sacramento. In January 1969, as an undergraduate student at University of California, Berkeley, he was a part of the Third World Liberation Front that went on strike (**the "Third World Strike"**) at the Berkeley campus to create the discipline of Ethnic Studies. During this transformative student strike, he was tear-gassed, shot at by the police, and most importantly, he learned the true meaning of creating a relevant education for all people. He is a pioneer in the field of Asian American studies.

Starting as a student, Dr. Mark was a community organizer and activist in Berkeley and Oakland. In 1969, in Oakland, he founded the East Bay Chinese Youth Council, which addressed the various challenges of Chinatown youth such as gangs. He continued this role as a community advocate and educator while a professor in San Jose, Honolulu, and Sacramento. He has fought for social justice, better education for the underserved, preventing youth violence in the Asian American community, and a broader and more correct interpretation of American history.

Dr. Mark is a pioneer in service learning, and in 2001, he founded the 65th Street Corridor Community Collaborative Project, which has served over 38,000 Sacramento residents. In 2021, this Project celebrates its 20th anniversary of service to the community.

This anthology, *ETHNIC STUDIES: An Introduction,* examines American history, education, ethnic identity, and the continued struggle for social justice through the lens of people of color in the United States. Last, the chapters in this publication, begin to bring to the forefront topics that have been largely ignored, but are essential for students to learn so that they can service their own communities.

Boatamo Mosupyoe

My name in itself tells a story. Boatamo, my name, means *Bonyana ba Mosupyoe bo ata mo, Ati.* I am the third born child and a girl of the six children born to Maropeng and Ramahatisa Mosupyoe. My two sisters, Mmule and Matshego (MG as we fondly refer to my elder second born sister), precede me in birth. As a third born child and girl my parents gave me a name that means I am a "part of the womanhood that enriches the Mosupyoe family." I was motivated by my mother's courage when I became aware of the oppressive system of apartheid that South African Blacks were subjected to. I have many memories of my mother confronting the inhumane treatment of Black people in South Africa by white South Africans. One of the earliest is when I witnessed in a grocery store my mother intervening when an older African Woman who could be about 80 years old miscalculated the cost of the items she had bought. It turned out she was short by R50.00 (approximately four dollars). The younger cashier, who happened to be white, verbally abused the woman with racist language and threatened to call the police. After failing to convince the white cashier to cancel the transaction, my mom gave the white cashier the R50.00 and the older African woman was able to get her items. My mom then asked my youngest sister—Morakane, and me to load grocery carts. By the time we finished, we had four carts full of groceries that we presented to the same cashier. The cashier spent about 45 minutes on the cash register entering "our" groceries. At the end, my mother told the cashier that she did not have enough money to pay for the groceries and dared her to call the police. As we walked away, my mom told the cashier to ask her boss to give her a lesson in "ubuntu" (humanity). Of course, my mom had enough money to pay for the groceries; she was not going to walk away without making a strong statement against the indignity visited upon the older African woman. The white cashier changed colors and her jaw dropped—she was speechless.

Such acts of resistance from my mom made me understand why I am named Boatamo Ati. I endure, question, resist, and strive for justice and equality. Majoring in anthropology for my undergraduate at University of the North in South Africa was not easy. It was hard to listen to a lecture that was a pure misrepresentation of our culture. It was even more difficult to listen to a lecture on racial classification presented as a scientific fact that Blacks are biologically inferior. I endured and continued with my education in the very discipline so that I should teach the same lecture differently. I do. I was motivated and obtained a PhD from University of California Berkeley. I became a professor at Sac State and a part of Ethnic Studies where I was not only able to teach and contribute toward the transformation of knowledge production and distribution but became the first Black woman to chair or head the department. I write books and articles, and organize international conferences on the prevention of genocide. Yes, the courage that I learned from my mother carried me when I lost my husband (Simmy) and a son (Thamsanqa) on the same day and while I was pregnant. I raised two girls, Palesa and Lesego, and lost Lesego. Today, Ethnic Studies is a requirement at the 23 California state universities. I was part of the Task Force that worked toward making this milestone a reality. These achievements did not come easy, but because I was named Boatamo Ati, a reflection of Mosupyoe womanhood, I endured. In one of the languages that I speak the saying goes *Leina lebe seromo*, your name most of the time reflects who you are.

Brian Baker

Howah!
Mashkiiziibii Kitchigami Anishinaabe

Aaniin! I am *Anishinaabe*, generally known as *Ojibway* or *Chippewa*. I am from *Odanah*, a tribal community located on the Bad River Indian Reservation in Wisconsin. Although I currently reside in Sacramento, California, Bad River remains relevant because it is connected to my indigenous homeland, the Lake Superior region, which became divided by the Canada–US boundary. I left Bad River to attend graduate school, a journey that led me to Stanford University where I completed my PhD. My experiences in graduate school, even when wrought with difficulty, were empowering and eye-opening, which I now understand as being integral to my journey. I remember having a conflict (aka *intellectual discourse*) over ideas and arguments having to do with perspectives on "race" and "ethnicity" with a tenured professor, a disagreement connected to how I experienced and understood the world as a Native person. It had been communicated to me that I should not be researching and writing about Native Americans because they were "too close" to me, albeit a strange and unfounded claim when you consider the fact that white people have been researching, writing, and teaching about white people since time immemorial. The disagreement became larger than life when that professor asserted authority and power, claiming that they were "recognized as the expert in the field of race and ethnicity" while refusing to answer my questions, dismissing my ideas, and kicking me out of their office. This went on for a few months, and unfortunately, I needed the approval of the expert. My advisor, who intervened and had previously pointed out that "conformity is your friend" in another instance where trouble happened to find me, told me that I had "a chip on my shoulder" and that it was in my best interest to listen to the expert. I quickly transformed their dominant cultural metaphor into an indigenous one, telling them about the *little people* in *Anishinaabe* oral tradition and storytelling where "a chip" being referenced by them was actually "a little Chippewa" on my shoulder who was my guide and voice of reason. In the end, while still entangled in a conflict with a tenured professor who withheld their approval yet supported by a glowing recommendation from my advisor, I was awarded a Fulbright Scholarship to support my dissertation research based on the ideas and arguments that got me into trouble with the expert in the field of race and ethnicity in the first place. I am a citizen of the Bad River (*Mashkiiziibii*) Band of Lake Superior (*Kitchigami*) Chippewa (*Anishinaabe*) Indians. *Howah!*

Why History Matters to Me

Julie López Figueroa, Ph. D.
Professor of Ethnic Studies

As the daughter of two Mexican-migrant parents (Macedonio and Maria), storytelling was so central to my life growing up. While I was too young to grasp the meaning of the storytelling, I so enjoyed listening to my parents individually and together share their lived experiences. The way they strung words together caused me to laugh, cry, or feel inspired. As a first-generation college student preparing to move away to college, living away from my family was not going to be easy. Reflecting on the lived histories my parents shared—about why and how they immigrated to the United States, my Dad's contribution as a Bracero during World War II, my Mom's courage to be the President of PTA at my elementary school with support of an interpreter, how they were migrant farmworkers that transitioned to cannery work to provide stability for their children—led me to realize that going to college would directly honor my parents' legacy of courage. Contending with a reality of being poor, not speaking English, and not having a formal education—as was the case for my parents—there is a level of vulnerability that could easily transform into fear. But, their lived histories were showing me how to live, really live with purpose, not fear.

Harnessing the courage, inspiration, and strength led me to graduate from the University of California, Davis with a double major in Chicana and Chicano studies and sociology, then evolved to completing an MA degree in education from the University of California, Santa Cruz, and finally led me to obtain a PhD in social and cultural studies in education from the University of California, Berkeley. While I am grateful for the numerous mentors and friends that I met along the way to show me how to academically succeed at each stage of my academic career, the emotional strength and tenacity that moved me forward as a first-generation student was nourished entirely by my parents' lived histories.

As a professor in ethnic studies, this discipline serves as one doorway to historical revisionism, while at the same time recovers dignity and humanity of the communities we study. History is not just about the past, but rather constantly being created through the ways we make sense of and respond to the world around us. Toggling between the past and the present generously positions us to make a choice to either appreciate what we have lived through or take for granted what has transpired. As someone who strongly believes that history manifests ideologies though action, I think it is extremely important to not only bridge the lives of my students to the broader events in history but also invite them to make an intimate connection through their lived experiences. To this point, I invite all of us to imagine a world where we can dare to appreciate, and dare to value history that may not be our own, but if we listen carefully provides us with a deeper sense of ourselves and greater connection to each other.

Introduction/
Perspectives

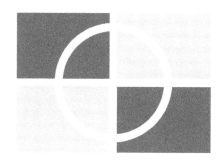

Dedication

In honor of the memory of Dr. Alexandre Kimenyi and his contribution to Linguistics, African Studies, Social Justice and Human Rights.

Photo courtesy of California State University, Sacramento.

Introduction to Ethnic Studies

Brian Baker and Julie López Figueroa

Between December 15 and 28, 2003, a group of 72 Lakota people traveled more than 300 miles on horseback in the cold South Dakota winter weather.[1] Why did they do this at this time of year? These *Future Generations Riders* of Lakota traversed the same path taken by Chief Bigfoot whose goal was to find refuge among relatives on the Pine Ridge Indian Reservation. On foot, and carrying only what they could take with them, Chief Bigfoot and over 350 Lakota, mostly women, children, and elders, made this journey in 1890. Many of the Lakota were weak due to illness and hunger; Chief Bigfoot himself was ill with pneumonia. Despite this, they continued walking through the winter snow because they had fled and were in search of safety.

Eventually, the U.S. Calvary caught up with this so-called band of *renegade Indians* at Wounded Knee Creek on the Pine Ridge Reservation. Completely surrounded by American troops, without weapons, and exhausted from their 300 mile trek on foot, the Indians wondered what would happen next on the morning of December 28. When a single gun shot was heard, the soldiers commenced shooting indiscriminately. The Lakota dispersed and ran in every direction. Unarmed, they were chased by soldiers on horseback. When the shooting stopped, more than a few hundred Lakota people were on the ground in an area that stretched nearly four square miles. Following this tragedy a blizzard set in and the Lakota who were not already dead were left there to die by the American military. For the Lakota who survived as witnesses to this act of terror, they had no choice but to follow a life defined by the laws and policies dictated by the American government toward American Indians.

In 2003, the descendants of those who survived the Wounded Knee massacre followed in the footsteps left by their relatives under the leadership of Chief Bigfoot in 1890. Along the way, the Lakota riders on horseback could feel the presence of their ancestors who lost their lives. The *Future Generations Riders* has become an annual journey of discovery and healing for many contemporary

Lakota since 1986, an important event that includes many children. This event not only reflects the relevance of historical memory and grief to contemporary identity; it is also an example of how an ethnic group asserts identity and culture.[2] According to Ron His Horse Is Thunder, president of Sitting Bull College, and one of the event organizers:

> *For 100 years, our young people have been taught that they needed to forget about being Indian in order to succeed. Today we're trying to reverse that by letting them know that our culture is important and that being Indian is a great thing. The ride is part of that process.[3]*

For the Lakota, the massacre continues to be an important memory and marker of their history and identity, and it has come to symbolize ethnic persistence and cultural pride.

Along with Lakota honoring of their ancestors, there are other examples of movements that have elicited controversy. A Day Without Immigrants March that occurred all over the United States on May 1, 2006, in which over one million Latinos from such cities as New York, Los Angeles, Sacramento, and Chicago, demonstrated for better immigration reform to challenge, contest, and recover lost, marginalized, and distorted histories. On this note, the use of Latinos versus Latina/o/x reflects the historical accuracy of the time in 2006. More specifically, this was a national grass-roots movement intended to bring public attention to the presence and contribution of immigrant workers in the U.S. economy.[4] Cities like Chicago and New York were especially important cities because they attempted to disrupt the practice of ascribing immigrant workers solely to Latinos. Non-Latino immigrant workers from Europe, Asia, and Africa marched in solidarity given their own understanding of how the same issues impact their quality of life differently. Anti-immigrant sentiments largely inform this nation's identity and process when confronting a new people. Tactics of intimidation against Latinos continue beyond the issue of the border to most recently include the dispersal of thousands of letters written in Spanish to Hispanics in Orange County, California, warning that immigrants could be sent to jail for submitting a ballot in the upcoming governor's election between Arnold Schwarzenegger and Phil Angelides.[5] No doubt a response to public acts of intimidation will forge a new beginning and bring an added complexity to the way we celebrate and practice culture.

These actions open up a public space to gain visibility in a world where these communities and its heroes and heroines are diminished into small paragraphs or conveniently lost in the history textbooks. When communities choose to respond, that is a prime opportunity to recover the truth and share a piece of shelved U.S. history. Ethnic Studies unapologetically puts forth the campaign that we must have a better and more accurate view of history in order to claim to truly be a United States. Beyond holidays and other significant events that define our culture and national identity as Americans, a number of unique and culturally specific ethnic events are held around the country. In fact, it would be impossible to list all of the cultural events that acknowledge and/or celebrate various aspects of the history, culture, and identity of all ethnic groups in America. Once subject to more extreme discrimination at the institutional and individual level in American history, contemporary African Americans, Asian Americans, Latino Americans, and Native Americans continue to assert their ethnic identities and play an important role in the remaking of contemporary American identity and culture. While America has always been a nation marked by racial and ethnic diversity, the difference in the contemporary world is that this diversity is now recognized and sanctioned as a vital and vibrant dimension of American society. America's future seems to be one that will be more multicultural and multilingual.

The Dynamics of Ethnicity, Ethnocentrism, and Racism

The 1960s and 1970s were important for many reasons, particularly due to the politics around race, class, and gender. Before the 1960s, *institutionalized racism,* supported by law and politics, defined and structured race relations in America. For example, it was *politically correct* for African Americans to sit in the back of the bus or eat at separate lunch counters before the civil rights movement in the American South. Americans of Asian, Latino, and Native (indigenous) descent were also the targets of such racism that shaped and limited their life opportunities in terms of education, housing, and occupation, among other things. In fact, dominant ethnocentric justifications played a key role in explaining and perpetuating racial and ethnic inequality. Dominant sentiments expressed in American culture defined Native Americans as ignorant and lazy people in need of protection, a powerful idea that was sanctioned in the historical development of Federal Indian law and policy under the guise of a *guardian* to *ward* relationship. Through the Bureau of Indian Affairs, Americans presumed that dominant society was burdened with the responsibility to care for American Indians because they could not do so on their own. In fact, the *white man's burden* and *manifest destiny* were the basic tenets of American political culture that also adversely impacted the daily lives of African Americans, Asian Americans, and Latinos. However, in the face of exclusion and oppression, and even under conditions of powerlessness, ethnic minorities survived and have successfully continued to define and assert their ethnic identity.

In a society where income and occupation continue to be important factors in how Americans gain access to health, housing, and education, to name but a few, socioeconomic status plays a central role in determining quality of life. Despite positive changes in recent decades, such as the implementation of Affirmative Action law and policy, to reconfigure race and ethnic relations in the United States, the fact is that racial socioeconomic inequality remains the reality. For example, the median family income for Hispanic ($26,502) and African American ($32,180) men was far below that for white men ($44,525) in 2001.[6] Do these income differences reflect something about the continuing role of race and ethnicity in the United States? How can we explain these differences? Further, while the median family income for white women ($31,575) is above that for Hispanic ($26,502) and African American women ($27,335), comparatively, women overall still earned less when compared to men in 2001. Do the differences in median family income between men and women reflect something about the continuing significance of gender inequality in the United States? How can we account for the differences? To what extent have the dynamics of ethnic and gender inequality been altered?

Culture, Experience and Contributions

The historical experience of African, Asian, Latino, and Native Americans relative to U.S. society is necessary to sufficiently understand current events and circumstances in the dynamics of ethnic relations. Due to their own unique historical circumstances and contributions to the making of America, each group possesses its own unique culture and historical memory. At the same time, we must take note of the fact that these groups are pan-ethnic identities. For example, the Asian American population as a group reflects something about dominant ideas regarding a race while simultaneously including distinct groups. Asian American as a category of ethnicity encompasses groups that have their own culture and identity, as in the case of people of Asian Indian, Japanese, Filipino, Korean, or Chinese descent. While this is not an exhaustive representation of all the distinct ethnic groups that come under the category of Asian American, there is something about American society that brings them together on some level *as* Asian American. While there is an element of experience and culture that brings a people together as Asian American on some level, it is also important to pay attention to the fact that there is diversity in the identities of the various groups that make up Asian Americans in the United States. This is also true for African Americans, Latino Americans, and Native Americans.

Through an understanding of their historical experience, we can also highlight the contributions that African Americans, Asian Americans, Latino Americans, and Native Americans have made to America. For example, although Japanese Americans were ousted from their homes and pushed out of their businesses to live in *evacuation camps,* and while Filipinos in America had the status of noncitizens, adult males from both groups joined the military and fought for the United States during World War II. Thus, while subject to conditions of oppression in the United States, Filipino and Japanese Americans made a positive contribution to the American war effort. In fact, a closer and more inclusive examination of American history reveals that Asian Americans, African Americans, Latino Americans, and Native Americans have all made a number of important contributions to the United States in addition to their own ethnic communities.

What Is Ethnic Studies?

The *National Ethnic Studies Association* defines Ethnic Studies as an "interdisciplinary forum for scholars and activists concerned with the national and international dimensions of ethnicity."[7] Given the politics of the 1960s and 1970s, coupled with the emergence of a vocal and visible population of African American, Asian American, Latino American, and Native Americans students attending colleges and universities, Ethnic Studies came into existence as an outcome of activism during this time period. As a discipline, Ethnic Studies has consciously cut across traditional academic disciplines as a necessary strategy to highlight the unique experiences of ethnic communities, and to build and strengthen connections with those communities outside of the academic institution. As a result, the voices and ideas of ethnic peoples, scholars and nonscholars alike, have changed academic institutions and affected the production of knowledge and ideas.

This volume, Ethnic Studies: An Introduction is designed to reflect the interdisciplinary nature of Ethnic Studies – the readings are drawn from academic fields in the humanities and social sciences. A few first-person narratives are also included, so we can get a sense of how individuals experience their ethnic group status. Overall, the readings in this book are meant to provide students with a foundation in Ethnic Studies. Since the last edition of this volume was published in 2011, we recognize that terms have changed such as Latina/o to Latina/o/x. However, we know that historically we must sustain the accuracy of the language for its period.

This book is divided into five sections. The first section, "Perspectives," is intended to provide students with theoretical concepts to foster critical view on the way U.S. society is constructed. This section openly invites the reader to examine and reexamine not just individual roles, beliefs, attitudes, and actions, but how the collective gathering of those individual voices can either lead to experiencing greater freedoms or can collective mislead us into thinking that a particular situation is normal because of the peer pressure of maintaining the status quo. The readings are meant to incite critical reflection to recognize the tensions of living within the United States given its ideal way of life versus the actual realities. In order to fully understand the significance of ethnic identity, we need to pay attention to the fact that ethnic identity is fluid and dynamic, subject to external and internal ethnic group pressures. Why do you believe what you believe about the world? In what ways is your world socially constructed that your perspective is justified?

The second section, "History," is intended to provide students with a basic understanding of the distinct histories of Asian Americans, African Americans, Latino Americans, and Native Americans. Comparatively, how are these histories similar on the one hand and dissimilar on the other? What can we learn from these histories?

The third section addresses the intersection of "Race, Class, and Gender" as the primary dimensions of stratification in the United States. The purpose of this section is not only to provide students with an understanding of how individuals and groups gain access to valued resources in society, but also to demonstrate that race, class, and gender play a key role in that process. In what ways do race, class, and gender continue to be important dimensions of inequality in the United States? In what ways do race, class, and gender intersect and why are those intersections important?

The purpose of the fourth section, "Identity and Institutions," is to demonstrate the various circumstances under which ethnic groups not only define themselves on their own terms, but also show how external conditions affect this process. This section helps bring complexity to the ongoing debate of explanations that want to relegate racial/ethnic issues to the category of cultural problems to resolve. Not only does this section highlight the coercive means by which institutions shape identity, but there is an example that illuminates how, even after institutions are physically dismantled, the psychological impact in terms of our own colonization is still in the process of recovery. How were communities racialized in order to justify the social workings of our society?

The final section, "Response and Responsibility," addresses the question, given that American society continues to manage and deal with politics relating to ethnic identity: What are the responsibilities of Americans as citizens? To what extent do Americans contribute to problems relating to ethnicity by participating in and accepting popularized images and stereotypes? For example, one issue has to do with the use of Native Americans as mascots in sports. Why is this a problem and what should be the appropriate response by society? Another issue has to do with the problem of gender inequality within social movement organizations during the Civil Rights movement of the 1960s. Why was gender inequality a problem in a movement that emphasized racial equality?

Notes

[1] Fedarko, Kevin (2004, May 16). This ride is about our future. *The Sacramento Bee,* Parade section, pp. 4–6.

[2] Yellow Horse Brave Heart, Mara, & DeBruyn, Lemyra (2000). The American Indian holocaust: Healing historical unresolved grief. *American Indian and Alaska Native Mental Health Research, 8*(2), 60–62.

[3] Fedarko, p. 5.

[4] Keen, Judy, & Kasindorf, Martin (2006, May 1). 1 million rally for immigrants. *USA Today.*

[5] Marquez, Jeremiah (2006, October 17). Intimidating voting letter to U.S. Hispanics investigated. *Herald Tribune.*

[6] Feagin & Feagin, page 82.

[7] National Ethnic Studies Association, http://www.ethnicstudies.org.

ETHNIC IDENTITIES RECONCILIATION VOICE MATTERS
INCLUSION EMPOWERMENT & DECOLONIZATION
STRUGGLE SOVEREIGNTY SOCIAL JUSTICE HOPE
ETHNIC STUDIES: AN INTRODUCTION

Questions for Ethnic Studies: An Introduction

The questions are intended to support the fostering of critical and engaged readers. Each section offers a set of framing questions and reflection questions. Framing questions are meant to prepare the reader for the coming section and invite world experiences while reflection questions at the end of each section inquire about what they learned, invite the reader to question what else could be learned from the experience, and assist in the transition to the following section.

Suggested questions have been identified to initiate a personal and classroom dialogue. Students are encouraged to address those questions for which space was provided. Faculty and students are invited to use these questions to build a rich discussion in reference to the readings. Faculty and students are invited to consider addressing optional questions to build upon personal and class discussions. Please select the questions that support students to become critical thinkers as well as skilled readers. All questions are meant to address the blank spots and blind spots as well as to maximize the instrumental value of this book. As faculty working within the discipline of Ethnic Studies, we mindfully assembled a volume that invites readers to engage both historical and contemporary issues informing and surrounding identity. Respecting the unique realities confronting the communities discussed in this volume, we intentionally aimed to evoke a sense of empathy and solidarity so that when you read the words like Black Lives Matter, Stop Asian Hate, Land Back, and No Borders listed, and capped off with the word Solidarity, these terms would reassert the humanity and dignity of someone else's lived experiences.

Pre-Book Exercise

1. What do you know or what have you heard about Ethnic Studies? Turn to a neighbor and share your impressions. Jot down three adjectives or thoughts.

2. What might be some assumptions made either by you or someone you know regarding who might best relate to this book? Please jot down at least two examples to discuss in class.

3. Upon reviewing the table of contents, the readings are combined historical and narrative accounts. Do you know the difference? Why do you think the editors offered this combined reading? Provide a brief explanation. (Optional)

4. Referencing the table of contents, which are the readings you think you might know something about and why? What are the readings you might know less about and why? Do the selected titles prompt images, sounds, stories, or adjectives? What are they?

5. Setting aside for one moment the question regarding familiarity with the readings, consider yourself a member within this society. How do you think you could use these readings to enrich your own life experiences as a member of this society and/or relate to someone you know nothing about? Turn to a partner and together come up with a list of four ways you could use the readings. (Optional)

Framing Questions

1. What is the value of telling and listening to history within family, among your friends, or people you consider to be important in your life? What is the role of history? Please share a piece of history that has influenced who you are today.

2. What are the various kinds of resources used to tell history? Do you rely on books, newspapers, oral traditions, movies, pictures? What is your cultural practice for learning and building knowledge? (Optional)

3. To what degree do you think not knowing about your history influences how you hear, interpret, and appreciate someone else's history? (Optional)

4. To what degree do you understand that how you speak or what is referred to as everyday discourse reflects your gender, race, class, and ethnicity? (Optional)

5. To what degree do you understand that your gender, race, class, and ethnicity influence how you interpret the readings in this particular kind of book? Please provide some examples to illustrate your point.

6. To what degree can you recognize that how you are perceived and treated in the world is mediated by gender, race, class, and ethnicity? (Optional)

Reflection Questions

1. Given the definition of Ethnic Studies, was it similar to or different from what you discussed prior to the introduction? (Optional)

2. To what extent do you think it is important for you to know the background of the author who writes about the history you read? (Optional)

3. Do you think any and all information is value-free? (Optional)

4. What is the process you employ to differentiate between biased and unbiased information? Provide a brief explanation to explain the process you employ to discriminate between biased and unbiased information.

5. To what extent do you know about the racial/ethnic history of your own community compared to the history of other racial/ethnic communities? What either facilitated or hindered your knowing more or less given your experience in school prior to college? Provide a brief explanation.

Framing Questions

1. How do you define perspectives? What is important about having a perspective? (Optional)

2. When you think of the elderly, the young, the poor, the wealthy, the college educated, which perspectives are valued more than others? Who gets to determine which perspectives are valuable and which can be dismissed?

3. What might be the reasons that some people have more than one perspective on the world versus others who do not? Do you think culture, language, age, generational differences, and so forth have anything to do with having multiple perspectives?

4. What are the elements that shape your perspective? Has your perspective changed with age and what are the positive sides and down sides of having a perspective? (Optional)

"We're Going Out. Are You With Us?" The Origins of Asian American Studies

Gregory Yee Mark

 Introduction

Scholars trace back the beginning of Ethnic Studies in the United States to the studentled strikes at San Francisco State College, now San Francisco State University (November 1968), and University of California, Berkeley ("Berkeley") (January 1969). At most universities and colleges, Asian American studies (AAS) is one of the major components of Ethnic Studies. I grew up in Berkeley and Oakland, California, and the beginning for me was the summer of 1968. I was a student at UC Berkeley and majored in criminology. Earlier that year, I transferred from Merritt Community College, which was on Grove Street (now Martin Luther King, Jr. Way) in Oakland. Three events that summer played key roles in creating and defining the Asian American Movement and my own lifelong interest and commitment to Ethnic Studies.

The first was a family journey that I still travel today. From age 6 to 19, I lived in Berkeley and my grandparents lived two blocks away on California Street. One day, in June 1968, my grandmother, Violet Wong, asked me to go downstairs with her to the basement and she pulled out an old film canister, which contained three reels of a 35 mm film. As she was pointing to the canister, grandmother told me, "Gregory, you do something with this." I took the film to Palmer's Camera Shop in downtown Berkeley to a childhood friend who worked there. From the decaying reels, he saved 30 minutes of film and transferred it to 16 mm film. Five years later, at our 1973 family Christmas party, 60 family members viewed a screening/showing of the 1916 silent movie *The Curse of Quon Gwon*, the very first Asian American film. Grandmother starred in the black/white film, which costarred her sister-in-law, Marion Wong. Marion played the villainess but, most importantly, *The Curse of Quon Gwon* was her creation. A unique aspect about this motion picture is that the key actors and people behind the scenes were Chinese American women. In fact, three generations of women in my family are in this pioneering film. Marion conceived the idea, raised the money, wrote the script, and directed the film. Today, I am still "doing something with it." In 2006, *The Curse of Quon Gwon* was selected to the Library of Congress's National Film Registry. I continue doing research on this motion picture, and I hope to transform the remnants of the film into an educational tool to examine the early Asian American community via film.

The second historical event was the founding of the Asian American Political Alliance (AAPA) in Berkeley by Yuji Ichioka and Emma Gee. I attended AAPA meetings and activities and considered myself a fringe member. The AAPA became the major political organizing arm of a large contingent of UC Berkeley's Asian American students and represented these students in the Third World Liberation Front coalition. AAPA played a key role on campus in Asian American student visibility and leadership.

The third historical event was the August 17, 1968 demonstration in San Francisco Chinatown (Umemoto, 2007, p. 33). The purpose of this demonstration, which was my first protest, was to bring attention to the numerous social problems that plagued San Francisco Chinatown. We wanted to push the Chinatown establishment to take action and make the public, especially government agencies, aware of these hidden social issues. I remember the sign that I held; it said, "Look around You, Chinatown is a **GHETTO**." This peaceful demonstration was especially important because it brought together community folks, university students (primarily from UC Berkeley and San Francisco State College), and even AAPA members.

The 1968 San Francisco Chinatown demonstration for the first time brought together Asian American community members and student activists advocating for their communities. Many of these students later became leaders in community mobilization efforts such as the International Hotel (I-Hotel) Struggle, Oakland Chinatown youth organizations, and Japanese American senior citizen programs in the cities of Berkeley and San Francisco. These community service projects have left their legacies through an extensive network of community-based organizations and created a pipeline for young Asian Americans to become involved in today's social justice issues and social services. For example, the multiservice Asian Health Services in Oakland Chinatown can trace its origins to 1970 and young Asian American activists.

The Asian Experience in America: Yellow Identity Symposium

In November 1968, 3 months after the San Francisco Chinatown demonstration, I was talking with five other Asian American students in the Chinese Students Club (CSC) office, on campus in Eshleman Hall. At that time, I was president of the CSC. In 1968–1969, Asian American students made up 10% of UC Berkeley's student population. There were four major Asian American student organizations: the CSC (primarily American born Chinese members); the Chinese Students Association (CSA; primarily Chinese Foreign born and immigrant students); the Nisei Students Club (NSC; Japanese American students); and Pi Alpha Phi (the Asian American fraternity). The first three organizations had offices on the fifth floor of Eshleman Hall.

On that November Friday afternoon, six male members from CSC, CSA, and NSC were talking about campus life. We started to talk about dating and one of the men, Gary, talked about a beautiful Asian American woman on campus who was from Sacramento. All the men knew who she was because she truly stood out on campus. In a dejected fashion, Gary told us that he had asked her out but she firmly said no. He then asked her why she wouldn't go out with him. Gary said that she told him, "I only go out with White men." Then, the six men let out a spontaneous groan. For the next 2 hours, I led my first discussion dealing with Asian American men and their relationships with Asian American women. A significant part of our discussion was about a topic, which later became known as "Asian American Identity." After our impromptu discussion, Gary and another friend said that they really enjoyed the discussion and gained a lot from it. As I was going down the elevator, I thought to myself, *Why not expand the discussion beyond the six of us?*

As president of the CSC, I called together a cabinet meeting and asked the members what they thought about the Club organizing a conference about Asian Americans. No one wanted to take the lead. At the first planning meeting, about 10 people attended; the next meeting, about twenty, and by December 1968, there were 60 people on the conference planning/implementation committee.

On January 11, 1969, CSC and some of the other Asian American clubs hosted the "Asian Experience in America: Yellow Identity Symposium" which was attended by 800 Asian Americans from around the United States, but mainly from California. This meeting was the first national conference that was organized by Asian Americans, about Asian Americans, and was for Asian Americans. I served as the emcee and we had three keynote speakers. They were Dr. Paul Takagi, Isao Fujimoto, and Dr. Stanford Lyman. The topics ranged from Asian American history to the socioeconomic political status of Asian Americans. Many of the Asian Americans who helped plan the conference and attended the meeting later also participated in the Berkeley Third World Strike.

From that Friday afternoon in November to the day of the conference, I knew the conference was going to be very important. I just did not realize how important. Nor did I comprehend its long-term importance. In fact, noted criminologist and Asian American scholar-activist Dr. Takagi, the symposium's lead keynote speaker, often laughed years later with the remark, "Can you believe that?" regarding the "boldness" in using the term "Yellow" for "Asian Americans," since it was not commonly used at the time. When Dr. Takagi was asked in May 2011 to reflect

asian experience / yellow identity

From: Asian Students of Chinese Students Club and Nisei Students Club 509-600 Eshleman Hall, University of California, Berkeley, 94720, 642-4216

Bring this, your invitation, to the 1st Asian Experience in America, Sat. Jan. 11, 1969, 9:00am-4:30pm Pauley Ballroom, ASUC Building UC Berkeley.

Asian Experience in America/Yellow Identity Symposium Program Heading, University of California, Berkeley, January 11, 1969

on his life's work, he wrote, "Perhaps Greg Mark asking me to keynote an event that he titled, The Yellow Symposium, was the beginning of my career!" (Takagi & Shank, 2012, p. 38). Here, Takagi was referring to his criminology career that took a significant turn from traditional and radical criminology to AAS scholarly activism. To Dr. Takagi, the Yellow Identity Symposium was so significant, that he stated, "That symposium was the true beginning of Asian American Studies" (Takagi & Shank, 2012, p. 39). By this, he meant the symposium was one of the primary catalysts in initiating the formation of the field of AAS.

The noted "Dean" of Chinese American Studies, historian Him Mark Lai, also attended. Just before he passed away in May 2009, in conversation at his home with the author of this chapter, Him Mark proclaimed this first-ever Asian American conference's historical significance when he said, "It was an awakening."

The Sacramento Connection

Another Asian American activist who attended the "Yellow Identity Symposium" was California State University, Sacramento (Sac State) student Wayne Maeda. In May 2011, Maeda wrote,

Sac State 42 years ago was a place that had its political awareness shaped by the Civil Rights Movement, the war in Vietnam and the Black Power movement. It was, after all, in Sacramento in 1967, that Black Panthers carried guns into the Capitol. However, it was events in 1968 that shaped many of us who were just students then. 1968 began with the Tet offensive where the Viet Cong attacked across Vietnam with impunity, followed by revelation of Mai Lai massacre cover up, assassinations of Martin Luther King and Robert Kennedy, Mayor Daly's thugs turned loose at the Democratic conventions in Chicago and San Francisco State and UC Berkeley campuses shut down in a push for Ethnic Studies. So there was a core of us becoming politically aware of issues of social justice and inequalities. But it was not until the 'Asian American Experience: Yellow Identity Symposium' held in January 1969 that we began to think in terms of Asians in American and our identity. A number of us came back from this first ever conference on Asian Americans even more focused and dedicated to push for Ethnic Studies at Sac State. We consolidated a coalition of Black, Chicano,

Native American and white radical students to push for hiring minority and women faculty, and fundamental change in curriculum.

The timing of the "Yellow Identity Symposium" was significant for another reason. During the symposium's lunch break, my fellow classmate in criminology, Maurice Williams, came by to see me. Maurice was a good friend who took me to African American parties and restaurants, and likewise, I took him to Asian American parties and restaurants. Originally, he was a student athlete recruited to play football at Cal (UC Berkeley). Maurice was the Black Student Union (BSU) liaison with other student groups. So Maurice told me that at last night's (Friday, January 10, 1969) BSU meeting, "We met last night and decided that we are going out. Are you with us?" I told Maurice, "Yes, we are with you." In other words, I was telling him that the Asian Americans students would be part of the strike, too. On January 19, 1969, the Third World Liberation Front began the Third World Strike at the University of California, Berkeley.

The Fight for Ethnic Studies:
The Third World Liberation Front

The Third World Liberation Front (TWLF) student coalition went on strike for the creation of a Third World College that would incorporate four programs: AAS, Black Studies, Chicano Studies, and Native American Studies. A significant part of the strike agenda was to achieve individual and community self-determination, social justice, service to the community, and to end racism. Third World (TW) was a term adopted from Frantz Fanon's (2004) book *The Wretched of the Earth*. To the strikers, TW meant not only the underdeveloped countries of the world but also the U.S. working class people of color.

In the first 2 weeks of the strike, it was exciting: peaceful picketing, marching around campus, listening to speeches from community folks and older student leaders, and handing out leaflets in front of classroom and administrative buildings. We had to have moving picket lines and not block the entrance to any buildings. We held our signs up proudly and over and over again shouted, "On Strike, Shut It Down, On Strike, Shut It Down!" and "Power to the People!" I remember the Asian American contingent holding long planning meetings to plan for the next days' strike events. Meetings sometimes lasted virtually the whole night. Our representatives also met with the other Coalition members to agree on the day's and even the week's strategies.

As the strike progressed, there was an increasing law enforcement presence. In the first week or so, it was the campus police and folks from the Dean of Students Office who monitored our activities. Next came the City of Berkeley Police Department, then a consortium of local police departments to augment the Berkeley Police Department, such as departments from Oakland and San Leandro, and then the California Highway Patrol joined them. Then the TWLF strategy changed from moving picket lines to what we called the "snake" which consisted of strikers moving around campus, making noise, and disrupting classes that still met. As the number of student strikers declined from the daily grind and stress, the "snake" tried to avoid law enforcement and be moving targets. As the strike progressed, the Alameda County Sheriffs or the "Blue Meanies" escalated the tension and violence even more. By the last few weeks of the Third World Strike, the National Guard was brought in with fixed bayonets attached to their rifles, and physical, violent confrontation became the daily standard mode of operation. They used tear gas and even brought in helicopters to tear-gas us. Of course, tear gas did not know the difference between a striker and a student going to class. The end result was the campus was shut down because of the increasingly heavy-handed law enforcement presence.

For the students the strike was very trying. In week six, I remember going to Cowell Hospital, the university student hospital, for treatment and the waiting area was filled with strikers. Everyone was just so tired, run down, and suffered from a lack of sleep and fatigue.

Around this time, I remember several personal low points in the strike. The first low point was the increasing violence. I personally believed in nonviolence and I still do. However, the strike was becoming increasingly more violent. Two major contributors were the Alameda County Sheriffs or the "Blue Meanies" and the National Guard. One day, from the fifth floor of Eshleman Hall, I looked down from the outdoor stairways balcony at the role of baton-carrying Sheriffs and fixed bayonets Guards trying to stare down protesters on the other side of Bancroft Ave. For some reason, one of the Sheriffs looked up and fired what I thought was a tear gas canister at me. I was not doing anything wrong or illegal, yet this man—this stranger—felt that he had the right to take a shot at me. It took all my self-control not to throw a chair down at him.

The second low point was a rumor that the strike was going to end—that the University Administration was going to meet our demands. One of the members of the Black Student Union, Charles wanted to celebrate on the steps of Sproul Hall (the administration building). He brought some watermelon and then he asked me if I had any opium. (And no, he wasn't joking about stereotypes of Blacks and Asian Americans.) I was so disappointed in Charles that he, a fellow striker, negatively stereotyped me with the old images of Chinese Americans as opium addicts and dealers. He thought that because I was Chinese American that I had access to opium. During the nineteenth century, the early Chinese pioneers to the United States were frequently accused of smuggling opium into the United States, operating opium dens and exposing/polluting White Americans to/with the drug.

Actually, in the late 1700s, the British, French, Americans, and most of the European powers smuggled opium into China, and by 1900, essentially, 27% of China's adult male population were opium addicts. So, when Charles asked me if I had any opium, I was really disappointed in him.

By week eight of the strike, the end of the Winter 1969 quarter, on March 15, 1969, the UC Berkeley Third World Strike ended. The TWLF and the University negotiated a compromise. The main demand was the creation of a Third World College. Instead, we ended up with four separate Ethnic Studies programs, which combined to become one department. Somehow, Black Studies worked out an independent arrangement with the administration and they became a separate Black Studies Program. I could not believe this—after this intense strike, a significant component of Ethnic Studies went off on its own.

By the end of the strike, I was getting tired from the daily demands to sustain the strike but also I was getting upset with outside elements in the Berkeley street community. As the strike progressed, they felt entitled to become involved with the TWLF strike. In the strike's last month, they used it as an excuse for violence and trashing the university. I felt that this outside element and law enforcement moved the strike more toward the confrontation mode than the strikers. Here, I learned a valuable lesson. Six years later, at San Jose State University, I was the director of the AAS Program. I led a takeover of President John Bunzel's office because he was threatening to take away some of the meager resources from AAS. During the takeover, in

the late afternoon, non-Asian Americans came to me and one of them said, "Let's break some windows and trash the administration building." I told them something to the effect of, "You don't tell us Asian Americans what to do. We determine our own strategies and our own destiny, and if you want, you can support us, but you don't tell us what to do." I never saw him or his friends again.

Sacramento State was highly impacted by the two Third World strikes. Professor Wayne Maeda recalled that

> *Beginning an Ethnic Studies program, hiring faculty, developing curriculum, and the general demand for fundamental change at the campus level was made infinitely less confrontational by enormous sacrifices of students and faculty at both SF State and UC Berkeley. Moreover, they provided us models for classes, curriculum, and they even came to Sac State to provide guidance and inspiration to us. Thus, we were able to institute the first Asian American course in the Fall 1970, which was team-taught.*

The Very First AAS Course in the United States

During the first week of the Winter 1969 quarter, we went "On Strike" and on Wednesday nights, the first ever AAS course, AAS 100X, met. Since we were "On Strike," we had to meet in one of the off-campus university's residence halls.

Of course, we could not violate our own strike by going to class on campus. There were 150 students enrolled in the class—and I was one of them.

Professor Paul Takagi was the instructor of record. However, it was a team-taught class in which the team included graduate students such as Floyd Huen, Ling-Chi Wang, Bing Tom, Alan Fong, and Richard Aoki. Class meetings were electric. There was this positive tension in the air that for the first time we were all meeting to learn about ourselves. Most students had attended Asian American weddings, baby parties, dances, and even funerals but now we were studying "Our History, Our Way" (the slogan of the University of Hawai'i at Manoa Ethnic Studies Department).

We, students, networked, studied, and discussed issues/topics that were relevant to our lives, and were simply awed by having the opportunity to validate our own and our family's lives. Since this was the first AAS class ever, there were no textbooks. Therefore, each week, we had lectures and frequently guest speakers were brought in such as Edison Uno who talked about the World War II Internment of Japanese Americans. Another time, a European American Anthropologist, George DeVos, spoke to the class. He came in with an arrogant attitude and was challenged by several students. The students questioned him regarding what gave him the right to tell us who we were. One of these students, Danny Li, is one of my close friends. He objected to the lecturer's "holier than-thou" tone and questioned "whether a non-Asian would have the insights of people of color who had experienced racial discrimination firsthand."

Danny later moved to Hawai'i in the fall of 1971 to continue graduate studies in Chinese History and he was involved in community-based organizations in Honolulu's Chinatown. These multiethnic residents were also facing "urban development" relocations, just like elderly Chinese American and Filipino American residents in the International Hotel (I-Hotel) in San Francisco's Chinatown. As with other involved Asian Americans, the strike and the movement provided Danny and many others a beginning of a lifelong commitment to end racism, fight for social injustice, and improve society.

Another person who was involved in the strike and AAS 100X was my childhood friend, Floyd Huen. Floyd was one of the early leaders for AAS. He wrote the first proposal for AAS and represented AAPA on the TWLF Central Strike Committee. This committee made the long- and short-run decisions for the Strikers and negotiated with the university administration. After AAS became a program at UC Berkeley, Floyd became its first program administrator (1969–1970).

Floyd had been one of the hardest working members of the Asian American student contingent. Prior to the TWLF Strike, Floyd fell in love with another student activist who was deeply involved in the strike, AAS 100X, and in general involved in the creation of AAS. Her name was Jean Quan. Jean was an undergraduate student in charge of communications during the Strike. At UC Berkeley, she cotaught the first Asian American Women's course with Emma Gee and edited and wrote the Asian Women's Journal. Later, in the mid-1980s, Quan was the Western Regional Coordinator of the Justice for Vincent Chin campaign. In 2011, Jean Quan became Mayor of Oakland.

January 1969 was truly a highpoint for me personally and for the Asian American Movement. "The Asian Experience in America: Yellow Identity Symposium" was not only successful but also the first national Asian American conference ever. AAS 100X was an amazing experience—it was very dynamic, exciting, and historical because it was the nation's first AAS class. I served as a volunteer teaching assistant (TA) for AAS 100X. In my section, I had 30 students. A group of the students and I compiled a resource directory, conducted an informal needs assessment survey, and started to network with individuals and organizations in Oakland Chinatown.

Service to the Community: Oakland Chinatown

During the middle of the strike, around February 1969, I started to reflect more about the roles that we, as Asian American students, should play to improve the quality of life in our communities. I thought about the needs in my own community—the community that had been a major part of my life—and what I could do as "an insider" to work on behalf of my own community. As a result, I started community service projects in the Oakland Asian American community, or specifically in the City's Chinatown.

I was born in Oakland and raised in both the cities of Oakland and Berkeley. As a child and young adult, my father frequently took me to Chinatown to visit with friends, eat Chinese food, and visit Chinese societies such as the Suey Sing Tong. As a young boy, I got haircuts from the barber on eighth Street, and this elderly Chinese woman barber gave children lollipops. I remember the corner grocery store at eighth and Webster. Its owners, Mr. and Mrs. Gee, frequently treated me to soda and salty plum crack seed.

As a part of the Asian American Movement, I felt that I could use my education to better serve my community. In fact, at this time, I decided to apply to the School of Criminology graduate program because I thought that I could be more effective in my community work with an advanced degree.

In 1965, Oakland began to experience what other major U.S. cities experienced as a result of the change in U.S. immigration policy created by the Civil Right movement inspired 1965 Immigration Reform Act. This dramatic increase in the Asian American population, in particular, initially impacted the Chinese American and Filipino American populations. As a result, by 1969, Oakland's Asian American community was undergoing a dramatic transition. Many new immigrants, especially Chinese, were moving into the Bay Area.

Oakland Chinatown attracted many newcomers, as demonstrated in the three Chinatown-serving neighborhood schools: Lincoln Elementary School, Westlake Junior High School, and Oakland Technical High School. As with San Francisco

Chinatown, there was a critical need for bilingual education, job training, and bilingual services such as in health, affordable housing, and youth programs. Inspired by the Civil Rights movement, the Asian American Movement and the Third World Strike, community-based organizations were created as early as the mid-1960s to address these needs.

During the last month of the Strike, I networked with Oakland Chinatown organizations such as the Chinese Presbyterian Church. I also attended board meetings of the Oakland Chinese Community Council (OCCC), which at that time was the primary social service organization in Chinatown, and I served as their youth representative.

Lincoln's principal, Mr. Moynihan, was on the OCCC board. At that time, two-thirds of Lincoln School students were Asian Americans, primarily Chinese Americans, many of whom were immigrants. At board meetings, Moynihan expressed his concern regarding the difficulties faced by these non-English speaking, new arrivals from Asia, and how these students needed special assistance. I volunteered to help, thinking of the many Asian American students involved in the emerging Asian American Movement who would likely answer to such a call for service.

In AAS 100X, I had worked with a small group of students. These students and I did a preliminary needs inventory of Oakland Chinatown. One of the greatest concerns was for the community's youth. The three primary public schools serving Chinatown expressed their concern for their recent Asian American immigrant students, and there was a growing youth violence and gang problem in this community.

In the spring 1969 quarter, three new additional AAS courses were offered. One of the courses was the "Asian American Communities" course, which was also referred to as the "Asian American Field Work" class. I was a TA for one of the sections, which was called the "Oakland Chinatown" section. There were 40 students in my section. In this course, we studied Oakland Chinatown needs, the community's history, and started a community service project. It was clear that one of the community's greatest needs was to expand social services for young people.

Considering the research findings coupled with Moynihan's appeal for help at Lincoln, I recruited students from the AAS Field Work course to tutor at Lincoln. As a result, the Lincoln Elementary School Tutorial Program was born.

The program was geared toward all Lincoln students, and its goals included improving reading and writing proficiency. However, for those students with limited English speaking abilities (primarily Asian American immigrant children), the program also aimed to improve their English verbal skills. In this way, the AAS Field Work course served as a direct pipeline to the Lincoln School Tutorial Program. My section of the Field Work course supplied the majority of the 35 tutors in the program.

The tutorial program was a success and continued for 4 more years. According to Moynihan, the immigrant children's English proficiency scores dramatically improved. Furthermore, this project was a manifestation of one of the first times an AAS course was directly involved with local Asian American communities. It literally applied theory and research to direct practice. In addition, it helped to jumpstart a new community-based organization, which focused on Oakland Asian American youth.

In August 1969, I founded the East Bay Chinese Youth Council (EBCYC), Inc. This wouldn't have been possible without my roots in this community, the partnerships that I had developed with youth in the community, and with the support from Reverend Frank Mar of the Oakland Chinese Presbyterian Church.

The East Bay Chinese Youth Council, Inc.

The East Bay Chinese Youth Council (EBCYC) was formed to improve the quality of education, provide employment training and opportunities, prevent youth violence, and provide recreational activities for Asian American youth in the East Bay. From 1969–1973, it ran an impressive array of youth programs and simultaneously sought to empower these Asian American youth. We were able to obtain funding from car washes, dances, and via the Neighborhood Youth Corps (NYC) subgrants from the Oakland Model Cities Program and the Oakland Unified School District.

One of EBCYC's nine programs was the summer NYC project that in 1970 and 1971 employed 133 and 230 Asian American youth, respectively between the ages of 14 and 18. Some of these programs were a community school for immigrant youth, community celebrations, film festivals, general community outreach, and the medical service outreach program.

In 1973, the Youth Council changed its location and name but continued many of the initial programs. The name changed to East Bay Asians for Community Action (EBACA). EBACA continued its health committee. In 1974, the health committee became Asian Health Services, which started as a one-room clinic. Asian Health Services has now become a multilingual, multispecialty community health center. Many consider it one of the nation's top community health centers/ clinics. It offers health, social, and advocacy services. It is an ever-expanding center, which annually offers primary health care services including medical care, dental care, and mental health services to 27,000 adults and children, and services to over 101,000 patients. Occupying two three-story building in the heart of Oakland Chinatown, AHS has 36 exam rooms and a dental clinic with seven chairs. Its staff is fluent in English and 12 Asian languages (Cantonese, Vietnamese, Mandarin, Korean, Khmer Cambodian, Mien, Mongolian, Tagalog, Karen, Karenni, Burmese, and Lao) (Asian Health Services, 2015)

The I-Hotel

One of the founding principles of Ethnic Studies was a commitment to service to our communities and "to do community work," which later became known as "community service." For the past 25 years, this model of bridging the community with mainly higher education has been more popularly called Service-Learning. Yet little acknowledgment is given to the contributions of Ethnic Studies to the development of the Service-Learning paradigm. In its purest form—community service—was actually a critical part of the original mission of Ethnic Studies and was, in fact, practiced as early as 1969 with the formation of Ethnic Studies.

The UC Berkeley AAS students focused their community work (service) on five projects in Berkeley, Oakland, and San Francisco. In Berkeley, the project centered upon the Issei (first generation Japanese Americans). In San Francisco, students worked with Issei in Japantown (J-Town), Chinatown with garment workers, a bookstore, and the International Hotel.

"Fight for the International Hotel" linocut with rubilith color overlay. Featured are I-Hotel tenants (left to right) Wahat Tampoa, Felix Ayson, and Mrs. Auguila. Slogan from a community-organized effort of supporters of the I-Hotel under the leadership of the tenants' association. Circa 1976. Artist: Rachael Romero, SF Poster Brigade.

The most immediate and high impact project was "Save the I-Hotel." In 1969, the Hotel was home to manongs (first generation Filipino American farmworkers) and elderly Chinese. One of the leaders to emerge from the struggle to save the I-Hotel and also, a key participant in the Berkeley Third World Strike, was Emil DeGuzman. He was born and raised in San Francisco. In April 2011, he said,

> *My father would take me down to Kearny Street as a little kid along with my younger brother. I had a godfather who had his photography shop under the Palm Hotel near Washington and Kearny Street. The Palm went down in 1968 and the I-Hotel was next. So I was very familiar with Manilatown growing up. When the fire happened that killed three manongs in March 1969, the Third World strike had just concluded . . . and we had fought so hard and learned so*

much, we were ripe to battle in the community . . . . Fortunately, my roommate Dwight Scott and myself organized students both from the strike and non-strikers who were anxious to be active to make a difference in the lives of their people. We did community work but it allowed us to join with the United Filipino Association representing the tenants to fight the owners. The success of the struggle which is true even today is the intergenerational unity where the young people unite with the elderly was the winning combination that drove the fight for eight years to stop eviction of the tenants at the I-Hotel . . .

It was the one of the best times in my early student years because the summer was hot and the campus was bustling with activity. The Third World Strike had ended after the Winter of 1969. This long fought struggle opened doors for minority students in the university. The victory to open an Ethnic Studies department was a major concession from the University Of California Board Of Regents. The TWLF movement had achieved new respect in the fight for the principle of self-determination in higher education.

In 1969, the Asian American population was 3,089,932 (U.S. Department of Commerce, 1973). This represented a significant increase from the previous decade. The three major Asian American groups were Japanese (591,290), Chinese (435,062), and Filipino (343,060).

The war in Southeast Asia was reaching a peak with the Tet Offensive just the year before. The Asian American Anti-War Movement was just beginning to take form and become visible in certain cities and campuses. This movement peaked a year later in April 1970 with the United States invasion of Cambodia and the increased intensity of the larger Anti-War Movement. At UC Berkeley, Asian Americans as a united group were highly visible in the Anti-War demonstrations and marches.

I remember at a planning meeting (April 1970) at the YMCA on Bancroft Avenue for one of the marches, there was a childhood friend who was attending this meeting. Ron, a Japanese American, was a Black Belt in Karate and a City of Berkeley Police Officer. I asked Ron, "Are you working now?" He embarrassedly said that he was working. We kind of laughed because it was obvious that he was working undercover to gather intelligence information on the pending march.

The summer of 1969 symbolized a critical time for the United Farm Workers Union (UFW) and their link to the Asian American Movement. Early Union leaders such as Larry Itliong, the original organizer and leader of the Delano Grape Strike, Philip Vera Cruz, and Cesar Chavez were utilizing Mahatma Gandhi's tactics of nonviolent protesting. Itliong and Vera Cruz, both Filipino Americans, also represented an important part of the 1969 Asian American population: the manongs. Many were retired farmworkers who worked in the fields with their Chicano counterparts. In order to improve farmworkers' wages and work conditions, the UFW utilized numerous nonviolent methods to achieve their goals such as strikes against nonunion farms, boycotts of supermarkets such as Safeway that sold grapes and lettuce from nonunion growers, a march to Sacramento, and Chavez's well-known hunger strikes.

A short time after the TWLF Strike, Professor Takagi organized a car caravan of Berkeley Asian American students and farmworker supporters to go to the UFW headquarters in Delano to show our support for the Union and delivered carloads of bags of rice. I remember arriving in Delano and going with Professor Takagi and a small group of students into the UFW headquarters. We walked into a back room and in a hospital bed was Cesar Chavez. He waved to us to come closer to him. My impressions for those 5 minutes were how kind he was, passionate about his cause, humble, and angelical. Although Chavez was weak and in poor health from his hunger strike, there was a peacefulness about this experience that I will never forget. This experience has left a lasting impression on me. To move people, to move mountains, one can do it with the positive, unflinching attitude of "Si, se puede (Yes, we can)."

The Third World Strike to establish Ethnic Studies at UC Berkeley was a hard-fought battle to establish a new discipline in higher education, but also in K-12. The College of Ethnic Studies was established at San Francisco State University and the Ethnic Studies Departments and Programs flourished at universities such as Sacramento State and the University of Hawai'i at Manoa. Ethnic Studies and related race and ethnicity courses sprang up all over the United States. Just as important was a new generation of community organizers and community-based organizations that for the past 48 years have truly impacted the communities they were meant to serve.

Concluding Thoughts

After Dr. Paul Takagi retired, he continued to actively write about, reflect on, and was a strong advocate for social justice. For over 47 years, he had been my mentor and friend. Paul passed away on September 13, 2015.

Him Mark Lai passed away May 2009. His research, publications, and mentoring of students about Chinese American history lives on.

Danny Li is semiretired on the Big Island of Hawai'i. He continues to fight for social justice and equal rights for all.

Floyd Huen, M.D., was recently medical director at Lifelong Medical Care and Over Sixties Health Center in Berkeley and Oakland. He continues to organize communities for social justice and equal rights.

Photo: © Christina Fa Mark

Dr. Paul Takagi and Dr. Greg Mark (left to right) at the Founding Meeting of the UC Berkeley Asian Pacific American Alumni Chapter, when Professor Takagi, professor emeritus of criminology, was honored "for his pioneering role in helping create Asian American Studies . . . ," October 11, 2008, Alumni House, UC Berkeley.

Jean Quan is the immediate past mayor of the City of Oakland. She was the City's first woman mayor and its first Asian American mayor, along with the first Asian American woman mayor of a major U.S. city. Mayor Quan brought her decades of training in the Civil Rights Movement to her public service positions on the Oakland School Board, Oakland City Council and as the Oakland City mayor.

Emil DeGuzman was a member of the City and County of San Francisco Human Rights Commission. He has also been a fair housing and public accommodations investigator/mediator. He continues to fight for social justice and is an activist in the Filipino American community.

Dwight Scott passed away November 2008. I have never forgotten his commitment, strength on the basketball court, and friendship.

Sac State had been very fortunate to have Wayne Maeda teach for 43 years in the Ethnic Studies Department. Since its inception, Wayne had been the foundation for AAS at Sacramento State—Brah, RIP.

I am now a professor of Ethnic Studies and the director of AAS at Sacramento State. My community service work in Oakland was followed by decades of service in Honolulu, and, even today, I'm engaged in community service programs that I have created in Sacramento. I continue to work for a more just and fair society for all.

Photo: © Christina Fa Mark

Gregory Mark, left, holding photo of Oakland Suey Sing Tong members in 1970, which included his father, then Oakland Suey Sing Tong President Byron Yee Mark. Standing on the right is Yi Ling Tsao, Oakland Suey Sing Tong President at the time of the photo. Taken during a presentation by Dr. Mark about Oakland's Suey Sing Tong to students at an Asian American studies field trip from Sac State to Oakland Chinatown, November 2013.

References

Asian Health Services. (2015). Retrieved from http://asianhealthservices.org/

Fanon, F. (2004). *The wretched of the earth*. Grove Press.

Takagi, P., & Shank, G. (2012). *Paul T. Takagi: Recollections and writings*. Crime and Social Justice Association.

Umemoto, K. (2007). "On strike!" San Francisco State College Strike, 1968–1969: The role of Asian American students. In M. Zhou & J. V. Gatewood (Eds.), *Contemporary Asian America* (2nd ed., pp. 25–55). New York University Press.

U.S. Department of Commerce. (1973, July). *Japanese, Chinese, and Filipinos in the United States: 1970 census of population*. Author.

Wei, W. (1993). *The Asian American movement*. Temple University Press.

Interviews

DeGuzman, Emil, April 2011.

Huen, Floyd, April 2011.

Lai, Him Mark, May 2009.

Li, Danny, August 2010.

Maeda, Wayne, May 2011.

Takagi, Paul, March 2011 and April 2011.

ETHNIC STUDIES: AN INTRODUCTION

Why Ethnic Studies Was Meant for Me

Rosana Chavez, M.S. (Ethnic Studies Alumna)

 ## My Golden Moment

I remember my graduation as if it were yesterday. Stepping foot into this huge stadium where the lights were so bright, all I could hear was the roaring crowd. I was instructed to move forward to take my photo, and then was hooded. I find myself standing next to these strong bronze women sharing this celebratory moment together. Everything is happening so fast and it's all just a huge blur. Then I hear my name being called into the mike, "Rosaaannna Chaveeeez". What! They said my name correctly! This was the first thought that rushed into my head. My goodness they actually said my God-given name the way it was meant to be pronounced! I shook the hand of the College of Education and my paper diploma was handed to me. This is it? I thought to myself out loud. This is truly it! I did it! I felt this huge sense of accomplishment take over my entire body. I felt as if I could fly and a huge weight had been lifted from me. Tears rolled down my cheeks as I looked for my family in the sea of people. With my diploma in hand, I waved it in the direction of my family. I yelled to my family, "This is for you!" This was my golden moment that I owned and that no one could take from me. I worked for the past seven years beginning with my undergraduate and ending with my graduate degree with fierce determination. Logistically, I earned a piece of paper that the University likes to call a Master's degree. But, oh boy, was it more than just a piece of paper with fancy writing. This was a piece of paper that symbolized much more.

Receiving this diploma embodied all of my and my family's hard work. Receiving this diploma represented overcoming many struggles and barriers that I had faced in addition to those that my family had endured. This piece of paper represented the blood and sweat of my Chicano gente involved in the Chicano

Movement and the many educational struggles it took before my time for me to be able to experience my golden moment. This piece of paper represented far more than what words can express. Receiving this diploma symbolized my new beginning as a first generation college graduate. I became the first woman in my entire family to earn a bachelor of arts degree, let alone a master of science degree. I reflect on my degrees hanging in my bedroom wall and relive the moment as much as possible. I relieve them to appreciate the past and present efforts to make education accessible. Sharing the graduation experience serves as a benchmark to remember that moment strongly influenced by my decision to major in Ethnic Studies as an undergraduate. Selecting the right major as an undergraduate is never an easy experience, especially a major few people generally understand. Just because people did not understand Ethnic Studies as a discipline did not deter me. In fact, the more I took courses in Ethnic Studies the more I recognized its universal applied value. I want to share my proud experiences for the sole purpose of educating those who are considering majoring in Ethnic Studies. However, my positive feelings about being an Ethnic Studies major also meant confronting many hurdles in order to experience academic success. But in order to understand my reflections I must rewind and share what life was like before my college journey began.

Where My Journey Began

What do you want to be when you grow up is a common question that many children have been asked while in grade school. Right? Some children might respond with wanting to be a doctor, a lawyer, an astronaut, or even a teacher. As very young children, our range of career choices are framed by the exposure we receive through school, in our home or even through our television sets. Although we might not realize at the time we are asked such questions as children, but those messages are informing part of our career development process. I am sure no child would answer (at least that I am aware of) that they want to major in Ethnic Studies and study social justice in a modern day society. As a child, I was definitely not the exception. However, I will tell you this: ever since I can remember I wondered why history books presented in classes always seemed to cover the same topics over and over and at the same time could never seem to locate my cultural history, or see people who looked like me, represented in my history books. As this learning experience continued, I became more eager and curious to learn and discover what was being hidden from me and why.

As an adult, I remember being in the second grade and the first book I checked out from my school's library was a book titled, Cesar Chavez. I did not know who he was or the history of the United Farm Workers Movement at age eight, but I choose this book because I read my last name "Chavez" on the front cover. I was so excited because my very own last name was written on a book. Now was this a coincidence? Or was I actually beginning the planning of my future major in

Ethnic Studies? Reflecting on this experience helps me to reinforce that even as a child I was eager to learn about socio-culture history. I was captivated by the title of this book simply because I could relate. These feelings I was exposed to at such a young age were the same feelings I felt as I discovered Ethnic Studies as a major.

My curiosity of my culture did not end in elementary school, but it definitely transferred into my high school years. I was a sophomore and I attended my first MEChA (Movimiento Estudiantil Chicano de Aztlan) Youth Conference at Sacramento State University. This was my first time stepping foot on to a college campus and I instantly fell in love. The campus felt welcoming and it was covered with many trees and buildings. There were many people walking from class to class and I remember seeing all the diverse faces. It was such a foreign world to me but all I knew was that I wanted to be part of it. This is when I first set the goal of graduating from high school and making college a part of my future plans. I did my research; I spoke with counselors and did everything possible in my power to make sure that I was eligible to apply for college. I was determined to attend Sacramento State even though my high school counselors told me that I was not university bound.

College Can Come True

In the fall semester of 2001 my dream became a reality when I began my college career at Sacramento State. I was a first-time freshman and scared out of my mind. I moved from a small local high school to this city size campus of 28,000 people overnight. I only knew one person from my high school that also began that same semester. Not knowing many people at the university was scary and I felt alone. I needed to make connections with students and the best way to do so was through my major. Initially I was majoring in apparel marketing and design. I wanted to be a fashion designer which in my mind translated into becoming rich and famous just like on television. This is what sounded good to me at the time because I had no other perception of what else was out there. I took classes in this major but did not find a personal connection. Before I discovered Ethnic Studies as a major I felt this huge emptiness and confusion about who I was as a person of color and where I was going with my life. I needed to find a major that matched my intellectual talents with my personal values and beliefs. A connection similar to the one I experienced as a child when I read my first book on Cesar Chavez. I knew that I had some type of purpose and mission to fulfill, but at the moment I was lost like many college students are during their first and even their sophomore year in college. What am I going to do with my life? I put this huge pressure on myself because it took so long for me to get into college and now I had no plan.

It was not until my beginnings of junior year at Sac State that I decided to take a class called Ethnic America with Professor Wayne Maeda. I chose this class because the description spoke to me. It was as follows: "Through an interdisciplinary approach, introduces the four major American ethnic groups – Black, American Indian, Chicano, Asian American. Focuses on themes common to all four groups (racism, economic and political oppression) and demonstrates the varied contributions of each culture to American social and economic life". Achieving my educational goal of beginning college also meant I could further educate myself on my culture, and I felt this class was my opportunity to do so. Since my ideas about having a career in fashion was steadily becoming uninteresting, I figured I had nothing to lose by exploring my personal interest. Little did I know that making this one simple decision, I was about to embark on a life changing experience that would impact my life path forever.

I still remember my first day of class. I couldn't find the building, I was late. I had to beg Professor Maeda to add me into his section. Luckily he did! Taking this course made me feel as if I was opening my eyes for the first time. Professor Maeda kept true to the description of the course. Learning about racism, oppression, and the various social justice movements of the four ethnic groups was empowering. Empowering in that I was learning about how and why these terms came into existence. My consciousness was being expanded. I stepped foot into this course that I was able to grasp an intellectual understanding and put into context how my own socially-lived experiences related to my history in the United States. My life began to make sense. Hearing what I like to call the other half of history made me feel complete. Like Professor Maeda would say "I was given a new pair of lenses to see the world through!" This statement carries so much meaning. Taking this course was like having a new pair of eyes and I could see life so clearly. My experiences as a woman of color began to make more sense to me. During that class Professor Maeda became a great mentor and actually convinced me in changing my major to Ethnic Studies. That is exactly what I did!

In the Process

Changing your major is not always the easiest process. Sure all it takes is a piece of paper with a few signatures, but there are social obligations and responsibilities that come along with receiving an education. Even though I found my calling and I knew Ethnic Studies was for me, I now had the duty to explain to my family and my peers what this major entailed. When asked what my major was going to be, my family and peers always responded with: "What are you going to do with that major?" Sound familiar? At the moment, I could honestly say I did not know how to answer that question. Or what was to become of me majoring in this field, but all I knew is that it felt right! With this deep-seated conviction, all I needed to know to keep moving forward without regret or doubt. I remember when I told my dad what I was studying he responded "Que es eso?" ("What is that")?

I slowly explained Ethnic Studies, but all he would ask is if I was going to make good money and if I was going to graduate fast. My mother, on the other hand, did not question me at all, she was just happy to see her daughter follow her path. My parents never really knew what this major was about, and I am not too sure if they still fully understand, but they were definitely proud of my renewed confidence as a student and daughter. My parents realized that selecting a major with this much enthusiasm meant I had direction to accomplish not just graduating from college but obtain a career that was personally and professionally fulfilling.

My Experience Matters

Ethnic Studies has built a strong foundation for my career and my everyday life. Learning about my cultural background in the classroom has been empowering to me. It was not until I stepped foot into an Ethnic Studies classroom that I was told my experience matters. One course in particular helped me conceptualize what it meant to be a woman of color and has facilitated my understanding of my different life roles. The course titled La Mujer Chicana (The Chicana Woman) taught by Dr. Julie Figueroa was a course where I literally studied and was invited to reflect on myself and the life I was living. In this course, the bar was consistently set to a high standard. Some of the most sensitive culturally taboo topics were addressed and it brought me out of my comfort zone. Topics included identity, feminism, sexuality, cultural tradition, language, religion, and art – just to name a few. Studying these types of topics in a classroom setting was mind blowing. It was through this course where I was able to ethnically identify myself through studying my own identity. I was never too sure how to ethnically define myself on campus until I met Dr. Figueroa. I knew that I was a hybrid of different cultures and that I was more than a person who was born in the United States, of Mexican descent. Like many first generation college students I struggled to understand my identity on a college campus and in my home. At home I was Mexicana, even though my aunt from Mexico begged to differ. She said I was a gringa with Mexican parents. On campus I did not identify as an American because this term did not embrace the whole me. This is when I decided to reject the pre-determined labels that were given to me and that I was going to take charge on how to ethnically identify myself. I was then able to link my two worlds and make it into my one entity. I identify as a Chicana woman because it personifies the full me and it represents my experience best in the United States. Overall this course supported my critical thinking skills and challenged what I thought I knew about myself and taught me what I needed to know. More importantly, it helped me understand where I wanted to go in life and how I was going to get there. Dr. Figueroa constantly pushed me towards academic success and she succeeded as a professor. My experience truly matters and I do have something worth sharing. Just as you do too.

My experiences with Dr. Maeda and Dr. Figueroa's courses illustrate how Ethnic Studies supported my critical thinking skills. I was able to develop this new-found consciousness and understanding of who I am as a Chicana woman. In respects to learning about myself, I also became aware of the diverse cultural backgrounds that surround me. I experienced various courses that shared the socially-lived experiences of a wide range of ethnic groups. Learning about social justice made me aware that different ethnic groups share a commonality with one another. We all faced and continue to face different oppressive social issues and struggles. Learning that when we unite as a people we can overcome hardships that cross our paths. This has enlightened me. More importantly, it has taught me the importance of celebrating diversity and as humans we actually have a lot more in common than what we think. Ethnic Studies has humbled me to appreciate not only myself, but the experiences of others. This is what Ethnic Studies can offer you.

Lessons Learned:

I currently work as a full time counselor for the College Assistance Migrant Program here at Sacramento State. I work with first year students who mostly are first generation college students just like me. Having Ethnic Studies as my foundation not only allowed me to understand my student's socio-cultural backgrounds, but I am able to share and relate my own experiences with them. As my students are going through their own self-exploration process I teach them to refuse what society has made of us and to become trend-setters within their families and communities. In so doing, they will find their purpose in life through fulfilling their own dreams. There are many lessons I learned while going through my college journey. They are the same lessons I pass down to my own students and that I will like to pass on to you. Lesson number one: follow your heart. Nowadays people seem to focus too much on their external influences and forget to give themselves permission to explore their likes and interest. It is through exploring yourself that you will find what is meant for you. Even though you may not know your calling it will shine through if you accept the exploration process. Lesson number two: trust yourself. It is completely natural to experience self-doubt and ask what I am doing? However, sometimes it takes this self-doubt to help you open your eyes and see what is truly right for you. Embrace this self-doubt and make it into a positive. How you may ask? Use this self-doubt as a motivator to do some of your own research as you are shopping for a major. Trust this process. Lesson number three: never settle for less. Don't go for the major that you randomly select with closed eyes, or the major your family and peers tell you to follow. Don't settle for what you think will be the easiest. You will not be fully satisfied with your career in the long run if you opt to take a short cut. Lesson number four: discover who you are through understanding were you come from. This has always been my motto. This helps keep you focused and humble. It will help you keep your priorities lined up and it will remind you why you are here in the first place? Coming to your realization and following these lessons will help you achieve academic and career success at Sacramento State.

The Journey Continues

As a counselor I enjoy working with first time freshmen and being part of their exploration process for my students. I am happy to give back and share what Ethnic Studies has given me. Over the years I have refused to be another negative statistic and decided to become a trend-setter for my family and my community. I decided to follow my dreams which created my path of success. I continue to give myself permission to explore for this process does not necessarily end once you graduate. I challenge you all to make similar efforts and create your path towards success. Refuse to be a negative statistic and create your own destinies and become trend-setters. Fulfill your life destinies so you too can experience your own golden moment. When in doubt follow your heart and your instincts and you will find that things will naturally unfold. Remember your experience does matter and you have a lot to share. You will come across your own lessons learned in your college careers that you too can share with future generations. Remember the journey still continues after you graduate, but it is up to you how you decide to navigate it. If you are deciding to purse Ethnic Studies and the next time someone asks you what can you do with that major, I would like for you all to please respond "What can you NOT do with that major" Now give yourself permission and go explore!

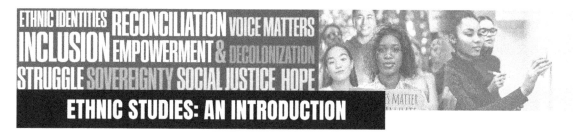

ETHNIC STUDIES: AN INTRODUCTION

"Ethnic Studies Embodies Activism"

Andrea L. Moore

Life for Ethnic Studies ain't been no crystal stair; however, with the teachings of those that came before us, "it's still climbing." In lieu of the 2020 global uprisings related to systemic racism, scholars are reflecting upon the 50+ year evolution of Ethnic Studies, beginning with origins of the discipline and what has supported its sustainment. One important fact about Ethnic Studies is that it was founded on the activism of a communal coalition made up of students, staff, and faculty who applied direct action organizing practices demanding the discipline to be offered in higher learning institutions and so on. Ethnic Studies focuses on the four federally protected groups, Native Americans, African Americans, Asian Americans, and Latino/a/x Americans, opening the door for conversations regarding science of the *social construction of race* and its function in the United States of North America. Ethnic Studies teaches about their immigration experiences in America over time, while acknowledging their panconnections. Each program in the discipline shares their narrative experiences of what led to the movement known as Third World Liberation Front in 1967 and after. "Most scholars point to 1967 or 1968 as the origin of the Black Studies Movement in academia and, ignoring the protests at historically Black colleges and universities (HBCUs), the previous 3 years and the dozens of protests in the spring of 1968, Benet (1971) and Rojas (2007) consider the San Francisco State strike, which kicked off in November 1968, as the first serious attempt to force the introduction of a Black Studies department" (Ibram Rogers, 2002). In 1968, the "coalition of the Black Students Union, the Latin American Students Organization, the Filipino American Collegiate Endeavor (PACE) the Filipino-American Students Organization, the Asian American Political Alliance, and El Renacimiento, a Mexican-American student organization, formed at San Francisco State" (UCB Center for Race & Gender, 2019) led a 5-month strike on campus to demand a radical shift in the curriculum as they deemed it disparate to BIPOC communities lived experiences in the United States. *Anti-Blackness* is a consistent concept in the genealogy of the fight for Ethnic Studies beginning with scholarships accounts that resisted the inclusion of the first program people were protesting for, Black studies. It is important to uplift the role that Black students, educators, and organizations had in the protests and activism prior to the 133-day strike. Arguably, that collective labor laid the foundation that created a base for TWLF known as the protest movement for an Ethnic Studies academic discipline. For over 50 years, academicians have had to continue this protest mode of activism to promote the systemic implementation of the discipline.

This chapter explores how the evolution of Ethnic Studies embodies collective and spiritual activism in the forms of organizing and protests during (1) *Inception of Ethnic Studies*, (2) *Commemorating the 50th anniversary of Ethnic Studies Scott's demand*, and (3) *the passing of AB 1460, the Ethnic Studies CSU requirement*. This work applies Cedric Robinson's "Black Radical Tradition" as the theoretical framework for understanding the response from Black communities in relation to the inception and evolution of Ethnic Studies. This Pan-African model is used to analyze the trajectory of values and principles that correlate with several Ethnic Studies learning objectives such as **Social Histories of Ethnic Groups** by "distinguishing the roles of community formations and institutions building among ethnic groups," **Service Based Community Learning** promoting community and civic engagement to provide service to others, and **Self-Development** when reflecting on "the value of social consciousness and personal responsibility" (CSUS Student Learning Objectives).

Inception of Ethnic Studies

There have been zero political wins that Black people have gained without protesting (abolition, citizenship, right to vote, equitable access to public spaces such as bathrooms, schools, etc.), and incorporating Black studies in academia has been one of them.

> *The movement for the discipline began in the spring of 1965, . . . Students developed and first presented the Black Studies idea to a group of professors in 1966. The nation's first program opened its doors in 1967 with students teaching most of the courses. The climax semester of protests for units was the spring of 1969. By the fall of 1969, the discipline had been forcibly institutionalized. In the spring of 1970, the effort to sustain the discipline and its hundreds of units became the primary aim of student activism, ending or more so shifting the mass movement of the previous 5 years to erect the discipline.*

Ethnic Studies embodies collective activism as an important element for transformation, "a process of change; the altering of one form into another, or the change of one condition into another" (Scott, 2008). What leads to the transformation is protest demands mobilizing organizing in an effort to ultimately not only educate people about the variance immigration experiences but also to eradicate systemic racism. "Ethnic Studies scholarship and activism as acts of social responsibility can be a welcome contribution to the age-old long march toward social justice" (Scott, 2008).

It is important to link the scholarship in Ethnic Studies curriculum with the people who first protested in support of Black studies because many of them would be the first teachers in the field. Ethnic Studies would embody the commitment to engage with the struggle to join in advocating for social change and social justice. This commitment is connected to the Pan-African Movement in that it uplifts a communal responsibility to advance the people.

Ibram H. Rogers's (NKA Ibram X. Kendi) work entitled "The Black Campus Movement and the Institutionalization of Black Studies 1965–1970" provides a narrative and analytical overview of the nationwide struggle of the Black students that began in 1965 and climaxed in the spring of 1969 to push and pull the discipline of Black studies into the academy. In the spring of 1966, the first Black Student Union emerged led by Jimmy Garrett who advocated for the organization in 1966 at San Francisco State. It would be the radical efforts made by the BSU to assist in the department win housed in a school of Ethnic Studies, and several BSU leaders served extended periods in jail (Rogers, 2011). These students would also serve by selecting the faculty, while Berkeley TWLF strikers gained a department.

On the east coast, in 1967 the historically Black college known as Howard, Professor Nathan Hare would begin a Black Student Union as a response to his critique that the HBCU was more interested in serving White populations than educating its Black students on their Pan-African history. Initial Black studies programs were directed to a White audience in what appeared to be geared to humanizing the "Black Experience." Hare was recruited to join San Francisco State eventually as the chair for Black studies, but was fired due to his activism (Barlow & Shapiro, 1971; Rogers, 2011).

Ethnic Studies embodies spiritual activism when analyzing the role of Black students, faculty, and so on. We see the generational sacrificial choices that they are willing to take in efforts to communally address racial injustice practices at their learning and employment institutions. Pan-African studies embodies the spirit of the people who engage in the praxis to fight, uplift, and uphold the value of a collective rooted in community. ***Pan-Africanism*** is a unified African diaspora ideology referring to the long-term historical process by which people of African descent have been scattered from their ancestral homelands to other parts of the world.[1] Often in Ethnic Studies, its scholarship and teaching are grounded and centered within lived pan-African experiences in the United States. Pan-African studies leaves space for spiritual knowledge for understanding the plight of human discovery. "By revisiting the roots of their religion and philosophy, those Africans in the continent and in diaspora begin to understand what it means to embrace African cosmology" (Karangi, 2019). Pan-Africanism directly connects to

African cosmology, which is a spiritual method in which some "Africans perceive, conceive and contemplate their universe; the lens through which they see reality, which affects their value systems and attitudinal orientations. It is the African's search for the meaning of life" (Kanu, 2017).

This focus on the evolution of the institutionalization of Ethnic Studies from a pan-African framework includes an accepted foundational understanding of "knowledge of self" as a life quest connecting present to past and future experiences. In relation to the emergence and advancement of the discipline, this work creates space for applying Cedric Robinson's Black Radical Tradition, "a collection of cultural, intellectual, action-oriented labor aimed at disrupting social, political, economic, and cultural norms originating in anticolonial and antislavery efforts. *This tradition is not only resistance against structures rooted in slavery, imperialism, and capitalism, but maintenance of an ontology (cultural traditions, beliefs, values)." (Robinson, 1983). It is here where the* "African Sage Philosophy" the name now commonly given to the body of thought produced by persons considered wise in African communities, and more specifically refers to those who seek a rational foundation for ideas and concepts used to describe and view the world by critically examining the justification of those ideas and concepts, comes into play.[2] These themes involve questions regarding the nature of the supreme being; the concept of the person; the meaning of freedom, equality, death; and the belief in the afterlife.[3]

The area that focuses on "the meaning of freedom, equality, death and the belief in the afterlife" speaks directly to the spiritual activism component apparent in the pan-African studies approaches to engaging with Ethnic Studies. These pan-African frameworks connect individual and communal values shared between past, present, and future generations. It also links the institutional beginnings of Ethnic Studies connection to direct action organizing as a method for creating social change. A change that encompasses human beings putting their lives and freedoms on the line so that their ancestors who contributed to the makeup of what we now refer to as United States of America not only had access to a democratically structured society but would also be included in the fabric of its origin stories.

This lends itself to what was originally shared as a sacred philosophical identification to directly connecting to those whom we come from, to an academic quandary where social science attempts to study humans' collective racial experiences in efforts to evolve consciousness. Oftentimes, it is the awareness of repetition in relation to the social dilemma that creates the response of protest, which continues to serve as one form of bringing awareness to an area that needs humanitarian growth.

Commemorating the 50th Anniversary of Ethnic Studies with Elder Scott's Reminder

Ethnic Studies embodied collective and spiritual activism during the 2019 commemoration of the 50th anniversary of Ethnic Studies.

As an associate professor, I often tread lightly around how transparent I become in the classroom. If applying a pan-African framework, then my transparency brings me into the communal circle, not completely eradicating the class structural hierarchy, but into encompassing the responsibilities of more than one role in the lives of the students and colleagues. As a professor in pan-African studies it is my responsibility to study and teach the history of the discipline, referring original works and thereby honoring the scholarship of those who have been advocating for Ethnic Studies since the beginning.

My other professional title includes the honor of directing the Cooper-Woodson College Enhancement Program, a pan-African retention program housed in Ethnic Studies founded by Dr. Otis Scott and the collective Black staff and faculty at Sacramento State in 1990.[4] In 2008, Dr. Scott honored the 30th anniversary of Ethnic Studies by reminding its supporters of the role that activism plays in the discipline. In honor of Dr. Scott for the 50th anniversary of Ethnic Studies as a discipline still fighting for academic support, I will be recounting some of his wisdom around collective activism in Ethnic Studies.

In an article entitled "Preparing for the Future" Elder Dr. Scott reminds us to employ activism because it is the *transformative* part of the discipline's longevity and our collective responsibility in improving human conditions. "The most critical objective of the discipline is to bring about changes in what is taught about the social, historical, and cultural experiences of ethnic groups. The objective of research and teaching in Ethnic Studies is to provide a deeper and wider reservoir of knowledge and perspectives about the experiences of ethnic groups" (Scott, 2008). Dr. Scott says by its 30th anniversary three themes had arisen on what he called the "Ethnic Studies movement": 1) "Ethnic Studies has a transformative mission. 2) Ethnic Studies is a corrective and redemptive project. 3) Ethnic Studies has generative capacities" (Scott, 2008).

When Scott refers to Ethnic Studies as a "corrective and redemptive project," I am arguing this also connects to a spiritual aspect of activism, as it was the spirit of the people in the honoring those that came before, to continue the legacy and praxis in Ethnic Studies.[5] All four groups revere ancestral lineage. This is seen in the content of information that is shared when teaching the discipline. Dr. Scott highlights the connection between the themes listed and social movements from the 1960s and 1970s requesting a restructuring of American institutions with a democratic implementation for citizenship equity that grossly impacted the lives of Native Americans, African Americans, Asian Americans, and Latino/a/x Americans. Personal stories play a role in allowing students to apply academic theory and vocab when analyzing concepts. This by way of practice is highlighting the lead experience of the generation that came before and many times have also transitioned. It is the legacies of those stories that are guiding the narratives of how the social construction of race impacted their everyday social, political, and economic realities. Ethnic Studies has shown its significance in the institutional context within which Dr. Scott spoke as perceptions of "people of color existed simply had to be changed from being discriminatory, alienating, and de-humanizing to one based on principles and practices recognizing the dignity and worth of human beings" (Scott, 2008). It is these stories that have "generative capacities" to speak truth to theory in that as a people we still have a lot more educating to do about the social variance in American histories/her stories/our stories.

The contribution I am adding to the conversation on spiritual activism is honoring the legacy of those that came before you and addressing racial issues with various forms of activism, which will create the transformation rooted in Ethnic Studies curriculum as praxis.

The origins of the discipline and its evolutions speak to the ancient practice of honoring community, as in holding community and elders as the center of life's transformation. Each program teaches their histories through a communal lens that honors the stories and experiences of the elders who then become ancestors. The academic conversation can travel beyond the academic theory and students begin to share their personal lived experiences juxtaposing how their ancestors lived may have impacted their own. When discussing this in the class setting it connects students with their ancestor's history and what they were going through during their times and how it's impacting our society today. This can be understood by identifying and connecting a spiritual understanding of transformation by connecting ancestral acknowledgment and communal responsibility with teaching the history of race and ethnicity's function in America.

1. Honoring the ancestors to continuing to include the struggles that they were fighting during previous social movements, that is, abolition, civil rights, Black Lives Matter, and so on.
2. Honoring their transition.
3. Building community and coalition

Applying Robinson's "Black Radical Tradition," spiritual activism as an ontological approach was embedded since enslaved Africans begin to collectively think about saving themselves while in a harmful situation.

It is at this juncture of self-reflection and awareness the students may connect with a sense of responsibility to continue in the historical challenges in the past to the present, by way of carrying the torch of coalition and community building. This brings in a spiritual component in the awareness and acknowledgment of looking to the ancestors for guidance in a very welcoming sense in that their stories are revisited and still being shared, keeping the energy of their spirits alive. Generationally the information being provided to students activates their agency to determine self-awareness in relation to the subject. There has been a direct link from our historical into the contemporary when we look at practices that are incorporated and demonstrated by people who call themselves activist, organizers, active leaders, and teachers. If we look at this within a spiritual context those people may be seen as sages, community healers, griots, shamans, priestess, and so on. It could be said that the information they are sharing is healing in our collective bodies that have been harmed due to racist practices. Ethnic Studies serves as the vanguard for generational transformation regarding systemic racism. Dr. Scott's guidance in sustaining the discipline's transformative power twenty years later would empower CSU students and the Ethnic Studies community educating the public about the significant impact one course can have on one's collegial experience.

After reading Dr. Scott's work I was empowered to know that I was a part of a historical moment in bringing the praxis of mobilization to assist in the support for an Ethnic Studies course requirement.

The passing of AB 1460, the Ethnic Studies CSU requirement

"When you stand on that history and you know it, you will appreciate it."
—Dr. Shirley Weber

Ethnic Studies embodied collective activism in March of 2019, when AB 1460 was introduced to legislature advocating for the *California State University graduation requirement: Ethnic Studies* (California State University, 2020). AB 1460 was authored by Dr. Shirley Weber. Weber made history by being the first African American to be elected to the California State Legislature south of Los Angeles. The Government of Newsom nominates Shirley Weber as California's first Black secretary of state (KCRA, 2020). The 31st secretary of the state of California (incumbent) and member of the California Legislative Black Caucus, she served as the assembly representative of the 79th district during the time of the authorship.

The same blueprint that was utilized during the 1960s protest for Ethnic Studies was applied again to push the AB 1460, Weber Bill.

The July 7, 2020 Ethnic Studies webinar series focused on the program of African American Studies in relation to Ethnic Studies, as part of a weeklong set of virtual panel discussions aired on the California Department of Education's Facebook live with Dr. Shirley Weber for a historical conversation on AB 1460. Weber spoke about the legacy of Africana studies, the very first HBCU beginning February 25, 1837 at Cheney University of Pennsylvania, the second one was in 1854 at Lincoln University also in Pennsylvania, and the third one was in 1856 Wilberforce. She talked about the fact that there are 107 HBCUs in the United States and that shows an investment of a population in education. Specifically, she spoke about the African American investment Black communities have in education otherwise as she stated, "we would not have invested so much into these schools."

What is fascinating about Dr. Weber's journey with Ethnic Studies is that it parallels the movement in that it was her learnings in pan-African studies that led her to become a supporter for Ethnic Studies and why she authored the bill. According to Weber, "Ethnic Studies is an important discipline because it changes how we see ourselves." Weber, like Scott, is a connecting thread to the protest for Ethnic Studies in 1960s, and an advocate for Ethnic Studies in educational curriculum from K-college. She serves as an elder and activist.

Weber stated on the heels of the protest in 1966 King was marching in Mississippi and Stokely Carmichael turned around and said, "well what we need is Black power." That wasn't the first time she remembers it being said but she remembers it being the first time she thought about it in a new way. She also mentioned how he talked about Black social, political, and economic power for self-determination. She then connected Carmichael to the teachings that came from Malcolm X that came from his iconic 1964 "The Ballot or the Bullet" speech. She also talked about how Ethnic Studies introduced her to Marcus Garvey and how Garvey is the person who actually fueled Malcolm X and the Black Panthers for Self Defense rhetoric. Weber acknowledged that people don't talk about Garvey who is heralded as a father in Pan-African revolutionary liberation thinking for the communal upliftment of the red, Black, and green.

Another beautiful aspect of Weber's gem-dropping conversation was when she shared how mentorship is an important component of Ethnic Studies and that Molefi K. Asante is still her mentor. Having faculty you can identify with sets a solid foundation for many freshmen and first-generation college students. In getting the audience to understand the plight faced by Ethnic Studies, Weber connects to a history of oppression regarding ethnic minorities agency in telling their own stories and how California should be so proud in leading some of the largest campuses offering Africana Studies. Weber sharing these stories honors the activism of the spirits that came before her.

The final push for AB 1460 occurred during the 2020 COVID-19 pandemic and the second wave of the Black Lives Matter movement. I argue that it was the social and historical climate that led the push and support Ethnic Studies. After the global uprisings due to the murders of Breonna Taylor and George Floyd, the rising of Asian hate crimes, the lack of respect for Native American sovereignty, and the increased number of children in cages under the Trump Administration, many looked to educational institutions for anti-racism accountability. Schools across the globe began to implement anti-racism initiatives and California State Sacramento was one of them. Thus, as the push to eradicate racism within the institution of academia, AB 1460 becomes the poster child for pulling colonial racist practices out of higher education. The practice played out in front of faculty and students when they learned about the Chancellor's office trying to dictate and appropriate what Ethnic Studies is and why it should require the approval from other disciplines to become a graduation requirement. Students, staff, and faculty lobbied at the Capitol, attended critical faculty senate meetings, used their social media platforms to create digital campaigns in support of AB 1460, as well as joined the Ethnic Studies Student Association to assist in writing and speaking about the need for the requirement.

The origins of Ethnic Studies as a curriculum model address the communal aspect of activism, organizing, and teaching. Similar to the initial groups who advocated for Ethnic Studies, the faculty in that department leaned into their relationships with the Black Student Union, other programs, clubs, and organizations that provide student services like Cooper-Woodson College, The Martin Luther King Center, Students for Quality Education (SQE led in pushing for abolishing campus police), The 65th Street Corridor, Full Circle Project, the Union for the California Faculty Association (CFA sponsored the bill), and many other departments and community members stepped into their roles of activists to helped bridge gaps and create communal understanding of learning about supporting Ethnic Studies.

The campaign for AB 1460 addressed not only the history of Ethnic Studies but revisiting the implementation of the Ethnic Studies graduation requirement, along with what can be done to decolonize the classroom and eradicate racism. It was the intersectional connections between original fight for an Ethnic Studies department and 50+ years later still fighting to incorporate just one Ethnic Studies course requirement. AB 1460 showed up as our ancestors reminding us it was time to educate ourselves more about the social construct of racism and how it continues to create social, political, class, and intersectional hierarchy. Requiring an Ethnic Studies course honors the legacies of the people by not only including them but allowing them to lead in the discussion and implementation of the requirement.

Conclusion

What can college departments do to support Ethnic Studies?

- The Faculty Senate should document that Ethnic Studies faculty and department will determine the implementation of the requirement.
- Departments should continue to support Ethnic Studies as it is an influential interdisciplinary study that can impact any professional role students go into.

What must Ethnic Studies faculty and program still do?

- Ethnic Studies faculty can review their chosen curricula and make the necessary modifications to ensure it does not uphold colonialism, imperialism, and or systemic racism.

The movement for pan-African studies (PAS) has another requirement.

- During the recent national uprisings the world watched as we saw an increase in national attention to the systemic epidemic of Black lives being taken by the police.
  - It must remain vigilant in its fight for Black lives by way of educating people about the history of the Black experience with institutional racism, and demand that the discipline be given financial support in hiring more Black staff and faculty to serve more students.
  - Black faculty and students must engage with pan-African research and share the findings.
  - PAS must advocate their educational institution financially invest in more Black student serving resources and increase the budgets of the current pan-African programs, clubs, and centers on campus.
  - Nourish Ethnic Studies' transformatory potential into actual capacity (Rogers, 2011).

So while we may be partaking in virtual libation, collective breaths, and land acknowledgments, it is imperative students overstand and connect the evolution of activism in Ethnic Studies with our ancestors guiding us along the way.

References

Articles

Kanu, I. A. (2017). Igwebuike as an Igbo-African philosophy for Christian–Muslim relations in northern Nigeria. *Spirituality and Global Ethics*, 300–310.

Maparyan, L. (2012). *The womanist idea*. Routledge.

Masolo, D. (2006). African sage philosophy.

Moore, A. (2019). Black gazing in digital communities as a form of collective activism. In *Race and ethnicity: Moving from sociological imagination to sociological mindfulness* (pp. 305–319). Cognella Academic Publishing.

Oruka, H. O. (Ed.). (1990). *Sage philosophy: Indigenous thinkers and modern debate on African philosophy* (Vol. 4). Brill.

Rogers. (2012). The Black Campus Movement and the institutionalization of Black Studies, 1965–1970. *Journal of African American Studies, 16*(1), 21–40. https://doi.org/10.1007/s12111-011-9173-2

Thompson, B. W. (1993). Review of *Transforming the Curriculum; Transforming Knowledge*, by J. E. Butler, J. C. Walter, & E. K. Minnich. *Gender and Society, 7*(3), 470–473. http://www.jstor.org/stable/189808

Books

Barlow, W., & Shapiro, P. (1971). *An end to silence: The San Francisco state college student movement in the 60s*. Pegasus Press.

Benet, J. (1971). *Introduction*. In D. Karagueuzian (Ed.), Blow it Up! The Black Student Revolt at San Francisco State College and the Emergence of Dr. Hayakawa. Gambit.

Butler, J. E., & Walter, J. C. (1991). *Transforming the curriculum: Ethnic Studies and women's studies* (edited by J. E. Butler & J. C. Walter). State University of New York Press.

California State University: Graduation Requirement: Ethnic Studies, Cal. Educ. Sec. 89032 (2020).

Rojas, F. (2007). *From Black Power to Black Studies: How a Radical Social Movement Became an Academic Discipline*. The Johns Hopkins University Press.

Scott, O. L. (2008). Ethnic Studies: Preparing for the future. In T. P. Fong (Ed.), *Ethnic Studies research: Approaches and perspectives* (pp. 17–32). Alta Mira Press.

Web Links

Du Bois, W. E. B. (1958, June 20). The early beginnings of the Pan-African movement. https://credo.library.umass.edu/view/pageturn/mums312-b206-i013/#page/1/mode/1up

Karangi, M. M. (2019, October). https://www.researchgate.net/publication/336445595_AFRICAN_COSMOLOGY. doi:10.13140/RG.2.2.35377.74082

UCB Center for Race & Gender. (2019). https://www.crg.berkeley.edu/research/third-world-liberation-front/

Notes

[1] Pan-African will be used interchangeably with Black when speaking about the Pan-African communal experience shared in Ethnic Studies.

[2] The expression acquired its currency from a project conducted by the late Kenyan philosopher Henry Odera Oruka (1944–1995), whose primary aim was to establish, with evidence, that critical reflection upon themes of fundamental importance has always been the concern of a select few in African societies.

[3] The evidence that Oruka collected regarding the rational elaboration of such themes by indigenous sages is contained in dialogues, many of which appear in his classic text *Sage Philosophy: Indigenous Thinkers and Modern Debate on African Philosophy* (1990).

[4] www.google.com/search?q=cwc+csus&oq=CWC&aqs=chrome.1.69i57j69i59l2j46i433j46i175i199j69i60l3.4237j0j7&sourceid=chrome&ie=UTF-8

[5] Maparyan writes about a womanism that looks at the elements of sacred feminine energy of creation in relation to actively engaging in social change. This work is adding the understandings of what can be included in spiritual activism when taking ancestral acknowledgment into consideration.

Framing the Value and Purpose of Perspectives

Julie López Figueroa

This section represents an opportunity to explore why you believe what you believe and consider deconstructing why your perspective at times strongly resonates with us while other times perspectives unintentionally cause eyebrows to be raised in disagreement or peak from curiosity.

By using a process commonly referred to as critical reflection, the collection of readings is fundamentally intended to have "learners begin to re-evaluate their lives and to re-make them" (Mezirow, 1990). Why? More than fulfilling an intellectual exercise, critically reflecting on perspectives in the United States enables a practice of accountability to insure that freedom operates in a contemporary and responsive manner in relationship to its ever-changing populations. The readings offer analytical and theoretical perspectives to frame the chapters in the other sections as well as broadly introduce an Ethnic Studies perspective to conceptualize the world in ways we might not otherwise consider. Because the quality of our questions is a measure of our critical thinking (Paul & Elder, 2005), the format of this section is guided by a series of basic questions that will hopefully prompt a journey of self-reflection and self-discovery.

What are perspectives and where do perspectives originate? We are not born with perspectives, but rather socialized into having perspectives. In the United States, the two most influential institutions that socialize and define our early perspectives in life are home and school (Bowles & Gintis, 1976). Even with the transcendence of these sociocultural spaces, school and home continue to serve as touchstones from which to compare and contrast other perspectives. No matter our backgrounds, we are all exposed to a variety of perspectives broadly classified as radical, liberal, progressive, mainstream, moderate, and conservative. For instance, presidential and gubernatorial platforms are public mediums that embody some of these perspectives. Though these perspectives are itemized, some people's perspectives blend together to become progressive conservative, or as moderately liberal.

This kind of discourse signals that perspectives can be multidimensional but also that life is more complex than our language can even capture.

In the case of Ethnic Studies, an Ethnic Studies perspective emerged in response to the unquestioned academic practice of solely functioning from a Eurocentric male perspective to examine all other experiences. These academic blinders would cast any lived experience that was non-eurocentric male as being deficient or inferior. Beginning in the late 1960s, Ethnic Studies amplified the rigor of analytical frameworks by centering the intersectionality race, class, gender, and sexual orientation issues. Ethnic Studies questions those ideas we take for granted for the purpose of creating a more equitable society. On this note Mark's chapter, *"We're Going Out. Are You With Us?" The Origins of Asian American Studies*, provides a first hand account regarding the experiences and conversations that led to what is historically known as the 'Third World Strike' at UC Berkeley. From this strike, Ethnic Studies as a discipline was born. What were the perspectives that needed to be challenged in order for true democracy to equally exist for all communities in this nation? Almost as an answer to this question, Chavez, a former undergraduate with an Ethnic Studies major, offers a contemporary perspective as to the personal and professional benefits of selecting an Ethnic Studies major in her chapter titled, *Why Ethnic Studies was Meant for Me*. As examples, these two chapters illustrate how a shift in perspectives carved powerful new inroads in knowledge to create and access from one generation to the next. With the establishment of Ethnic Studies, future generations could access the true inheritance promised by democracy. This book is an invitation to juxtapose an Ethnic Studies perspective with your own perspectives to encourage a greater understanding about the way prejudice and discrimination formulate perspectives.

What role and function does our cultural practice of individualism play in shaping our perspective? Although we see the world through our individual perspectives, we also need to remember that our individual perspectives are porous to larger social perspectives. Another way of talking about perspectives is to consider the terms, micro and macro. Micro perspecties are individual whereas macro perspectives speak to societal or to a global level influence. Micro perspectives are always couched in macro perspectives therefore our individual perspectives are permeated by society's messages. Certainly, we have choices to believe certain things or see the world in a particular way but this is not always constant. For example, in my courses white and non-white students often demonstrate great apprehension to develop or let go of perspectives because changing perspectives somehow threatens family loyalty and/or they do not want to risk losing social acceptance among peers. In this way, students will distance themselves from critically thinking about the world and yet recognize that injustice is being experienced or do not want to think of injustice as working in their favor. Even though we live in a democratic nation, we make no apologies for not equally valuing and marginalizing the perspective of various communities throughout history. Because our perspectives are shaped by lived experiences, sometimes those lived experience are perceived to be the same or different. When individual differences are very different, that difference can either surface that harm of traditional practices or confirm the value of traditional practices.

Perspectives that operate at a macro level publicly declare and delineate appropriate social and cultural standards for viewing, framing, and engaging in a particular society. To insure macro perspectives are firmly interwoven in the society's structure, macro perspectives must permeate and define cultural norms and traditions in order to organize and regulate human behavior to insure "identity" is sustained, or socially reproduced throughout many generations (Bowles & Gintis, 1976). For example in a social and cultural context like the United States, the mainstream perspective is expressed in the commonly known phrase, the American Dream. The American Dream is nominally associated with being White and middle class, living a heterosexual lifestyle where father works and mother (assuming they are married) takes care of children in their purchased home where English is the preferred language. Collectively, these items represent a standard or ideal way of life indicating success. More often than not these standards are detached from the everyday realities that confront single mothers, single fathers, divorced parents, unmarried parents, gay and lesbian parents, gay and lesbian communities, grandparents raising grandchildren, adopted children, the homeless, adoptive parents, active racial/ethnic enclaves, and working poor. Having an ideal life identified creates the temptation to readily sort our lifestyles and perspectives into mainstream or non-mainstream bins. There is a real danger in oversimplifying how life happens. When we have an ideal by which to measure our level of success, very few people actually stop to consider what it takes to live up to the American Dream.

For example, in the United States where mainstream perspectives are intimately linked with representing good American traditional values and the norm, the majority of folks in this country can never be allowed to achieve the American Dream. Why? Our social outlook and cultural practice explicitly confirms that Americans in the United States revere and admire what cannot be commonly attained. In other words, the notion of exclusivity assigned to an experience or owning a rare material good is highly prized and admired in our nation. Maintaining glamour in practical terms requires that the common person not have full access to that particular experience or item. That is, inequality is a required condition that must exist in order for the American tale of meritocracy to exist.

The language of meritocracy rationalizes the exclusive experiences as an outcome of working harder and having more ability than others to achieve. Wing Sue defines and illustrates with examples how meritocracy can be the greatest American myth to shroud privilege and entitlement. Meritocracy, of course, assumes a level playing field and institutions are inherently fair. Because meritocracy is not only a cornerstone of our American identity, but a cultural ideology that informs our practice, we fail to critically recognize that inequality must exist in order for meritocracy to keep operating. That is, meritocracy cannot exist without making sure there is a group of folks that can be referenced as having less so the story of people pulling themselves up by the boot straps does not lose its luster. The earlier discussion of home and school is another example of how meritocracy emerges based on inequality and notions of neutrality. Home and school are social and cultural contexts that may or may not always coincide with one another (Delgado-Gaitan, 1992; Erickson, 1987; Villegas, 1994). When the home culture and school culture coincide, the experience of individuals for whom it coincides (Phelan, Davidson & Yu, 1993) very rarely is framed as unearned privilege. Instead, we continue to push the idea that everyone has a fair chance and that education is the great equalizer. No one stops to consider the differences in access to resources and opportunities (Oakes, 1994; Rios, 1996), the varying degrees in quality of schooling (Kretovics & Nussel, 1994), the lack of qualified teachers being directed to poor schools (Payne, 1994), or the fact that networks and mentoring can hugely make a difference in the lives of students (Stanton-Salazar, 1997). The tensions that centrally inform our lives hopefully inspires some realization that the ideal way of life can be detached from the complex realities through which life happens. While we need to celebrate our individuality, we also need to recognize our failures and successes are not solely determined by sheer will but are also mediated by active social structures.

What purpose does having a perspective serve in shaping identity? We must have the courage to contemplate the role of privilege when we cannot find value in one another's perspectives or essentialize someone else's experience. Privilege can be a hard term to apply to ourselves mostly because we do not set out to purposefully diminish or under value people. Yet, historically we can point to processes like assimilation, genocide, colonization, and conquest that occurred like slavery, Boarding Schools, and Manifest Destiny that violently divided communities. Generations later, some of us benefited from this outlook whereas others folks were severely disenfranchised. Certainly the progress in our communities releases us from having to live in the binary of winners and losers even though society insists that we all live in the binary to measure progress and tell stories of then and now.

How can social movements help us evaluate our individual perspectives? When individual perspectives are reticent to change, social movements are critical sites of accountability that keep inclusion and social justice as a priority. Social movements remind us that mainstream American perspectives have the inability to progressively transform given that they are color-blind, male-centric, and class-blind, among other things. While social movements may not entirely abolish the issues targeted, social movements invite us to recognize that working collectively rather than individually can transform our world. Without different civil right and social movements the once normal American traditions of slavery, conquest, colonization, segregation, xenophobia, denying a woman's rights to vote, eugenics, anti-miscegenation laws, and anti-Semitism might not otherwise be disrupted at a monumental scales. In some instances, communities are still surviving and/or recovery from these life changing events. We have to make more responsible choices no matter the level of fear that overcomes us and no matter the threat of social alienation. I want to invite you to sit in silence to contemplate what you contribute to the world around you and what kind of movement you belong to by virtue of your (un)conscious choices, or rather your individual perspectives.

I recently attended a speaking engagement in which Dr. Angela Davis (2006) was the featured speaker. Dr. Davis reflected on growing up during segregation in Birmingham, Alabama and shared how her mother would tell her at a very young age, "Things aren't suppose to be this way, this is not how things are supposed to be." I have to believe that there are more people in the world who would agree with this but perhaps feel it is enough to live comfortably and conveniently as long as one's needs are addressed and success is happening.

When we cling to our beliefs or become apprehensive to evaluating our perspectives, we do not build new knowledge or become critical thinkers. While it is important to celebrate what we know, it is even more essential to surface those power dynamics that refrain us from thinking there is nothing wrong or worse yet we cannot do anything to make substantive changes. If we feel at all inspired by Martin Luther King Jr., Dolores Huerta, Mahatma Gandhi, Jimmy Carter, Barbara Jordan, Gloria Anzaldúa, let us remember feeling inspired by these and other folks happens not just because we stand in agreement for what they do but I want to suggest that it is also because a part of us potentially recognizes our capacity to have the same courage. We need multiple voices and multiple perspectives to bring the same perspective of social justice to build awareness.

The collection of authors in this section invites readers to consider their outlook on society. More specifically, the readings examine the role and purpose of culture, the organizational structure of society, the intersection of race, class, and gender, the nature and purpose of meritocracy, the role of heterosexism, and the workings of racial formation. The readings refute the notion that perspectives emerge in happenstance way, and instead highlight the processes that silently inform but explicitly influence our perspectives. To this end, it is the hope of this author that these readings synergistically foster a habit of critical reflection among its readers to imagine a world where diversity is not viewed as a threat to American life, but gives life to Americans in the United States.

References

Bowles, S. and Gintis, H. (1976). *Schooling in capitalist America: Educational reform and contradictions of economic life*. New York: Basic Books.

Davis, Angela. (2006). *Making Real Change*. (Talk given at the University of California at Davis on October 10, 2006)

Delgado-Gaitan, C. (1992). School matters in the Mexican-American home: Socializing children to education. *American Educational Research Journal*, *29*(3), pp. 495–513.

Erickson, F. (1987). Transformation and school success: The politics and culture of educational achievement. *Anthropology and Education Quarterly, 18* (4), 335–356

Hurtado, A., Haney, C and Garcia, E. (1999). Becoming the mainstream: Merit, changing demographics and higher education in California. *La Raza Law Journal, 10*(2), 645–690.

Mezirow, J. (1990), "How critical reflection triggers transformative learning", in Mezirow, J. (Eds), *Fostering Critical Reflection in Adulthood. A Guide to Transformative and Emancipatory Learning* (pp.1–20). Jossey-Bass, San Francisco, CA.

Neill, D. M. & Medina, N. J. (1994). Standardized testing: harmful to educational health. In J. Kretovics & E. J. Nussel (Eds.) *Transforming urban education* (pp. 128–145). Boston: Allyn and Bacon.

Oakes, J. (1994). Tracking, inequality, and the rhetoric of reform: Why schools don't change. In J. Kretovics & E. J. Nussel (Eds.), *Transforming urban education* (pp.146–164). Boston: Allyn and Bacon.

Paul, R. & Elder, L. (2005). *Critical thinking: Concepts and tools.* Dillion Beach: Foundation for Critical Thinking.

Payne, R. S. (1994). The relationship between teacher's beliefs and sense of efficacy and their significance to urban LSES minority students. *Journal of Negro Education, 63* (2), 181–196.

Phelan, P., Davidson, A. L., & Yu, H. C. (1993). Students' multiple worlds: Navigating the borders of family, peer, and school cultures. In P. Phelan & A. L. Davidson (Eds.), *Renegotiating cultural diversity in American schools*, (pp. 52–88). New York: Teachers College Press.

Rios, F. (1996). Teachers' principles of practice for teaching in multicultural classrooms. In F. Rios (Ed.) *Teacher thinking in cultural contexts* (pp.129–148). Albany, NY: State University of New York Press.

Stanton-Salazar, R. D. (1997). A social capital framework for understanding the socialization of racial minority children and youths. *Harvard Educational Review, 67* (1), 1 – 39.

Villegas, A. M. (1994). School failure and cultural mismatch: Another view. In J. Kretovics and E. Nussel (Eds.), *Transforming urban education* (pp. 347–359). Boston: Allyn and Bacon.

Reflection Questions

1. How can we use some of the concepts to evaluate the perspectives we hold to be true? (Optional)

2. What aspects of the readings do you agree or disagree with and why?

3. Reflecting on the readings, what are the perspectives that dominate and define our life in the United States? (Optional)

4. What are the solutions and challenges we can draw from the readings to positively influence our quality of life?

5. Which perspectives do you hold on to and which have you let go of at this point in your life? What process or guidelines did you apply to negotiate your perspectives? Do you think these readings can enrich this process?

History

Framing Questions

1. What is the purpose of Ethnic Studies given the author's discussion? Provide a brief explanation using two examples to illustrate your viewpoint.

2. Do you believe the law is objective? If so, what are the strengths and limitations of a color-blind law given the diversity in our society?

3. Have you ever read history books by scholars who are nonwhite? If not why, not? If so, then explain what were the circumstances. (Optional)

4. Do you think that reading focused on the lived experiences written by nonwhite scholars might be different or the same as those written by white scholars? Provide a brief explanation. (Optional)

5. If you consider the works of white scholars and nonwhite scholars to be similar, how might you explain that in college the preferred way of telling history is often through the perspective of white scholars? (Optional)

ETHNIC STUDIES: AN INTRODUCTION

Introduction

Wayne Maeda (in memoriam) and Brian Baker

Ethnic Studies as a program and as a field of study was really born during the Third World Liberation strikes at San Francisco State College from November 1968 to March 1969 and University of California, Berkeley from January 1969 to March 1969.[1] African American, Chicano, Asian American, Native American and other students demanded, among other things, that institutions of higher learning provide access to poor and minority students, hiring minority faculty, administrators, and provide relevant curriculum. For those in the burgeoning field of Ethnic Studies, relevant curriculum broadly meant developing new perspectives, different methods of analysis, reconsidering what constituted "facts" and "interpretations" that shaped social realities for America's racial groups.

One of the most important functions envisioned over four decades ago in the field of Ethnic Studies was to provide a scholarly critique of the methods, theories, and practices of framing "the minority" experience by mainstream disciplines. This new breed and generation of historians challenged the notion that interpretation of history rested on dates, great men, and that "facts" speak for themselves in this grand narrative that passed as "the" definitive national history of America. In reality, the actual interpretation of history is affected by which facts are used, omitted, falsified, distorted, and known by the historian. More importantly, historical interpretation depends as much on the historian's own assumptions, biases, and agendas as it does on "facts." Because student activists of the late 1960s realized that the facts in the histories of African, Asian, Chicano, and Native Americans were often distorted, buried or simply "MIH" (missing in history) they argued that it was necessary to recover, re-interpret, and revise those histories. Ethnic Studies still commits itself to the goal of recovering, re-interpreting, and revising our past so that we can make sense of the present in order to prepare for the future that will become even more diverse.

Contributed by Wayne Maeda. © Kendall Hunt Publishing Company

The problem of the twentieth century is the problem of the color line. Although this prophetic statement was made by W. E. B. Du Bois in 1903, it remains one of the most salient and intractable issues in the twenty-first century. When he published *The Soul of Black Folks*, Du Bois was well aware of the Chinese who journeyed to "Gold Mountain" in the 1850s were denied naturalization rights and prevented from intermarrying with whites. In fact, the Chinese held the distinction of being the first ethnic group in the United States to be persecuted and excluded from immigration based on race in 1882. The Japanese, who followed the Chinese immigrants beginning in 1880s, not only inherited the anti-Asiatic sentiment but also faced the same fate of denial of citizenship and ownership of land, as well as ultimate exclusion in 1924. Moreover, by the time Du Bois's book was published, America was on the verge of concluding its first imperialistic venture into Asia with the military conquest and occupation of the Philippines. Under the guise of "benign assimilation," American imperialistic policy brought civilization to the "brown monkeys," "savages," and Filipino "niggers" in the Philippines. Du Bois recognized the depth, complexities and nuances of navigating the issue of the "color line" across the color spectrum: the challenge for all of us in the twenty-first century remains . . . *the problem of the color line-the relationship of the darker to the lighter races of men in Asia and Africa, in America and the islands of the sea.*[2]

This section on History begins with a special, albeit not complete, focus on California Indians in the middle decades of the nineteenth century when settler colonial policies facilitated many instances of genocide and where indigenous claims to their homelands were blatantly and convenient ignored. In "Returning Home," Annette Reed shares an account of the challenges faced by the Tolowa Dee-ni' people in maintaining their traditional connections to their homeland in northern California. Although California Indians had already experienced a myriad of political, economic, and social problems brought on by manifest destiny and settler colonialism, an already problematic situation was worsened with the discovery of gold at Sutter's Mill in 1848. Within a period of seven years, more than 300,000 settlers invaded the indigenous landscape, and as an outcome of their desire for gold thousands of California Indians were brutally killed in many documented instances of genocide. When California achieved statehood in 1850, state-sponsored genocide and settler colonial initiatives intensified the marginalization of Native nations and communities. However, despite existing amid circumstances where they faced their "world turned upside down" Reed highlights the significance of her Tolowa Dee-ni' ancestors as "decision makers" who managed to express and assert their sense of indigeneity. According to Reed, despite repeated attempts by colonial decision-makers to forcefully remove them from their homeland, the actions and strategies initiated by her Tolowa Dee-ni' ancestors "ensured our lives as Native peoples today."

Steven Crum provides the reader with a focus on broad federal policies that impacted the Native American people from the nineteen-century to recent times.

While these federal policies may be familiar to many, Crum explores the complexities of Native Americans as not merely victims but agents. Native Americans in the past have been constructed as one-dimensional "savages" or as victims of federal policies. Crum demonstrates that Native Americans responded, reacted, and, even more importantly in the processes became actors forcing the federal government to become the "reactors."

Timothy Fong, in *The History of Asians in America* demonstrates with a grand sweep, the diversity that makes up this group labeled "Asian Americans" and divides them into four general historical epochs. In doing so, Fong situates various Asian American groups throughout our history beginning in 1840s, through War World II, to Southeast Asian refugee groups fleeing the effects of Vietnam War, and the "new immigrants" who have invigorated the pre-1965 Asian American communities. Asian Americans, with changes in immigration laws and growth of globalization, are now posed to become, in more urban and suburban cities in California, the majority population.

In *Recent African Immigration History*, Boatamo Mosupyoe illuminates little known or understood immigration from Africa and the Caribbean. So much emphasis has been focused on Asian immigration and their growth in America that recent immigrants from Africa and the Caribbean have not been on our radar. Even with President Barack Obama's father, a Kenyan, our simplistic view of "the" African American experience continues. Mosupyoe, however, examines the complex relationships of identity formation of these recent immigrants from Africa and the Caribbean, as well as the nuances between the new immigrants and the long-established African American communities.

As a Hmong refugee born in Thailand after the Vietnam War and before coming to the United States as a child with parents and family members, Bao Lo addresses themes of resilience, resistance, and survival in "The Hmong in the United States." Following the passage of the Indochina Migration and Refugee Assistance Act of 1975, Hmong refugees started arriving in the United States and through the 1980s. The largest communities of Hmong Americans formed in Central Valley region of California in cities such as Fresno and Merced, and the Minneapolis and St. Paul area of Minnesota. Lo provides us with detailed discussion of demographics related to the Hmong Americans and an overview of data related to income, poverty rates, homeownership, and educational attainment. The data reveals that the Hmong population, which today includes first, second, and third generations, experiences economic hardship overall when compared to "all Americans." Hmong Americans have built an infrastructure of community organizations, especially in California and Minnesota. The building of organizations that have engaged in political and civic engagement as well as cultural identity has fostered empowerment within and throughout Hmong communities. Due to war and displacement the Hmong were pushed from their homelands and became refugees, and those who came to the United States managed to re-establish themselves and form communities. Despite using their agency to form Hmong communities in cities like Fresno, California, and Minneapolis, Minnesota, data shows that they continue to experience economic hardships when compared to all Americans.

This introductory section on history is meant to be just that — an introduction. There are many more areas to be studied, explored, recovered, re-interpreted, and even continually re-written. It is hoped that the seed of curiosity, a desire to question, and the valuing of a critical approach have been sown, for there is much work to be done in all fields of Ethnic Studies to be engaged in by future generations of historians, researchers, and writers.

Notes

[1] William Wei, *The Asian American Movement* (Philadelphia: Temple University Press, 1993), 15.

[2] Du Bois, 23.

"Returning Home Tolowa Dee-ni'"

Annette L. Reed, Ph.D.

Enrolled at Tolowa Dee-ni' Nation (Northwestern California)
Department of Ethnic Studies Professor in Native American Studies and
Ethnic Studies California State University, Sacramento

In reflection of Tolowa (Huss or Dee-ni) history and the histories of other Native Nations, our ancestors faced "a world turned upside down" by White contact and intrusion into traditional homelands.[1] Their lives, forever changed, under the controlling paternalism of the U.S. government and surviving devastating genocidal practices, it appeared that Native Americans or American Indians became helpless victims. However, nothing could be further from a Native reality. Our ancestors, while they endured horrific conditions, including diseases, massacres, and removals from homelands, while maintaining their powerful role as "decision makers." In fact, their decisions, their responsible ways of taking actions, and their deep connection to homeland, ensured our lives as Native peoples today.

This chapter focuses on the story of Indian–White relations between the Euro-Americans and the Tolowa between 1858 and 1868. Despite White invasion and intrusion in the mid-19th century, the Tolowa people of northwestern California and southwestern Oregon, remained Native over the years because of their cultural persistence and a deep-rooted attachment to their land. Through resistance efforts, Tolowa people shaped their own destiny and that of their future generations. This piece seeks to illuminate Native response to non-Indian invasion and colonial control of their homeland and to further present Native people, our ancestors, as active agents, decision makers, in their own tribal histories.

Contributed by Annette L. Reid. © Kendall Hunt Publishing Company

Years before the establishment of the Smith River Reservation in 1862, the American government enacted two Indian policies: removal and reservation. Indian removal was first applied to Native American tribes east of the Mississippi River. In the decade of the 1830s, the government removed approximately 75,000 tribal people of the Southeast—Cherokees, Choctaws, Chickasaws, Creeks, and Seminoles—to Indian Territory (today's Oklahoma). Congress made Indian removal official in 1830 with the passage of the Indian Removal Act.[2]

Euro-Americans favored the removal act for several reasons. First, they could not accept Indian nations within a larger nation because of the belief in one nation "indivisible." Second, the United States wanted to open Native land for farms and homesteads of White citizens and for business interests, including railroads. Third, White Americans wanted their country to be homogeneous with everyone speaking the same language, operating under the same laws, and having the same customs and beliefs. Because Indian tribes remained culturally diverse, they could not be a part of America's cultural and social homogeneous order without giving up their ways of life. White Americans also maintained that it would be too expensive and time-consuming to try to Americanize Indians. The quick solution, they argued, was to remove them outside the physical boundaries of the United States. Indian Territory became the logical choice for Indians since it was located west of the Mississippi River.[3]

Removing tribes westward also affected Native groups living in the far western region. Beginning in the early 1860s the government considered gathering up tribal groups in California and removing them to particular reservations. In 1862, Senator Milton Latham of California submitted a bill into Congress which, if passed, would have gathered up all the tribes west of the Sierra Nevada mountains in California and placed them on one big reservation located in Owens Valley, California.[4] This idea failed to be carried out, but others continued to be proposed. Two years later, some White Californians suggested gathering up all California Indian tribes and placing them on some offshore island. More specifically, they had in mind the Santa Catalina Islands, not far from Santa Barbara.[5] Again this idea fell to the wayside. However, Indian removal was successfully carried out in 1863 when some Indians in Butte County, California were accused of stealing White-owned cattle. Four hundred and sixty-one Indians of the Concow Maidu tribe around Chico were gathered up and removed to Mendocino County on the newly established Round Valley Reservation.[6]

The removal policy became this nation's official Indian policy in the 1830 and 1840s. By the late 1940s, however, some White American policy makers began to question the policy of removing tribes further west. If the nation continued to carry out westward removal, then the tribes would eventually drop into the Pacific Ocean. The White Americans therefore came up with a new alternative Native plan by 1848. In that year, William Medill, the Commissioner of Indian Affairs of the Bureau of Indian Affairs (BIA), suggested creating "colonies" for Indians. He had in mind setting aside gigantic reserves of land in the American heartland and then removing tribes to those reserves. Medill wanted one reserve located in the northern Great Plains region and the second reserve on the southern plains.[7] By creating these sizable colonies, the American people would open the middle part of the continent as a major travel artery for Americans to move from east to west.

Eventually, Medill's idea of colonies became the new reservation policy for Indians in the decade of the 1850s. In this period the government negotiated treaties with the tribes of the Great Plains area which brought into existence reservation land for Indians to move to. For agreeing to surrender their large hunting ranges and consenting to move to reservations, the Indians were to be paid in the form of annuity goods (clothing, food, etc.) and services (education, health services, etc.). Once the government acquired Indian land by land cession treaties, it created new western territories. In 1854, Congress passed the Kansas-Nebraska Act which brought into existence these two territories. Thus, the reservation policy came into existence in the 1850s and largely replaced the earlier policy of removing Indians further west.[8] However, Indian removal was not eliminated completely, for it continued to be carried out since the government wanted all Indians to remove to newly established reservation located throughout the far western region. The notion of Indian removal therefore became intertwined with the reservation policy.

By the late 1850s, both policies became visible in the far west. The Federal government removed many Indians from southwestern Oregon and northwestern California to west-central Oregon in the 1850s due to the Rouge River War. The government placed them on the Siletz Reservation located in west-central Oregon. Moreover, the U.S. Government forcibly removed most Tolowa to move to the newly established Klamath Reservation in northern California in 1857.

As part of a larger national policy of removal, the American government forced Tolowa to leave their homelands and move to a variety of places already inhabited by Native peoples from other tribal groups. Local White citizens sought the rich agricultural lands of the Smith River valley. The beginning of removal took place from 1852 to 1856 when the federal government, with local White support, removed some Tolowa to Wilson Creek, a locality approximately 25 miles south of Smith River. But the significant removals of Tolowas started in the mid-1850s and thereafter.

In June 1855, Stephen Gerald Whipple, a federal Indian agent, proposed Tolowa removal to a reservation at the lower the Klamath River. Whipple and other Indian agents along with the U.S. military decided that the Indians in the area needed to be moved to the Klamath Reservation to make the Smith River Valley available for White settlement. The U.S. Army thus moved the Tolowa onto the lower Klamath reservation, but without food. In Tolowa traditional society, each family possess the "rights of usage" their own fishing, hunting, and gathering areas. With this in mind, moving the Tolowa onto the Yurok's homeland left them without resource areas to obtain food and caused friction between the two Native Nations.

The U.S. Army established Fort Ter-waw on the lower Klamath River in October 1857 under the command of Lieutenant George Crook. Crook and approximately 50 soldiers arrived at the Klamath River reservation on October 13, 1857.[9]

Lieutenant Crook explained to his superior, Major Mackall, in a letter dated October 21, 1857, that upon his arrival to the Klamath River Reservation he found Tolowas dissatisfied with their new location on the Klamath River and they escaped in small groups to return to their homeland on the Smith River. Crook and his men, however, forcibly removed approximately 100 Tolowas from Smith River back to the Klamath reservation.[10]

Lieutenant Crook quickly assessed the state of Tolowas and Yuroks on the Klamath Reservation and incorrectly gave his reasons why Tolowas returned to Smith River:

> As far as I can learn of present, the Indians [Yuroks] who have allways [sic] lived in the land occupied by this Indian Reservation, are perfectly contented, and it is only those moved here from Smith River and its vicinity, who are discontented and that this disaffection is principally caused from misrepresentations of ill disposed whites, whose interest it is to have the Indians back on Smith River.[11]

While some Whites did urge Tolowas to return to Smith River, their main reason for returning home persisted to be their deep-rooted connection to their ancestral homeland. A secondary reason was the lack of food and supplies on the lower Klamath. Acting upon their own initiative, they repeatedly escaped Klamath Reservation and returned home.

> Major,
>
> I have the honor to report, that, since my communication to you of Oct 21st, the Smith River Indians here, have made repeated attempts to leave the reservation, and a large number succeeded by stealing off in small parties: they said they were not afraid of one, as the white men told them I would not dare fire on them, and that they were going back to their country ....[12]

Indeed, Tolowas viewed the area around Smith River as "their country" and made all efforts to return. After several efforts to escape, but finally being rounded up by the Army and forcibly returned to the Lower Klamath Reservation, the Tolowas developed a larger plan.

Tolowa leaders and elders most likely gathered to discuss the best strategies to escape to their homeland. Facing a military force with their families, including children must have been of great consideration. Yet even in arms way of life-threatening danger, they created a plan and carried it through.

Lieutenant Crook learned of the plan in time to alter but remained unable to stop the Tolowas efforts to return home.

> Finding however that they could not all get away by this method [escaping to Smith River in small groups] they formed a conspiracy, first to kill me, destroy the boats between here and Man-kill and leave for Smith River. Being apprized [sic] of this conspiracy, and that a large number of warriors had already arrived from Smith River, for the purpose of carrying their plan into execution. I posted a guard at Man-kill on the 7th inst. to await the issue. On the 17th inst. the Indians

sent for the agent to come to their houses, to see a sick Indian: the agent went accompanied by one white man! Immediately upon their arrival, the Indians made an attack from all sides with knives and bows and arrows, fortunately the two succeeded in keeping them off until the guard came to their rescue, who after firing two or three volleys succeeded in driving the Indians to the brush. A dispatch was sent for me, but after my arrival, I could only get an occasional shot at them in the bush.[13]

In their struggle to return to the Smith River area, the Tolowas did not kill Crook and the Indian agent, but they did leave the Klamath Reservation in record numbers, approximately 600-700, and returned Smith River.[14]

Tolowa men, women and children returned to the Smith River to make their stand in their sacred homeland. They chose to not submit to the federal government policy of removal and remained determined. In a letter dated, December 25, 1857, Lieutenant Crook wrote,

The number of warriors on Smith River are about one hundred and they say they will not come back here alive and if I want to fight I will find them on Smith River.[15]

As a result of this and subsequent stands, Tolowas played an active role in remaining within their ancestral homeland. They refused to submit to removal policy and continued to escape in small groups to their homeland.

These powerful responses insured the continuation and survival of Tolowas people in the place where they now reside. If they had submitted to removal to Klamath River reservation, they would have effectively assimilated or at least acculturated to a greater degree. It can be speculated that they would have ceased to be a culturally distinct group, known as Tolowa.

Later, Indian Agent Stephen Whipple attempted to obtain $2,000 from the federal government to purchase "rights of usage" from the Yuroks, but he was unsuccessful. The Tolowa were starving and therefore many returned to Smith River. Only a handful remained for one year at the lower Klamath Reservation. H. P. Heintzleman, sub–Indian Agent, reported to Thomas J. Henley, superintendent of Indian affairs in San Francisco, on July 1, 1858: "Of the Tolana [Tolowa] Indians who were removed to the reservation during the past year about eighty of them remain, the balance have returned to their old haunts."[16]

It is rather ironic that Whites commonly used the term "old haunts" in reference to Tolowa returning to their homeland. They did not realize how accurate a term this became to reflect the perspective of Native people. Smith River area remained their indigenous homeland with the graves of their ancestors embedded in the very soil since the beginning of time, thereby giving irony to the use of the word "haunts," ghosts, and thereby ancestors. Thus, they returned to the land of their ancestors. Also, as mentioned that most had returned to their Native homeland, that demonstrated that the ancestors made the decision to return home and they carried out their decisions even in the case of U.S. military forces in the area.

After the Klamath Reservation experience, the Federal Government, removed the Tolowa northward, especially after the Rogue River war broke out between Indians of southwestern Oregon. Local militia groups and White settlers targeted all Indians of the area, including Tolowas for removal to distant reservations. White citizens and military officers repeatedly expressed concern that Tolowas would join their southwestern Oregon tribal cousins in open warfare against non-Indians. The federal government, as well as local militia units, used the Rogue River war of the mid-1850s as a springboard for Tolowa removal policy.

In 1860, the military force marched six hundred Tolowa to Siletz Reservation in Oregon. During the march, a woman gave birth, but she was allowed to stop only long enough to squat down and bear the baby. The woman died and other women took the baby and nursed it.[17] The military herded Tolowa onto Battle Rock at Port Orford and stayed there for nearly a year. After near starvation, the government removed them to Siletz, but most hid and returned to Smith River Valley.

Basically, at this point in time, the Tolowa were scattered in many directions, but many made their way back to their homeland. Finally, on May 3, 1862, the federal government created a reservation at Smith River, as well as Camp Lincoln, a military fort in Elk Valley, near Crescent City, to "supervise" this reservation and act as a buffer between the Tolowa and Crescent City White settlers. Obviously, the Indian women needed protection from White men. Sexual assaults by White men upon Native women were common. In a letter to William Dole, commissioner of Indian affairs, Indian Agent George Hanson wrote, "It was quite apparent that more married men should be brought into the service as soon as possible and those who are unmarried discharged."[18] (The underline emphasis is Hanson's, not mine.)

By the beginning of the 1860s it became clear that the Tolowa people remained deeply rooted to their homeland. Even after the devastating massacres and more than one removal, the Tolowa continued to return to their "old haunts."[19] The reasons they returned were based on their spiritual beliefs and culture. These reasons are part of a collective memory of the Tolowa people. The creation account embedded religious significance between the land and people. The physical land was tied in with traditional stories which connected the Tolowa people to their land. Used for education, the stories of the land and animals cemented the Tolowa with their land.

In 1862, Tolowa forced the BIA to create a reservation for Tolowa people at Smith River, although it was short-lived. The BIA abolished the reservation in July 1868 to save money. It first considered taking the 370 residents of the reservation and removing them to the Round Valley Reservation in Mendocino County. But the government concluded that the trip would be too far and expensive. Therefore, it removed the Indians to the Hoopa Valley Reservation, established in 1864 and located some 150 miles southeast of Smith River.[20] On December 6, 1868, the government moved Smith River Indian residents out of the valley, and they arrived on the Hoopa Reservation on December 20. About 100 of the above number ran away before arriving at Hoopa but were soon captured and brought to Hoopa.[21]

As previously discussed this was not their first removal from their ancestral home-lands. By 1871, not one Tolowa remained at Hoopa, for they had all left over a two-year period and returned to Smith River. Only 50 former residents of once-existing Smith River Reservation remained at Hoopa in the early 1870s, but they were all former Natives of Humboldt County, perhaps Yurok.[22]

Thus, up to 1870, the Tolowa had experienced living on three different Indian reservations: first the Klamath Reservation (1857–58), then the Smith River Reservation (1862–68), and finally the Hoopa Reservation (1868–71). The nation's Indian policies certainly had an impact on the Tolowa in the 1860s.

In 1908 the federal government established a small 163-acre reservation at the mouth of the Smith River along the Pacific coast. The government purchased the land for a price of $7,200.00 from William Westbrook, a White landowner whose family-owned sizable amounts of property in the Smith River Valley. Payment was made possible by the congressional appropriation of June 21, 1906.[23]

Tolowas from Smith River maintained a sense of deep connection to the land of their ancestors. At every attempt to remove Tolowas, they made decisions to return to their homeland. If they had not stood strong and actively carried through with their plans to escape and return home, today's people of Smith River Rancheria, now renamed Tolowa Dee-ni' Nation, most likely would not have remained a culturally distinct people. Native people are a land-based people. Today, the Tolowa Dee-ni' Nation continues to grow and develop, both as a people and a land-base for our Nation. Over the years, when I returned home, I saw my mother Adrienne Thomas working in the fields, the cannery or with children at her own home day care. I attended Nay-Dosh, our ceremonial dances, and watched the young people singing and giving thanks to creator. I went for walks with my uncle to gather plants used by our people. I constantly think of the great sacrifices, determination and decision making that our ancestors did to ensure that we exist today. I hope the decisions we make today will be ones by which future generations will look back and say, "our ancestors' way back in 2021 made decisions and actions that ensured our continuance in a good way, as Native people."

 ## Notes

[1] I will use the term "Tolowa" in my chapter, although there is no clear tribal consensus regarding what we would traditionally refer to ourselves as. Huss or Dee-ni are also terms used meaning "the people." In precontact times, Tolowa people would have had more of an identity with the villages of their parents and family.

Tolowa world embroiled in rapid societal change. Tolowa elders thus referred to the 1850s as "the time the world was turned upside down." Reed Interview with Loren Bommelyn, Crescent City, California, January 1983.

[2] Francis Paul Prucha, *The Great Father*, Vol. 1 (Lincoln: University of Nebraska Press, 1984), pp. 179–242; Arrell Morgan Gibson, The American Indian: Prehistory to the Present (Lexington, Mass.: D.C. Heath and Company, 1980), pp. 303–331.

[3] Prucha, pp. 179–242; Gibson, pp. 307–331.

[4] A bill," Visalia Weekly Delta, June 5, 1862, p. 2; P.H. Wentworth to William P. Dole, August 30, 1862, ARCIA, 1862, Serial 1157, p. 471.

[5] Byron Nelson, Jr., *Our Home Forever: The Hupa Indians of Northern California* (Salt Lake City: Howe Brothers, 1988), p. 88.

[6] Dorothy Hill, The Indians of Chico Rancheria (Sacramento: State of California, Resources Agency, 1978), pp. 39–41.

[7] Ibid.

[8] Annual Reports Commissioner of Indian Affairs, 1858 serial 997.

[9] Strobridge, William. *Regulars in the Redwoods: The U.S. Army in Northern California 1852-1861.* Spokane, Washington: The Arthur H. Clark Company, 1994. p. 154.

[10] RG 393, Returns From Military Post, Camp Lincoln, M617-627 Lt. George Crook to Major Mackall, October 21, 1857.

[11] Ibid.

[12] RG 393, Returns From Military Post, Camp Lincoln, M617-627 Lt. George Crook to Major Mackall, November 21, 1857.

[13] Ibid.

[14] RG 393, Returns From Military Post, Camp Lincoln, M617-627 Lt. George Crook to Major Mackall, November 25, 1857.

[15] Ibid.

[16] Annual Reports Commissioner of Indian Affairs, 1858 serial 997.

[17] Reed, Annette, Interview with Loren Bommelyn, Crescent City, California, August 1991.

[18] George, Hanson, Letter Received Office of Indian Affairs (M234,Roll 39, F260-266), RG 75, NA.

[19] The term "they returned to their old haunts" was used repeatedly by Indian agents, local militia, and government officials regarding the Tolowa returning to their homeland.

[20] Nelson, Our Home Forever, p. 89.

[21] Henry Orman, Jr., to N.G. Taylor, December 31, 1868, LR (M234, Roll 43, f 376), RG 75, NA.

[22] D.H. Lowry to Commissioner of Indian Affairs (CIA), September 1, 1871, ARCIA, 1871, Serial 1505, p. 747.

[23] Letter to Attorney General, May 6, 1908, Central Classified Files (CCF), 77389-07-California Special-311, RG 75, NA.

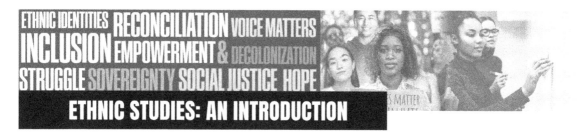

ETHNIC STUDIES: AN INTRODUCTION

The History of Asians in America
Timothy Fong

 ## Visibility and Invisibility

On October 14, 2000, Miss Hawaii, Angela Perez Baraquio, was crowned Miss America 2001, becoming the first Filipino American and Asian American ever to hold the title. Miss California, Rita Ng, the first Asian American to hold that state's beauty title, was selected as the second runner-up. This seemingly innocent historical event was not lost to many Asian Americans, especially Filipino Americans. "After years of invisibility in the mainstream and being seen as inferior to accepted standards of beauty, we now have a sudden validation of the multicultural in America," beamed *Asian Week* columnist Emil Guillermo. Despite his celebratory mood, Guillermo also touched on an important irony. Baraquio was never referred to as Filipino American or Asian American. Instead, she was referred to as Hawaiian. On the surface, this would seem to make sense because she is from Honolulu. "So what explains Miss Louisiana being reported as 'black' . . . and Baraquio's Hawaiian?" Guillermo asked incredulously. "The significance is that since their arrival on the scene in America at the turn of the century, Filipinos have toiled quietly and invisibly. It seems when they get face time, they don't get the credit they deserve."[1]

Guillermo's observation speaks loudly to the fact that Asian Americans are at once visible, yet invisible. This is particularly true with regards to the history of Asians in the United States. The historical experience of Asian Americans is not at all atypical of other minority groups. As a distinct racial minority group, and as immigrants, Asian Americans faced enormous individual prejudice, frequent mob violence, and extreme forms of institutional discrimination. But Asian Americans have not merely been victims of hostility and oppression; indeed, they have also shown remarkable strength and perseverance, which is a testimony to their desire to make the United States their home.

Fong, Timothy P., *Contemporary Asian American Experience, The: Beyond The Model Minority,* 2nd Edition, © 2002, pp.15–35. Reprinted by permission of Pearson Education, Inc., Upper Saddle River, NJ.

Immigration

Between 1848 and 1924, hundreds of thousands of immigrants from China, Japan, the Philippines, Korea, and India came to the United States in search of a better life and livelihood. Although this period represents the first significant wave, these immigrants were by no means the very first Asians to come to America. Recent archaeological finds off the coast of Southern California have led to speculation that the West Coast may have been visited by Buddhist missionaries from China in the fifth century. Direct evidence of this claim is still being debated, but it is known that the Spanish brought Chinese ship-builders to Baja California as early as 1571, and later Filipino seamen were brought by Spanish galleons from Manila and settled along the coast of Louisiana. Chinese merchants and sailors were also present in the United States prior to the discovery of gold in California in 1848. Most people are unaware that Asian Indians were brought to America during the late eighteenth century as indentured servants and slaves.[2]

The California gold rush did not immediately ignite a mass rush of Chinese immigrants to America. In fact, only a few hundred Chinese arrived in California during the first years of the gold rush, and most of them were merchants. However, large-scale immigration did begin in earnest in 1852 when 52,000 Chinese arrived that year alone. Many Chinese came to the United States not only to seek their fortunes but also to escape political and economic turmoil in China. As gold ran out, thousands of Chinese were recruited in the mid-1860s to help work on the transcontinental railroad. Eventually more than 300,000 Chinese entered the United States in the nineteenth century, engaging in a variety of occupations. During this same period Chinese also immigrated to Hawaii, but in far fewer numbers than to the continental United States.[3]

Large capitalist and financial interests welcomed the Chinese as cheap labor and lobbied for the 1868 Burlingame Treaty, which recognized "free migration and emigration" of Chinese to the United States in exchange for American trade privileges in China. As early as 1870 Chinese were 9 percent of California's population and 25 percent of the state's work force.[4] The majority of these Chinese were young single men who intended to work a few years and then return to China. Those who stayed seldom married because of laws severely limiting the immigration of Chinese women and prohibiting inter-marriage with white women. The result was the Chinese were forced to live a harsh and lonely bachelor life that often featured vice and prostitution. In 1890, for example, there were roughly 102,620 Chinese men and only 3,868 Chinese women in the United States, a male to female ratio of 26:1.[5] Despite these conditions, Chinese workers continued to come to the United States.

Following the completion of the transcontinental railroad in 1869, large numbers of unemployed Chinese workers had to find new sources of employment. Many found work in agriculture where they cleared land, dug canals, planted orchards, harvested crops, and were the foundation for successful commercial production of many California crops. Others settled in San Francisco and other cities to manufacture shoes, cigars, and clothing. Still others started small businesses such as restaurants, laundries, and general stores. Domestic service such as house boys, cooks, and gardeners were also other areas of employment for the Chinese. In short, the Chinese were involved in many occupations that were crucial to the economic development and domestication of the western region of the United States.[6] Unfortunately, intense hostility against the Chinese reached its peak in 1882 when Congress passed the Chinese Exclusion Act intended to "suspend" the entry of Chinese laborers for ten years. Other laws were eventually passed that barred Chinese laborers and their wives permanently.[7]

The historical experience of Japanese in the United States is both different yet similar to that of the Chinese. One major difference is that the Japanese immigrated in large numbers to Hawaii, and they did not come in large numbers to the United States until the 1890s. In 1880 only 148 Japanese were living in the U.S. mainland. In 1890 this number increased to 2,000, mostly merchants and students. However, the population increased dramatically when an influx of 38,000 Japanese workers from Hawaii arrived in the U.S. mainland between 1902 and 1907.[8] The second difference was the fact the Japanese were able to fully exploit an economic niche in agriculture that the Chinese had only started. The completion of several national railroad lines and the invention of the refrigerator car were two advancements that brought tremendous expansion in the California produce industry. The early Japanese were fortunate to arrive at an opportune time, and about two thirds of them found work as agricultural laborers. Within a short time the Japanese were starting their own farms in direct competition with non-Japanese farms. By 1919 the Japanese controlled over 450,000 acres of agricultural land. Although this figure represents only 1 percent of active California agricultural land at the time, the Japanese were so efficient in their farming practices that they captured 10 percent of the dollar volume of the state's crops.[9]

The third major difference was the emergence of Japan as a international military power at the turn of the century. Japan's victory in the Russo-Japanese War (1904–1905) impressed President Theodore Roosevelt, and he believed a strategy of cooperation with the Japanese government was in the best interest of the United States. Roosevelt blocked calls for complete Japanese exclusion and instead worked a compromise with the Japanese government in 1907 known as the "Gentleman's Agreement." This agreement halted the immigration of Japanese laborers but allowed Japanese women into the United States. With this in mind, the fourth difference was the fact that the Japanese in the United States were able to actually increase in population, start families, and establish a rather stable community life.[10]

Filipino immigration began after the United States gained possession of the Philippines following the Spanish-American War in 1898. The first Filipinos to arrive were a few hundred *pensionados*, or students supported by government scholarships. Similar to the Japanese experience, a large number of Filipinos went directly to Hawaii before coming to the U.S. mainland. Between 1907 and 1919 over 28,000 Filipinos were actively recruited to work on sugar plantations in Hawaii. Filipinos began to emigrate to the United States following the passage of the 1924 Immigration Act, which prohibited all Asian immigration to this country, and there was a need for agricultural and service labor.[11]

Because Filipinos lived on American territory, they were "nationals" who were free to travel in the United States without restriction. In the 1920s over 45,000 Filipinos arrived in Pacific Coast ports, and a 1930 study found 30,000 Filipinos working in California. These Filipinos were overwhelmingly young, single males. Their ages ranged between 16 and 29, and there were 14 Filipino men for every Filipina. Sixty percent of these Filipinos worked as migratory agricultural laborers, and 25 percent worked in domestic service in Los Angeles and San Francisco. The rest found work in manufacturing and as railroad porters. Unlike the Japanese, Filipinos did not make their mark in agriculture as farmers, but as labor union organizers.[12] Both Filipino farm worker activism and Japanese farm competition created a great deal of resentment among white farmers and laborers.

Koreans and Asian Indians slightly predated the Filipinos, but arrived in much smaller numbers. Between 1903 and 1905 over 7,000 Koreans were recruited for plantation labor work in Hawaii, but after Japan established a protectorate over Korea in 1905, all emigration was halted.[13] In the next five years, Japan increased its economic and political power and formally annexed Korea in 1910. Relatively few Koreans lived in the United States between 1905 and 1940. Among those included about 1,000 workers who migrated from Hawaii, about 100 Korean "picture brides," and a small number of American-born Koreans. The Korean population in the United States during that time was also bolstered by roughly 900 students, many of whom fled their home country because of their opposition to Japanese rule. Like other Asian immigrant groups, Koreans found themselves concentrated in California agriculture working primarily as laborers, although a small number did become quite successful farmers.[14]

The first significant flow of Asian Indians occurred between 1904 and 1911, when just over 6,000 arrived in the United States. Unlike the other Asian groups, Asian Indians did not work in Hawaii prior to entering the American mainland, but they worked primarily in California agriculture. Similar to the Chinese, Filipinos, and Koreans, they had an extremely high male to female ratio. Of the Asian Indians who immigrated to the United States between 1904 and 1911, there were only three or four women, all of whom were married.[15] Eighty to ninety percent of the first Asian Indian settlers in the United States were Sikhs, a distinct ethnoreligious minority group in India. Despite this fact, these Sikhs were often called Hindus, which they are not. Sikhs were easily recognizable from all other Asian immigrant groups because of their huskier build, their turbans, and their beards. But like other Asians in the United States at the time, they also worked primarily in California's agricultural industry. Asian Indians worked first as farm workers, and like the Japanese, they also formed cooperatives, pooled their resources, and began independent farming.[16] Immigration restrictions, their relatively small numbers, and an exaggerated male to female ratio prevented Asian Indians from developing a lasting farm presence. One major exception can be found in the Marysville/Yuba City area of Northern California, where Asian Indian Sikhs are still quite active in producing cling peaches.[17]

Anti-Asian Laws and Sentiment

The United States is a nation that claims to welcome and assimilate all new-comers. But the history of immigration, naturalization, and equal treatment under the law for Asian Americans has been an extremely difficult one. In 1790 Congress passed the first naturalization law limiting citizenship rights to only a "free white person."[18] During the period of reconstruction in the 1870s following the end of the Civil War, Congress amended the law and allowed citizenship for "aliens of African nativity and persons of African descent."[19] For a while there was some discussion on expanding naturalization rights to Chinese immigrants, but that idea was rejected by politicians from western states.[20] This rejection is exemplary of the intense anti-Chinese sentiment at the time.

As early as 1850 California imposed the Foreign Miners Tax, which required the payment of $20 a month from all foreign miners.[21] The California Supreme Court ruled in *People v. Hall* (1854) that Chinese could not testify in court against a white person. This case threw out the testimony of three Chinese witnesses and reversed the murder conviction of George W. Hall, who was sentenced to hang for the murder of a Chinese man one year earlier.[22] In 1855 a local San Francisco ordinance levied a $50 tax on all aliens ineligible for citizenship. Because Chinese were ineligible for citizenship under the Naturalization Act of 1790, they were the primary targets for this law.[23]

The racially distinct Chinese were the primary scapegoats for the depressed economy in the 1870s, and mob violence erupted on several occasions through to the 1880s. The massacre of 21 Chinese in Los Angeles in 1871 and 28 Chinese in Rock Springs, Wyoming, in 1885 are examples of the worst incidents. It is within this environment that Congress passed the 1882 Chinese Exclusion Act. The act suspended immigration of Chinese laborers for only ten years, but it was extended in 1892 and 1902. The act was eventually extended indefinitely in 1904.[24] The intense institutional discrimination achieved the desired result: The Chinese population declined from 105,465 in 1880 to 61,639 in 1920.[25]

Anti-Chinese sentiment easily grew into large-scale anti-Asian sentiment as immigrants from Asia continued to enter the United States. During the same period that the Chinese population declined, the Japanese population grew and became highly visible. As early as 1910 there were 72,157 Japanese Americans compared to 71,531 Chinese Americans in the United States.[26] Japanese farmers in California were particularly vulnerable targets for animosity. One of the most sweeping anti-Asian laws was aimed at the Japanese Americans but affected all other Asian American groups as well. The 1913 Alien Land Law prohibited "aliens ineligible to citizenship" from owning or leasing land for more than three years. Initially the Japanese Americans were able to bypass the law primarily because they could buy or lease land under the names of their American-born offspring (the Nisei), who were U.S. citizens by birth. The law was strengthened in 1920, however, and the purchase of land under the names of American-born offspring was prohibited.[27]

Several sweeping anti-immigration laws were passed in the first quarter of the twentieth century that served to eliminate Asian immigration to the United States. A provision in the 1917 Immigration Act banned immigration from the so-called "Asian barred zone," except for the Philippines and Japan. A more severe anti-Asian restriction was further imposed by the 1924 National Origins Act, which placed a ceiling of 150,000 new immigrants per year. The 1924 act was intended to limit eastern and southern European immigration, but a provision was added that ended any immigration by aliens ineligible for citizenship.[28]

Asian Americans did not sit back passively in the face of discriminatory laws; they hired lawyers and went to court to fight for their livelihoods, naturalization rights, and personal liberties. Sometimes they were successful, but oftentimes they were not. In the case of *Yick Wo v. Hopkins* (1886), Chinese successfully challenged an 1880 San Francisco Laundry Ordinance, which regulated commercial laundry service in a way that clearly discriminated against the Chinese. Plaintiff Yick Wo had operated a laundry service for 22 years, but when he tried to renew his business license in 1885 he was turned down because his storefront was made out of wood. Two hundred other Chinese laundries were also denied business licenses on similar grounds, although 80 non-Chinese laundries in wooden buildings were approved. The Supreme Court ruled in favor of Yick Wo, concluding there was "no reason" for the denial of the business license "except to the face and nationality" of the petitioner.[29]

The inability to gain citizenship was a defining factor throughout the early history of Asian Americans. The constitutionality of naturalization based on race was first challenged in the Supreme Court case of *Ozawa v. United States* (1922). Takao Ozawa was born in Japan but immigrated to the United States at an early age. He graduated from Berkeley High School in California and attended the University of California for three years. Ozawa was a model immigrant who did not smoke or drink, he attended a predominantly white church, his children attended public school, and English was the language spoken at home. When Ozawa was rejected in his initial attempt for naturalization, he appealed and argued that the provisions for citizenship in the 1790 and 1870 acts did not specifically exclude Japanese. In addition, Ozawa also tried to argue that Japanese should be considered "white."

The Court unanimously ruled against Ozawa on both grounds. First, the Court decided that initial framers of the law and its amendment did not intend to *exclude* people from naturalization but, instead, only determine who would be *included*. Ozawa was denied citizenship because the existing law simply didn't include Japanese. Second, the Court also ruled against Ozawa's argument that Japanese were actually more "white" than other darker skinned "white" people such as some Italians, Spanish, and Portuguese. The Court clarified the matter by defining a "white person" to be synonymous with a "person of the Caucasian race." In short, Ozawa was not Caucasian (although he thought himself "white") and, thus, was ineligible for citizenship.[30]

Prior to the *Ozawa* case, Asian Indians already enjoyed the right of naturalization. In *United States v. Balsara* (1910), the Supreme Court determined that Asian Indians were Caucasian and approximately 70 became naturalized citizens. But the Immigration and Naturalization Service (INS) challenged this decision, and it was taken up again in the case of *United States v. Thind* (1923). This time the Supreme Court reversed its earlier decision and ruled that Bhagat Singh Thind could not be a citizen because he was not "white." Even though Asian Indians were classified as Caucasian, this was a scientific term that was inconsistent with the popular understanding. The Court's decision stated, "It may be true that the blond Scandinavian and the brown Hindu have a common ancestor in the dim reaches of antiquity, but the average man knows perfectly well that there are unmistakable differences between them today."[31] In other words, only "white" Caucasians were considered eligible for U.S. citizenship. In the wake of the *Thind* decision, the INS was able to cancel retroactively the citizenship of Asian Indians between 1923 and 1926.

Asian Americans also received disparate treatment compared to other immigrants in their most private affairs, such as marriage. In the nineteenth century, antimiscegenation laws prohibiting marriage between blacks and whites were common throughout the United States. In 1880 the California legislature extended restrictive antimiscegenation categories to prohibit any marriage between a white person and a "negro, mulatto, or Mongolian." This law, targeted at the Chinese, was not challenged until Salvador Roldan won a California Court of Appeals decision in 1933. Roldan, a Filipino American, argued that he was Malay, not Mongolian, and he should be allowed to marry his white fiancee. The Court conceded that the state's antimiscegenation law was created in an atmosphere of intense anti-Chinese sentiment, and agreed Filipinos were not in mind when the initial legislation was approved. Unfortunately, this victory was short-lived. The California state legislature amended the antimiscegenation law to include the "Malay race" shortly after the Roldan decision was announced.[32]

World War II and the Cold War Era

For Asian Americans, World War II was an epoch, but the profound impact was distinct for different Asian American groups. For over 110,000 Japanese Americans, World War II was an agonizing ordeal soon after Japan's attack of Pearl Harbor on December 7, 1941. The FBI arrested thousands of Japanese Americans who were considered potential security threats immediately after the Pearl Harbor bombing raid. Arrested without evidence of disloyalty were the most visible Japanese American community leaders, including businessmen, Shinto and Buddhist priests, teachers in

Japanese-language schools, and editors of Japanese-language newspapers. Wartime hysteria rose to a fever pitch, and on February 19, 1942, President Franklin Roosevelt issued Executive Order 9066. This order established various military zones and authorized the removal of anyone who was a potential threat. Although a small number of German and Italian aliens were detained and relocated, this did not compare to the mass relocation of Japanese Americans on the West Coast of the United States.[33]

The order to relocate Japanese Americans because of military necessity and the threat they posed to security, was a fabrication. Even military leaders debated the genuine need for mass relocation, and the government's own intelligence reports found no evidence of Japanese American disloyalty. "For the most part the local Japanese are loyal to the United States or, at worst, hope that by remaining quiet they can avoid concentration camps or irresponsible mobs," one report stated. "We do not believe that they would be at least any more disloyal than any other racial group in the United States with whom we went to war."[34] This helps explain why 160,000 Japanese Americans living in Hawaii were not interned. More telling was the fact that Japanese Americans in the continental United States were a small but much resented minority. Despite government reports to the contrary, business leaders, local politicians, and the media fueled antagonism against the Japanese Americans and agitated for their abrupt removal.[35]

With only seven days notice to prepare once the internment order was issued, and no way of knowing how long the war would last, many Japanese Americans were forced to sell their homes and property at a mere fraction of their genuine value. Japanese Americans suffered estimated economic losses alone of at least $400 million. By August 1942 all the Japanese on the West Coast were interned in ten camps located in rural regions of California, Arizona, Utah, Idaho, Wyoming, and Arkansas. Two thirds of the interned Japanese American men, women, and children were U.S. citizens, whose only crime was their ancestry; even those with as little as one-eighth Japanese blood were interned. The camps themselves were crude, mass facilities surrounded by barbed wire and guarded by armed sentries. People were housed in large barracks with each family living in small cramped quarters dubbed "apartments." Food was served in large mess halls, and toilet and shower facilities were communal. Many of the camps were extremely cold in the winter, hot in the summer, and dusty all year round. The camps remained open for the duration of the war.[36]

After the first year of the camps, the government began recruiting young Japanese American men to help in the war effort. The military desperately needed Japanese Americans to serve as interpreters for Japanese prisoners of war and translators of captured documents. But to the military's incredulity, most American-born Japanese had only modest Japanese-language skills and needed intense training in the Military Intelligence Service Language School before they could perform their duties.[37] It was, however, the heroic actions of the 100th Infantry Battalion, which later merged with the 442nd Regimental Combat Team, that stand out the most among historians. The two segregated units engaged in numerous campaigns and served with distinction throughout Europe. By the end of the war in Europe, for example, the Nisei soldiers of the 442nd suffered over 9,000 casualties, and earned over 18,000 individual decorations of honor. The 442nd was the most decorated unit of its size during all of World War II.[38]

Compared to the Japanese American experience, other Asian American groups fared far better during and after World War II. Changes for Chinese Americans were particularly dramatic. Prior to the war, the image of the Chinese was clearly negative compared to the Japanese. A survey of Princeton undergraduates in 1931 thought the top three traits of the Chinese were the fact they were "superstitious, sly, and conservative," whereas Japanese were considered "intelligent, industrious, and progressive."[39] Immediately after the bombing of Pearl Harbor, Chinese store owners put up signs indicating they were not Japanese, and in some cases Chinese Americans wore buttons stating, "I am Chinese." To alleviate any further identification problems, *Time* magazine published an article on December 22, 1941, explaining how to tell the difference between Chinese and "Japs." The article compared photographs of a Chinese man and a Japanese man, highlighting the distinguishing facial features of each.[40] Just months later, a 1942 Gallup Poll characterized the Chinese as "hardworking, honest, and brave," and Japanese were seen as "treacherous, sly, and cruel."[41]

Employment opportunities outside of the segregated Chinatown community became available to Chinese Americans for the first time during the war and continued even after the war ended. Chinese Americans trained in various professions and skilled crafts were able to find work in war-related industries that had never been open to them before. In addition, the employment of Chinese American women increased threefold during the 1940s. Leading the way were clerical positions, which increased from just 750 in 1940 to 3,200 in 1950. In 1940 women represented just one in five Chinese American professionals, but by 1950 this increased to one in three. On another level, Chinese actors suddenly found they were in demand for film roles—usually playing evil Japanese characters. Shortly after the war, writers such as Jade Snow Wong and Pardee Lowe discovered the newfound interest and appreciation of Chinese Americans could be turned into commercial success through the publication of their memoirs.[42]

On the military front, Asian Americans also distinguished themselves. Over 15,000 Chinese Americans served in all branches of the military, unlike the Japanese Americans who were placed only in segregated infantry units and in the Military Intelligence Service. Similarly, over 7,000 Filipino Americans volunteered for the army and formed the First and Second Filipino Infantry Regiments. About 1,000 other Filipino Americans were sent to the Philippines to perform reconnaissance and intelligence activities for Gen. Douglas MacArthur.[43] Equally significant was the War Bride's Act of 1945, which allowed war veterans to bring wives from China and the Philippines as non-quota immigrants. This resulted in a rapid and dramatic shift in the historic gender imbalance of both groups. For example, between 1945 and 1952, nine out of ten (89.9 percent) Chinese immigrants were female, and 20,000 Chinese American babies were born by the mid-1950s.

Similarly, between 1951 and 1960 seven out of ten (71 percent) Filipino immigrants were female.[44]

On the broad international front, alliances with China, the Philippines, and India eventually began the process of changing the overtly discriminatory immigration laws against Asians. The Chinese Exclusion Law was repealed in 1943, and an annual quota of 105 immigrants from China was allotted. In 1946 Congress approved legislation that extended citizenship to Filipino immigrants and permitted the entry of 100 Filipino immigrants annually. Also in 1946, the Luce-Cellar Act ended the 1917 "Asian barred zone," allowed an immigration quota of 100 from India, and for the first time permitted Asian Indians to apply for citizenship since the *United States v. Thind* case of 1923. Although these changes were extremely modest, they carried important symbolic weight by helping create a favorable international opinion of the United States during and immediately after the war.[45]

Geopolitical events during the Cold War era of the 1950s and 1960s immediately following World War II continued to have important ramifications for Asian Americans. After the 1949 Communist Revolution in China, about 5,000 Chinese students and young professionals were living in the United States. These "stranded" individuals were generally from China's most elite and educated families and not necessarily anxious to return to China because their property had already been confiscated and their livelihoods threatened. They were eventually allowed to stay in the United States.[46] Several other refugee acts in the late 1950s and early 1960s allowed some 18,000 other Chinese to enter and also stay in the United States. Many of these refugees were well-trained scientists and engineers who easily found jobs in private industry and in research universities. These educated professionals were quite distinct from the vast majority of earlier Chinese immigrants because they usually were able to integrate into the American mainstream quickly, becoming the basis of an emerging Chinese American middle class.[47]

The Cold War affected immigration from Asian countries as well, but in a very different fashion. During and after the Korean War (1950–1953), American soldiers often met and married Korean women and brought them home to the United States. Between 1952 and 1960 over 1,000 Korean women a year immigrated to the United States as brides of U.S. servicemen. At the same time, orphaned Korean children, especially girls, also arrived in the United States in significant numbers. Throughout the 1950s and up to the mid-1960s, some 70 percent of all Korean immigrants were either women or young girls. Korea was the site of the actual conflict, but large numbers of troops were also stationed in nearby Japan. Even higher numbers of Japanese women married American soldiers, left their home country, and started a new life in the United States. Roughly 6,000 Japanese wives of U.S. servicemen annually immigrated to the United States between 1952 and 1960, which was over 80 percent of all immigrants from Japan. These Korean and Japanese war brides and Korean orphans were spread throughout the United States and, as a result, had very little interaction with other Asian Americans already living in this country.[48]

These war bride families were, however, a significant part of the biracial Asian American baby boom that is discussed in greater detail in Chapter 7.

Post-1965 Asian Immigrants and Refugees

A number of factors have clearly influenced Asian immigration and refugee policies, including public sentiment toward immigrants, demands of foreign policy, and the needs of the American economy. World War II and the Cold War years were epochal for Asian Americans, but the period since the mid-1960s has proven to be even more significant. An overview of U.S. immigration statistics shows just how important recent immigration reforms and refugee policies have affected Asian Americans.

Official records on immigrants entering the United States did not exist before 1820, but since that time it is quite obvious that the largest number of immigrants come from European countries. Between 1820 and 1998 over 38.2 million Europeans immigrated to the United States (see Table 1-1). In contrast, only 8.3 million immigrants came from Asia during the same period of time. Looking at this figure more closely, however, we find over 6.6 million immigrants from Asia arrived in the United States in the period between 1971 and 1998. Although the Chinese and Japanese have the longest histories in the United States, the largest group of Asian immigrants since 1971 has come from the Philippines. Over 1.4 million Filipino immigrants entered the United States between 1971 and 1998. It is also significant to note that over 90 percent of Filipino, Asian Indian, Korean, and Vietnamese have entered the United States since 1971.

This next section focuses on three broad events that have directly influenced both the numbers and diversity of Asians entering the United States since 1965: (1) the passage of the 1965 Immigration Reform Act, (2) global economic restructuring, and (3) the Vietnam War.

The 1965 Immigration Reform Act

Why did the dramatic increase in Asian immigration take place? What changes in the law or public attitudes facilitated such a rapid influx of immigrants from Asia? One important reason was the civil rights movement of the 1960s, which brought international attention to racial and economic inequality in the United States—including its biased immigration policies. This attention is the background for the passage of the 1965 Immigration Reform Act, the most important immigration reform legislation. This act, along with its amendments, significantly increased the token quotas established after World War II to allow the Eastern Hemisphere a maximum of 20,000 per country, and set a ceiling of 170,000.

This act created the following seven-point preference system that serves as a general guideline for immigration officials when issuing visas: (1) unmarried children of U.S. citizens who are at least 21 years of age; (2) spouses and unmarried children

Region	Total 1820–1998	1971–1998	% of Immigrants Since 1971
All countries	64,599,082	18,836,444	29.2
Europe	38,233,062	2,693,920	7.0
Asia	8,365,931	6,673,085	79.7
China*	1,262,050	818,747	64.9
Hong Kong†	398,277	298,129	74.9
India	751,349	710,553	94.6
Japan	517,686	152,302	29.4
Korea	778,899	738,305	94.8
Phillippines	1,460,421	1,337,519	91.6
Vietnam	699,918	692,243	98.9
North America			
Canada and Newfoundland	4,453,149	484,441	10.9
Mexico	5,819,966	4,115,959	70.7
Caribbean	3,525,703	1,435,703	40.7
Central America	1,242,394	985,240	79.3
South America	1,693,441	1,200,740	70.9
Africa	614,375	537,902	87.6
Oceana	250,206	132,031	52.8
Not specified	290,679	24,264	.8

*Beginning in 1957, China includes Taiwan.
†Data not reported separately until 1952.
Source: U.S. Immigration and Naturalization Service, 1998 *Statistical Yearbook of the Immigration and Naturalization Service* (Washington, DC: U.S. Government Printing Office, 2000), Table, pp. 8–10.

of permanent resident aliens; (3) members of the professions, scientists, and artists of exceptional ability; (4) married children of U.S. citizens; (5) brothers and sisters of U.S. citizens who are at least 21 years of age; (6) skilled or unskilled workers who are in short supply; and (7) non-preference applicants.

U.S. immigration policy also allowed virtually unrestricted immigration to certain categories of people including spouses, children under 21, and parents of U.S. citizens. These provisions served to accelerate immigration from Asia to the United States. The primary goal of the 1965 Immigration Reform Act was to encourage family reunification, however, a much higher percentage of Asian immigrants initially began entering the United States under the established occupational and nonpreference investment categories. In 1969, for example, 62 percent of Asian Indians, 43 percent of Filipinos, and 34.8 percent of Koreans entered the United States under the occupational and investor categories. By the mid-1970s, however, 80 to 90 percent of all Asian immigrants entered the United States through one of the family categories.[49] Studies clearly show that most post-1965 Asian

TABLE 1-2 Percentage of Immigrants Admitted by Region, Fiscal Years 1901–1998

Decade	Europe	Asia	North America	South America	Africa
1901–10	91.6	3.7	3.2	.2	.1
1911–20	75.3	4.3	19.2	.7	.1
1921–30	60.0	2.7	35.9	1.0	.2
1931–40	65.8	3.1	28.8	1.5	.3
1941–50	60.0	3.6	32.2	2.1	.7
1951–60	52.7	6.1	36.0	3.6	.6
1961–70	33.8	12.9	43.9	7.8	.9
1971–80	17.8	35.3	37.5	6.6	1.8
1981–90	10.4	37.3	43.0	6.3	2.4
1991–98	14.9	30.9	43.8	5.8	3.7

Source: U.S. Immigration and Naturalization Service, *Naturalizations, Fiscal Year 1998* (Washington, DC: U.S. Government Printing Office, 2000), Chart B, p. 4.
Note: Figures may not add to 100 due to rounding. Oceana and unspecified regions represent no more than 1 percent of legal immigration each decade.

immigrants tend to be more middle-class, educated, urbanized, and they arrive in the United States in family units rather than as individuals, compared to their pre-1965 counterparts.[50]

The framers of the 1965 law did not anticipate any dramatic changes in the historical pattern of immigration, but it is clear Asian immigrants have taken advantage of almost every aspect of the 1965 Immigration Reform Act. Asians were just 6.1 percent of all immigrants to the United States between 1951 and 1960; this rose to 12.9 percent between 1961 and 1970, and increased to 35.3 percent between 1971 and 1980. The percentage of Asian immigrants peaked at 37.3 percent between 1981 and 1990 but declined to 30.9 percent by the 1990s (see Table 1-2). This decline was due to the sudden increase of mostly Mexicans who were able to apply for legal status following the passage of the Immigration Reform and Control Act of 1986 (IRCA). By the late 1990s, about 3 million aliens received permanent residence status under IRCA.[51]

This "amnesty" provision was only a part of IRCA, which was fully intended to control illegal immigration into the United States. IRCA also required that all employers verify the legal status of all new employees, and it imposed civil and criminal penalties against employers who knowingly hire undocumented workers.[52] While IRCA closed the "back door" of illegal immigration, another reform, the Immigration Act of 1990, was enacted to keep open the "front door" of legal immigration. Indeed, this law actually authorizes an *increase* in legal immigration to the United States. In response to uncertain economic stability at home, growing global economic competition abroad, and the dramatically changed face of immigration, the 1990 law sent a mixed message to Asian immigrants.

First of all, the law actually authorized an increase in legal immigration, but at the same time placed a yearly cap on total immigration for the first time since the 1920s. For 1992 to 1995, the limit was 700,000 and 675,000 thereafter. This appears to be an arbitrary limit, but it still allows for an unlimited number of visas for immediate relatives of U.S. citizens. This may not have a negative effect on Asian immigration because, as a group, Asians have the highest rate of naturalization compared to other immigrants.[53] Second, the law encourages immigration of more skilled workers to help meet the needs of the U.S. economy. The number of visas for skilled workers and their families increased from 58,000 to 140,000, and the number for unskilled workers was cut in half to just 10,000. This may prove to be a benefit to Asians who, since 1965, have been among the best educated and best trained immigrants the United States has ever seen. Third, the 1990 immigration law also seeks to "diversify" the new immigrants by giving more visas to countries who have sent relatively few people to the United States in recent years. This program has been popular with lawmakers who want to assist those from Western European countries at the expense of Asians. For example, up to 40 percent of the initial visas allocated for the diversity category were for Ireland. Noted immigration attorney Bill Ong Hing found sections of the Immigration Act of 1990 "provide extra independent and transition visas that are unavailable to Asians."[54]

The lasting legacy of the civil rights movement on immigration policy was the emphasis on fairness, equality, and family reunification. But the increased emphasis on highly skilled immigrants found in the 1990 immigration law indicates some loosening of those ideals and priorities. It is clear from the descriptions of Asian American history here that the conditions for the post-1965 Asian migrants are quite distinct from pre-1965 migrants. This seemingly obvious observation reflects the fact that international migration is not a simple, stable, or homogeneous process. Even with this in mind, the most popular frame of reference for all movement to the United States continues to be the European immigrant experience throughout the nineteenth and early twentieth centuries. The popular European immigrant analogy is highlighted in the words of welcome written on the Statue of Liberty:

Give me your tired, your poor
Your huddled masses yearning to breathe free
The wretched refuse of your teeming shore.
Send these, the homeless, tempest-tost to me,
I lift my lamp beside the golden door!

The European immigrant experience, however, is by no means universal, and it is only part of what scholars today see as a much broader picture of the international movement of people and capital. Understanding the broader dynamics of global economic restructuring is useful in comparing and contrasting post-1965 Asian immigrants with other immigrants and minority groups in the United States.

Global Economic Restructuring

What makes people want to leave their home country and migrate to another country? The most commonly accepted answer is found within what is known as the push-pull theory. This theory generally asserts that difficult economic, social, and political conditions in the home country force, or push, people away. At the same time, these people are attracted, or pulled, to another country where conditions are seen as more favorable. On closer examination, however, this theoretical viewpoint does run into some problems. Most significantly, the push-pull theory tends to see immigration flows as a natural, open, and spontaneous process, but it does not adequately take into account the structural factors and policy changes that directly affect immigration flows. This is because earlier migration studies based on European immigration limited their focus on poor countries that sent low-skilled labor to affluent countries with growing economies that put newcomers to work. The push-pull theory is not incorrect, but is considered to be incomplete and historically static. Recent studies have taken a much broader approach to international migration and insist that in order to understand post-1965 immigration from Asia, it is necessary to understand the recent restructuring of the global economy.[55]

Since the end of World War II, global restructuring has involved the gradual movement of industrial manufacturing away from developed nations such as the United States to less developed nations in Asia and Latin America where labor costs are cheaper. This process was best seen in Japan in the 1950s through 1970s, and accelerated rapidly in the 1980s to newly industrialized Asian countries, namely Taiwan, Hong Kong, Singapore, and South Korea. Other Asian countries such as India, Thailand, Indonesia, Malaysia, and the Philippines also followed the same economic course with varying degrees of success. In the 1990s mainland China increased its manufacturing and export capacity dramatically and was steering on the same economic path of other Asian nations.

Among the effects of global restructuring on the United States is the declining need to import low-skilled labor because manufacturing jobs are moving abroad. At the same time, there is an inclining need to import individuals with advanced specialized skills that are in great demand. According to research by Paul Ong and Evelyn Blumenberg (1994), this phenomena is evidenced in part by the increasing number of foreign-born students studying at U.S. colleges.[56] In the 1954–1955 academic year the United States was host to just 34,232 foreign exchange students; this number increased to over 440,000 in 1994.[57] Today over half of all foreign students in the United States are from Asian countries, and most major in either engineering, science, or business. In 1997 foreign students earned 53 percent of the doctorates in engineering, 50 percent of doctorates in mathematics, and 49 percent of doctorates in computer science.[58] Many of these foreign graduate students planned to work in the United States and eventually gained permanent immigrant status. Companies in the United States have, of course, been eager to hire foreign-born scientists and engineers. Not only are highly skilled immigrants valuable to employers as workers, but many also start their own high-tech businesses. For example, Vinod Khosla is the co-founder of Sun-Microsystems, and Gururaj Deshpande is co-founder of a number of high-tech businesses worth around $6 billion.[59]

The medical profession is another broad area where Asian immigrants have made a noticeable impact. Researchers Paul Ong and Tania Azores (1994) found that Asian Americans represented 4.4 percent of the registered nurses and 10.8 percent of the physicians in the United States in 1990. Ong and Azores estimate that only a third of Asian American physicians and a quarter of Asian American nurses were educated in the United States. Graduates of overseas medical and nursing schools have been coming to the United States since the passage of the 1946 Smith-Mundt Act, which created an exchange program for specialized training. Although this exchange was intended to be temporary, many medical professionals were able to become permanent immigrants. A physician shortage in the United States during the late 1960s and early 1970s, coupled with the elimination of racial immigration quotas in 1965, brought forth a steady flow of foreign-trained medical doctors from Asian countries. A 1975 U.S. Commission on Civil Rights report found 5,000 Asian medical school graduates entered the United States annually during the early 1970s. But, under pressure from the medical industry, Congress passed the 1976 Health Professions Educational Act, which restricted the number of foreign-trained physicians who could enter the United States. Despite the passage of this law, almost 30,000 physicians from Asia immigrated to the United States between 1972 and 1985, and data up to 1990 show roughly half of all foreign-trained physicians entering the United States have come from Asia.[60]

Asia is also the largest source for foreign nurses. In particular, over half of all foreign-trained nurses come from the Philippines. One 1988 study conservatively estimated 50,000 Filipino nurses were working in the United States at the time. Filipino nurses find work in the United States attractive because they can earn up to 20 times the salary they can make in the Philippines, and their English-speaking abilities make them highly desired by employers. Filipino nurses are also attracted to the United States because of liberal policies that eventually allow them to stay permanently. Most foreign-trained nurses are brought to work initially on a temporary basis, but the passage of the Immigration Nursing Relief Act of 1989 allows nurses to adjust to permanent status after three years of service.[61]

The general explanations for the origins of migration found that the push-pull theory continues to have some value today. Opportunities for large numbers of professionals in Asian countries are still difficult and limited, and opportunities and relatively high salaries are available in the United States. Political instability throughout Asia also continues to be an important push factor for Asian immigrants and refugees. At the same time, this immigration process is not totally natural or spontaneous, as witnessed by foreign student and immigration policies encouraging well-trained individuals to come to the United States. Overall, the changing character of the push and pull in terms of the types of immigrants entering the

United States and the new skills they bring are very much a result of dynamic global economic restructuring. Global economic restructuring is an important context for understanding not only why Asian immigrants have come to the United States but also how well they have adjusted and been accepted socially, economically, and politically. Note that not all Asian immigrants are middle-class and successful professionals; a sizable number of other Asian immigrants, especially refugees, have also found their lives in America extremely difficult. The extreme diversity among Asian Americans is due in large part to the third major event affecting migration from Asia—the Vietnam War.

The Vietnam War and Southeast Asian Refugees

Since 1975 large numbers of Southeast Asian refugees have entered the United States, and today California is the home for most of them (see Table 1-3). Roughly three quarters of all Southeast Asian refugees are from Vietnam, with the rest from Laos and Cambodia. Unlike most other post-1965 Asian immigrants who came to the United States in a rather orderly fashion seeking family reunification and economic opportunities, Southeast Asian refugees arrived as part of an international resettlement effort of people who faced genuine political persecution and bodily harm in their home countries. Southeast Asian refugees to the United States can be easily divided into three distinct waves: the first arrived in the United States in 1975 shortly after the fall of Saigon; the second arrived between 1978 and 1980; and the third entered the United States after 1980 and continues to this day. The United States has accepted these refugees not only for humanitarian reasons but also in recognition that U.S. foreign policy and military actions in Southeast Asia had a hand in creating much of the calamity that has befallen the entire region.

TABLE 1-3 States with the Largest Southeast Asian Populations, 1990

State	Vietnamese	Cambodian	Laotian	Hmong	Total
Washington	18,696	11,096	6,191	741	36,724
California	280,223	68,190	58,058	46,892	453,363
Texas	69,634	5,887	9,332	176	85,029
Minnesota	9,387	3,858	6,381	16,833	36,459
Massachusetts	15,449	14,050	3,985	248	33,732
Virginia	20,693	3,889	25,899	7	27,178
Pennsylvania	15,887	5,495	2,048	358	23,788
Wisconsin	2,494	521	3,622	16,373	23,010
New York	15,555	3,646	3,253	165	22,619
Florida	16,346	1,617	242	7	20,379

Source: U.S. Bureau of the Census, *1990 Census of the Population, General Population Characteristics, United States Summary* (Washington, DC: U.S. Government Printing Office, 1993), CP-1-1, Table 262.

U.S. political interests in Southeast Asia actually began during World War II, although for years efforts were limited to foreign aid and military advisers. Direct military intervention rapidly escalated in 1965 when President Lyndon B. Johnson stepped up bombing raids in Southeast Asia and authorized the use of the first U.S. combat troops in order to contain increasing communist insurgency. The undeclared war continued until U.S. troops withdrew in 1973 at the cost of 57,000 American and 1 million Vietnamese lives. The conflict also caused great environmental destruction throughout Southeast Asia and created tremendous domestic antiwar protests in the United States.[62]

As soon as the U.S. troops left, however, communist forces in Vietnam regrouped and quickly began sweeping across the countryside. By March 1975 it was clear that the capital of South Vietnam, Saigon, would soon fall to communist forces. As a result, President Gerald Ford authorized the attorney general to admit 130,000 refugees into the United States.[63] In the last chaotic days prior to the fall of Saigon on April 30, 1975, "high-risk" individuals in Vietnam, namely high-ranking government and military personnel, were hurriedly air-lifted away to safety at temporary receiving centers in Guam, Thailand, and the Philippines. This group marked the first wave of Southeast Asian refugees, who would eventually resettle in the United States. The first wave is distinct in that they were generally the educated urban elite and middle class from Vietnam. Because many of them had worked closely with the U.S. military, they tended to be more westernized (40 percent were Catholics), and a good portion of them were able to speak English (30 percent spoke English well). Another significant feature is the fact that roughly 95 percent of the first wave of Southeast Asian refugees were Vietnamese, even though the capitals of Laos and Cambodia also fell to communist forces in 1975.[64]

Once these first-wave refugees came to the United States, they were flown to one of four military base/reception centers in California, Arkansas, Pennsylvania, and Florida. From these bases they registered with a voluntary agency that would eventually help resettle them with a sponsor. About 60 percent of the sponsors were families, while the other 40 percent were usually churches and individuals. Sponsors were responsible for day-to-day needs of the refugees until they were able to find jobs and become independent. The resettlement of the first wave of refugees was funded by the 1975 Indochinese Resettlement Assistance Act and was seen as a quick and temporary process. Indeed, all the reception centers closed by the end of 1975, and the Resettlement Act expired in 1977.

The second wave of Southeast Asian refugees was larger, more heterogeneous, and many believe even more devastated by their relocation experience than the first wave. The second wave of refugees were generally less educated, urbanized, and westernized (only 7 percent spoke English and only about 7 percent were Catholic) compared to their predecessors; at the same time they were much more ethnically diverse than the first wave. According to statistics, between 1978 and 1980, about 55.5 percent of Southeast Asian refugees were from Vietnam (including many ethnic Chinese), 36.6 percent from Laos, and 7.8 percent from Cambodia. The second wave consisted of people who suffered under the communist regimes and were unable to leave their countries immediately before or after the new governments took power.[65]

In Vietnam, the ethnic Chinese merchant class was very much the target of resentment by the new communist government. Many of the Chinese businesses in Vietnam were nationalized, Chinese language schools and newspapers were closed, education and employment rights were denied, and food rations were reduced. Under these conditions, about 250,000 escaped North Vietnam, seeking refuge in China. Roughly 70 percent of the estimated 500,000 boat people who tried to escape Vietnam by sea were ethnic Chinese. The treacherous journey usually took place on ill-equipped crowded boats that were unable to withstand the rigors of the ocean or outrun marauding Thai pirates. The U.S. Committee for Refugees estimates at least 100,000 people lost their lives trying to escape Vietnam by boat.[66] Along with the Chinese, others in Vietnam, particularly those who had supported the U.S.-backed South Vietnamese government and their families, were also subject to especially harsh treatment by the new communist leadership. Many were sent to "reeducation camps" and banished to work in rural regions clearing land devastated by 30 years of war.

The holocaust in Cambodia began immediately after the Khmer Rouge (Red Khmer) marched into the capital city of Phnom Penh on April 17, 1975. That same day the entire population of the capital was ordered to the countryside. After three years it has been broadly estimated between 1 and 3 million Cambodians died from starvation, disease, and execution out of a population of less than 7 million. In 1978 Vietnam (with support from the Soviet Union) invaded Cambodia, drove the Khmer Rouge out of power, and established a new government under its own control. Famine and warfare continued under Vietnamese occupation, and by 1979 over 600,000 refugees from Cambodia fled the country, mostly to neighboring Thailand. In Laos, the transition from one government to another was initially rather smooth compared to Vietnam following the fall of Saigon. After over a decade of civil war, a coalition government was formed in April 1974 that included Laotian communists, the Pathet Lao. But shortly after communists took power in Vietnam and Cambodia, the Pathet Lao moved to solidify its full control of the country. It was at this time that troops from both Laos and Vietnam began a military campaign against the Hmong hill people, a preliterate ethnic minority group that lived in the mountains of Laos who were recruited by the U.S. government to serve as mercenaries against communist forces in the region. The Hmong were seen as traitors to the communist revolution, and massive bombing raids were ordered against them that included the dropping of napalm and poisonous chemicals. Thousands of Hmong were killed in these fierce assaults, and those who remained had little choice but to seek refuge in neighboring Thailand. The Hmong were not the only people in Laos who were persecuted. By 1979 roughly 3,000 Hmong were entering Thailand every month, and as late as 1983 an estimated 75 percent of the 76,000 Laotians in Thai refugee camps were Hmong people.[67]

The world could not ignore this massive outpouring of refugees from Southeast Asia, and in 1979 President Jimmy Carter allowed 14,000 refugees a month to enter the United States. In addition, Congress passed the Refugee Act of 1980, which set an annual quota of 50,000 refugees per year, funded resettlement programs, and allowed refugees to become eligible for the same welfare benefits as U.S. citizens after 36 months of refugee assistance (this was changed to 18 months in 1982).

Many of the Southeast Asians who came in the third wave are technically not considered refugees, but are in actuality immigrants. This has been facilitated by the 1980 Orderly Departure Program (ODP), an agreement with Vietnam that allows individuals and families to enter the United States. ODP was a benefit for three groups: relatives of permanently settled refugees in the United States, Amerasians, and former reeducation camp internees. By the end of 1992, over 300,000 Vietnamese immigrated to the United States, including 80,000 Amerasians and their relatives, as well as 60,000 former camp internees and their families.[68] The resettlement experience, the development of Southeast Asian communities, as well as the influx of Amerasians to the United States are respectively discussed in greater detail in Chapters 2 and 7.

It is obvious that Southeast Asian refugees/immigrants have been a rapidly growing and extremely diverse group. According to the 1990 census, there were 1,001,054 Southeast Asians in the United States, or 13 percent of the total population of Asian Americans. Individually, the census counted 614,547 Vietnamese, 149,014 Laotians, 147,411 Cambodians, and 90,082 Hmong. Some have argued that these census figures are an undercount of the actual numbers of people from Southeast Asian countries. Researchers point to the fact that the total number of arrivals to the United States from Southeast Asia is roughly the same as census figures. This is an anomaly because the census figure should be about 20 percent larger to reflect the number of American-born Southeast Asians. There are, however, several reasons for this disparity. First of all, new arrivals from Southeast Asia who have little knowledge of the English language may simply not have responded to census questionnaires. This certainly is a general concern for all Asian American groups. Second, and probably most important, an estimated 15 to 25 percent of those from Vietnam, Cambodia, and Laos are actually ethnic Chinese. It is quite possible that many ethnic Chinese from Southeast Asia answered the appropriate census question of ethnicity without regard to their nationality. Third, no one is exactly sure how Amerasians identified themselves on the 1990 census or if they even participated at all. Although a factor, note that most of the Amerasians from Vietnam did not actually enter the United States until after the 1990 census was taken. In all references to the Southeast Asian population, keep these considerations in mind.[69]

Conclusion

This chapter briefly describes the history and recent growth of the Asian population in the United States. It also highlights the significance of the 1965 Immigration Reform Act, global economic restructuring, and the Vietnam War as three broad events that profoundly impacted both the number and type of migrants who have come to the United States from Asian countries. In order to examine post-1965 Asian Americans comprehensively, it is particularly important to look at the rapid growth of the population, personal history, nativity, length of time in the United States, premigration experiences and traumas, education, socioeconomic class background, and gender. Chapter 2 details the social and economic diversity of immigrant and American-born Asians, as well as their settlement patterns and impact on various communities across the United States.

Notes

[1] Emil Guillermo, "From Miss America to Mr. President," *Asian Week,* October 19, 2000.

[2] Shih-shan Henry Tsai, *The Chinese Experience in America* (Bloomington: Indiana University Press, 1986), p. 1; also see Stan Steiner, *Fusahang: The Chinese Who Built America* (New York: Harper & Row, 1979), pp. 24–35; Elena S. H. Yu, "Filipino Migration and Community Organization in the United States," *California Sociologist 3:2* (1980): 76–102; and Joan M. Jensen, *Passage from India: Asian Indian Immigrants in North America* (New Haven: Yale University Press, 1988), pp. 12–13.

[3] Sucheng Chan, *Asian Californians* (San Francisco: MTL/Boyd & Fraser, 1991), pp. 5–6.

[4] Ronald Takaki, *Strangers from a Different Shore* (Boston: Little, Brown, 1989), pp. 79, 114.

[5] Stanford Lyman, *Chinese Americans* (New York: Random House, 1974), pp. 86–88.

[6] Chan, *Asian Californians,* pp. 27–33.

[7] Lyman, *Chinese Americans,* pp. 63–69.

[8] Yuji Ichioka, *The Issei: The World of the First Generation Japanese Immigrant's, 1885–1924* (New York: Free Press, 1988), pp. 64–65.

[9] Roger Daniels, *Concentration Camps: North American Japanese in the United States and Canada During World War II* (Malabar, FL: Robert A. Kreiger, 1981), p. 7.

[10] Bill Ong Hing, *Making and Remaking Asian America Through Immigration Policy, 1850–1990* (Stanford, CA: Stanford University Press, 1993), pp. 28–30.

[11] Chan, *Asian Californians,* p. 7.

[12] Edwin B. Almirol, *Ethnic Identity and Social Negotiation: A Study of a Filipino Community in California* (New York: AMS Press, 1985), pp. 52–59; and H. Brett Melendy, "Filipinos in the United States," in Norris Hundley, Jr. (ed.), *The Asian American: The Historical Experience* (Santa Barbara: Cleo, 1977), pp. 101–128.

[13] Takaki, *Strangers from a Different Shore,* pp. 53–57.

[14] Chan, *Asian Californians,* pp. 7, 17–19, 37; and Warren Y. Kim, *Koreans in America* (Seoul: Po Chin Chai, 1971), pp. 22–27.

[15] Joan M. Jensen, *Passage from India: Asian Indian Immigrants in North America* (New Haven: Yale University Press, 1988), pp. 24–41; and Rajanki K. Das, *Hindustani Workers on the Pacific Coast* (Berlin and Leipzig: Walter De Gruyter, 1923), p. 77.

[16] Das, *Hindustani Workers,* pp. 66–67.

[17] Bruce La Brack, "Occupational Specialization Among Rural California Sikhs: The Interplay of Culture and Economics," *Amerasia Journal* 9:2 (1982): 29–56.

[18] Naturalization Act of 1790, I Stat. 103 (1790).

[19] Act of 14 July 1870, 16 Stat. 256.

[20] Roger Daniels, *Asian Americans: Chinese and Japanese in the United States* (Seattle: University of Washington Press, 1988), p. 43.

[21] Chan, *Asian Californians,* p. 42.

[22] Robert F. Heizer and Alan F. Almquist, *The Other Californians: Prejudice and Discrimination Under Spain, Mexico, and the United States to 1920* (Berkeley: University of California Press, 1971), p. 129.

[23] Takaki, *Strangers from a Different Shore,* p. 82.

[24] Lyman, *Chinese Americans,* pp. 55–85.

[25] Takaki, *Strangers from a Different Shore,* pp. 111–112.

[26] Juan L. Gonzales, *Racial and Ethnic Groups in America,* 2nd ed. (Dubuque, IA: Kendall/Hunt, 1993), p. 136; and Juan L. Gonzales, *Racial and Ethnic Families in America,* 2nd ed. (Dubuque, IA: Kendall/Hunt Publishing Co., 1993), p. 3.

[27] Chan, *Asian Californians,* pp. 44–45.

[28] Hing, *Making and Remaking Asian America,* pp. 32–39.

[29] *Yick Wo v. Hopkins,* 118 U.S. 356 (1886); and Lyman, *Chinese Americans,* p. 79.

[30] *Takao Ozawa v. United States,* 260 U.S. 178 (1922); Heizer and Alquist, *The Other Californians,* pp. 192–193; and Ichioka, *The Issei,* pp. 210–226.

[31] *United States v. Bhagat Singh Thind,* 261 U.S. 204 (1923); Jensen, *Passage from India,* pp. 255–260; and Gurdial Singh, "East Indians in the United States," *Sociology and Social Research* 30:3 (1946): 208–216.

[32] Megumi Dick Osumi, "Asians and California's Anti–Miscegenation Laws," in Nobuya Tsuchida (ed.), *Asian and Pacific American Experiences: Women's Perspectives* (Minneapolis: Asian/Pacific American Learning Resource Center, University of Minnesota, 1982), pp. 1–37; and Takaki, *Strangers from a Different Shore,* pp. 330–331.

[33] William Petersen, *Japanese Americans* (New York: Random House, 1971), pp. 66–100; Roger Daniels, *Concentration Camps, U.S.A.* (New York: Holt, Rinehart & Winston, 1971), pp. 75, 81–82; and Jacobus tenBroek, Edward N. Barnhart and Floyd W. Matson, *Prejudice, War, and the Constitution* (Berkeley: University of California Press), pp. 118–120.

[34] Cited in Commission on Wartime Relocation and Internment of Civilians, *Personal Justice Denied* (Washington, DC: U.S. Government Printing Office, 1982), pp. 52–53.

[35] Takaki, *Strangers from a Different Shore,* pp. 379–392.

[36] Commission on Wartime Relocation and Internment of Civilians, *Personal Justice Denied,* p. 217; tenBroek, Barnhart, and Matson, *Prejudice, War, and the Constitution,* pp. 155–177, 180–181; and Daniels, *Concentration Camps: North America.*

[37] Chan, *Asian Californians,* p. 101.

[38] Petersen, *Japanese Americans,* p. 87.

[39] Cited in Marvin Karlins, Thomas L. Coffman, and Gary Walters, "On the Fading of Social Stereotypes: Studies of Three Generations of College Students," *Journal of Personality and Psychology* 13 (1990): 4–5.

[40] *Time,* December 22, 1941, p. 33.

[41] Cited in Harold Isaacs, *Images of Asia: American Views of China and India* (New York: Harper & Row, 1972), pp. xviii–xix.

[42] Chan, *Asian Californians,* pp. 103–104; and Lyman, *Chinese Americans,* pp. 127, 134.

[43] Takaki, *Strangers from a Different Shore,* pp. 357–363, 370–378; Manuel Buaken, "Life in the Armed Forces," *New Republic* 109 (1943): 279–280; and Bienvenido Santos, "Filipinos in War," *Far Eastern Survey* 11 (1942): 249–250.

[44] Harry H. L. Kitano and Roger Daniels, *Asian Americans: Emerging Minorities,* 2nd ed. (Upper Saddle River, NJ: Prentice Hall, 1995), p. 42, Table 4–2; and Monica Boyd, "Oriental Immigration: The Experience of Chinese, Japanese, and Filipino Populations in the United States," *International Migration Review* 10 (1976): 48–60, Table 1.

[45] Chan, *Asian Californians,* pp. 105–106.

[46] Diane Mark and Ginger Chih, *A Place Called Chinese America* (San Francisco: The Organization of Chinese Americans, 1982), pp. 105–107.

[47] Chan, *Asian Californians,* pp. 108–109.

[48] Ibid., pp. 109–110.

[49] Hing, *Making and Remaking Asian America,* Appendix B, pp. 189–200; Table 9, p. 82.

[50] Hing, *Making and Remaking Asian America,* pp. 79–120; Luciano Mangiafico, *Contemporary American Immigrants: Patterns of Filipino, Korean, and Chinese Settlement in the United States* (New York: Praeger, 1988), pp. 1–26; James T. Fawcett and Benjamin V. Carino (eds.), *Pacific Bridges: The New Immigration from Asia and the Pacific Islands* (Staten Island, NY: Center for Migration Studies, 1987); and Herbert R. Barringer, Robert W. Gardner, and Michael J. Levine (eds.), *Asian and Pacific Islanders in the United States* (New York: Russell Sage Foundation, 1993).

[51] U.S. Immigration and Naturalization Service, *Statistical Yearbook of the Immigration and Naturalization Service, 1993* (Washington DC: U.S. Government Printing Office, 1994), p. 20.

[52] Roger Daniels, *Coming to America* (New York: HarperCollins, 1990), pp. 391–397.

[53] U.S. Immigration and Naturalization Service, *Statistical Yearbook of the Immigration and Naturalization Service, 1994* (Washington, DC: U.S. Government Printing Office, 1996), p. 126, Chart O.

[54] Hing, *Making and Remaking Asian America,* pp. 7–8.

[55] Paul Ong, Edna Bonacich, and Lucie Cheng (eds.), *The New Asian Immigration in Los Angeles and Global Restructuring* (Philadelphia: Temple University Press, 1994), pp. 3–100; and Edna Bonacich, Lucie Cheng, Norma Chinchilla, Nora Hamilton, and Paul Ong (eds.), *Global Production: The Apparel Industry in the Pacific Rim* (Philadelphia: Temple University Press, 1994), pp. 3–20.

[56] Paul Ong and Evelyn Blumenberg, "Scientists and Engineers," in Paul Ong (ed.), *The State of Asian Pacific America: Economic Diversity, Issues & Policies* (Los Angeles: LEAP Asian Pacific American Public Policy Institute and UCLA Asian American Studies Center, 1994), pp. 113–138. Note that I am distinguishing between foreign exchange students who are overseas nationals from Asian American students who happen to be foreign born.

[57] Ibid., p. 173; and U.S. Department of Commerce, *Statistical Abstract of the United States, 1995* (Washington, DC: U.S. Government Printing Office, 1995), p. 188, Table 295.

[58] U.S. Department of Commerce, *Statistical Abstract of the United States, 1999* (Washington, DC: U.S. Government Printing Office, 2000), p. 625, Table 1004.

[59] "The Golden Diaspora: Indian Immigrants to the U.S. Are One of the Newest Elements of the American Melting Pot—and the Most Spectacular Success Story," *Time Select/Global Business,* June 19, 2000, pp. B26–27.

[60] Paul Ong and Tania Azores, "Health Professionals on the Front-Line," in Paul Ong (ed.), *The State of Asian Pacific America: Economic Diversity, Issues & Policies,* pp. 139–164.

[61] Paul Ong and Tania Azores, "The Migration and Incorporation of Filipino Nurses," in Ong et al. (eds.), *The New Asian Immigration in Los Angeles and Global Restructuring,* pp. 166–195; and Mangiafico, *Contemporary American Immigrants,* pp. 42–43.

[62] Literature on the Vietnam conflict is voluminous. For an excellent and readable overview, see Stanley Karnow, *Vietnam: A History* (New York: Penguin, 1991).

[63] The quota for refugees under the 1965 Immigration Reform Act was only 17,400, so President Gerald Ford instructed the attorney general to use his "parole" power to admit the 130,000 refugees. The use of parole power was also used to bring European refugees to the United States during the 1950s. For more detail, see Hing, *Making and Remaking Asian America,* pp. 123–128; and Paul J. Strand and Woodrow Jones, Jr., *Indochinese Refugees in America: Problems of Adaptation and Assimilation* (Durham, NC: Duke University Press, 1985).

[64] Chan, *Asian Californians,* p. 128; and Chor-Swan Ngin, "The Acculturation Pattern of Orange County's Southeast Asian Refugees," *Journal of Orange County Studies* 3:4 (Fall 1989–Spring 1990): 46–53.

[65] Ngin, "The Acculturation Pattern of Orange County's Southeast Asian Refugees," p. 49; and Ngoan Le, "The Case of the Southeast Asian Refugees: Policy for a Community 'At-Risk,' " in *The State of Asian Pacific America: Policy Issues to the Year 2020* (Los Angeles: LEAP Asian Pacific American Public Policy Institute and UCLA Asian American Studies Center, 1993), pp. 167–188.

[66] For more details, see Strand and Jones, *Indochinese Refugees in America;* Barry L. Wain, *The Refused: The Agony of Indochina Refugees* (New York: Simon & Schuster, 1981); and U.S. Committee for Refugees, *Uncertain Harbors: The Plight of Vietnamese Boat People* (Washington, DC: U.S. Government Printing Office, 1987).

[67] Chan, *Asian Californians,* pp. 121–138; Kitano and Daniels, *Asian Americans: Emerging Minorities,* pp. 170–191; U.S. Committee for Refugees, *Cambodians in Thailand: People on the Edge* (Washington, DC: U.S. Government Printing Office, 1985); and U.S. Committee for Refugees, *Refugees from Laos: In Harm's Way* (Washington, DC: U.S. Government Printing Office, 1986).

[68] U.S. Committee for Refugees, *Uncertain Harbors,* pp. 19–20; and Ruben Rumbaut, "Vietnamese, Laotian, and Cambodian Americans," in Pyong Gap Min (ed.), *Asian Americans: Contemporary Trends and Issues* (Thousand Oaks, CA: Sage, 1995), p. 240.

[69] Ruben Rumbaut and J. R. Weeks, "Fertility and Adaptation: Indochinese Refugees in the United States," *International Migration Review* 20:2 (1986): 428–466; and Rumbaut, "Vietnamese, Laotian, and Cambodian Americans," pp. 239–242.

ETHNIC STUDIES: AN INTRODUCTION

Recent African Immigration

Boatamo Mosupyoe

 ## Introduction

Current immigration policy in the United States and the manner in which it has operated have created more opportunities for citizens of other nations to immigrate into the country (Nag, 2005), which has manifested in an increasing number of immigrants since the 1970s as natives from other countries continue to migrate to the United States. The immigrants often arrive in search of opportunities to improve their standard of living (Lee, Myers, Ha & Shin, 2005; Nag, 2005). Many of these immigrants are well-educated, holding managerial and professional positions in their native country prior to immigrating (Buzdugan & Halli, 2009; Nag, 2005). On their arrival in the United States, some of these professionals are forced to take on jobs that are considered "low skill" in spite of their educational background (Adamuti-Trache & Sweet, 2005).

While this article draws from my unpublished research of recent African immigrants in Washington State and the San Francisco Bay area of California and the state's capitol, Sacramento, my discussion also draws from other sources. The article should not be seen as a report on my research, since it just borrows and does not even begin to give an exhaustive account of the research.

Areas of focus are the lives and experiences of recent African immigrants entering the United States of America relative to the following issues:

● the immigration pattern of Africans in the United States
● the motivations for immigrating to the United States
● collective and multiple identities (e.g., how and to what extent ties to the African continent affect the group's identity; the extent to which their views converge and diverge with their children's; their respective achievements and failures and the extent to which these are ideological or structural; issues like school performance are considered as well as the relevance of Ogbu's theory of voluntary and involuntary minority)

- the assertion that recent African immigrants are favored by institutions and are benefiting from Affirmative Action more than African American descendants of former enslaved people
- the relationship of African Americans with their recent African counterparts
- the challenges that recent African immigrants face, including domestic violence
- an overview of their contribution of to the U.S. economy

Immigration Patterns

The United States is always defined as a country of immigrants. Native Americans have been very generous in accommodating people from different countries, a point never acknowledged. The United States immigration pattern reveals a historical preference towards European immigration into the United States and varied degrees of less preference towards immigrants from other parts of the world, including Africa. Salih Omar Eissa (2005) accurately observes that the 19th and 20th century immigration policy was discriminatory and heavily Eurocentric, despite the migration of Black Cape Verdean mariners to Massachusetts during this period.

Even when the McCarran-Walter Act of 1952 eliminated all racially specific language from the Immigration and Nationality Act (INA), and the Hart-Cellar Act of 1965 passed, national quotas remained and migration from the African continent was set at the lowest quota of 1,400 annually. Eissa (2005) further argues that of all people admitted to the United States between 1990 and 2000 only ten percent were Africans. This notwithstanding, the number of Africans in the United States has been increasing. An examination of immigration figures show that 30,000 Africans came legally into the United States in the 1960s, 80,000 in the 1970s, and 176,000 in the 1980s (Khalid El-Hassan, 2005). Since the 1980s the number has more than quadrupled. The figures from the Immigration and Naturalization Services (INS) reveal that between 1981 and 2000 the number stood at 531,832. It is important to note that some scholars, including myself, believe the U.S. Census Bureau 2000 report fails to capture the actual number of recent African immigrants. The possibility exists that the report underreported the number of Africans by hundreds of thousands. Africans who are in the country illegally exhibit the same behavioral pattern as other immigrants. They would not participate in the census exercise or even seek government help in other matters. At all costs they avoid authorities since they seek to hide their statuses.

Motivations for Immigrating to the United States

U.S. Census 2000 show that most recent African immigrants come from West Africa at 35 percent a year, 26 percent from East Africa, 20 percent from North Africa, seven percent from South Africa, and less than two percent from

Central Africa. They are found in major metropolitan cities as well as in small towns and are not necessarily clustered in one part. The reasons for their immigration to the United States are varied and will be discussed. However, to give a context to the many issues that the recent Africans face, a very brief overview of the first African immigrants and their contribution is in order. We all know that the majority of first people of African descent to come into the United States came as people who were later enslaved. Any account about African immigrants that fails to acknowledge the foundation laid by these first Africans would be disingenuous (Mosupyoe, 2005).

Europeans traded with Africans as early as 1450. In the 17th century the British started transporting Africans to North America. They were also captured from different parts of Africa, including Bight of Benin, Senegambia, and the Gold Coast in West Africa, Angola, et al. Their labor and presence transformed the sociocultural and economic patterns of the United States. By the mid 1800s the positions they occupied and the kind of work they performed varied to include teamsters, porters, domestics, and plantation workers. At this time European immigration was encouraged and favored. European immigrants were also granted citizenship, a right that was denied to Africans, through the 1857 Dred Scott decision (Mosupyoe, 2005).

The decision declared Africans as "beings of an inferior order," and therefore deserving to be denied rights by the Constitution, including the right of citizenship. In addition, many other laws denied Africans their basic human rights. Although January 1, 1808, became the date designated for the prohibition of trade with African people, the capture and enslavement of African people continued well into the mid-19th century. The Emancipation Proclamation of 1863 permanently ended enslavement of African people. Thereafter, in 1868, the 14th amendment to the U.S. Constitution guaranteed citizenship, due process, and equal protection under the law for people of African descent, thereby overturning the Dred Scott decision (Mosupyoe, 2005).

In spite of all these gains, discrimination against African Americans continued in various ways, Jim Crow laws in the South being one of those. Through different organizations, such as the National Association for the Advancement of Colored People (1909), National Urban League (1911), and United Negro Improvement Association (1916), African Americans and institutions such as Howard University, Morehouse College, and Spelman University, African Americans were able to secure for themselves their rightful place in the U.S. landscape.

These remarkable people and their descendants, who have endured tremendous adversity and displayed admirable temerity, unquestionably laid the foundations of opportunity for a new wave of immigration after slavery and desegregation. Their struggles against and triumphs over slavery, Jim Crow, and segregation, through the civil rights movement and other means have been instrumental in transforming the sociopolitical climate in the United States. Pertinent to this discussion is the 1965 Hart-Cellar Immigration Act. The act advocates admission of immigrants based on their skills, professions, and familial relations.

The ideology of the act, in origin, substance, and final passage as law, mirrors the spirit of the civil rights movement as well as the thoughts of other Pan African activist who preceded the movement. Moreover, the African American involvement could be attributed to the direct success of a series of post-1965 immigration policy shifts that opened the doors to a steady increase in African immigration in the latter part of the 20th century. African Americans, descendants of enslaved Africans, created benefits through their struggle, which recent African immigrants like me enjoy. They produced an environment far more accepting of new immigrants. Today, approximately 50,000 Africans arrive annually from different parts of Africa for different reasons (Mosupyoe, 2005).

The post-enslavement period migration of Africans falls within the purview of Ogbu's voluntary immigrants' classification (Ogbu, 1993). The voluntary African immigrants came to the United States for many different reasons. In the 1950s and 1960s many Africans migrated to Europe; however, during the 1970s and 1980s most European countries experienced recessions that went along with aversion to immigration and culminated in the tightening of immigration laws. Meanwhile with the passage of the 1965 Hart-Cellar Immigration Act the U.S. immigration policies became somewhat liberalized. The United States then became the country of choice for Africans to immigrate to.

The push to immigrate stems from various factors. In the 1970s high unemployment and devalued currencies in most African countries resulted from failed economic policies engendered by poor management and "structural adjustment" programs demanded by the World Bank and International Monetary Fund. These conditions caused disappointment in the wake of newly acquired freedoms from European domination. Some parts of Africa, like South Africa, had racist governments that blatantly and legally discriminated against blacks. Opposing the racist policies led to detention and even death. In addition, civil wars in some parts of Africa precipitated immigration into the United States. In view of this and also taking into consideration civil wars in other parts of the world, such as Bosnia, the U.S. Congress reformed its policy towards refugees.

African immigrants benefited from the Refuge Act of 1980 and the immigration Reform and Control Act of 1986. One offered new refugees permanent resident status after one year while the other legalized the status of 31,000 Africans living in the United States since 1982. It could be argued that such a step encouraged African immigrants to stay in the United States. The Temporary Protected Status (TPS) that is part of the Diversity Visa Lottery Act of 1990 also acted as an impetus for African immigration from African countries such as Sudan, Sierra Leone, Liberia, Somalia, and Burundi. The act has a provision that gives temporary refuge status to foreign nationals present in the United States who would be subject to either violence due to armed conflict or environmental disaster if repatriated.

This Diversity Visa Lottery Act of 1990, further, offers immigrant visas to high school graduates in an attempt to increase the low rates of underrepresented nations in the United States. The visa lottery thus became another vehicle through which Africans primarily immigrated to the United States. Some Africans come to the

United States to study or on exchange programs and then decide to stay because they have developed love relationships that culminate in marriages. Others come with babies who grow into children and teenagers while parents are attending school. Having raised their children here, they then decide to stay. Their decision is mainly based on their conclusion that their children will find it hard to adapt to their countries of origin. Yet others come to the United States through family reunification programs.

In the 1960s and 1970s most Africans who came to the United States had strong desires to go back and contribute towards their respective countries nation building. The trend has changed in the last two decades. Recent African voluntary immigrants chose to stay, build a life for their families, and find ways of integrating into the U.S. society – the focus of the next section.

Challenges, and Collective and Multiple Identities

The recent African immigrants are not a monolithic group; they come from various countries in Africa and the Caribbean. Although they speak English, they also speak different languages that are not mutually intelligible. African cultures have as many similarities as they have differences. Ideological diversity also abounds. A case in point is the view of how South Africans should deal with the post-apartheid society, how Nigeria should mediate the corruption in that country, how to raise children in the U.S. culture, and how to best integrate into U.S. society.

In most part Africans will associate and form strong alliances with those who come from the same African countries. You will also find organizations formed along those lines (e.g., you will find an Igbo organization, a Somali organization, South African in the Bay Area, et al.). Organizations formed along African country of origin lines are mostly support system groups designed to strengthen relationships and help one another in times of need. In addition, such communal organizations offer ties with people from respective homes who share a common language. It also important to note that some alliances are formed based on the different regions from the same country (e.g., in the case of South Africans, people from the eastern Cape will feel closer to one another than they would with people from Gauteng), although, survival, the need for community, and fear of isolation often force collective identity based on the country of origin to be stronger and more enduring.

In addition to this collective identity defined by specific countries of origin, Africans from different parts of Africa do share a collective identity based on a continent of origin, the differences notwithstanding. Africans tend to come together to an "African party" to share their respective vibrant cultures and also to discuss difficult issues that they face as immigrants. Some of the challenges that recent African immigrants face are the same as those faced by African Americans. To start with they share some phenotypes, and in the United States discrimination on the basis of how you look persists.

Police brutality (as in the case of the death of Amadou Diallo, an African immigrant who was killed by police) and racial profiling affect them, as does the subtle perception as inferior and less than others. Additionally, Africans accents are described as heavy (although as an African immigrant myself, I never understood that); this tends to invite both intrigue and repulsion from others. I personally have had students' evaluation where one student asked that the school should make me change my accent. I have also had people admire "my heavy accent."

Discussions with some of the immigrants have revealed that they are often told that "you have an accent." To some, to the extent that having an accent suggests ignorance and stupidity, this observation becomes troubling – particularly since we all have accents, a point that most U.S. people miss, in my experience. One immigrant related how a taxi driver attempted to take advantage of her in terms of pricing because he thought that since she "had an accent" her knowledge of the place and the pricing was minimal and therefore she was a prime target for exploitation.

Other problems are presented by men and women's relationships as they try to adapt to the new culture. Domestic violence is a reality in the communities of recent African immigrants. Some men come with their cultural beliefs about women as inferior and subservient. In 2005 professor Uwazie of the Criminal Justice Department at California State University, Sacramento, called a meeting that was triggered by a series of domestic violent acts committed by men on women in the Sacramento area and other parts of the United States. I was asked to be the co-moderator of the discussions.

In one of the Sacramento incidents a Ghanaian man reportedly stabbed his wife 22 times to death, after an argument between the estranged couple. In another case, a Nigerian man drove all the way from Atlanta, Georgia, to stalk his Ondo-born wife living separately in Dallas, Texas. He eventually shot her to death in her car. Also, in August 2005 a Nigerian man used a hammer to murder his Sierra Leonean-born wife at their home in a Dallas suburb. The murder reportedly occurred in front of the couples' seven-year-old daughter. Ben Edokpayi reported on the meeting in the newspaper Times of Nigeria in an article entitled "An Elephant in the House." I am going to briefly summarize his report to give you insights into the thinking of recent African immigrants from different countries, both men and women on this issue.

Edokpayi acknowledges the existence of patriarchy and male chauvinism as an epidemic in Africa. He reports that while incidents of domestic violence in African communities in the diaspora are only now coming into the limelight, the problem has long been an entrenched epidemic in African countries where male chauvinism rules. He writes that "the dominant thread that ran through many of the evening's contributions on the subject was the juxtaposition of the African and American cultures and how the two can be effectively combined by recent transplants from across the Atlantic." He goes on to give a sampling of the discussions that reflected the variety of opinions:

"The *support system you have back home doesn't exist here. In order to feel comfortable here we need to know our limitations. The rules of the game are not the same as you might have say in Ghana*," said Ngissah.

A Nigerian auditor who's been married to his wife for 30 years had a different perspective. *"We already know the problem. First of all you can't put old wine into new wine. You can think you can bring your Igbo culture and enforce it here? It just won't work,"* he said, adding rather humorously, *"You go to our African parties and take a look at the face of our women. They look worn out and don't want to dance. Why? Because they spend most of their time cooking, cleaning and taking care of the home all by themselves. That's abuse!"*

Another Nigerian, Sylvester Okonkwo, presented an interesting angle to the clash of cultures and how it frames the issue. *"Let's not make this sound as if it's an African problem,"* he said. *"The African culture has its own pluses and minuses. Most of us studied here and gained employment here. We have a proverb that says when you are in a foreign land, 'learn all the good things there and leave the bad ones alone,'"* said Okonkwo.

I agree with Edokpayi' s observation that "most participants agreed that it was tough to balance the two cultures, all were in agreement that the African culture was intrinsically sound and could be a good insulation against the pressures of today's microwave world where materialistic pursuits and the hurry for results tend to obfuscate everything else." The discussions offer hope to the extent that the domestic violence is acknowledged, discussed, and the determination to come with solutions salient. In her article "What it means to be an Asian Indian Woman," Y. Lakshmi Malroutu posits that among the recent Asian Indian immigrants, domestic violence is hidden and denied. This should speak well of the recent African immigrants.

Mediating the tension brought by raising children who grow up in the United States also presents paradoxes. An experience of children who grow up in the United States and have minimal to zero experience of Africa is often the discussion of common experiences. Children assume a different identity from their parents and most likely identify as African Americans, proclaiming more of an affinity in cultural experiences to African American children who are descendants of former enslaved Africans than to their parents. Often parents have to decide which behavior should be accepted and which not. In the research that I am currently conducting on this topic, a student from Ethiopia relates how her mother preferred that she and her siblings associate with other recent immigrant children who have better manners than the rest of American kids. It is only recently, she says, that her mother has accepted that they are culturally American and have chosen their identity accordingly.

I have two daughters, too, who grew up here. When I first came one was two weeks old and the other just a year-and-a-half old. They identify with no hesitation as African Americans. We also have different views and perspectives on things in addition to those engendered by generational differences. I would like them to offer people food when they come to visit without asking if they want food or not. People will then reject the food politely afterwards if they choose to, but they constantly remind me that they have to ask since this is "America." Most parents have a variation of these cognitive dissonances to deal with. In most part parents identify with Africa more than their children do. In my research I found that African adults will identify as "Africans in America" and children will identify as African Americans.

Relationships with African Americans

It has also been argued that recent African immigrants perform well in school, have better study habits, and have excellent job performance rates. This behavior pattern parallels that of other immigrants of different continental origin. An assessment of the applicability of Ogbu's theory on voluntary and involuntary minority then becomes relevant here. This assessment should also take into consideration that the late Ogbu was also a recent African immigrant who came to the United States in the 1960s from Nigeria. Ogbu asserts that in understanding the performance of minorities in the United States a distinction between the types of minority status and the different types of cultural differences should be taken into account (Ogbu, 1993).

Voluntary minority refers to immigrants like the recent African immigrants who came to the United States through other reasons than U.S. enslavement. Involuntary minority refers to the status of African Americans who are descendants of enslaved people. Ogbu argues that there is an absence of persistent basic academic difficulties among the voluntary minorities despite the primary cultural differences with the Euro-American culture. Involuntary minorities, on the other hand, Ogbu further posits, have difficulties because of the nature of their responses to their forced incorporation and subsequent persistent mistreatment by the Euro-American power structures. Despite the phenomenal strides that have been made, legacy of sanitized unequal treatment still endures. Ogbu argues that African Americans have thus formed oppositional identity and cultural frame of references that tend to impact performance.

If we are to follow Ogbu's argument, if indeed, recent African immigrants are performing better, than their success could be attributed to the fact that they have a better response to the structural discrimination and unwelcoming school environments. What Ogbu's theory fails to take into consideration is the fact that some Euro-Americans feel more comfortable with recent African immigrants than they do with African Americans. When I first came to the United States as a student, an African American professor at Denison University in Ohio, at an orientation into the U.S. society, explained that in his experience there is less guilt whether subconscious or salient, for Euro-Americans towards recent African immigrants. As a result they tend to be more receptive and friendlier to recent African immigrants. Obviously this friendly attitude has its unfair benefits. The friendly atmosphere contributes towards a learning environment conducive to producing good results, or conversely a friendly working environment. This then becomes a structural and institutional hurdle for others who are not afforded the same courtesy to overcome.

I have personally experienced this, as this discussion will later show. The fact that African immigrants enter the country mostly with more than a high school diploma, should also explain their relatively high level of educational attainment.

African immigrants are not immune to the adverse impact of competition for resources that often manifest in xenophobia. They have been looked at as taking away jobs from those already here and have also been victims of hate crimes. The other challenge that they have to face pertains to their relationship with African Americans who are descendants of former enslaved people. Professors Lani Guinier and Henry Louis Gates, Jr., a Harvard law professor and the chairman of Harvard's African and African-American Department, respectively, spoke at the third Black Alumni Weekend of Harvard University, which took place October 3–5, 2003, and drew more than 600 former students. Their comments illustrate the tension and challenge.

According to the Harvard University news of January–February, 2004, university officieals were pleased with an eight percent increase in black students (530) from the 2003 enrollment. However, the celebratory mood of the evening was broken by Professor Guinier, whose mother is white and whose father immigrated from Jamaica, when she advised that Harvard should reconsider its celebration since the majority of the black students were not true African Americans, but West Indian and African immigrants or their children, or to a lesser extent, children of biracial couples. Professor Gates, Jr., supported her assertions and charges (Onyeanyi, 2006).

Such comments by highly visible African Americans continued when Mr. Alan Keyes, a former right-wing Republican presidential candidate, accused Mr. Barack Obama, a senator from Illinois, of not being a true African American since his father was from Kenya. Alan Keyes is quoted in a *New York Times* article of August 27, 2004, titled "'African-American' Becomes a Term for Debate," as saying, "Barack Obama claims an African-American heritage." Mr. Keyes said on the ABC program "This Week" with George Stephanopoulos, "Barack Obama and I have the same race — that is, physical characteristics. We are not from the same heritage."

Yet another prominent African American, an administrator at the University of Columbia, Dr. Bobby Austin, was quoted in the same *New York Times* article of August 27, 2004, saying, "some people feared that black immigrants and their children would snatch up the hard-won opportunities made possible by the civil rights movement." Dr. Austin further said, "We've suffered so much that we're a bit weary and immigration seems like one more hurdle we will have to climb. People are asking: 'Will I have to climb over these immigrants to get to my dream? Will my children have to climb?'" Perceptions and thoughts like this permeate to the other parts of the community. Oftentimes in my classes I will have African American students asking me why do Africans hate them and vice versa. I often tell them that I do not wish to participate in this divide-and-conquer mentality that does not benefit us.

The workplace also fails to help bridge the gap between the two. I am a recent African immigrant, as I have mentioned before. Prior to coming to California State University, Sacramento, I was employed in Washington, in an institution that was predominately Euro-American. For years I was the only faculty of African descent. Efforts to encourage a hire of African Americans were often met with, "but we have you." For years the institution and some of its people felt comfortable with me and did not find it necessary to hire an African American who was born and raised in the United States.

When I discussed my concerns about this with some of my former colleagues and expressed that I felt like a token because of their attitude and refusal to hire African Americans, they would tell me how they did not see me as a token but as a strong, highly opinionated woman. As can be expected, they missed the point. Their behavior made me fully understand what the professor in Denison meant, that hiring an African American evokes feelings that they would rather not deal with. When they did subsequently hire an African American, they displayed such racist behavior towards her that, among other issues, she was forced out.

Recently, I spoke with one of my former colleagues, Vicki Scannell, who is also a friend from the same institution. She told me that the problem still persists and the excuse that is now being made is that the institution does not pay enough to attract African Americans. The impression created then remains that African Americans will not work for less pay while hardworking Euro-Americans would. Of course, my friend, who is also Euro-American, made a point to remind them that institutional racism, and not pay, accounts for the absence of African American professors.

African Americans, as I mentioned earlier, paved the way for contemporary African immigrants — it would benefit both groups to unite and work together. Students where I am teaching seem to do a better job of bridging the gap. Two years ago they invited me to speak at an event they organized and the thesis was "bridging the gap between people of Africans descent from the continent and the diaspora."

Despite all the challenges that I have mentioned, African immigrants do share a life with their native-born counterparts. There are many intermarriages between them. Their offspring and their unions provide an element of diversity in the United States that should not be ignored since it bridges the gap between the native born and foreign born. Second-generation Africans are commanding leadership roles in arenas large and small throughout the country. Whether members of Congress such as Barack Obama, leaders of black community and student organizations, or even up-and-coming hip-hop artists such as Akon, African second-generation immigrants are wholehearted participants in and even creators of today's African American culture.

Continuously infused with new influences from their own diaspora, Africans are contributing to the fluid adaptability of U.S. dynamic urban culture. In the process of redefining their race and culture in a social order far different from that of their parents, African immigrants are both giving to and taking from African American tradition in a reciprocal and mutually advantageous relationship (Salim Omar Eisa, 2005).

They have embraced the economic opportunities offered by the United States. According to the Schomburg Center for Research in Black Culture, "Some highly educated [African] immigrants, realizing that their limited proficiency in English and their foreign degrees would make it difficult to get the American jobs they coveted, have instead opened their own businesses. This entrepreneurial spirit is deeply ingrained in Africa, where the informal economic sector is particularly dynamic." The Bay Area and Sacramento, like many other U.S. cities, have African restaurants, African hair braiding salons, nightclubs, music stores, and many other entrepreneurial ventures that provide economic stability.

Although there were about 100,000 highly educated African professionals throughout the United States in 1999, many more are also involved in jobs where less education and often less skill may be required. They work as cab drivers, parking lot attendants, airport workers or waiters, waitresses, and cooks in restaurants. Even African women who have traditionally been in the background of most traditional African family structure now find themselves at the forefront of economic opportunities in the United States and thus are playing important economic roles in maintaining the family structure both for the family members who are still in Africa and those in the United States.

References

Africa News Service (1999, November 21).

[The] African Sun Times (2006, February 6).

Daff, Marieme (2002, August 9). Women-migration: Women taking their places in African immigration. *Inter Press services.*

Diouf, Sylviane (2005). The new African diaspora. From *In Motion: The African American Migration Experience* (p. 1). New York: Schomburg Center for Research in Black Culture.

Edokpayi, Ben (2006). *The Times of Nigeria.*

Eissa, Salih Omar (2005). *Diversity and transformation: African Americans and African immigration to the United States.* Immigration Policy Brief.

Halter, Marilyn (1993). *Between race and ethnicity: Cape Verdean American immigrants 1860–1965* (pp. 67–98). Champaign, IL: University of Illinois Press.

Logan, John R., & Deane, Glenn (2003, August 15). *Black diversity in metropolitan America.* Lewis Mumford Center for Comparative Urban and Regional Research, University of Albany, p. 4.

Mosupyoe, Boatamo. *Recent African immigrants in the U.S.*, unpublished manuscript.

Ogbu, John (1993). Difference in cultural frame of references. *International Journal of Behavioral Development, 16*(3), 483–506.

Onyeanyi, Chika A. (2006, February 6). *The African Sun Times.*

Schomburg Center for Research in Black Culture (2005, February). The waves of migration. From *In Motion: The African American Migration Experience. www.inmotionaame.org*

Takougang, Joseph. Recent African immigrants to the United States: A historical perspective. *The Western Journal of Black Studies*, 19(1).

U.S. Census, 2000.

ETHNIC STUDIES: AN INTRODUCTION

Native Americans and the United States, 1830–2000 Action and Response

Steven J. Crum

Introduction

In this chapter, I will focus on federal government policies toward Native American people from the early nineteenth century forward. Although this story has been told numerous times, and scholars have called it an old-fashioned historical approach to the writing of Indian history–an assessment I agree with–I will work hard not to repeat the same examples others have given over the years. Instead, I will provide some new examples as much as possible. My main argument is that the history of federal government policy toward Indian people is one of action on one side and response and reaction on the other. More often than not, the federal government initiated the action and the Indians responded or reacted to it. At times, however, the Indians served as actors and persuaded the federal government what to include in its interactions with tribal people, including treaty provisions of the nineteenth century.

Indian Removal

In 1830, Congress passed the Indian Removal Act, which paved the way for the mass-scale physical removal of thousands of Native Americans who lived east of the Mississippi River. In the southeast alone, the federal government moved roughly 60,000 tribal people to the area we now call eastern Oklahoma (Indian

Contributed by Steven J. Crum. © Kendall Hunt Publishing Company

Territory up to 1907). Those of us who study Native American history know the historical accounts of the removed Cherokee, Choctaw, Creek, Chickasaw, and Seminole. We are fully aware of the Trail of Tears of 1838 in which thousands of Cherokee died en route from their former homeland.[1]

Although Indian removal was a case of the American government having its way, at the same time, some of the tribes made certain that favorable provisions ended up in the removal treaties. In the Treaty of Dancing Rabbit Creek of 1830, negotiated with the Choctaw of Mississippi, the Choctaw leadership persuaded the government to include a provision for the education of Choctaw people. The tribe viewed education as a means of "survival" and a way of dealing with the white Americans. With the funds coming from the treaty, the tribe eventually created the Forty Youth Fund, which helped several Choctaws pursue a higher education. Some earned college and university degrees from eastern postsecondary institutions and returned home to help maintain their Choctaw Nation. Concerning the educational provision of the 1930 treaty, it was a case of the Choctaw leadership calling the action and the treaty negotiators responding.[2]

When we read about Indian removal of the nineteenth century, we typically think about eastern Indians being removed west of the Mississippi River. What we seldom read about are the number of far western tribes who were also subjected to the same policy. In the state of California alone, the government applied its removal policy to the tribes of this state, especially in the 1860s. In 1863, California state troops gathered up roughly 400 Concow Maidu of Butte County (about 100 miles north of Sacramento) and marched them across the Sacramento Valley, over the coastal range, and placed them on the Round Valley Reservation in Mendocino County. The descendants of the Maidu still live at Round Valley.[3] In another case, the military gathered up 800 Owens Valley Paiute from eastern California and placed them at Fort Tejon in the mountains overlooking the San Joaquin Valley. Because the military did not have the strength to manage the Paiutes, every one of them eventually escaped and most returned to Owens Valley. A few ended up on the Tule River Reservation between Fresno and Bakersfield.[4]

Along with these actual removal cases in California, there were also removal proposals made by federal officials. In 1862, Senator Milton Latham of the state submitted a bill into Congress which, if passed, would have paved the way for the tribes of the state to be removed over the Sierra Nevada Mountains and placed in Owens Valley. This bill never made it out of Congress. There was also a removal proposal to colonize the tribes of California on some of the off-shore islands near Santa Barbara.[5]

The Reservation Policy

Around the mid-nineteenth century, the government created a new policy called the reservation policy. Its objective was to gather up the tribes of the North American continent and place them on reserves where they could be managed and controlled. Under the supervision of federal agents, the tribes could slowly be subjected to so-called American "civilization" since the white Americans viewed Indians as savages. The new reservation policy did not replace the earlier removal policy entirely. Instead, the federal sector carried out both simultaneously, with the tribes being removed to reservations. The only noticeable difference was that the government did not move the eastern tribes farther west.[6]

Some tribal individuals showed their extreme dislike of the reservation policy by eventually rejecting reservation life. The Office of Indian Affairs (today's BIA), the federal agency given the responsibility to run Indian affairs, required the Modoc of extreme northern California to move across the state line and settle on the newly established Klamath reservation of southern Oregon in the 1860s. At first the tribe went along with the plan. However, the Modoc felt uncomfortable living in a foreign area. Not willing to face confined reservation life, the Modoc left and returned to their ancestral homeland in northern California. The government branded the Modoc as lawbreakers and declared war against them. This led to the well-known Modoc War of 1873 in which the American military finally won.[7]

To punish the Modoc, the government carried out three forms of punishment. In the first instance, it hung the major leaders and sent their skulls to Washington, D.C., for so-called scientific study. Next, it confined two leaders on Alcatraz Island as prisoners. Third, it removed the larger number of Modoc to eastern Indian Territory, where they remained as prisoners of war of the government until 1909. Removal thus became a form of punishment for tribes that did not accept the reservation policy.[8]

Other Native Americans refused to move to newly established reservations when asked. For example, in 1877, the government created the Duck Valley Reservation, which straddles the Idaho-Nevada border. The plan was to induce all the Western Shoshones of the Great Basin region to move there in the years immediately thereafter. But this effort was largely a failure, for only one-third of the tribe moved, those tribal groups and bands that lived closest to Duck Valley. The other two-thirds publicly refused to move and used the aboriginal argument of their deep attachment to particular valleys and mountain ranges where their ancestors had lived "since time immemorial." Their form of punishment was deliberate indifference; that is, the government largely pretended that nonreservation Indians did not exist in the Basin area. Thus they received little or no services from the Indian bureau. Not until the 1930s would the BIA give these Shoshones consistent federal attention.[9]

Assimilation

Around 1880, the American government came up with a third generalized Indian policy called assimilation with the objective to Americanize those Indians living on reservation land. The assimilation campaign had several components. The Indian bureau created on-reservation police forces and tribal courts to make adult Indians give up their native ways. The police forces consisted of tribal members who were bought off by BIA agents. Agents provided them various benefits and services, which included wood-frame houses, firewood, and extra food provisions. Under the supervision of the agent, the police tried to make their own kind surrender their Indian ways and become good Americans.[10]

Many tribal individuals outsmarted the assimilation plan by pretending to become responsible Americans. They joined Christian churches, learned rudimentary English, and displayed different forms of American patriotism. Some reservation Indians organized Fourth of July Grounds where they camped out for days to celebrate American independence and democracy. But in reality these encampments were a way for the Indians to create underground cultures that allowed the participants to perpetuate native dances and social practices, including indigenous forms of gambling. To this day, the descendants of the nineteenth-century reservation Indians still remain native to varying degrees.[11]

One of the most visible forms of assimilation for young Indians was formal schooling. The government developed three kinds of schools in the last quarter of the nineteenth century: reservation day schools, reservation boarding schools, and off-reservation boarding schools. Typically, the youngest children started their schooling in the reservation schools. As they became older, the bureau removed them from their families, kinship groups, and tribes and sent them to large off-reservation schools located hundreds or even thousands of miles away from home. In other instances, very young children spent all their schooling in distant off-reservation boarding schools.[12]

In the government schools, the government subjected the students to a detribalization process. It stripped them of their native dress and issued military uniforms for young boys and Victorian dresses for the girls. It suppressed tribal languages and required the students to speak and read English. It made the students follow American values and practices, which included the puritanical work ethic, Christian values, and die-hard individualism.[13]

As for the students, they reacted to forced schooling by expressing various forms of resistance, which can be classified as "overt" and "covert." Perhaps the most popular form of overt resistance was running away. Unable to cope with institutionalized schooling, an unspecified number of students ran away with the objective of returning home. Most were captured, but some succeeded in returning to their families and tribes. Covert forms of resistance included "work slow down," talking tribal languages behind the scenes, and stealing food from the cafeteria.[14]

Although the vast majority of students ended up learning English and wearing American clothing, they still remained native to varying degrees, and most returned home to their Indian communities. There they lived out their lives by being both American and native. They built wood-frame houses and acquired horses and cattle. Yet, at the same time, they continued to speak their native languages and relied on indigenous medicinal remedies. In short, their schooling was only a partial success.[15]

Another form of assimilation was the breaking apart of Indian reservation land. To carry out this initiative, Congress passed the Dawes Act (General Allotment Act) of 1887, which allowed the federal sector to subdivide reservation land and issue individual allotments to the tribal members. For the most part, adult heads of households received 160 acres of land since this specific acreage represented the size of a nineteenth-century American homestead. The BIA expected the Indian allottees to farm the land and become American-style homesteaders. Once the government surveyed and allotted a reservation, it sold any remaining surplus land. By carrying out these initiatives, it hoped to destroy the tribal way of life and make Indians think and act individualistically rather than communally or tribally.[16]

Many tribal people did not passively accept the allotment process. They expressed their dislike in a number of ways. One person, Lone Wolf of the Kiowa tribe in Indian Territory, took the American government to court because of his opposition to the 1887 act. In the Supreme Court decision *Lone Wolf v. Hitchcock* (1903), Lonewolf argued that the Dawes Act could not be applied to the Kiowa because of prior treaty rights. He was correct, for some years earlier, under the Medicine Lodge Treaty of 1867 made with the Kiowa and other tribes of the southern Great Plains area, the treaty specified that the only way the government could alter the landbase of the reservation given to the Kiowa was if the majority of adults agreed to any form of alteration. But years later, the Kiowa never agreed in the majority to have their reservation subdivided by the Dawes act. Thus the act violated Kiowa treaty rights. However, the Supreme Court disregarded treaty rights and argued that the federal government had superior power over Indian tribes.[17] Therefore, Congress could apply an act to Native Americans, regardless of prior treaty rights.

To show their anger over the Dawes Act, which of course led to substantial land loss, other Native Americans considered leaving the United States completely in the late nineteenth and early twentieth centuries and moving to Mexico. Several tribal individuals from Indian Territory made trips to Mexico between 1890 and 1938 to look for a new homeland where Indian tribes could be free from negative governmental laws and policies. In the opening decade of the twentieth century, Crazy Snake and his followers of Creek Indians of eastern Oklahoma talked about moving to Mexico. As late as the 1930s, some Seminoles of Oklahoma met with the president of Mexico to discuss Mexico as a future home. In the end, these delegations chose to remain in the U.S.[18]

Other aspects of the overall assimilation policy surfaced after the turn of the century. One was the BIA's in-house regulation called Circular 1665 of 1921 and 1923. This BIA regulation either suppressed or prohibited Native American religious practices. It allowed Indians to have only one monthly traditional dance, which could be held from September to February. No dances could be held from March to August. Moreover, the monthly dance could take place only during the day time. No nighttime dance could take place. Only those fifty years and older could participate in the monthly daytime dance. Lastly, Indians could no longer carry out their traditional giveaways.[19]

Most Native American people rejected Circular 1665 and found ways to maneuver around the regulation. Some tribal individuals held dances in remote areas where BIA agents could not find them. Some joined the dances of other tribes held in outlying areas where agents would not or could not visit. Others practiced public exhibition dancing for white audiences, thus enabling them to practice traditional dances throughout the year. The BIA did not prohibit exhibition dances because these dances were nonthreatening and pleased the white crowds that wanted to observe what it labeled "exotic" Indians. Some Indians performed popular forms of white dances and entertainment during early evening hours to convince watchful agents that they were becoming good Americans. Once the officials left, and late at night, the Indians resorted to their traditional dances. All these tactics allowed tribal individuals to outwit the BIA in the early years of the twentieth century.[20]

Cultural Pluralism and the Indian New Deal

As time moved forward in the twentieth century, some white people realized that the government's campaign to assimilate the Indians had largely failed. Native Americans simply could not be completely transformed because of their deep-rooted cultures and traditional beliefs. White reformists advanced the argument that because the U.S. was a democracy where people are given choices, then Indian people must be given the choice to remain native if they wanted. One of the noted reformers was non-Indian John Collier who created the American Indian Defense Association in 1923 with a two-fold purpose: that Indians must be given their religious freedom and that the Indian landbase must be preserved. Besides private individuals such as Collier, even some federal officials concluded that the BIA needed to change some of its policies toward Indian people. In response, Hubert Work, the Secretary of the Interior in 1926, authorized the establishment of a ten-member team to study the "so-called Indian problem" and make recommendations in a published report of how the BIA could be improved.[21]

In 1928, the Meriam team released its lengthy study called *The Problem of Indian Administration*, or popularly known as the Meriam report. The report pointed out the serious problems within Indian affairs, including the substantial land loss of Indian people since the passage of the Dawes Act in 1887, poor health care, and the poor quality of education and life students had received in the BIA boarding schools. At the same time, the report team made positive recommendations of how life could be improved for Native Americans. The federal government needed to provide improved health care for Indians, Indian students needed to be given a quality education in the Indian schools, and the Indian students needed to be taught native subject matter. Here was a case of reformists rejecting the half-century assimilationist policy.[22]

One of the ten members of the Meriam team was Henry Roe Cloud of the Winnebago tribe in Nebraska. After experiencing the boarding school process as a youngster, Cloud made the decision to go to college. He earned more than one college degree, including the bachelor's degree from Yale in 1910. Aware that the BIA did not give Indian students a full high school education in the early twentieth century, he established the American Indian Institute, an all-Indian high school in Wichita, Kansas, for those students who aspired to a full secondary education. Cloud encouraged his students to appreciate their Indianness, and it became obvious why the Meriam report favored the teaching of native subject matter in the Indian schools.[23]

One important end result of the reform sentiment of the 1920s and early 1930s was the Indian Reorganization Act (IRA) of 1934. The provisions of this congressional act were largely the work of John Collier, who became the new commissioner of the BIA in 1933. As a federal official, Collier put his reformist ideas into action by making sure Congress passed the IRA. Some of the provisions of the act were as follows: it ended any further allotment of Indian reservations; it returned to reservation status any remaining surplus land; it allowed tribes to organize politically with tribal constitutions and charters, or it gave tribes a kind of quasi-sovereign status; it provided loans so that tribal individuals could create business enterprises and become better off economically; it provided loans so that Indian students could pursue a college or university education; and it introduced "Indian preference," which was a measure to employ qualified Indians to work in the BIA.[24]

The majority of Indian tribes voted to become IRA tribes since they liked the provisions of the act. Specifically, 181 of them voted in favor of the act. However, 77 tribes voted against it for their own reasons.[25] As a case in point, the Paiutes of Owens Valley voted against the act in large numbers, not because they disliked the act, but because of the BIA's recent rhetoric of Indian removal. Both before and at the time of the act's passage, the BIA had considered removing the Owens Valley Paiutes completely from their ancestral valley in eastern California. The bureau used the argument that the Indians could not really make a living there because the city of Los Angeles had taken much of the water from the Owens River for its California Aquaduct, channeling the river water across the desert to Los Angeles. Thus the BIA wanted the Paiutes to move either to the Walker River Reservation in western Nevada or to move over the Sierra Nevada Mountains and settle down near Merced in the San Joaquin Valley. Insecure about possible removal, the Paiutes voted against the act. In the end, the bureau backed away from removal, allowed the Paiutes to remain, and even created three small reservations for them in the second half of the 1930s: Bishop, Big Pine, and Lone Pine.[26]

The Hupa of northern California also voted against the IRA. Unlike the Paiutes of Owens Valley, the Hupa voted against the act for completely different reasons. First, the tribal leaders favored land allotment, which the IRA ended. Secondly, the Hupa already had a tribal council in operation for some years before Congress passed the act. Thus, there was no need to create a new one under the IRA. Lastly, the Hupa, as well as other tribes of California, had impending claims against the American government. This claims matter was rooted in the eighteen treaties that the Senate did not ratify in the mid-nineteenth century, which would have set aside over seven million acres of land for California Indians. Six years before Congress passed the IRA, it had approved the California Indian Jurisdiction Act of 1928 to allow the California tribes to file suit for past injustices, including the unratified treaties. The Hupa in the mid-1930s felt that the IRA might somehow disrupt the current claims case even though the act itself specified that cases would not be affected.[27] Here was a case of government action and tribal reaction.

Since the passage of the IRA in 1934, tribal individuals have expressed a wide range of views about the act. Some leaders pointed out that despite the act's limitations, it still had some good outcomes. Tim Giago (Lakota), former editor of *Indian Country Today*, stressed that "there wouldn't be any reservations left today if it wasn't for the IRA."[28] Another Lakota, Pat Spears, leader of the Lower Brule Sioux, stated.: "It's better than what it replaced. . . . I don't think we're better off by the IRA. . . . It's been the only vehicle we had, but I think it's time we trade it in."[29] Webster Two Hawk, chairperson of the Rosebud Sioux Tribe, expressed a similar view: "I have mixed opinions regarding the IRA. I have to support it because I work for an IRA government. . . . The IRA was a child of the federal government and did not really contain Indian ideas. . . . In redoing it, I would remove many of the restrictions."[30] Some Lakota leaders were much more critical of the IRA. Robert Fast Horse, tribal judge from Pine Ridge, stressed that the IRA "wouldn't recognize our traditional form of government."[31] Bertha Chasing Hawk of Cheyenne River argued that "the tribal court is useless to us because the [IRA] tribal council can overrule the tribal court's decisions."[32] All of the above individuals are from reservations in North and South Dakota.

Regardless of the IRA's shortcomings, it did create some new directions. The Indian preference clause made it possible for more Indians to be employed by the BIA, especially those who were college educated. By the mid-1940s, the following individuals were superintendents of BIA agencies and reservations: Henry Roe Cloud (Winnebago), Kenneth Marmon (Laguna Pueblo), George LaVatta (Shoshone), Archie Phinney (Nez Perce), Frel Owl (Cherokee), and Gabe Parker (Choctaw).[33]

Termination

In the late 1940s and early 1950s. the BIA inaugurated a new Indian policy called Termination. Its basic purpose was the end of the "long-term historic relationship" the Indian tribes had with the American government. The government wanted Indians to assimilate into the larger dominant society. To carry out the new policy, the BIA and other branches of the government came out with several components of termination. The first was the congressional Indian Claims Commission

Act of 1946. Under it, the government wanted to compensate the Indian tribes for all unjust acts committed against Indian people. The tribes would be given the opportunity to develop shopping lists and submit documented examples of injustices before the Indian Claims Commission. If a tribe won suit, it was awarded a monetary settlement or claims money. The BIA distributed this money in the form of per capita payments.[34]

Another component was House Concurrent Resolution (HCR) 108 in 1953, which paved the way for the elimination of various Indian reservations across the country. Under HCR 108, the Indians lost 1.3 million acres of land in the postwar period. The BIA wanted the more successful tribes to be terminated first, including the Menominee of Wisconsin and the Klamath of Oregon. But in the end, most of the tribes terminated were small and defenseless. This included forty small Indian rancherias of California and four Southern Paiute bands of southwestern Utah.[35]

Another component of termination was Operation Relocation (1952) in which the BIA induced reservation people to leave their respective reservations and move to urban areas. The BIA provided incentives, including paid transportation; rent money for the first few months; short-term educational training that included auto mechanics, welding, licensed practical nursing, and dental assistant training; and the overall promise of a better way of life, which included jobs, education, and recreation.[36]

From a statistical standpoint, relocation was extremely successful, for thousands of Indians across the nation moved to various big cities that had BIA-run relocation centers. Some of the cities included Chicago, Dallas-Fort Worth, Denver, Detroit, Los Angeles, Oakland, San Francisco, and San Jose. As a result of relocation, Native Americans became markedly urbanized from the 1950s forward. In 1950, only 13.4 percent of the Indian population lived in cities, whereas by 1980, fifty percent of them were urbanites. The Indian population of California alone skyrocketed after 1950. In 1950, only 19,000 Indians lived in the state. By 1960, it was 39,000. By 1980, it stood at 200,000 with relocation being the huge factor.[37]

The relocation component was both a success and a failure. On the success side, if the BIA's plan was to amalgamate Indians into the overall population in urban America, this effort led to urban Indians having one of the highest out-marriage rates in the nation. Those in the cities have a 50/50 chance of marrying non-Indians. On the failure side, many urban Indians did not melt into urban white America. Instead, they looked for ways to remain native. Some worked hard to live in certain neighborhoods so that families could visit one another. Christian Indians established all-Indian churches in the inner city. Those who were more traditional held sweat ceremonies in their backyards and carried out Peyote ceremonies.

Most attended intertribal pow wows. Others sponsored all-Indian sports, which included basketball and softball tournaments. Others gathered at intertribal urban Indian centers that provided various services, including job referral and social gatherings. In short, urban Indians reacted and created ways to remain native and never surrendered their identities, both tribal and intertribal.[38]

Self-Determination

After 1960, the American government came up with still another Indian policy called self-determination. This policy in certain ways was the opposite of termination. The government encouraged Indians to remain on reservations if they chose. The BIA wanted the tribes to become involved in running their own affairs with federal financial support. Like termination, self-determination had a number of components. The Department of Housing and Urban Development (HUD) helped tribal families build "self-help" houses to replace the older substandard houses that lacked indoor running water and other basic necessities. These new houses of the 1960s forward eventually became known as HUD houses, named after the federal department.[39]

Reservation Indians also benefitted from aspects of the Office of Economic Opportunity (OEO) which was intended for poor people in general, regardless of race. Young Indian students entered preschool programs called Headstart, and high school students lived on college campuses during summer months under Upward Bound. This latter program sought to encourage the high school students to consider higher education after graduating from high school.[40]

The BIA also encouraged the teaching of Indian languages and culture in reservation-based schools run by the tribes themselves. The Rough Rock Demonstration School of the Navajo reservation in Arizona was an example of the Navajos creating their own school to emphasize native culture. The school received financial support from the BIA. Several other tribes would also build their own tribally run schools to provide elementary and secondary education. These schools received support from the congressional Indian Self-Determination and Education Assistance Act of 1975.[41]

Self-determination also encouraged tribal people to develop reservation-based higher education programs because of the shortcomings of mainstream higher education. The Navajo Nation established its Navajo Community College in 1968 (renamed Dine College in 1997). This tribally controlled college inspired dozens of other tribes also to establish tribal colleges.[42] As of 2000, thirty-three tribally run colleges existed throughout the U.S. They are run largely by college-educated tribal people, and they offer Indian courses to the students. The colleges receive funding from a number of sources, including the congressional Tribally Controlled Community College Act of 1978.

Congress supported the notion of self-determination in the late 1960s and 1970s by passing more than one act. The Indian Civil Rights Act of 1968 applied certain aspects of the U.S. Bill of Rights to Indian reservations. This meant that reservation-based Indian people possessed certain constitutional guarantees, including the freedom of religion, the freedom of the press, and the right to assemble. The Indian Child Welfare Act of 1978 provided a preference of who could adopt Indian children. First preference is given to the child's extended family, second to other members of the child's tribe, third to members of other tribes, and fourth to non-Indians if no one adopted from the three higher categories. Congress passed this law to make sure an adopted Indian child would remain connected to his native culture. In the same year, Congress passed the American Indian Religious Freedom Act which allowed Indian people to possess sacred objects (e.g., eagle feathers), overall freedom to practice traditional religions both on and off reservation, and the right to practice ceremonies at traditional places.[43]

Self-Governance

The most recent federal Indian policy is self-governance, which emerged in the late 1980s. For the most part, self-governance is an extension of self-determination but with some big differences. Under it, the BIA wants to shift its long-term functions over to the tribes themselves. One example of this action is higher education, which has been a BIA function since the early 1930s. From the 1950s forward, the BIA's regional area offices administered higher education grants and loans to Indian students pursuing a postsecondary education. But under self-governance, the tribes themselves receive BIA funds to run their own higher education programs. The BIA is no longer involved except to channel funds.[44]

Conclusion

In this brief account of the history of Indian policy, we have looked at the pattern of government action and native responses and reactions. Although this has been the prevalent pattern for almost two centuries, there are also times when the process is reversed with the Indians as actors and the government as the reactor. For example, in 1916, the BIA began to add the higher high school grades to its off-reservation boarding schools, which went only to the eighth grade. This BIA action was in response to the Indian members of the intertribal organization Society of American Indians, which asserted that Indians should be given more education instead of being educated as simple laborers in the Indian schools.[45] More recently, in 1988, Congress passed the Indian Gaming Regulatory Act, which determines what tribal nations can do in the domain of gaming. The act designates three classes of gaming: (1) traditional gaming, which tribes can carry out without restriction; (2) gaming such as bingo and card games, which Indian tribes can have in their casinos but would be regulated by a national Indian gaming commission; and (3) Nevada-styled gaming, which the tribes can carry out but only if these forms are legal within a given state where the Indian casino is located. Congress passed the law because it wanted to regulate the rising tide of Indian gaming that started in 1979 with the Seminole tribe in Florida. As of the late 1990s, 148 tribal groups had casinos with class three gaming. They introduced them for two reasons in the 1980s. The first was to move away from the state of poverty that many tribes had lived in for decades. Second, in the early 1980s, President Reagan's administration reduced substantially federal funds for poverty programs. The tribes sought new sources of funding for tribal survival, and one means was the revenue from new casinos. But when casinos started to become too numerous, the government stepped in with its regulations.[46] Here was a case of Indian action and government reaction.

Notes

[1] Philip Weeks, *Farewell My Nation: The American Indian and the United States, 1820–1890* (Arlington Heights, IL: Harlan Davidson, Inc., 1990), 22–23; Francis Paul Prucha, *The Great Father: The United States Government and the American Indians,* abridged edition (Lincoln: University of Nebraska Press, 1984), 64–93.

[2] 7 Stat. 315; Grayson B. Noley, "The History of Education in the Choctaw Nation from Precolonial Times to 1830," (Ph.D. dissertation, Pennsylvania State University, 1976), 172; Clara Sue Kidwell, *Choctaws and Missionaries in Mississippi, 1818–1918* (Norman: University of Oklahoma Press, 1995), 96; 136; James D. Morrison, *Schools for the Choctaws* (Durant, OK: Choctaw Bilingual Education Program, 1978), 240.

[3] Dorothy Hill, *The Indians of Chico Rancheria* (Sacramento, CA: Department of Parks and Recreation, 1978), 39–42.

[4] Steven Crum, "Deeply Attached to the Land: The Owens Valley Paiutes and Their Rejection of Indian Removal, 1863 to 1937," *News From Native California,* 14 (summer 2001): 18.

[5] "A bill . . ." *The Visalia (Weekly) Delta,* 5 June 1862, p. 2; "About Indian Affairs," *The Visalia (Weekly).Delta,* 17 December 1983, p. 2; James J. Rawls, *Indians of California: The Changing Image* (University of Oklahoma, 1984), 169.

[6] Prucha, *The Great Father,* 116, 129–132, 181–197; Weeks, *Farewell My Nation,* 60, 159, 170, 178, 208.

[7] Lucille J. Martin, "A History of the Modoc Indians: An Acculturation Study," *The Chronicles of Oklahoma,* 47 (winter 1969–70): 398–417.

[8] Ibid., 420–421, 441.

[9] Steven Crum, *The Road on Which We Came* (Salt Lake City: University of Utah Press, 1994), 43–84.

[10] Prucha, *The Great Father,* 195–197, 218–219; Weeks, *Farewell My Nation,* 217–232.

[11] Crum, *The Road,* 52.

[12] David Wallace Adams, *Education for Extinction: American Indians and the Boarding School Experience, 1875–1928* (Lawrence: University Press of Kansas, 1995), 21–24, 28–59.

[13] Ibid., 97–163.

[14] Ibid., 232–238; K. Tsianina Lomawaima, *They Called It Prairie Light: The Story of Chilocco Indian School* (University of Nebraska Press, 1994), 115–126.

[15] Adams, *Education for Extinction,* 273–306.

[16] Prucha, *The Great Father,* 224–228.

[17] Blue Clark, *Lone Wolf v. Hitchcock: Treaty Rights and Indian Law at the End of the Nineteenth Century* (University of Nebraska, 1994).

[18] Steven Crum, " 'America, Love It or Leave It': Some Native American Initiatives to move to Mexico, 1890–1940," *The Chronicles of Oklahoma,* 79 (winter 2001–02): 408–429.

[19] Peggy V. Beck and Anna L. Walters, *The Sacred: Ways of Knowledge, Sources of Life* (Tsaile: Navajo Community College Press, 1977), 158–161.

[20] Annette Louise Reed, "Rooted in the Land of Our Ancestors, We Are Strong: A Tolowa History," (Ph.D. dissertation, University of California, Berkeley, 1999), 155–163.

[21] Kenneth R. Philp, *John Collier's Crusade for Indian Reform, 1920–1954* (Tucson: University of Arizona Press, 1977), 55–91; Peter Iverson, *'We Are Still Here,' American Indians in the Twentieth Century* (Wheeling, IL: Harlan Davidson, Inc., 1998), 58–76.

[22] Prucha, *The Great Father,* 277–279; Iverson, *'We Are Still Here,'* 75.

[23] Steven Crum, "Henry Roe Cloud: A Winnebago Indian Reformer: His Quest for American Indian Higher Education," *Kansas History,* 11 (autumn 1988): 171–184.

[24] Prucha, *The Great Father,* 311–339; Philp, *John Collier's Crusade,* 135–186; Iverson, *'We Are Still Here,'* 77–102.

[25] Philp, *John Collier's Crusade,* 163; Prucha, *The Great Father,* 324.

[26] Crum, "Deeply Attached to the Land," 19.

[27] Joachim Roschmann, "No 'Red Atlantis' on the Trinity: Why the Hupa Rejected the Indian Reorganization Act," paper presented at the Sixth Annual California Indian Conference, 27 October 1990; George H. Phillips, *The Enduring Struggle: Indians in California History* (San Francisco: Boyd & Fraser Publishing Company, 1981), 50, 69.

[28] Quoted in "Lakotas Have Different Views on Indian Reorganization Act," *Lakota Times,* 28 November 1984, 7.

[29] Ibid.

[30] Quoted in "Fifty Years of IRA–Working or Not?" *Lakota Times,* 4 July 1984, 1.

[31] "Lakotas Have Different Views," 7.

[32] Ibid.

[33] *Interior Department Appropriation Bill for 1947,* 97th Congress, 2nd session, Part I (Washington, D.C.: Government Printing Office, 1946), 822.

[34] Donald L. Fixico, *Termination and Relocation: Federal Indian Policy, 1945–1960* (Albuquerque: University of New Mexico Press, 1986), 3–21; Larry W. Burt, *Tribalism in Crisis: Federal Indian Policy, 1953–1961* (UNM, 1982); Prucha, *the Great Father,* 340–356; Iverson, *'We Are Still Here,'* 103–138.

[35] Fixico, *Termination and Relocation,* 91–110; Prucha, *The Great Father,* 340–356.

[36] Ibid., 137–157; Donald L. Fixico, *The Urban Indian Experience in America* (University of New Mexico, 2000), 8–25.

[37] Prucha, *The Great Father,* 394; Francis Paul Prucha, *Atlas of American Indian Affairs* (University of Nebraska Press, 1990), 142; Russell Thornton, *American Indian Holocaust and Survival: A Population History Since 1492* (University of Oklahoma, 1987), 227.

[38] Thornton, *American Indian Holocaust,* 236; Fixico, *The Urban Indian Experience,* 74, 80, 125, 127, 133.

[39] George Pierre Castile, *To Show Heart: Native American Self-Determination and Federal Indian Policy, 1960–1975* (University of Arizona Press, 1998), 23–42.

[40] Ibid, 35–42.

[41] Margaret Connell Szasz, *Education and the American Indian: The Road to Self-Determination,* 3rd ed. (University of New Mexico, 1999), 169–187.

[42] Wayne J. Stein, *Tribally Controlled Colleges: Making Good Medicine* (New York: Peter Lang, 1992).

[43] Iverson, *'We Are Still Here,'* 170–171; Prucha, *The Great Father,* 379.

[44] David E. Wilkins, *American Indian Politics and the American Political System* (New York: Rowman & Littlefield Publishers, Inc., 2002), 105, 117–118.

[45] "Editorial Comment," *Quarterly Journal of the Society of American Indians,* 2 (April–June 1914): 99; *Annual Report of the Department of the Interior, 1915, Vol. II: Indian Affairs and Territories* (Washington, D.C.: GPO, 1916), 7.

[46] W. Dale Mason, *Indian Gaming: Tribal Sovereignty and American Politics* (University of Oklahoma, 2000), 44, 47, 64–65; Wilkins, *American Indian Politics,* 164–172.

Iu Mien—We the People

Fahm Saetern

Important Words and Concepts in This Chapter

There are several important words and concepts throughout the upcoming chapter. The words appear several times in different places in order to help you remember the words and understand the chapter. The words are defined several times.

- Right before the chapter begins
- In text boxes throughout the chapter
- In red and boldfaced within the chapter
- In a glossary in expanded form at the end of the units

Some of the words also appear in other chapters. Talk about the words with other students, teachers, friends, and family members before you read, while reading the chapter, and after you have read the chapter.

Ethnicity

Membership or affiliation in a particular ethnic group.

Totemic Ancestor

An object (such as an animal or plant) serving as the emblem of a family or clan and often as a reminder of its ancestry.

Immigrate

The movement of peoples into a country or territory (movement of people within countries is referred to as migration). Some immigration is voluntary and some immigration is forced. Immigration can involve small number or masses of people in orderly or chaotic, dangerous conditions.

Migrate

The act or an instance of moving from one place to another, often on a regular basis.

Southeast Asia

Southeast Asia consists of a vast territory encompassing 11 countries that span from eastern India to China and is generally divided into mainland and island zones. Burma, Thailand, Laos, Cambodia, and Vietnam are in the mainland zones. Malaysia, Singapore, Indonesia, and Philippines are part of the island zone.

Sinocentric

Any ethnocentric political ideology that regard China to be central or unique relative to other countries. A hierarchical Sinocentric model of international relations, dominated by China, prevailed in East Asia until the weakening of the Qing Dynasty and the encroachment of European and Japanese imperialists in the second half of the 19th century.

Refugee

A person who flees to a foreign country or power to escape danger or persecution.

Refugee Camps

Temporary shelters for people fleeing their home country. The United Nations High Commissioner of Refugees administers camps sheltering a vast population displaced people. World conflicts often result in scores of refugees around the world seeking shelter in camps. Contrary to popular belief, many of these settlements are far from temporary, and today most of the largest ones are in Africa and South Asia.

Linguistic Diversity

Different forms of verbal communication based on ethnicity, geography, culture, and age.

Myths

Sacred stories from communities around the world that help explain how things were created and how they came to be.

Theories

Beliefs, policies, or procedures that guide action.

Transliteration

To represent or spell the characters from an alphabet different from your own.

Fred Korematsu, Min Yasui, Gordon Hirabayashi

Korematsu from Oakland, California failed to report to an assembly center. Yasui from Portland, Oregon violated a curfew order. Hirabayashi from Seattle, Washington violated a curfew order and failed to report to an assembly center.

All three cases were appealed to the U.S. Supreme Court but all lost. The U.S. Army stated that evacuation and incarceration were carried out because of Military Necessity.

In the late 1960s, after the Federal Freedom of Information Act was passed, documents were discovered which showed the U.S. Army knew there was no Military Necessity. Government prosecutors had these documents, but did not disclose this information. All three cases were re-filed under a rarely used legal procedure. They used *coram nobis*, which means to right a wrong. This time they won.

When people ask what **ethnicity** I am, I say, "I am Iu Mien." They then ask who are the Iu Mien and where are we from? My short response is "we do not have a country of our own but we originated from China." Often times, this response is enough to satisfy their curiosity. However, for many Iu Mien Americans, this answer does not suffice.

Although they **immigrated** to the United States over four decades ago, there are limited resources exist about the Iu Mien. As I explore my identity and feed my own curiosity about "who, what, when, where, and why" of the Iu Mien, I realize that I must do my part in ensuring that our rich traditions, customs, and culture survive the impact of past, current, and future social, political, and economic events. This chapter examines Iu Mien history, statistical data regarding the Iu Mien, and includes my personal experiences as an Iu Mien American.

Iu Mien History and Background

The Iu Mien are one of "the smallest major refugee groups in the United States and the least known in the refugee literature" (MacDonald, 1997, p. 3). Due to the **Sinocentric** biases of the mostly Chinese records, the early history of the Iu Mien is obscure and unclear. There is no reliable history of the Iu Mien before the tenth century AD (MacDonald, 1997, p. 70). Before the tenth century AD, the Han did not distinguish among the different ethnic minorities. All southern China **ethnic** minorities were labeled "Man" (蛮). "Man" is derived from the ancient Chinese word for "barbarian" (Eberhard, 1982; Fortune, 1939; Wiens, 1967). In modern China, the Iu Mien are more commonly known as "Yao" (瑶). "Yao" is a government classification given to ethnic minority groups in China. In the United States as well as other parts of the Western world, the "Yao" identify themselves as Iu Mien or Mien.

Origin of Iu Mien Surnames

"The Iu Mien have various **myths** concerning the origin of the world, of the gods, of the Iu Mien, and other humans." Influences from the highland cultures and Han Chinese culture have contributed to the various versions that exist (MacDonald, 1997, p. 75).

A popular legend states that the Iu Mien's 12 surnames derived from the sons and daughters of Bienh Hungh, the Iu Mien **totemic ancestor.** The first six clans descend from the six sons of Bienh Hungh. The other six clans descend from the six daughters of Bienh Hungh.

Iu Mien surnames include Saephan (Bienh), Saelaw (Lorh), Saelee (Leiz), Saechou (Zuoqv), Saetern (Dangc), Saeyang (Yaangh), Saechao (Zeuz), Saelio (Liouh), Saefong (Bungz), Saechin (Zanh), Saetang (Dorngh), and Saehu (Huh). Although it is believed that there are 12 clans, there are other surnames that exist. This is not an inclusive list of Iu Mien surnames and variations in spelling do exist.

When Iu Mien migrated to Thailand, Thai authorities added "Sae" as the prefix to all Iu Mien last names. "Sae" in Thai means "last name." Today, it is more difficult to distinguish Iu Mien from other ethnicities solely based on their surnames since many Iu Mien Americans are reverting to their traditional names by dropping the prefix "Sae."

Iu Mien Migration to Southeast Asia

The Iu Mien **migrated** across national boundaries long ago. Records indicate that the first southward **migration** from China to Vietnam occurred during the seventeenth and eighteenth century. Throughout the late nineteenth and early twentieth century, the Iu Mien migrated into Laos, Burma (formerly Myanmar), and Thailand. Reasons for these **migrations** remain controversial varying from political to socioeconomic ventures (Saeteurn, n.d.).

A large number of Iu Mien families settled in the mountains of northern and central Laos. Here, the Iu Mien practiced slash and burn agriculture, which involves cutting down trees and brush, burning the area to clear it, and then planting. They grew rice and other crops such as squash, beans, and poppies. Men crafted beautiful silver jewelry and women embroidered intricate designs on clothing and accessories (Gogol, 1996, p. 20).

© Popartic/Shutterstock.com

The Secret War

The simple and serene lives of the Iu Mien were abruptly interrupted by a civil war. "When the French struggled to retain control of Laos from 1945 to 1954, the Central Intelligence Agency (CIA) starting in 1958 began heavy recruitment among the hill tribes in order to counteract the Chinese and Vietnamese communists across the border and the Pathet Lao in Laos" (Gross, n.d.). By the early 1960s, a full-fledged civil war broke out in Laos. This war in Laos "quickly became part of a larger regional conflict known in the United States as the Vietnam War. Supported by the United States, the Royal Laotian government opposed Communist forces. An anti-Royalist group in Laos known as the Pathet Lao received military aid from North Vietnam, a neighboring Communist country" (Gogol, 1996, p. 20).

This civil war is known by many Iu Mien as the "Secret War." During this war, "Iu Mien men were recruited as anti-guerrilla forces by the CIA" (MacDonald, 1997, p. 88). In the documentary, *Voices from the Mountains*, Eric Crystal stated, "the United States dropped more conventional bombs in Laos than has ever been dropped in any country in the history of warfare, more than were dropped in Japan in World War II" (Saeliew, 2007). Many hill tribes including the Iu Mien fought a bloody secret war for the United States. Iu Mien men and teenage boys fought bravely and suffered many casualties.

In 1975, Pathet Lao forces won the war in Laos. Because the Iu Mien fought alongside the United States, they became targets for persecution. "Over 70% of the Iu Mien in Laos were forced to leave, abandoning their livelihood and walking two to three months to settle in large camps where they survived on the limited supplies provided by the American army" (Moore-Howard, 1989, p. 75). To escape danger, many families and even entire villages began to flee Laos. The majority of the Iu Mien population fled to Thailand resettling in **refugee camps**. "After several years, the United States returned to fulfill their contract made with the ethnic minorities. They offered a **refugee** rescue program, which gave the Iu Mien and other groups the choice to resettle in the United States" (Saeteurn, n.d.). U.S. residents aided by sponsoring Iu Mien families from the refugee camps. In 1976, the first Iu Mien families reached the United States to settle in Portland, Oregon.

Iu Mien Migration to the United States

The first significant group of Iu Mien arrived in the United States during the late 1970s. The number of arrivals increased in the 1980s. The majority of Iu Mien families settled on the West Coast in California, Oregon, and Washington. A smaller number of families settled in Alabama, North Carolina, Illinois, Minnesota, Kansas, Texas, and Oklahoma. Between 1980 and 1982, approximately seven families settled in Sacramento, California (Saechao, 1992).

Although the Iu Mien community grew significantly since their first arrival, the U.S. Census fails to recognize them as a separate ethnic group. The U.S. government includes the Iu Mien in the subgroups, "Laotian" and "Other Asian." One main reason why the Iu Mien are not recognized as an independent group is due to the fact that this community has yet to establish a consensus on one specific name. Some individuals from the community identify themselves as Iu Mien while others identify themselves as Mien. Variations of the spelling of Iu Mien include

Iu-Mien, Iu Mienh, Iu-Mienh, Yiu Mienh, and Mien. Since the Iu Mien remain aggregated under the "Laotian" and "Other Asian" categories, exact numbers for the Iu Mien population are unknown. Estimates vary from as little as 30,000 to as much as 150,000 Iu Mien residing in the United States.

Fahm Khouan-Saelee Saetern's Personal Experiences

I, Fahm Khouan-Saelee Saetern, was born in Ban Vinai refugee camp located in Loei, Thailand. On June 27, 1988, at the age of 2, my family and I migrated to the United States. My parents, Wern Khouan Saelee and Khae Luang Saelee, raised their children with traditional Iu Mien values and norms. They communicated with us in Mien. My parents expected my siblings and I to

Iu Mien—We the People ▶ **135**

understand, participate, and respect Iu Mien traditions. We retain the ability to speak Mien today.

While studying abroad at Peking University (北京大学) in Beijing, China from August 2006 to July 2007, I encountered many people who asked what nationality I am. Very few thought I was Chinese—most assumed I was Korean or Japanese. When I told them I was American, some were immediately surprised and asked how could that be since I have the black hair, a petite stature, and the face of someone from the East, not the West. I couldn't claim I was Thai. Sure, I was born in Thailand, but I left the country at age 2 and never learned the language or culture. I couldn't tell them I was Chinese. I knew my ancestors descended from China, but how long ago and exactly from where, I wasn't sure. I realized then that my uncertainty about my identity was why I was in China.

After a few months in China, I began to seek out Iu Mien living in China. I contacted an Iu Mien woman, Li Shaomei, a professor at the Central University for Nationalities (CUN) (中央民族大学). To my surprise, Mien literacy classes are offered at this university. I also discovered the Museum for Nationalities of CUN. This museum, created in 1951, is a professional museum that collects, displays, and researches the culture relics of 56 **ethnic groups** in China (Beijing, n.d.). I was both astonished and excited that I was surrounded by an abundance of resources that could potentially help me find answers I've been searching for.

After my studies in China ended in 2007, I continued on this journey of self-reflection and self-discovery. In 2014, I returned to China for a short visit. I traveled to Thailand in 2014 and 2017 to visit family members, continue my research about the Iu Mien, and collect artifacts and artwork created by the Iu Mien.

Fortunately, since I speak Mien, I am able to communicate with the Iu Mien of China and the Iu Mien of Thailand. I can connect with my parent's generation and can communicate in Mien with my cousins and distant relatives who live in Thailand. So many of the Iu Mien youth today struggle to speak and understand Mien. This is a reality in the United States, China, Vietnam, Laos, and Thailand. It is my goal as a parent to pass down my mother tongue to my children so that they too can describe the world in the one language their great-grandparents once spoke and understood.

Survey on Iu Mien Language

When the Iu Mien fled China, they brought with them "an Iu Mien spoken dialect, which had no written characters, and Mandarin, which was both spoken and written by a select, male, educated elite" (Egert, 2009, p. 5). Today, the Iu Mien language, Mien, has a form of Romanized **transliteration** that was developed in the late twentieth century. Mandarin survives among the Iu Mien in the United States only as written characters of texts for ceremonies, which can be interpreted by shamans (Egert, 2009, p. 5).

In November 2007, shortly after returning from China, I surveyed 135 Iu Mien currently living in California. The results indicate that the majority of Iu Mien Americans cannot speak Mien. Eighty-six percent of those surveyed have lived in the United States for less than 25 years. Fourteen percent have been in the United States for over 25 years. The data show half are fluent in Mien and 92% are fluent in English. Eighty-two percent feel most comfortable speaking English, while only 18% indicate that they feel most comfortable speaking in Mien. Within just a few decades, the Iu Mien language is on the brink of extinction in California. The relevance of learning Mien has been replaced by the need to learn English. Many Iu Mien, especially the 1.5, second and third generation Iu Mien Americans are losing their ancestral language despite the fact that 99% of first generation Iu Mien Americans are fluent in Mien.

As alarming as these survey results are, Iu Mien Americans show an interest in preserving their language. Many are not fluent in Mien, but are interested in learning the language. The survey asks, "If Mien language courses are offered at a community college, a university, or a place nearby you, will you consider taking a course?" Seventy-one percent responded yes. Twenty-two percent were unsure and only 7% responded no. Ninety-seven percent believe it is important for Iu Mien people to be able to speak their ethnic language. One particular individual stated, "Language is one of the most critical factors for ethnic association. Without our language, we essentially would lose part of our identity. Further, our future generations need to be able to speak Mien to prevent our own extinction. Once a language is extinct, it is impossible to revive it as we have seen with many other extinct languages." He also feels it is important for Iu Mien to read and write Mien. It is important for the Iu Mien to learn the Romanized script "because of the nature of societal changes that necessitate us to have our language in a written form to make it useful. Furthermore, that would be one way of trying to increase usage and perhaps preserve what is left of our language." The overall consensus is it is important to take measures in preserving the Mien language. The Iu Mien have concerns about the availability of resources for them to maintain and learn the language. Ninety-one percent of the Iu Mien surveyed don't think there are enough learning materials available.

Conclusion

The Iu Mien struggle to maintain our community and culture in the United States. It is our responsibility as Iu Mien and Iu Mien Americans to preserve our identity. We need to contribute to the resources by doing academic research and oral history projects. We need to work together and advocate for our community. It is vital that we diligently record and document the different facets of Iu Mien life. Let's preserve **linguistic diversity**. Let's preserve our cultural heritage. Let's not allow scholars to draw conclusions about the Iu Mien based on assumptions and **theories**. We can take measures today to combat the loss of the Iu Mien language

Photo courtesy of Fahm Khouan-Saelee Saetern. © Kendall Hunt Publishing Company.

and culture. With our combined efforts, future Iu Mien Americans can more accurately define who we are and who they are. Until then, there are more questions to be explored and more research to be done.

References

Beijing Museum for Nationalities of Central University for Nationalities, Beijing Museums-Beijing China Travel Agency. (n.d.). *Beijing Tours, Beijing Tour, Beijing China Tours—Beijing Travel Agency and China Tour Operator.* Retrieved from www.tour-beijing.com/museums_guide/museum_for_Nationalities_of_central_university_for_nationalities.php

Eberhard, W. (1982). *China's minorities: Yesterday and today.* Wedsworth.

Fortune, R. (1939). *Yao society: A study of a group of primitives in China.* Department of Sociology, Lingnan University.

Gogol, S. (1996). *A Mien family.* Lerner.

Gross, M. (n.d.). Wildflowers Institute—Iu Mien Community Portrait. *Wildflowers Institute—Home page.* www.wildflowers.org/community/IuMien/portrait2.shtml

MacDonald, J. L. (1997). *Transnational aspects of Iu-Mien refugee identity.* Garland.

Moore-Howard, P. (1989). *The Iu Mien: Tradition and change.* Patricia Moore-Howard.

Saechao, S. (1992). *The Iu Mien community.* Asian Community Center of Sacramento Valley.

Saeliew, J. (2007). Voices from the Mountain by Jai Saeliew | IMMIEN—Connecting Iu Mien with the world. IMMIEN.com—Connecting Iu Mien people with the world. www.immien.com/entertainment/arts-and-entertainment/videos/voices-from-the-mountain-by-jai-saeliew-2/

Saeteurn, F. F. (n.d.). United Iu-Mien Community, Inc.—Iu-Mien History. *United Iu-Mien Community, Inc.* www.unitediumien.org/MienHistory.php

Wiens, H. J. (1967). *Han Chinese expansion in South China.* Shoe String Press.

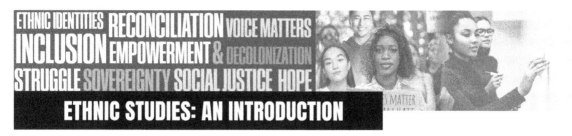

ETHNIC IDENTITIES RECONCILIATION VOICE MATTERS
INCLUSION EMPOWERMENT & DECOLONIZATION
STRUGGLE SOVEREIGNTY SOCIAL JUSTICE HOPE
ETHNIC STUDIES: AN INTRODUCTION

The Hmong in the United States
Bao Lo

As a child of Hmong refugees, I was born in a Thailand refugee camp and came to the United States at a young age. I grew up and attended K-12 schools in Stockton, California, home to the country's sixth-largest Hmong population. The central valley of California constitutes the highest concentration of Hmong Americans in the country. However, I did not receive any formal education about the history and experiences of my community in K-12. In college, there was some reading and discussion in my Asian American History course that mentioned Hmong refugees who migrated to the United States after the Vietnam War. Scholarship on Hmong Americans from the perspectives of Asian American studies and Ethnic Studies is relatively few and research on Southeast Asian Americans has largely documented the experiences of the Vietnamese who constitute the largest group (Caplan et al., 1991; Wilcox et al., 2015; Zhou & Bankston, 1998). Traditional disciplines such as History, Anthropology, and Area Studies, specifically Asia or Southeast Asia Studies largely dominate scholarship about Hmong Americans that privileges Western knowledge, or a white male epistemology, to repress Hmong knowledge and decenter their voices and agency (Hillmer, 2010; Symonds, 2004; Tapp et al., 2004). For instance, this scholarship often tells the story of Hmong refugees as victims that Western culture and society need to save (Faderman, 1998; Fadiman, 1997; Mote, 2004). Emerging scholarship by Hmong Americans are challenging these problematic framings of Hmong American experiences and centering Hmong knowledge, voices, and agency (Lo, 2016; Vang, 2016, 2021). The need for more critical scholarship about Hmong Americans, the lack of education about Hmong Americans and other Southeast Asian Americans in K-12, as well as my background and experiences are reasons why I became a scholar of Ethnic Studies.

Given its origins and purpose, it is imperative to produce scholarship about Hmong Americans through Ethnic Studies and Asian American studies perspectives. Ethnic Studies emerged in the late 1960s under the Third World Liberation

Front (TWLF) that consisted of student coalitions of African American, Mexican American, Asian American, and Native American students. As a subdiscipline of Ethnic Studies, Asian American studies adopted terms such as self-determination to challenge historical practices of racism that excluded Asian Americans from membership and citizenship within the United States. The field also emphasized history, identity, and community, particularly engaging scholars and students with working-class communities (Zhou et al., 2016, p. 5). With changing demographics and increased diversity in Asian American communities, the field has expanded in curriculum and research to include groups such as Southeast Asian Americans including Hmong Americans. The following sections provide an overview of Hmong American experiences and a centering of our community's history and agency.

The Hmong in the United States: History and Community Building

Hmong refugees who came to the United States were from Laos (Vang, 2008, p. 1). The origins of the Hmong is unclear due to lack of historical evidence. However, many scholars believe the Hmong in the United States originated from southern China and settled in Laos in the early 1800s (Chan, 1994; Donnelly, 1994; Faderman, 1998; Hamilton-Merritt, 1993; Quincy, 1998). As a result of their involvement during the Vietnam War as U.S. allies, Hmong refugees largely resettled in the United States and began arriving in the mid-1970s. Like other Southeast Asian refugees, the Hmong were widely dispersed throughout the country during resettlement efforts (Chan, 1994; Loescher & Scanlan, 1986). Today, Hmong Americans are concentrated in the twin cities of Minneapolis-St. Paul, Minnesota and the Central Valley of California, from Fresno to Sacramento, making this group important in these places.

War, Migration, and Resettlement

The Hmong people of Laos were recruited by the Central Intelligence Agency (CIA) during the Vietnam War as war allies and became targets of genocide for aiding the United States after the Vietnam War ended. An array of scholarship speaks about the recruitment of Hmong tribesmen in the mountains of northern Laos by the CIA to combat communist Pathet Lao forces in the "Secret War." The CIA recruitment of the Hmong in Laos remained "secret" to avoid violating the agreements of the Geneva Accords of 1954 and 1962 that prohibited foreign intervention in Laos, which was established as a neutral and sovereign state after the fall of French colonial rule in 1954 (Chan, 1994; Hillmer, 2010; Morrison, 1999; Pfaff, 1995; Quincy, 2000). American political interests and military intervention in the Vietnam War were driven by the "domino theory," or the perception that countries in Southeast Asia standing like a row of dominoes, would all fall one after another, if one country fell to Communism (Chan, 1994, p. 23). This containment policy of the Cold War explains American intervention in Laos and their recruitment of the Hmong in the Secret War. From 1961, General Vang Pao led the Hmong in the Secret War, which went on for nearly 15 years until the communist took over Laos in 1975. Once the United States decided to pull out of Laos, some 12,000 to 15,000 Hmong were evacuated by the CIA and taken to refugee camps in Thailand. However, most fled on their own to neighboring Thailand (Pfaff, 1995, p. 51). The Hmong who reside in the United States today are a result of U.S. foreign policy and militarization in Southeast Asia.

U.S. intervention resulted in the largest migration of Hmong refugees to the United States. The majority of Hmong refugees that left Laos have been resettled to the United States. Others were resettled to various parts of the world including Australia, France, Germany, French Guiana, Argentina, and Canada (Yang, 2013, p. 4). Hmong refugees like other Southeast Asian refugees from Vietnam, Laos, and Cambodia, shared a similar fate of displacement and resettlement in the United States after the Vietnam War. Under the Indochina Migration and Refugee Assistance Act of 1975, Hmong refugees began arriving to the United States by 1976 with high ranking military officers and their families who were involved with the American military receiving priority (Pfaff, 1995, p. 62). The peak of Hmong refugee arrivals occurred between 1979 and 1980 (Olney, 1986, p. 180). An estimated 130,000 Hmong refugees had arrived in the United States and spread out over many parts of the country, with dense concentrations in particular cities such as Fresno, California or St. Paul, Minnesota by the mid-1990s. As Thailand refugee camps closed by 1995, the processing and resettlement of all Hmong refugees came to a halt (Vang, 2008, p. 10). Hmong refugees were forced to leave because the Thai government never officially allowed Hmong resettlement within its borders. Those who remained in the camps at the time of their closure were sent to transit camps to await repatriation to Laos. Several thousand, however, fled to rural areas of Thailand or to Wat Tham Krabok, a Buddhist monastery where a local religious leader organized shelter and services. Wat Tham Krabok Hmong refugees are the newest refugees to be resettled in the United States. An additional 15,000 of these refugees have been resettled since 2004 (Yang, 2013, p. 4).

Similar to other Southeast Asian refugees, initial placement of Hmong refugees was determined by the location of American families and sponsoring agencies. The first Hmong refugees to arrive were sponsored by voluntary agencies (VOLAGs), churches, and individual American residents (Vang, 2008, p. 11). The U.S. refugee resettlement policy dispersed refugees throughout the country to accelerate acculturation into American life and to avoid economic burden on one region (Yang, 2013, p. 13). However, California experienced a dramatic growth in the Hmong population in the early to mid-1980s as a result of secondary migration, particularly in the Merced and Fresno counties. Reasons for secondary migration among Hmong refugees to California included unemployment, reduction in cash assistance for refugees, family reunification, and farming. Farming was an important livelihood for the Hmong in Laos and without formal education, many Hmong could not find employment to live sufficiently in the United States. Many of them decided to migrate to Fresno, CA and other parts of California's central valley for farming opportunities (Finck, 1986). The initial concentrations of the Hmong population were Fresno (over 8,000), Stockton (4,000), and Merced (5,000). An additional 20,000 Hmong settled into the central valley between 1981 and 1983. By the end of 1986, more than half of the U.S. Hmong population had settled in California (Yang, 2013, p. 13). In the mid-1990s, a third Hmong migration resulted in a significant decrease of the Fresno and central valley Hmong population, as people moved to Minnesota, Wisconsin, and other Midwestern states to escape high unemployment and poor economic conditions. The Twin Cities of St. Paul/Minneapolis became the largest urban concentration of Hmong in the United States (Yang, 2013, p. 22).

The history of resettlement and secondary migration explains the large concentration of the Hmong today in states such as California and Minnesota. The three largest states of the U.S. Hmong population are California (94,454), Minnesota (75,565), and Wisconsin (55,792). Compared to the total U.S. population and other immigrant groups such as the Mexicans, Asian Indians, Vietnamese, the Hmong population is not as large. However, the concentrations of the Hmong population in cities such as Fresno and Sacramento, California and St. Paul and Minneapolis, Minnesota, make this population important in these places (Pfeifer et al., 2012). In Minnesota, the Hmong population is concentrated in the twin cities of Minneapolis and St. Paul. In California, the Hmong mainly reside in the cities of the Central Valley, from as far north as Chico and Yuba City, to the south of Fresno and Visalia.

A Demographic Overview

The American Community Survey 2017 estimates the U.S. Hmong population at 309, 564, a slight increase of the Census 2010 count of 256,430 persons. The gender distribution is about even as there are 49% females and 51% males. The average household size is four to five people. Of the total U.S. Hmong population, 66% are American born, with 36% of this population under the age of 18. In addition, 15% of the population are between 18 and 24 years of age, 23% are between 25 and 34 years of age, and 11% are between 35 to 44 years of age. Only 15% are 45 years and over, who constitute the first generation of Hmong refugees who migrated to the United States after the war. Given that the flow of Hmong refugees stopped in the early 1990s, with the exception of the latest wave to resettle in 2004 and 2005, the U.S. Hmong population is largely American-born and relatively young or young adults. Since the arrival of the first Hmong refugees in the mid-1970s, Hmong Americans now comprise of first, second, and third generations.

The American Community Survey 2017 suggests that income, poverty rates, homeownership rates, and educational attainment have improved for Hmong Americans. Comparing data from the American Community Survey 2017 and

Census 2010, the average household income is $61,348 compared to $49,399, and 16% of Hmong families live below the Federal Poverty Level compared to 27% in 2010. Of the U.S. Hmong population, 49% owns a home compared to 46% in 2010. Among those of 25 years or older, about 25% of Hmong Americans have obtained a bachelor's degree or higher compared to only 11% in 2010. Additionally, 23% of Hmong Americans have less than a high school diploma compared to 38% in 2010. When compared to the U.S. general population, Hmong Americans still have not reached economic parity. Although the average household income for Hmong Americans is $61,348 compared to $60,336 for all Americans, the average household size is higher among Hmong Americans (4.6) than all Americans (2.6). Additionally, the poverty rate of Hmong families (16%) is almost two times that of all Americans (10%). Fewer Hmong Americans (49%) own a home compared to all Americans (67%). The educational attainment of Hmong Americans is still lower compared to all Americans. Only 25% of Hmong Americans have a bachelor's degree compared to 32% of all Americans and 23% of Hmong Americans have less than a high school compared to 12% of all Americans. Since their arrival in the United States more than forty years ago, Hmong Americans continue to experience economic hardship.

Building Community

Mutual assistance associations or ethnic-based organizations were formed in the 1980s and 1990s to help Hmong refugees with acculturation, unemployment, poverty, and cultural and language barriers, as Hmong refugees were unprepared educationally, technologically, and linguistically to adapt to life in the United States (Yang, 2013, p. 6). Moreover, the insufficiency of resettlement programs justified the need for ethnic-based organizations (Vang, 2008, p. 71).

As migration disrupted the clan and kinship system that traditionally provided support for Hmong families, Hmong refugees were forced to utilize available resources to create new support systems. These organizations were essential for building the community and provided information and assistance with housing, English, health, and employment, served as a place to maintain Hmong culture and identity, and focused on homeland politics (Vang, 2010, p. 69). Faith-based organizations were also important for community building, as they provided religious and social support to families who did not have extended kinship networks. Hmong American National Catholic Association, the Lao Evangelic Church, and the Association of Hmong Community United Methodist Church are some examples of these formal institutions (Vang, 2010, p. 87).

With the largest concentrations of the U.S. Hmong population in Minnesota and California, formal institutions have become essential for the development and progress of Hmong communities in these locations. The St. Paul Hmong community has developed over 10 community-based organizations that provide complete social services to the Hmong community of St. Paul. These include the Center for Hmong

Arts and Talents (CHAT), Hmong American Partnership (HAP), Hmong Cultural Center (HCC), and the Center for Hmong Studies (Vang, 2008). CHAT is the first Hmong arts organization in the country and has contributed to the Twin-Cities' reputation as an international arts community. HAP was founded in 1990 and provides English classes and job placement for Hmong refugees and has become one of the largest Hmong social service organizations in the country. HCC and the Center for Hmong Studies participate in creating an academic community of Hmong scholars and scholarly writing of the Hmong in the United States and around the world.

In California, more than thirty organizations were developed to support the largest U.S. Hmong population. In Fresno, the largest city of California's Hmong population, there were numerous mutual assistance associations and faith-based organizations to support members of the community until 2017 such as Lao Family Community, Inc. and the International Hmong New Year Committee. Lao Family Community, Inc. was one of the eight Lao Family Organizations in the nation which was founded by General Vang Pao, general of the Hmong army that fought with the CIA during the Vietnam War. The first Lao Family Community Based Organization was founded in Santa Ana, California in 1977, to help transition Southeast Asian refugees, particularly the Hmong, into American society (Yang, 2013, p. 9). The International Hmong New Year Committee organized the nation's largest Hmong New Year festival in Fresno. Although these organizations were instrumental in helping the largest Hmong population in the country transition and develop, challenges such as the lack of long-term, sustainable funding forced the closure of many of these organizations. Remaining organizations such as Fresno Interdenominational Refugee Ministries (FIRM), Stone Soup Fresno, and the Fresno Center provide job placement and training, English classes, and social services related to health and cultural adjustment.

In Sacramento, the second largest city of California's Hmong population, the two organizations that have been the most influential include Hmong Women's Heritage Association and Lao Family Community, Inc. Hmong Women's Heritage Association was a nonprofit, community-based organization that started as a support group in 1993 for Hmong women and their children after significant arrivals of Hmong refugees in Sacramento. The organization provided support for Hmong families such as crisis intervention, paraprofessional counseling, and referrals to other county and federal agencies and community-based organizations. As a response to the growing Southeast Asian refugee population, a Lao Family Community was formed in 1982 to assist the growing Lao, Hmong, and Mien population in Sacramento and Yolo counties. They provided English language courses, assisted with job placement and training and helped refugees through the process of becoming a U.S. citizen. They have also helped to resettle the newest Hmong refugees coming from Thailand since 2004. These two community based organizations have been instrumental to the transition and adjustment of the Hmong in Sacramento since many of their goals have focused specifically on addressing the needs of the Hmong community in Sacramento. Unfortunately, due to limited funding these two organizations have closed. Currently, Hmong Youth and Parents United (HYPU), focusing on strengthening the Hmong American community with programs focused on health, culture, youth, and elders, opened the first community center (HOPE) in the north Sacramento neighborhood for Hmong Americans. Also, Hmong Innovating Politics, a grassroots organization in south Sacramento empowers Hmong and other communities of color through political and civic engagement.

Community Empowerment

Political and civic engagement are evident among the two largest states of the U.S. Hmong population of Minnesota and California. Community mobilization in electoral politics in Minnesota set the stage for the rest of the U.S. Hmong population. As the first Hmong to be elected to and hold political office in the nation, the election of Choua Lee as a member of St. Paul's School Board in 1991 was a defining mark of Hmong political participation. The successful elections of Mee Moua into the State Senate and Cy Thao into the House of Representatives in 2002 were significant milestones for Hmong Americans. Kazoua Kong-Thao was elected in 2003 to serve on the Board of Education of St. Paul Public Schools and became the president of the Board in 2008 (Yang, 2013, pp. 30–32). Many more Hmong American candidates have since been elected to public office and are a political force in the Twin Cities. The critical mass and large concentration of the Hmong population are key factors in Hmong American candidates' success in politics in this region of the United States (Vang, 2010, p. 133). Additionally, the Hmong community of Minnesota played an important role in the passage of the Hmong Veteran's Naturalization Act of 2000, which provided special exemptions to Hmong veterans when they applied for naturalization (Vang, 2010, p. 129). In 2012, queer Hmong Americans in Minnesota organized and engaged their own community to defeat a state-wide ballot initiative that challenged the movement to legalize same-sex marriage (Pha, 2019). These achievements are evidence of the political influence and community power of the Hmong in Minnesota.

The political progress of the Hmong community in California has been slower than the Hmong community of Minnesota. However, California's Hmong population showed its political power with the successful election of its first Hmong official in California in 2001, Paul C. Lo, a member of the Board of Trustees of Merced School District. Tony Vang was elected as a member of the Board of Trustees of Fresno Unified School District in 2002, the first elected Hmong American official in Fresno. Blong Xiong was elected as a Fresno City council member in 2006 (Yang, 2013, pp. 30–32). Noah Lor was the first Hmong American elected to the Merced City Council in 2007 and served for two terms. Steve Ly was elected as mayor of Elk Grove in 2016. Lee Lor was the first Hmong American woman elected to serve on the Merced County Board of Supervisors in 2016. Mai Vang was elected in 2016 as a member of the Sacramento City School Board and was recently elected in 2020 as a member of the Sacramento City Council. Despite these achievements, California's Hmong community still lags behind Minnesota's Hmong community in the world of politics. The electoral turnouts are lower and the Hmong population of California make up only a small percentage of California's Asian American population, the largest in the nation, making it harder for California's Hmong population to have a strong political voice. California's larger and more racially diverse population also makes the Hmong communities of California less visible. In addition to participating in electoral politics, Hmong Americans in California demonstrated their community mobilization to pass California Assembly Bill 78 in 2003. The bill encourages the teaching of Hmong history in California's public schools, specifically social science curriculum in grades 7 to 12, to teach about the Vietnam War including the "Secret War" in Laos and the role of Southeast Asians (Xiong, 2018, p. 65). Hmong community activists successfully utilized community infrastructure, including Hmong kinship networks and Hmong-language radio stations, to galvanize support for the bill.

Conclusion

The Hmong in the United States demonstrate much resilience, resistance, and survival. Through war and displacement, Hmong refugees resettled in the United States. With limited support from the government and little to no formal education, Hmong refugees utilized their own community infrastructure and support networks to create new ones. Their capacity to influence politics and policies are evident in the two largest states of the U.S. Hmong population. Although Hmong Americans employ remarkable agency in their efforts toward inclusion, data shows that Hmong Americans continue to experience economic hardship. It is unfortunate that the history and extraordinary lives of Hmong Americans is not yet part of the standard curriculum of K-12 education. Hmong Americans understand the importance and need to center the knowledge and voices of their community, especially if they want to be visible and have their community's needs addressed. They exercised their community mobilization to pass California Assembly Bill 78 to have Hmong history taught in California's public schools. Hopefully, we can learn and build upon these efforts in our continued fight for Ethnic Studies in K-12 and beyond.

References

Caplan, N., Choy, M. H., & Whitmore, J. K. (1991). *Children of the boat people: A study of educational success*. The University of Michigan Press.

Chan, S. (1994). *Hmong means free: Life in Laos and America*. Temple University Press.

Chan, S. (2004). *Survivors: Cambodians refugees in the United States*. University of Illinois Press.

Donnelly, N. (1994). *Changing lives of refugee Hmong women*. University of Washington Press.

Faderman, L. (1998). *I begin my life all over again: The Hmong and the American immigrant experience*. Beacon Press.

Fadiman, A. (1997). *The spirit catches you and you fall down: A Hmong child, her American doctors, and the collision of two cultures*. Farrar, Straus, and Giroux.

Finck, J. (1986). Secondary migration to California's Central Valley. In G. L. Hendricks, B. T. Downing, & A. S. Deinard (Eds.), *The Hmong in transition* (pp. 184–187). The Center for Migration Studies of New York.

Hamilton-Merritt, J. (1993). *Tragic mountains: The Hmong, the Americans, and the secret wars for Laos, 1942–1992*. Indiana University Press.

Hillmer, P. (2010). *A people's history of the Hmong*. Historical Society Press.

Lo, A. (2016). Reel women: Diasporic cinema and female collectivity in Abel Vang's *Nyab Siab Zoo*. In C. Y. Vang, F. Nibbs, & M. Vang (Eds.), *Claiming place: On the agency of Hmong women* (pp. 220–245). University of Minnesota Press.

Loescher, G., & Scanlan, J. A. (1986). *Calculated kindness: Refugees and America's half-open door*. Free Press and Collier Macmillan.

Morrison, G. L. (1999). *Sky is falling: An oral history of the CIA's evacuation of the Hmong from Laos*. McFarland.

Mote, S. M. (2004). *Hmong and American: Stories of transition to a strange land*. McFarland.

Olney, D. (1986). Population trends. In G. L. Hendricks, B. T. Downing, & A. S. Deinard (Eds.), *The Hmong in transition* (pp. 179–184). The Center for Migration Studies of New York.

Pfaff, T. (1995). *Hmong in America: Journey from a secret war*. Chippewa Valley Museum Press.

Pfeifer, M. E., Sullivan, J., Yang, K., & Yang, W. (2012). Hmong population and demographic trends in the 2010 census and 2010 American Community Survey. *Hmong Studies Journal, 13*(2), 1–31.

Pha, K. P. (2019). The politics of vernacular activism: Hmong Americans organizing for social justice in Minnesota. *Amerasia Journal, 45*(2), 207–221.

Quincy, K. (1998). *Hmong: History of a people*. Eastern Washington University Press.

Quincy, K. (2000). *Harvesting Pa Chay's wheat: The Hmong and America's secret war in Laos*. Eastern Washington University Press.

Symonds, P. V. (2004). *Calling in the Soul: Gender and the cycle of life in a Hmong village*. University of Washington Press.

Tapp, N., Michaud, J., Culas, C., & Lee, G. Y. (2004). *Hmong/Miao in Asia*. University of Washington Press.

U.S. Census Bureau. (2010). *2010 Census of population: General population characteristics of the United States*. Bureau of the Census.

U.S. Census Bureau. (2017). *2017 American Community Survey 1—Year estimates*. Bureau of the Census.

Vang, C. Y. (2008). *Hmong in Minnesota*. Minnesota Historical Society Press.

Vang, C. Y. (2010). *Hmong America: Reconstructing community in diaspora*. University of Illinois Press.

Vang, M. (2016). Writing on the run: Hmong American literary formations and the deterritorialized subject. *MELUS, 41*(3), 89–111.

Vang, M. (2021). *History on the run: Secrecy, fugitivity, and Hmong refugee epistemologies*. Duke University Press.

Wilcox, H., Schein, L., Vang, P. D., Chiu, M., Pegues, J. H., & Vang, M. (2015). Displacing and disrupting: A dialogue on Hmong studies and Asian American studies. *Hmong Studies Journal, 16*, 1–24.

Xiong, Y. S. (2018). The dynamics of discursive opportunities in the Hmong campaign for inclusion in California. *Amerasia Journal, 44*(2), 65–87.

Yang, K. (2013). The American experience of the Hmong: A historical review. In M. E. Pfeifer, M. Chiu, & K. Yang (Eds.), *Diversity in diaspora: Hmong Americans in the twenty-first century* (pp. 1–53). University of Hawaii Press.

Zhou, M., & Bankston, C. L., III. (1998). *Growing up American: How Vietnamese children adapt to life in the United States*. Russell Sage Foundation.

Zhou, M., Ocampo, A. C., & Gatewood, J. V. (2016). Introduction: Revisiting contemporary Asian America. In M. Zhou, A. C. Ocampo, & J. V. Gatewood (Eds.), *Contemporary Asian America: A multidisciplinary reader* (pp. 1–24). New York University Press.

Reflection Questions

1. Upon reading this chapter, what do you consider to be legitimate knowledge? (Optional)

2. In your view, when is knowledge only information and when is knowledge a resource? How do you make the distinction? Please offer a brief explanation using two examples to illustrate your point.

3. Who in your view benefits from publishing distorted knowledge? Why do you suppose this knowledge is still used despite its distortion? (Optional)

4. How can you be sure that the knowledge you hold about someone else's racial/ethnic community is not distorted? Please offer a brief explanation using two examples to illustrate your point.

5. How can you be sure that the knowledge that someone holds about you is accurate? (Optional)

Race, Class
and Gender

Framing Questions

1. Define the terms *race, class,* and *gender*.

2. Why do you think the authors up to this point have emphasized awareness regarding race, class, and gender? (Optional)

3. In what ways do you see or not see the ways race, class, and gender influence the way you are perceived and/or treated by others? Please offer a brief explanation using two examples to illustrate your point.

4. Are there instances that you can name when race, class, and gender matter most and least? Please offer a brief explanation using two examples to illustrate your point.

5. Why do you suppose race, class, and gender are often discussed as being interlinked as opposed to being discussed individually? (Optional)

ETHNIC IDENTITIES RECONCILIATION VOICE MATTERS
INCLUSION EMPOWERMENT & DECOLONIZATION
STRUGGLE SOVEREIGNTY SOCIAL JUSTICE HOPE
ETHNIC STUDIES: AN INTRODUCTION

Introduction
Boatamo Mosupyoe

The articles in this section *focus* on women and their experiences. The accounts about women and their experiences show women's thinking, knowing, and being manifest in multicentric ways. From these multicentric contexts the articles show (a) women of different descents' relative position in a hierarchy of status, (b) the interactional process that tends to perpetuate inequality, (c) the experience resulting from participating in those interactions, (d) the importance of relations between women and women, men and women, and men and men, in shaping the character of inequality and dominance, (e) the impact of the legacy of the past on the present forms of inequality, (f) the function of internalized sexism, classism and racism, and (g) how raising level of consciousness to the intersection of race, class, generational differences, transformational resistance, physicality, spatial differences, and gender can enhance the understanding and offer hope for reaching solutions. Further, the articles inquire into various social practices, historical processes, and the multiple cultural logics of gender relations.

The intersection of race, class, and gender gives a historical development of thought on the three concepts. The article starts by giving definitions of the terms. The definitions were coined by the dominant group that also benefited from the definitions in real life. Race has been defined as a biological concept when in reality it is a social construct that has functioned to engender systems of inequality that favored groups of Euro descent. Class is described as a system that ranks people according to their relative economic status. Since the top ranking group because of racial classification is the one that controls resources and access, it tends also to be favored by classism. Gender refers to the experiences of women and men, cultural definitions of womanhood and manhood and the interconnections between race, gender, sexual orientation, age, class, and other forms of oppression.

The article cites examples from different communities to illustrate the importance of the intersection of race, class, and gender. The importance of addressing the intersection is emphasized. However, addressing the intersection becomes very difficult since both men of color and women of Euro descent tend to refuse to acknowledge its existence. Men of color, understandably, also face brutality and discrimination from oppressive Euro-male structures. Consequently, they feel that addressing gender inequality as they practice it is a further unfair attack on them. Similarly, some women of Euro descent find it difficult to acknowledge that they enjoy privilege because of their skin color, because they too are discriminated against by the male Euro-structures.

In "What It Means to be an Asian Indian Woman," Y. Lakshmi Malroutu shows the diversity of the Asian Indian society but most importantly she discusses how traditional gender roles of the Asian Indian societies have transferred to the Asian Indian immigrant societies in the United States. Examples of these are having arranged marriages and considering the wishes of parents as primary when choosing a spouse, etc. Patriarchy and sexism continue to prevail even in the 21st century among Asian Indian immigrants. Men are still considered the primary immigrants, Lakshmi Malroutu argues, and women enter the country as their dependents. She further posits that the success of woman is still defined by her "ability" to maintain the marriage and keep the family together irrespective of abuse. This kind of attitude valorizes women's suffering by discouraging divorce and encouraging perceptions of single motherhood as detrimental to and unfit for proper child development.

The article "Is the Glass Ceiling Cracked Yet" reflects that change towards gender equality is possible but you have to go through a process of mediation and tension. The article trace the challenges and achievements of Rwanda and South Africa on gender equality and compares in some instances to the USA. In terms of representation in government it seems that while Hilary's 18 million votes have delivered some cracks in the glass ceiling Rwanda and South Africa have gone beyond and their reality challenges the gluey floors/glass ceiling dichotomy to include metaphors that reflect the change. Change is possible; the mere fact that cracks were made in the "highest, hardest, glass ceiling" is an indication of a movement towards change. Change is achieved by acknowledgement that informs mechanism to redress and transform. The discourse requires an understanding of paradigms and variables that function to either perpetuate or promote gender equality.

Marietess Masulit article on Tungtong gives us insights into how most Filipino, like her mother, immigrated to the United States for better opportunities. More importantly immigrating to the United States was also a means for Filipino immigrants to provide help for those they left in the Philippines. We learn from Masulit that some, like her mother, would come to the United States while they were pregnant so that their children would be born American Citizens. To navigate the new environment and new challenges, families shared multigenerational homes and formed part of the communities that provided support and resources. Masulit continues to shed light on how the Hawaiian Sugar Planters Association (HSPA) recruited males to the United States to work on sugarcane plantations. They were successful because of gender roles and "expectations within families" that favored sons. Masulit posits, "It was common for families to utilize their resources to assist their sons to emigrate, while it was expected for Filipino women to have their primary goals be marriage and having a family." Masulit concludes her chapter by making a connection between her experiences as a Filipina American and the knowledge that she gained from Ethnic Studies discipline.

This sections comprises small articles by students who took ETHN 14: Introduction to Asian American Studies course. In the chapter "Fiji and Fijians in Sacramento" the authors of that chapter share their experience as Fijian Americans. They share an intersectional range of experiences as they learned to adjust to the United States' way of life. Mitieli Gonemaituba, for example, appreciated the absence of corporal punishment, marveled at the lack of school uniform expectations, and understood that parents in Fiji are stricter than parents in the United States. Neha Chand as a fifth-generation Indo-Fijian Californian maintains the connection with Fiji by going to the Hindu Temple. One way that Chand's parents navigated their new environment was by maintaining the religious connection to their former homeland. Similarly, Naidu's parents made sure that they passed on their Indo-Fijian culture to the next generation. Darsha Naidu states, "I wear my traditional Indian clothes and jewelry to represent my Indo-Fijian roots." From Jenisha Lal, we learn about the dance and music of Fiji in the United States. Brigham Young University, according to Lal, has a display featuring cultural dances of Fiji. Lal draws our attention to the lack of literature on Fijian Americans, but appreciates the information in ETHN 14: Introduction to Asian American Studies. Singh continues the experience by discussing how food builds community and bridges the gap. This piece reminds us to celebrate food. Shayal Sharma discusses the research on Indo-Fijians and taxi industry. Singh, like Lal, makes us understand the lack of journals, articles, and written records on Fiji Indians.

These articles suggest to us how to mediate the tension. They inform us of the importance of a multicentric approach to gender issues. In a multicentric environment parties will have to exercise the ability to move from the center to the margin in a fashion that will include similarities and differences in a lineal, circular, and spiral fashion. They remind us that the coexistence of multiple centers should also be encouraged. The concept of humanity entails differences and similarities. The reduction of humanity to commonalities has historically ended up in Genocides and persecution of those who were different and perceived as inhuman, because they were different.

We have to learn to live with differences. The Eurocentric, sexist, classist, and patriarchal approaches have been unable to do that in many ways. The realities of the differences are obvious. Implicit in these articles is an important message: the construction and reconstruction of relationships, whether they are racial, sexual, heterosexist, or based on class, require a multicentric approach that can engender understanding and resolution of the challenges.

ETHNIC STUDIES: AN INTRODUCTION

The Intersection of Race, Class and Gender

Boatamo Mosupyoe

The Purpose

The purpose of this article is to offer an introductory definition and explanation of what the intersection of race, class and gender means. The article will trace the historical development of thought on the three concepts and briefly analyze their impact on men and women relationships and status.

Much has been written about the impact of racism on people of Asian, African, Mexican, Native American descents. The debate about what is important in gender relations has spanned the discourse for ages. Views have varied from looking at race as the most salient, and class and gender as less salient. As time progresses views changed, in other words views moved from isolating the three to putting them on the same par. Progressive feminists and scholars like bell hooks, (1984) Cornell West (1993) and most recently Cole and Guy-Sheftall (2003) have stressed the importance of an analysis that focuses on the confluence of race, class, and gender in understanding the complexities of communities of color in the U.S. and the challenges that they face. In order to fully understand the impact, the three variables have to be considered. Institutionalized racism, economic injustices, and gender all play a role in the relegation of people to secondary status in societies like the United States.

Explaining the Topic

Historically race has been defined on the basis of how people look. In other words, race has been defined around intrinsic criteria that use phenotypes attributes ascribed by birth to distinguish people from one another. The classifications went a step further to assign and associate certain behavior and skills with certain races. Some scholars of European descent argued that Euro phenotypes reflect highest forms of beauty, in other words people of Euro-descent are the most beautiful of all the people on earth. They are the standards of beauty against which everybody should be measured. Their "fine" hair, sharp noses, "pink skin" which they described and still describe as "white," represented the ultimate forms of beauty. White also came to mean "pure," "innocent," and "less likely to do evil and wrong deeds." Further, it was argued that because of the size of their skulls people of Euro-descent possess superior intellect. The logic centered around the intrinsic nature of the phenotypes, and therefore were presented and explained as biologically determined. Since they are biologically determined, they cannot be changed and have to be accepted as factual and static.

This way of thinking influenced how important political, economic, educational, social, cultural, etc. decisions were made. People of Euro descent were said to be the "norm," the "supreme," the "yard stick," and the "natural." Other people who are not of Euro-descent were not only classified but were also described in comparison with the Euro model in the most unfavorable ways. People were looked upon as inferior precisely because they were not of Euro-descent. Much has been written to dispel the myth of race as a biological construct. Race is a social construct. Although the classification uses obvious physical characteristics to group people, it is very illogical and arbitrary to conclude that the shape of somebody's nose, the color of their skin and the size of their skull give them genetic advantage in terms of intellect, beauty, and behavior over the others.

The definition of race in biological terms was clearly designed to institute and maintain a system of social inequality that ensured and still ensures the preservation of racism. It guaranteed that only people who look a certain way will have access to resources and maintain control. Moreover, this classification influences how people interact with one another. Associating physical characteristics with behavior often leads to discrimination based on race. Joy James in her article "Experience, Reflection, Judgment and Action: Teaching Theory, Talking Community," writes in part:

> "I seem continuously challenged to "prove" that I am qualified. Comparing my work experiences with those of other African American Academics, I notice that in spite of being hired through a highly competitive process, we seemed to be asked more routinely, almost reflectively, if we have Ph.D. We could attribute this and have to our "diminutive" height, youngish appearances, or casual attire. Yet I notice that white women about our height, unsuited, and under sixty seem not to be interrogated as frequently about their qualifications." (D Bell and Klein Radically Speaking, 1996, p 37).

Clearly from this quote Joy James qualifications and credentials are questioned precisely because she is not of Euro descent. In simple terms, the motivation of questioning her qualifications are racist. This explains and indicates the unfair and irrational privilege the color of the skin confers on people of Euro-descent. As much as I want to write about this in the past tense, the fact of the matter is, it still happens today.

Together with race, class can function and has functioned as a form of discrimination. The tendency to socially rank people according to their relative economic system gives rise to classism. The class ranking system, unlike race, is often considered extrinsic to the individual. It is also looked upon as situational and fluid and therefore allows an individual to choose her or his position in the class hierarchy system. This is not necessarily true since class does not happen in a vacuum. It intersects with other variables that influences the status of people in a society. More often than not, in all systems of stratification, the top ranked group controls the economic resources and also enjoys the highest prestige and privilege. Historically, in societies where race has been used to rank people, people who were favored by the race classification as superior, become the people who are also favored by the class system. In societies like the United States and South Africa male of Euro-descent have been the favored group that also defined and determined policies. Policies favored those who looked like them skin wise and gender wise. This favoritism resulted in systems of race and gender inequality that take struggles to penetrate and overcome.

Gender refers to a social construct whereby certain characteristics, behavior, and actions are assigned and associated with people based on their biological sex. "Gender also refers to the experiences of women and men, cultural definitions of womanhood and manhood and the interconnections between race, gender, sexual orientation, age, class, and other oppression." (Cole and Guy-Sheftall, 2003, pxxii). Gender constitutes one of the most salient modes of organizing inequality among the sexes. Vouching for gender as the most quintessential of the three undermines the interconnection of the three, that is, race, class and gender. The three have to be considered in an analysis of discriminatory practices. Experiences of the system and of the intersection of the different systems articulating the actual experiences of inequality, will necessarily be different from man to man, woman to woman, and man to woman. In addition, the experience will be different from one group to another, as well as from groups within a society. Women and men's experiences across class and race have both similarities and differences. It is important not to deny the differences of experiences.

Feminism as a Concept

This section examines the development of the concept of feminism and global feminism from the 1960's onwards. The examination best exemplifies the complexities of the confluence of race, class, and gender. The efforts of the United Nations Commission on the status of women are well known. Despite sometimes fruitless attempts, the Commission was relentless in its efforts to represent women's issues to the United Nations. It's efforts were eventually successful. The advocates of women's rights eventually managed to convince the United Nations General Assembly to declare 1976–1985 the decade of women. In addition, the advocates and women were able to convince the United Nations to fund an International Women's Conference in 1975 in Mexico City. The theme of the conference was "Equality, Development, and Peace." The theme was intended to be inclusive of world's women's issues; however, what it achieved was a clear picture of dissimilarities of women's experiences world wide.[1]

The conference highlighted the differences in thought and experiences between women of Euro-descent, who I will refer to as women of the north and the others, who I will refer to as women of the south.[2] The theme Equality became the focal point of women of Euro descent. Their definition of equality in relation to men formed an important area of focus for them. Other women could not identify with the priorities and the agenda as determined by women of Euro- descent. They looked upon them as, and indeed, they were, part of the oppressive dominant structures that women of the south sought equality from. After all, most of the governing structures where the delegates came from composed of people of Euro-descent. That also meant to most if not all women at the time, women of Euro-descent represented an extension of those oppressive structures. In addition, their priorities were to be liberated from racial oppression and not gender oppression. **At that time,** race and not gender seemed to form the salient variable for women of the south. Of course, later the approach would evolve to recognizing the importance of the intersection of race, class and gender, as this discussion will later illustrate.

Conversations about feminism centered around the definition of the term. To women of the south the term would be irrelevant to their experiences if its translation meant to "be like a man and act like a man." It sounded to women of the south as if women of Euro-descent wanted to be men, in a nutshell. The women of the south did not want to be men; instead they saw an urgent need just to be treated like human beings, to have roofs over their heads, to earn wages that would enable them to feed their children, as priorities. The women of the south's arguments have been articulated outside of the conference by scholars like Lewis (1977). She describes the way in which race is more often a salient feature of oppression in African American women's lives. Lewis **then,** further argued that gender relations in communities of color cannot be interpreted in the Euro-centric terms that reflect the experiences of women of Euro-descent. Historically, African American women have tended to see racial discrimination as a more powerful cause of their subordination. In the 1980's and 1990's scholars like bell hooks also articulate experiences that are similar to those articulated by women of the south at the Mexico conference. In her book *Feminist Theory*, from margin to center (1984), bell hooks writes in part:

> *When I participated in feminist groups, I found that white women adopted a condescending attitude towards me and other non-white participants. The condescension they directed at black women was one of the means they employed to remind us that the women's movement was "theirs"—that we were able to participate because they allowed it, even encouraged it, we were needed to legitimate the process. They did not see us as equals. They did not treat us as equals. And though they expected us to provide first hand accounts of black experiences, they felt it was their role to decide if these experiences were authentic. Frequently, college-educated black women (even those from poor and working*

*class backgrounds) were dismissed as mere imitators. Our presence in movement
activities did not count (p 11).*

Sentiments such as these articulated by hooks, were present in the Mexico
conference. The agenda and the access were seen as determined by women of
Euro-descent. These actions clearly indicated and proved to others that women of
Euro descent were oppressive. Others in discussing Chicana women's experiences
also confirmed the primacy of race in determining an individual's position in the
economic order in the United States. Similar experiences by women of Asian descent and Native American women also abound.

The other two themes, Peace and Development, seemed to resonate more with
women who were not of European descent. The different themes and the different
experiences of women in these contexts then brought into question the universal
applicability of the term feminism to women's issues. The visibility of the differences intensified during the mid-decade world conference on women held in Co-
penhagen in 1980. Women were determined to unite and resolve their differences.
The determination, notwithstanding, the difference were present and they needed
to be confronted. As part of the solution the intersection of race, gender, together
with their implication on access and privilege had to be acknowledged. The discourse and the process proved difficult then as it does today in the 21st century.
Cole and Guy-Sheftall (2003) notice the difficulty even today. These two remarkable women have been involved both in the civil rights and women's movements,
and have been committed to the elimination of racism, sexism, classism and heterosexism in all of their professional lives. They write in part,

> *We have been engaged in difficult dialogues with white feminists about the
> importance of understanding the particular experiences of women of color, and
> the need to take seriously the intersection of race, class and gender in the lives
> of all women, not only women of color"* (xxviii)

Arguably, most women of Euro-descent refuse or find it difficult to acknowledge the
privilege their skin color confers to them in societies like the United States. Much
has been debated about the origin or root of the denial. I will posit the views of
two Euro-American women, one that I know personally and have interacted with
extensively, and the other who I am acquainted with through her work. The first
woman Kyzyl-Fenno-Smith is a respected librarian and scholar; she often articulates how as a woman of Euro-descent she recognizes the tremendous effort spent
in maintaining the advantage accorded by the 'pink' Euro skin by Euro-American
women.

From Fenno-Smith's point of view the unconscious claim reflects one symp-
tom of the concerted effort to maintain the privilege. She succinctly points out that
women we are talking about are smart and articulate in ways that demonstrate a
deeper level of understanding sexual discrimination, institutionalized and otherwise, what then blinds them to racial discrimination? Fenno-Smith argues that
some women of Euro-descent become so skilled in the art of perpetuating their

own privilege that they believe it is natural and self perpetuating. What complicates matters is the undeniable fact that women of Euro descent have also been discriminated against by Euro-male dominated structures. However, Fenno-Smith cautions that this should not be confused with or equated to something in the unconscious level. The often uttered phrase "I am doing the best I can," in the discussion of the intersection proves that the domain where the privilege exists is the conscious level. Fenno-Smith also says that it benefits Euro-American women to maintain the privilege, since most of the time Euro-American men, and not women, are blamed for the exclusion and discrimination. It is, she concludes, to the benefit of the women to maintain the status quo.[3]

Peggy Mackintosh in her article "White Privilege, Unpacking the Invisible Knapsack," posits a different view from Fenno-Smith's. Her divergent view is mirrored in her statement:

After I realized the extent to which men work from a basis of unacknowledged privilege, I understood that most of their oppressiveness was unconscious. Then I remembered the frequent charges from women of color that white women whom they encounter are oppressive.

Mackintosh and Fenno-Smith with their divergent views represent those women of Euro-descent who recognize the existence of racism in woman to woman relationship and therefore, offer hope for the achievement of an ideal. Problems of denial or lack of awareness or consciousness resulted in women from the south's reluctance to embrace the term feminism. The problems had linguistic, definition, and substantive implications as well. English constituted the first language of some and not all of the delegates; this impacted the efficacy of translation. The different experiences and agendas impacted the substance of the term.

The controversy surrounding the relevance of the concept feminism to "poor people" precipitated the International Women Tribune Center (IWTC) to hold a forum made up primarily by women from North and South America on "What is Feminism?" These group of women decided that feminism should not be viewed as a list of separate issues, but as a political perspective on women's lives and the problem of domination. Focusing on the problem of domination, then women have to contend with the domination of women of Euro-descent over other women. In the United States, Australia, New Zealand, and South Africa, for example where systems still use skin color to confer privilege, women of Euro-descent had to acknowledge the privilege and its implications. When this is achieved then women can work for a definition with the contribution from everybody. This then eliminates confusion and engenders common ownership of the word.

It is worth mentioning here that it is now ten years since South Africa has been freed from a brutal blatant racist system of apartheid that classified and treated people based on the color of their skin. The progress in South Africa remarkable as it is, it takes more than ten years to transform or even eradicate a system that has been in place for 342 years. Further, Euro-Africans will be super humans to just automatically and miraculously rid themselves of the deeply socialization process that taught them that they are superior because of their race. South Africa and the United States are comparable. In spite of the civil rights movement, the U.S. is still battling different manifestations of racism, classism, and sexism.

Towards the Intersection of Race, Class and Gender

Increasingly, recent scholarship suggests a shift without denying race as one of the important variables in understanding gender and racial relationships. The scholarship has no choice but to shift, since the intersection dates from time immemorial. What has been missing is the acknowledgement of its existence. In the case of the United States like in South Africa, with racist pasts, it became difficult for women and men of color to acknowledge the intersection. Instead, what happened in such situations racial oppression seemed to take primacy over gender oppression. This is true for most communities of color in the United States and elsewhere. Women were faced with a difficult choice, (that should not have been a choice at all), of addressing either gender oppression and risk being labeled collaborators with the Euro enemy or just sticking to addressing racial oppression in the face of patriarchy and sexism from men of color. Anyway, the intersection manifested in various forms. I will first examine the intersection as it found articulation between women and women and then between men and women.

The experiences of Sojourner Truth and Francis Gage best exemplify the intersection that was present in the long history of racial, class, and gender relationships in the United States. Their experiences also prove the complexities of the relationships and the difficulty of assigning hierarchies to oppression. However, I am very much aware that some women of color in the United States will still maintain that in a racially divided society, race and not gender becomes more prominent in creating experiences of discrimination. This paradigm becomes clear in the analysis of Sojourner Truth's experiences in Akron Ohio. At this conference that was attended mostly if not exclusively (except for Sojourner) by Euro-American women and men, men were giving reasons why Euro-American women should not be given the right to vote. One man after the other stood in the podium and justified the exclusion of women from participating in making decisions that affected their daily lives.[4]

Arguments for the exclusion of Euro-American women included the sin of the first mother, Eve was created second and sinned first, that was a powerful reason for the exclusion, one man reasoned. One man referred to the birth of Jesus Christ. Jesus Christ was not a woman; therefore, women should not be given the right to vote. Other arguments pertained to the physical weakness of Euro-American women, since men helped them over puddles of water, opened doors for them, and pulled chairs for them to sit. Arguments about women's inferior intellect were also cited as the reason. After the men made their arguments, Euro-American women were paralyzed into silence, until Sojourner Truth decided to go to the podium to respond. When she stood up, Euro-American women protested, not the men, but the women. They whispered to Francis Gage to stop Ms. Truth from going to the podium because they did not want their course to be mixed up with "the Negro's" course, they declared, very upset.

Francis Gage, an equally remarkable Euro-American woman ignored the Euro-American women's pleas and did not stop Sojourner from going to the podium. Once on the podium Sojourner addressed every argument that men cited. When she said that Jesus Christ was made by a woman and God, and man had nothing to do with it, there was a thundering applause even from those who had earlier on objected. She continued to even more applause when she addressed the sin of the first mother, by saying that, if one woman was able to turn the world upside down like that, then the women of the north and of the south will be able to turn it back right, if men would allow them.

Perhaps the most applause came when she declared that nobody helped her over puddles of water, and nobody opened doors for her; she could work from sun rise to sun set with somebody, a slave owner, beating her up on her back with a lash; not only that, she also saw most of her children sold into slavery and continued to ask, "And, Aint I a woman?" Sojourner rescued Euro-American women from the men that day in Ohio. Initially, her race as an African American woman, invoked rejection from Euro-American women. To them she was a Negro, period, her gender and her support for their course was irrelevant. Sojourner knew that she would not be part of those who would be granted the right to vote. The struggle for the right to vote at that time was for women of Euro-descent. That notwithstanding, she saw the struggle as that of all women. She and Miss Gage saw the intersection that others failed to see. In this context one would be justified to say that race seem more salient here than gender. Be that as it may, they both exist in the equation.

Rollins (1985), in her ethnographic work on black domestics in the United States, shows a different manifestation of the intersection of race, class and gender between women and women. Aspects of inequality as played out in the relationship between an African American woman employee and her Euro-American woman employer manifest in ways that blends the three variables. Phenotype distinctions, that is, race becomes an instrument that the employer uses to dehumanize her African American employee. The Euro-American employee treated the African American as invisible, as though she does not exist. The employers' skin color translated into a symbol of success, which made it easier for her to achieve with her African American employee than with other women of Euro-descent. Further, gender (female to female) blended together with class (/servant/employee to master/employer) and phenotypes (skin color, etc.) in determining the dynamics of the relationship. The African American employee would exhibit extreme forms of deference to the Euro-American employer, on one hand. On the other hand the Euro-American employer will display condescending maternalism towards her African-American employee. In addition, the employer will feel entitled to intrude into her employee's life.

The invasion served to empower the employer and reaffirmed her self worth as she continued to demean her employee who was under pressure to develop affective bonds. One other dynamic that manifested in this relationship was the need for the African American employee to perpetuate the false notion of their employer's superiority and their (African American) inferiority in their employer's mind. They would not reveal their economic successes to their Euro-American women employers, e.g., children in college, owning a car. They understood the need of their employer to feel superior in the face of the Euro-American male patriarchy and sexism. Similarly, Segura (1994) in her discussion of Chicana' women's triple oppression in the contemporary USA also sees race as playing a decisive role in the access of Chicana women to jobs. Segura sees the confluence as important and like the others she acknowledges that racial discrimination sometimes makes race more salient in determining an individual's position in the economic order in the USA.

The intersection of gender relations is very complex. The complexity increases as it relates to men and women of color relationships, especially in a racially divided society like the United States and South Africa. In their book Gender Talk, Cole and Guy-Sheftall (2003) write:

> *"We have also been engaged in difficult dialogues with Black men about their sexism, problematic conceptions of Black manhood, and their own gender privilege, even within a culture that continues to be deeply racist and demonizes them" (xxxii).*

Confronting sexism and forms of patriarchy in communities of color has historically posed a challenge. The saliency of race functioned to both preclude and undermine the importance of addressing the forms of patriarchy and sexism as practiced by men of color. Both Chicana and African American women talk about how the men in their communities will label them traitors and collaborators with the Euro system that brutalizes them on the daily basis when they attempted to address sexism as they experienced it from the men of color. The same dynamic also manifested in Asian American communities. Chow in her article "The Development of Feminist Consciousness Among Asian American Women" writes:

> *As Asian women became active in their communities, they encountered sexism. Even though many Asian American women realized that they usually occupied subservient positions in the male-dominated organizations within Asian communities, their ethnic pride and loyalty frequently kept them from public revolt. More recently some Asian American women have recognized that these organizations have not been particularly responsive to their needs and concerns as women. They also protested that their intense involvement did not and will not result in equal participation as long as the traditional dominance by men and the gendered division of labor remain (Ngang-Ling Chow, 1987, p288).*

The arguments varied. In the video *Black is Black Ain't*, (1995) bell hooks clearly articulates the presence of gender inequality in the African American communities and the energy that is directed at making it a taboo subject. She recalls an incident where her father unilaterally ordered her mother to leave the house. The incident confused her and conflicted with her perception of marriage as a partnership. In the same video bell hooks continues to take issue with males of color equating the reclamation of the race to the redemption of an emasculated male identity. Ironically, when male identity is defined as such, it encompasses forms of oppressions that marginalize women of color. In the same video Angela Davis also talks about how women subordination in the African American community needs to be addressed, and how African American males should take equal responsibility.

Often men will cite traditional values to justify sexism, even in the U.S. Chicana women will be told that they are betraying La Rasa. Elizabeth Martinez (1998) notes that in situations where Chicano and Chicana are faced with racism, fighting for women's rights is relegated to secondary status. She states "women will feel an impulse towards unity with rather than enmity towards their brothers" p. 183. Confronting sexism in the communities of color also translated for men into the desire by women of color to be like women of Euro-descent, adopting their values and ideals. This was just another way of silencing the women from addressing the sexism and patriarchy in their communities. Examples of instances where women of color are silenced when they try to address sexism within their own communities are many. Women are often told that they should not air dirty linen in public, because the enemy will use it against the race. Again here this quote from Cole and Guy-Sheftall elucidates the issue; *"whatever differences that we have as Black brothers and sisters should and can be worked out behind closed doors, and not be aired in public, as if we need to be validated by whites or the white media."* (xxxii). This was said by an African American male journalist, reacting to statements made by an African American woman about O. J. Simpson and Clarence Thomas.

In the Asian American women's protest against sexism within the community will be criticized as *"weakening of the male ego, dilution of efforts and resources in Asian Communities, destruction of working relationships between Asian men and women, setbacks for the Asian American cause, cooptation into the larger society—in short the affiliation with the feminist movement is perceived is perceived as a threat to solidarity within their own community."* (Ngan-Ling Chow, 1987, p2).

Since there are similarities and also differences in the experience of women of color with South African women, I will in the next section examine the experiences of women in South Africa for comparative purposes.

The South African Case

For a long time indigenous African women in South Africa faced the same dilemma. It became very difficult for women to address the subordination of women within the movements that were fighting against the racist policies of the South African Apartheid Government. Apartheid was the system that divided people based on the color of the skin and treated them accordingly. The indigenous Africans were placed at the bottom of the ladder in the hierarchical structure of oppression hierarchy and relegated to the margins. It was a brutal racist system that treated Africans as secondary citizens with no rights at all. The apartheid racist system was also very sexist. Women were denied many legal rights. At some point African women were legally denied the right to occupy a house if the husband died and the woman did not have a son. An African woman could not purchase anything on credit unless her husband also co-signs. Outside of the apartheid sexist and racist laws, African women were also faced with forms of patriarchy from within their own culture. Much has been debated about the origin of the sexism and patriarchy. Granted some of it was inherited and imposed by the Euro-Africans during colonialism and apartheid era. Be that as it may, it existed and it impacted women's lives. It needed to be addressed.

The preference was to talk about the contributions of women to the liberation struggle, but not to address the gender inequality among the Africans. Often three different views prevailed. One view preferred that the close door or closet resolution of the problem. In other words, if men and women publicly confronted patriarchy and sexism, the evil apartheid agents will use it against them. The second view opted for the problem to be left to individual couples married or single to resolve. The advocates of the view opposed turning the issues into a systemic problem within the movement. The last view saw women's subordination and exclusion as an important but not as an urgent problem; or as unimportant. To them overthrowing the racist regime superceded any kind of struggle.

The then liberation movements in South Africa made efforts and strides in gender issues. Indeed, the African National Congress Women's Charter and the Women's League bear testimony to this. However, on a daily basis, women did face some of the similar difficulties that women in the United States faced. Shahrazad Ali's ideas in her book *The Black Man's Guide to Understanding Black Women* (1990), about the relationship between African American men and women, echoed what African women had to face when they dared address sexism within their own community. Ali posits that men must rule and women must submit to their natural and traditional roles, as well as to the man's will. These ideas are presented as traditional roles. Any woman who was seen to violate these roles was then described as embracing evil Western ideas. In South Africa women faced the same obstacles as well.

What should be understood is, women experience sexism and patriarchy. The experience and not the western ideas prompts their objection to the dictates that put them in the situation. It is common knowledge that I lost a husband and son on the same day, and at the time when I was expecting one of my daughters. During that period I was required to sit in a very hot room with my head bowed to show my grief. I was pained in the most terrible way; I did not need to have my head bowed all the time. I felt I needed to go outside and get some fresh air. I was pregnant and it was very hot. While my mother was very reluctant to go against the dictates of my late husband's mother, and could not bring herself to rescue me, I was fortunate that my sister was there. Mary Grace, my sister would tell everybody that I needed to take a walk and needed fresh air. That caused a lot of tension that my mother avoided, but to my sister my comfort was most important. She knew I was grieving. She could not even comprehend the extent of my grief, because she said to me after the tragedy, "Ati (my name) I am feeling so much pain, and Simmy (my late husband) and Thami (my late son) are just my brother-in-law and nephew, I cannot even imagine what pain you are feeling right now." My sister knew I was grieving whether my head was bowed 24 hour a day or not. A widow then was not allowed to go outside because that would undermine the extent of her grief, while a widower could go about and even sit under a tree, in a shade. If this was tradition, it was a tradition that was oppressing me and I needed it changed. I was experiencing it as oppressive that is why I wanted it changed, not because some Euro-woman told me it was oppressive. I don't need a Euro-woman to tell me about my experience.

In 1996 I was invited to speak to a multiracial audience at University of Witwatersrand on my research that focused on the mediation of patriarchy and sexism by women in South Africa. During the talk I referred to the differential treatment of widows and widowers, and to this experience. While I love my culture very much, I am aware of oppressive tenants in it. At the end of my talk an African man stood up and berated me on embracing Western values and undermining the fundamentals of the African culture. He told me that he would be damned to listen to somebody who has just come from the US to lecture him on sexism. Needless to say, I did not have to respond to this man, because all the women in the audience of all descents and colors responded to him and lectured him on patriarchy and sexism. The only thing that I said at the end was to ask the women if they have been to the U.S. and the answer was no. That was an attempt to silence me. The man was obviously oblivious to the intersection of racial and sexual oppression.

Conclusion

Clearly, attempts to silence existed and still exists when the intersection of race, class, and gender are addressed. This should not be the case. Acknowledging the existence of sexism, patriarchy, and gender inequality will lead us to solutions and better relationships. The call to the recognition of the intersection does not constitute an oblivion to women of Euro-descents' subordination. However, it is important for Euro-American women to recognize the existence of privilege for a true sisterhood and brotherhood to be forged. It is in order here that I conclude by referring to MacKinnon (1996) disturbing claims that really prove her lack of awareness to the intersection of race, class and gender.

MacKinnon fails to understand or see the presence of race when she was given the statistics that African American women are raped twice as Euro-American women by Euro-American men. She asked "when African American women are raped twice as white women are they not raped as women." Her question indicates that she marginalizes the racial component in the whole equation. Her lack of awareness becomes even more apparent when she continues to claim that she views the whole experience as a composite rather than a divided unitary whole. Her line of argument still fails to acknowledge the meaning of the intersection of race, class, and gender. To the extent that patriarchal atrocities sometimes affect other women more than the others, points to different contexts created by multiple factors. Those multiple factors, race and class being the two of them need to be addressed together with sexual inequality. The fact that the tendency is to subject women of color with PhD's to more interrogation than women of Euro-descent to proof their qualifications, the fact that Euro-American women ideas will be embraced quicker, the fact that African American or Mexican women are raped twice more than Euro-American women, demand the approach that takes race, class, and gender into account.

Men of color too should take responsibility. Addressing sexism and patriarchy does not mean women hate men. I personally love men to death, and that should not stop me from addressing sexism in as much as it should not stop me from addressing racism, classism, and heterosexism and their intersection.

Notes

[1] Mosupyoe (1999).

[2] The north and south characterization follows the debate at the United Nations in the 1970's. The intention was to move away from the political and economic valuation of other countries as inferior. People claimed confusion with New Zealand and Australia. They were both regarded as northern and therefore part of the west. The north in this article refers to "western-Euro" and the south to indigenous and/or different from western-Euro."

[3] ibid.

[4] Mosupyoe, (1999).

References

Cole, J. B. and Guy-Sheftall 2003, *Gender Talk, The Struggle for Women's Equality in African American Communities,* New York: Random House Publishing Group.

hooks, bell 1984, *Feminist Theory from margin to center,* Boston: South End Press.

Joy James 1996, "Experience, Reflection, Judgment and Action Teaching Theory, Talking Community," in D. Bell and Klein *Radically Speaking: Feminism Reclaimed,* p 37 ed. Australia: Spinifex Press.

MacKinnon, P. 1996, "From Practice to Theory, or What is White Anyway" in Bell, D. and Klein, R. *Radically Speaking: Feminism Reclaimed,* pp 45–54 ed. Australia: Spinifex Press.

MacKintosh, P. 1990, White Privilege: Unpacking the Invisible Knapsack" an excerpt from working papers 189. *White Privilege and Male Privilege: A Personal Account of Coming to See Correspondence through Work in Women's Studies.*

Marlon Riggs et al. 1995, *Black is Back Ain't.* California: California Newsreel.

Martínez E. De Colores Means All of Us Latina Views for a Multi-Colored Century. Cambridge: South End Press.

Mosupyoe, B. 1999, *Women's Multicentric Ways of Knowing, Being, and Thinking, 2nd* Edition. New York: McGraw-Hill Companies, Inc.

Ngan-Ling, E 1987, "The Development of Feminist Consciousness Among Asian American Women" in *Gender and Society, Vol. 1. No. 3 September 1987* 284–289, 1987 Sociology for Women Society.

Segura, D. A. 1994 Working at Motherhood: Chicana and Mexican Immigrant Mothers and Employment. London: Routledge.

What It Means to Be an Asian Indian Woman

Y. Lakshmi Malroutu

"India émigré Indra Nooyi named first female CEO of PepsiCo" read headlines in the business section of major newspapers. On August 14, 2006, Nooyi became the first Asian Indian woman CEO of a Fortune 500 company joining a small but elite group of 11 women CEOs of Fortune 500 companies. Does this appointment symbolize the emergence of a new era and a chink in the corporate glass ceiling that many feel hinders ambitious Asian Indians from landing the top jobs in corporate America? According to some news reports, Nooyi landed the top job because she is a leader who is capable of leading a conglomerate in a global society and not because of her gender or ethnicity. So we are left grappling with the question of where Asian Indians stand in mainstream America and among other Asian groups. Why do we remain an overlooked minority despite our significant contributions in the fields of technology, science, and business? What do these sporadic moments in the sun mean for the Asian Indian group as a whole? While we celebrate the achievements of our successes, we seem to be at a loss to collectively confront issues facing us as a group especially when confronted with questions about our identity and inclusion in the Asian society.

To consider how Asian Indian immigrants are faring in the United States, I refer back to an essay that I wrote nearly 10 years ago, highlighting my experiences as a first-generation immigrant. Revisiting the topic of what it means to be an Asian Indian woman in the United States, I go over some of my experiences in this narrative. Although some experiences in the narrative continue to be the same, some things have changed; some are positive while others are not so rosy. Since the narrative expounds my personal experiences and perspective, it is not possible to use this essay as a representation of the Asian Indian group experience. Even though the challenges that I face are unique to my situation there is a thread of universality in the echoes of our voices.

Contributed by Y. Lakshmi Malroutu. © Kendall Hunt Publishing Company

Contemporary Demographic Portrait of Asian Indians

First and foremost, I expound the issue of identity and representation in the context of the Asian milieu. This narrative is an attempt to extricate the term "Asian Indian" from "Asian" and focus specifically on that group, a group that is not often recognized nor represented. The Census 2000 reports that more than 1.6 million Asian Indians and nearly 1.9 million Asian Indians in combination with at least one other race make their home in the United States (Reeves & Bennett, 2004). Even though they are the third largest Asian group, Asian Indians do not seem to benefit from the largeness of their group. The significant increase in numbers has not helped the group leave its footprints within the Asian context as they still remain on the periphery mostly obscured or omitted when stories of Asians are narrated. Even in the 21st century, Asian Indians remain the forgotten Asians and their experiences in the United States receive minimal consideration.

To understand the identity of Asian Indians one has to recognize the makeup of the group and the ambiguity that they experience regarding their multiple identities. Most Americans tend to perceive Asian Indian immigrants as a homogenous group. This perception is prevalent in the studies on Asian Indians where group differences are not adequately identified and discussed. In reality, Asian Indian immigrants have more subgroup differences than any other Asian immigrant group. While the term "Asian Indians" refers to people from India, the prevalent term used often is "South Asian," which encompasses people who trace their heritage to India, Pakistan, Bangladesh, Nepal, Sri Lanka, and other places on the Indian subcontinent. The broader term South Asians acknowledges common interests of the group while allowing for intragroup differences.

As South Asian people from the Indian subcontinent increasingly started participating in the complex and often heated debates about race and ethnicity in the United States, they confronted questions about naming and claiming an identity that designates their group in this country. Claiming any single identity omits the significant political, historical, economic, and religious differences between their countries of origin. This construction process parallels the gradual recognition of the term "Asian American" for peoples of East and Southeast Asian ancestry.

The Heterogeneity of the Asian Indian Society

The Asian Indian society is very diverse with linguistic, regional, caste, class, and religious differences. The subethnic division based on regional and linguistic differences follow a long legacy of regional and linguistic movements in India. While differences such as place of origin, caste, and language do not play a determining role within small groups of Asian Indians living in towns in the United States, these factors do play a decisive role in bigger cities such as New York City, Jersey City, Chicago, and San Jose and others, where organizations are formed based along these lines. Also evident among the Asian Indian groups are religious differences and tensions.

In Corvallis, Oregon, where I attended graduate school there were about 25 families of Indian origin. The families came from several states in India and religious, state, and caste differences were evident within the group. Because of the small numbers there was limited possibility of forming separate organizations in Corvallis and the families were forced to congregate as a whole and form social friendships. However, the friendships were out of necessity and underneath the friendly façade I could sometimes experience the aggressive and fragmented nature of Indian subcultures. Since I grew up in Calcutta, a busy metropolis of India, I was unaccustomed to dealing with the nuances of the subethnic differences. Growing up, the class distinction was very much in place in India. I attended private schools and had little or no contact with people beneath my socioeconomic status. The household help who assisted with chores at home and the chauffeur who drove us to and from our school and around were part of the household makeup, but my siblings and I did not have much contact with their children.

Interestingly, subgroup identity was a strong presence in New York City. After completing my graduate studies in Oregon, I moved to New York City in 1992, where I started my university teaching career at Queens College, City University of New York. There were dozens of Indian organizations based on religion, class, and region. Indian and South Asian immigrants transplanted three major non-Christian religions – Hinduism, Sikhism, and Islam, and several minor religions such as Jainism, Buddhism, and Zoroastrianism. Because of the distinctiveness of their cultures and religions, Asian Indians seem to have multiple identities. The majority of my Indian friends in New York belonged to several organizations based on religious and regional differences and most of them were comfortable in their multiple identities.

The Immigration of Asian Indians

The first wave of South Asian immigration occurred at the tail end of the 1800s from an India still under British colonial rule. Scientists and technocrats comprised most of the second wave, who came to the United States after the relaxing of the immigration policies in 1965. In early 1900s when Asian immigrants were not eligible for U.S. citizenship, Indian leaders organized the "citizenship movement" to get Indian immigrants considered Caucasian and thus eligible for citizenship. However, when the U.S. Census Bureau classified Indian as white in 1970, Indian community leaders lobbied the U.S. government to reclassify them as Asian Indians. They wanted Indians to be classified separately as a minority group partly because minority groups were entitled to a number of benefits in the post-civil rights era. The U.S. Census Bureau has classified Asian Indians as one of the Asian and Pacific Islander groups since 1980. Although Indians and other South

Asians culturally and physically differ from other Asian groups, the governmental classification of Indians and other South Asians into the Asian and Pacific Islander category has influenced their ethnic and panethnic identities.

The Recent Asian Indians

The former Immigration and Naturalization Service (INS), now called the U.S. Citizenship and Immigration Services, radically structured the homogeneity of the community as it consciously selected technically trained and English educated individuals from South Asia. The rapid financial success that this group achieved in the United States is now a matter of undisputed record. In 1999, the median family income of Asian Indians was the second highest of all Asian groups at $70,708, slightly less than the Japanese median family income (Reeves & Bennett, 2004). Along with its quest for financial stability, the community also became preoccupied with maintaining its cultural integrity and consequently, established numerous linguistically and regionally specific "cultural" associations.

It was only in the 1980s and with the help of the Family Reunification Act that the community demographics started to turn heterogeneous. Individuals who were kin to the first group or were displaced from other regions of the world such as Africa began migrating to the United States. Vocationally, the later immigrants moved into blue-collar work and local businesses as shopkeepers, taxi drivers, and motel owners. During this time, the Asian Indian community became divided by a chasm that was formed along class lines based on education, occupation, and economics.

In recent years, in response to the events in India and in this country, the Asian Indian community has segued into two major platforms with thrusts towards being "South Asian" and "pan-Hindu." The first group is more inclusive and has a secular and multicultural view of India. They focus on the similarities of South Asians and the issues facing them, especially in the aftermath of 9/11 terrorist attacks. On the other hand, the pan-Hindu group focuses on India and its culture, and feels strongly in the exclusion of other South Asian communities because they do not share the same history.

Gender Expectations for Asian Indian Women

The second area that I will develop to help understand Asian Indian immigrants is the expectations that the group sets for itself: expectations for their women and expectations for success. Being an Asian Indian has certain advantages; for example, one's life is clearly laid out. All one has to do is just follow the red brick road and he or she is rewarded with approval and acceptance. One is expected to follow the few identified status professions – doctor, engineer, or computer scientist.

As a freshmen orientation advisor, I meet many first- and second-generation Asian Indians and their parents to assist with scheduling of courses. Parents with single-minded determination steer their children into completing premedicine, preengineering, and computer science or natural science degrees at the exclusion of the arts and the humanities. In many instances, the son or daughter do not have much say in selecting a major–they just follow the expectations laid down by their parents and the society.

I am single, and much of my life revolves around my career and this makes me an oddity among most Asian Indians. Though most Indians will not say outright that I have chosen to live an unconventional life by remaining single, they say as much through their unspoken words. Marriage provides a woman with her primary identity and in India, as in many other South Asian cultures, marriage and motherhood provide women with their primary identities (Malroutu, 1999).[1]

Marriage is undoubtedly the central priority in the Asian Indian's social life, and is the end toward which all girls are conditioned to achieve. The fact of my life is that as a single, professional woman I command more awe than understanding, more questions than solutions, more isolation than inclusion. It is not just a social disconnect that I experience; it is an emotional one as well because most Asian Indians have yet to accept or even comprehend the possibility of someone, especially a woman, being both single and content.

The concept of marrying for love is still foreign to most Asian Indians. Most of my friends had arranged marriages. Relatives or friends would suggest a suitable match or a man's family would inquire about a young woman after spotting her at a social function. Some of my friends selected their own spouses, but they usually chose someone who was from the same region, caste, and socioeconomic background, out of deference to their parents' wishes and social pressures. Another determining factor in mate selection is the color of one's skin. It is an exasperating yet amusing experience to read matrimonial advertisements in Indian newspapers and websites. In the ads, the gradations of color quoted include "white," "very fair," "wheat," and "dark wheat" (Malroutu, 1999).[2]

Even on the celluloid screen, the paradigm of woman/wife/mother remains monotonously unchanged from the 20th century. Despite the spirited and unconventional carrying-ons before marriage, once married, the leading lady suddenly transforms herself into a conventional wife draped in a "sari" or "salwar-kameez" and an epitome of goodness, sweetness, and virtue. The deeper message within the film remains the same, that is, the unshakable conviction that this is the way a good wife or daughter-in-law behaves.

My female friends, those who had arranged marriages and those who chose their partners, generally seem to fall into the category of good wife and mother. Even though all of them have graduate degrees and hold professional careers, their home lives seem to follow a predictable pattern of making sure that the meals are prepared on time, dishes washed, parties organized, and the other humdrum of life. On the surface, my Asian Indian friends have an ideal family – a successful husband, their own careers, nice children, and a nice home in a nice neighborhood, but I feel the frustration and disappointment that some experience in their marriage.

But they are hesitant to elaborate on their problems lest they upset the façade of blissful life. Divorces and separations are few and far between and I personally know of only a handful of women who are divorced. An Indian acquaintance of mine ran away with a Caucasian because her husband did not measure up to her expectations but sadly found that the other man did not either.

In addition to their commitment to retaining cultural identity, Asian Indian community leaders become strongly engaged in upholding an impeccable image of the community and thus deny the existence of social problems such as sexual assault, mental illness, homelessness, intergenerational conflict, unemployment, and delinquency. Absorbed in affirming group cohesion, all social problems are relegated to the periphery. Although the community turns a blind eye to many troublesome issues, it denies abuse of women in particular, because it presumes that being away from the structural oppressions of extended families and strict gender hierarchies prevalent in South Asian countries, women's independence and liberation are heightened in the United States. However, not all is well within the women's community.

In the South Asian community, men are the primary immigrants, whereas women enter the country as their dependents: wives, daughters, or on a few occasions, mothers and sisters. The women's community that congregate in the United States, educationally and financially have more in common with the later immigrants than the more prosperous early group. For instance, according to Census 2000, although 54 percent of Asian Indian women over 16 years old worked outside their families, the annual median earnings was $35,173, an amount that was significantly lower than the median earnings of men in the community ($51,904) (Reeves & Bennett, 2004).[3] However, it is more than financial dependency that plagues South Asian women in the United States. Underneath the veneer of the placid and companionable family, domestic violence lurks silently taking its toll on South Asian women.

A woman is judged to have failed in her role if she cannot maintain her marriage and provide her children with a father, regardless of his conduct. An encouragement to keep one's family intact comes from the belief that being a single mother is detrimental to her children's proper development. Divorce is still unacceptable in the Asian Indian community and the percentage of divorced couples in the United States (2.4%) is indicative of this conviction (Reeves & Bennett, 2004).[4] Thus, the main burden of keeping the family intact primarily rests on women. An added incentive to keep the family together at all costs comes also from the cultural glorification of women's suffering. South Asian societies tend to extol women who endure violence for the sake of their families' togetherness.

In addition, the pervasive notion of "karma" plays a crucial role in intensifying women's tolerance of domestic violence. Many South Asian women tend to believe in "karma," one's predestination or fate. Thus, they may feel that their situation in an abusive relationship is their destiny. Several of these barriers interacting in complex ways make South Asian women feel helpless to change their situations and accept abuse as inevitable. My involvement with Sakhi, an organization that assists South Asian women escape domestic violence in New York City, opened my eyes to the horrors that women were forced to endure by their husbands. At one of their annual fundraisers, I heard the testimony of a woman who survived burns to 60 percent of her body and face when her husband poured kerosene, threw a match on her, locked their apartment door from the outside, and left her to die because he had found another woman and did not want to stay married. While women are held to higher standards in keeping their families intact, men have more latitude in deciding whether they want to remain in the marriage.

Acculturation Problems of Elderly Women

Another group of Asian Indians that has not received much attention is the elderly, especially elderly women. I conducted an exploratory research study on the acculturation problems and service needs of Asian Indian elderly in New York City in 1997 to gather data on key issues associated with the adjustment and coping mechanisms of elderly Asian Indian immigrants. In 2000, nearly 4 percent of the Asian Indian population in the United States was 60 years or older (Reeves & Bennett, 2004). Because the Asian Indian elderly come to this country with different cultural expectation, they face many problems because of differences in their expectations and the treatment they receive.

Individual problems for the Asian Indian elderly in this country include the psychological and emotional conflict between retaining their position in the family and society and loss of identity and power. The majority of elderly, more than half, are married or widowed women, live with their adult children, and experience overcrowding, lack of privacy, the emotional strain of three generations residing in a two- or three-bedroom apartment or house, and further dilution of financial resources (Malroutu, 1999a).[5] Social problems involve the older person's interaction with the social environment, such as language barriers, illiteracy, isolation, and immobility. In the study, it was found that elderly, especially women, have limited access to the outside world because of their fear to venture outside on their own in their traditional clothes. Besides overcrowding, lack of language fluency is a major problem for the majority of elderly women (Malroutu, 2001).[6]

The number of new older immigrants who are entering the United States as dependents do not demonstrate a proficiency in English and are dependent on family members to act as interpreters of both language and culture. In the absence of familial help, the elderly (mostly women) feel isolated and lonely even when they live in neighborhoods predominantly occupied by Asian Indians. Many elderly women have immigrated as dependents of their professional adult children and as caregivers of grandchildren, while some immigrated for financial and medical reasons. In contrast to recent immigrants, Asian Indian elderly who have worked in the United States are fluent in English and have access to health and other social services (Malroutu, 2001).[7]

The elderly immigrant women frequently talk about their relatives, friends, and social networks in India, returning home to India, and in general, feel lonely and depressed. This group is reluctant to develop close associations with neighbors unless they have similar linguistic and religious beliefs. So even when the elderly women find themselves among others of their own kind, they still experience loneliness and isolation (Malroutu, 1999b).[8]

Institutional problems include inadequate knowledge of social services, poverty, immigration status, and lack of culturally sensitive social services. The addition of the elderly immigrants into the household results in financial strain on families that may already be strapped for money (Malroutu, 1999a).[9] Many elderly women feel a debt of gratitude to their children who they feel have made sacrifices to help them immigrate, and are reticent to complain or seek assistance if their families are unable to adequately provide for them. The Welfare Reform Act also plays a significant role in limiting access to health care for recent immigrants.

This narrative is an attempt to highlight the Asian Indian dilemma within the Asian context. Asian Indians are frequently subjected to and subject themselves to the model-minority thesis with the belief that they are a financially successful group with no or few problems. Marginalization of individuals and families who do not fit the mold is common with limited recourse to addressing the issues.

References

Malroutu, Y. L. (1999). The balancing act. In P. G. Min & R. Kim, (Eds.), *Struggle for ethnic identity.* Walnut Creek, CA: AltaMira Press, Sage Publications.

Malroutu, Y. L. (1999a). Factors affecting retirement income sources and financial dependency of Asian Indian elderly in New York City. In G. Olson (Ed.), *Proceedings of Asian Consumer and Family Economics Association,* 17–22.

Malroutu, Y. L. (1999b). Acculturation problems and service needs of Asian Indian elderly in New York City: Executive summary. Unpublished report.

Malroutu, Y. L. (2001). Predictors of elderly Asian Indians' dependence on informal support systems. In J. Fan and L. Malroutu (Eds.), *Proceedings of Asian Consumer and Family Economics Association,* 163–171.

Reeves, T. J., & Bennett, C. E. (2004). We the people: Asians in the United States. Washington, DC: U.S. Census Bureau.

Y. Lakshmi Malroutu, Ph.D. is a Professor in the Department of Family and Consumer Sciences, California State University, Sacramento. Her research interests include Financial Adequacy for Retirement, Money Attitudes and Behaviors of College Students, and Asian-Indian Elderly.

Is the Glass Ceiling Cracked Yet? Women in Rwanda, South Africa and the United States, 1994–2010

Boatamo Mosupyoe

> *"Making gender equality a reality is a core commitment of UNDP. As a crosscutting issue, gender must be addressed in everything the organisation does. Why? Because equality between women and men is just, fair and right—it is a worthy goal in and of itself, one that lies at the heart of human development and human rights; and because gender inequality is an obstacle to progress, a roadblock on the path of human development. When development is not 'en-gendered' it is 'endangered'. . . . There are two complementary approaches to achieving gender equality: mainstreaming gender and promoting women's empowerment. Both are critical." (United Nations Development Programme, 2002)*

We are in the 21st century and the issue of gender equality remains salient in global education, economic, political, scientific, cultural, academic, and other discourses and agendas. As recent as in 2008 when Hillary Clinton lost to Barack Obama she remarked that although the effort to shatter the glass ceiling failed, it, however, culminated with 18 million cracks (Milbank 2008). Her failure to reach the highest office in the United States of America indicates the strength and formidability of the glass ceiling, even in a country that perceives itself as the leader of the world. Hillary's 18 million votes failed to break the glass ceiling, prompting Mosupyoe to assert "one area in which the USA has failed to lead is in having a person other than a male of European descent to its highest office. It is also worth mentioning that the second office, that of the Vice President has suffered the same fate" (2008: v). The glass ceiling refers to the challenge women face to achieve equal and fair representation with men in senior executive positions in the workplace. Berry and Frank (2010) define the glass ceiling as an invisible obstruction that stands in the way of women's ability to occupy the highest executive jobs.

This invisible obstruction mutually operates with the problematic sticky floors that locate women at the bottom of the economic pyramid. In variable forms the obscured glass ceiling is discernable in different parts of the world, manifesting in and informed by different contexts. Equally true, cracks have been made to the ceiling, to borrow Hillary Clinton's words, in different ways. Turning to Africa, this paper examines how two African countries, Rwanda and South Africa, have negotiated and attempt to synthesize the tripartite and mutually constitutive paradigms: glass ceilings, sticky floors, and cracks. The analysis also makes few comparisons with the United States. The question remains, have Rwanda and South Africa delivered a crack or completely crumbled the imperceptible stubborn configurations of women's inequality? Have the two countries advanced beyond the metaphorical glass ceiling, cracks, and sticky floor variables to new realities and emblematic formations that will offer novel descriptions?

An analysis of the following can help us formulate our understanding: (1) a brief historical background of the events of 1994 that led to self-determination in both countries; (2) post-conflict approaches to gender equality and men's and women's participation in the reconstruction; (3) the pronouncement of the constitutions of both countries on the status of women, (4) the function of the dual legislative/electoral voluntary/involuntary allocation of percentages to gender shared governance, and (5) the representation of women in government, informal, and private sector. Both countries have made a concerted effort to address gender equality. Akin to the UNDP statement on gender, in principle both countries seem to understand that "when development is not `en-gendered' it is `endangered.'" In development transformation is achieved by an acknowledgment that informs mechanisms to redress inequalities. The discourse requires an understanding of paradigms and variables that function to either perpetuate gender inequality or promote gender equality. To give context to Rwanda and South Africa's achievements and challenges on gender equality, a brief history is in order.

A juxtaposition of the 1990 events of the two countries reveals that at the end of April while South Africa celebrated its independence from centuries of discrimination of indigenous people by a white minority, Rwanda experienced genocide that culminated in the death of almost a million Tutsis. It could even be argued that the attention of the world on the "miraculous" transformation in South Africa contributed toward the diverted focus from the inhumane genocide in Rwanda. Nevertheless, the Rwandan Patriotic Front (RPF) managed to gain military victory in July 1994. The post-conflict reconstruction in both countries assumed forms and approaches that included security, justice and reconciliation, individual healing, governance, etc. In an effort to bridge the divide engendered by race, class, ethnicity, gender, etc., the two countries established somewhat similar administrative processes. The processes' main intent was to build consensus and avoid further division among the citizens of the respective countries.

The 1994–2003 Rwandese Broad Based Government of National Unity mirrors in principle and intent the 1994–1997 South African provision for a Government of National Unity. In the South African election of April 27, 1994, the African National Congress obtained the majority of seats in the National Assembly, and together with the other parties, including those that supported and perpetuated the racist apartheid system, formed a Government of National Unity. Clause 88 of the interim Constitution of South Africa made a provision for broad participation of political parties. Any party with 20 or more seats in the National Assembly was entitled to one or more cabinet portfolios as membership in the government. More pertinent to the theme of my analysis, both the interim and final constitution states in part that "The Republic of South Africa is one sovereign democratic state founded on the value of Non-Racialism and non-sexism" (Mosupyoe 1999: 53). Furthermore, the part of the Constitution on Commission on Gender Equality states:

(1) There shall be a Commission on Gender Equality, which shall consist of a chairperson and such number of members as may be determined by an Act of Parliament. (2) The Commission shall consist of persons who are fit and proper for appointment, South African citizens and broadly representative of the South African community. (3) The object of the Commission shall be to promote gender equality and to advise and to make recommendations to Parliament or any other legislature with regard to any laws or proposed legislation which affects gender equality and the status of women. (Constitution of the Republic of South Africa Act 200 of 1993, repealed by Constitution of the Republic of South Africa, [No. 108 of 1996], G 17678, December 18, 1996)

An examination of the processes of Rwanda reveals the same spirit of commitment to gender equality. According to http://www.gov.rw/ page.php, the official website of the government of Rwanda, on July, 19, 1994, the RPF established the Government of National Unity with four political parties: the Liberal Party (PL), the Social Democratic Party (PSD), the Christian Democratic Party (PDC), and the Republican Democratic Movement (MDR). Subsequently a 70-member Transitional National Assembly consisting of representatives of the RPF, the four other original parties plus three other smaller parties—namely, the Islamic Party (PDI), the Socialist Party (PSR), and the Democratic Union for Rwandese People (UDPR)—as well as six representatives of the Rwandese Patriotic Army (RPA) came into being. Here again relevant to the thesis of my investigation, the 2003 Rwandan Constitution adopted on May 2003 clearly and unequivocally pronounces gender equality as follows:

"Reaffirming our adherence to the principles of human rights enshrined in the United Nations Charter of 26 June 1945, the Convention on the Prevention and Punishment of the crime of Genocide of 9 December 1948, the Universal Declaration of Human Rights of 10 December 1948, the International Convention on

the Elimination of All Forms of Racial Discrimination of 21 December 1965, the International Convention on Civil and Political Rights of 19 December 1966, the International Covenant on Economic, Social and Cultural Rights of 19 December 1966, the Convention on the Elimination of all Forms of Discrimination against Women of 1 May 1980, the African Charter of Human and Peoples' Committed to ensuring equal rights between Rwandans and between women and men without prejudice to the principles of gender equality and complementarity in national development." (http://www.rwandahope.com/ constitution.pdf)

In addition, Article 9 of the Rwanda Constitution obligates 30% of posts for women in decision-making bodies and Article 82 reserves 30% of seats in the Senate for women. Rwanda's legislative milestone also reflects in the bills aimed at ending domestic violence and child abuse. Thus, while Rwanda's constitution has a constitutional involuntary gender-shared governance allocation, South Africa does not. However, both countries have clear and precise constitutional pronouncements on gender equality and the status of women, but approach shared governance allocation differently.

The notion of gender-based shared governance percentage allocation in Africa has been common since the 1990s. Kandawasvika-Nhundu (2009) notes that the desire for visible impact of women's contribution necessitates the practice. The efficacy of the constitutional mandate becomes evident with an analysis of Rwanda's achievements. Rwanda occupies the highest position in the world, with its highest number of women parliamentarians, also leading Europe, North America, and Asia. Women constitute 56.3% of parliamentarians in the Lower House and 34.6% in the Senate. The latter is an improvement from 48.8% and 30%, respectively, before the 2008 elections. The South African constitution, unlike the Rwandese constitution, does not mandate a percentage of gender-shared representation for elected public officials. Even in the absence of such a provision South Africa in terms of numbers has made strides. The representation of women in the local government has improved from 19% after 1995 to 40% after the 2007 elections (Letsholo & Nkwinika 2006: 21; Chikulo & Mbao 2006: 54); and from 27.5% in 1994 to 43% in the National Assembly in 2009. Compared to the United States, both countries, with Rwanda leading, possess a decisive numerical strength of women representation in parliament. As of October 2010, of the 100 members of the U.S. Senate only 17 are women, while the 111th United States Congress consists of 541 elected officials, only 75 are women. Furthermore, in the U.S. federal government, women occupy 44.1% of available positions but only hold a mere 13% of Senior Executive Service (SES) positions (Annual Report on the Federal Workforce, 2009). In this area it is safe to say that Rwanda and South Africa have delivered a much more powerful blow to the ceiling than the United States, with Rwanda's glass ceiling at a more advanced stage of destruction. The glass might be cracked, but sticky floors remain, as persistent gender inequalities can still be traced to other areas in government. Both Rwanda and South Africa have not had a woman occupying the highest office of the presidency. However, South Africa has had two women Vice Presidents, and three women Speakers of the House. Rwanda has a woman as the Speaker of the House, and of course the United States also has a woman as a speaker of the house. While change is evident, it would be premature to declare a total destruction of the glass ceiling with its complimentary opposite sticky floors.

The South Africa ruling party, the African National Congress (ANC), has adopted a voluntary gendered shared governance to negotiate the sticky floors. This is done on the party and not the government level. The results of the 2008 census underscored the need. The 2008 census reveals that while women outnumber men across all salary levels in government at 54.76%, men still hold 67.8% of senior management positions. The census also shows that in the private sector the employment of women in executive positions has slightly improved but leaves a lot to be desired. The other area to measure achievements and challenges is the informal economy sector. The informal economy sector is "the part of economic activity that is neither taxed nor monitored by government, and it is not included in government's Gross National Product (GNP); as opposed to a formal economy" (Phalane 2009: 2). South African women make up 40.4% of the street traders according to the 2007 national estimates (Phalane 2009: 43; Braude 2004: 7; StatsSA 2007: 33).

The informal economy sector also offers a clear indication of persistent inequalities that still demand a consideration of the intersectionality of race and class 16 years after South African indigenous people freed themselves from white oppression. In this sector low wages and lack of benefits locate women at the bottom of the economic ladder. African (black) women make up 50% of people employed in the informal economy sector, domestic sector, and subsistence agriculture. These statistics—11.4% of African women work as domestic workers as compared to 7.7% of Colourdes, .03% of Indians, and 0.2% of white women (Phalane 2009: 45)—remind us that aftermaths of white privilege accorded to white women during apartheid remain part of the discourse and tension to be negotiated. The ANC purposeful 50/50 2005 Get the Balance Right campaign produces visible impact on government gender equity; the informal economic sector and the private sector need more attention, perhaps a gendered campaign that also takes the intersectionality into consideration.

As in South Africa, in Rwanda women also constitute the majority in the informal sector. Inter Press Service News Agency (2010) reports that the Rwandan government aims to register 900,000 informal businesses to increase tax revenue. To that effect they have embarked on registering the informal sector businesses through an agency called Rwanda Development Board. One of its tasks is "the sensitisation and mobilisation of women to invest in doing business" (http://ipsnews .net/africa/nota.asp?idnews=51756).

Rwandese women also form cooperatives that allow them to sell their goods to stores like Macy's in the United States. The famous peace basket has improved how women conduct business and has allowed them to get loans through the

Women's Guarantee Fund. Some rural women have complained about the efficacy of the program but that notwithstanding Rwanda has made progress in the informal sector and through legislation it has repealed laws that prevented women from inheriting land, and thus improving economic growth and freedom for Rwanda's women. The new laws also allow them to sign for bank loans.

The discussions show that although gender inequalities persist, the gluey floors/ glass ceiling dichotomy experienced a shift that calls for new definitions of the degree and intensity of formidability. The transformation in Rwandan and South African governments defy the crack allegory because of the visible gaping holes in some places. The application of the metaphor should not obscure areas where gender parity exists as a result of transformation. In countries where women's involvement with knowledge production and construction transcends party affiliation and engagement with the media intensified to provide a gender sensitivity lens, the glass ceiling metaphor demands a definition that highlights the achievements of gender parity in areas where it has occurred. In conclusion, one must acknowledge that the glass ceiling/gluey floor dichotomy works with patriarchal traditions that also need mediation as they contribute to the slow progression of women into senior-level positions. The latter include society's social expectations of women entering traditionally male-dominated positions (Gherardi & Poggio 2001) and internalized sexism where women locate themselves at the bottom of the hierarchy (Conrad et al. 2010). This personal orientation regarding the hierarchical structure may affect the chances of women advancing more so than the glass ceiling. Conrad et al. (2010) state that anything that is perceived as real is real in all of its consequences.

References

Aimable Twahirwa and Kudzai Makombe 2010 *Inter Press Service News Agency*, "Women Win by Formalising Businesses.

Annual Report on the Federal Workforce. 2009. http://www1.eeoc.gov//federal/reports/ fsp2009/ index.cfm?renderforprint=1, accessed October 2010.

Berry, P. & Franks, T. 2010. Women in the world of corporate business: Looking at the glass ceiling. *Contemporary Issues in Education Research*, 3(2), 1–9. Retrieved May 19, 2010 from EBSCOhost database.

Braude, W. 2004. *South African Country Analysis, A Naledi Global Poverty Network Workforce Development Study*. South Africa: Naledi.

Chikulo, B., and Mbao, M. 2006. North West: Gender. In *EISA Election Update: South Africa*.

Conrad, P., Carr, P., Knight, S., Renfrew, M. R., Dunn, M. B., and Pololi, L. 2010.

Hierarchy as a Barrier to Advancement for Women in Academic Medicine. *Journal of Women's Health* 19(4): 799–805.

Constitution of the Republic of Rwanda, http://www.rwandahope.com/constitution .pdf, accessed July 2010.

Constitution of the Republic of South Africa Act 200 of 1993, repealed by Constitution of the Republic of South Africa, [No. 108 of 1996], G 17678, 18 December 1996, http://www.info.gov.za/documents/constitution/ index.htm, accessed July 2010.

Gherardi, S., and Poggio, B. 2001. Creating and recreating gender order in organizations. *Journal of World Business 36*: 245–259.

Kandawasvika, Nhundu, R. 2010. Expert Opinion: Strategies and Legislation Adopted in Africa that Call for the 30% Quota, http://www.iknowpolitics.org/en/ node/9289.

Letsholo, S., and Nkwinika, T. 2006. Gauteng Gender Issues. In *EISA Election Update: South Africa.*

Milbank, D. 2008, June 8. A Thank-You for 18 million cracks in the glass ceiling. *Washington Post*, p. 1.

Mosupyoe, Boatamo. 1999. *Women's Multicentric Way of Knowing, Being, and Thinking.* New York: McGraw-Hill.

Mosupyoe, Boatamo. 2008. Introduction. In Rita Cameron-Wedding and Y. Boatamo (Eds.), *Institutions, Ideologies, and Individuals,* eds. Dubuque, IA: Kendall/ Hunt.

Phalane, Manthiba, M. 2009. *Gender, Structural Adjustment and Informal Economic Sector Trade in Africa: A Case Study of Women Workers in the Informal Sector of North West Province, South Africa.* PhD dissertation, University of the North.

Statistics South Africa (Stats SA) 2007: 33.

The UN Development Programme (UNDP). 2002. Gender Equality Practice Note. New York: United Nations Development Programme.

Tungtong: Share Your Stories

Marietess Masulit

Ethnic Studies has shaped my life in ways that I never knew it would. As a first-generation college student, who identifies as a Pinay from a low-income, working-class household, I had no idea what Ethnic Studies was until I began my higher education journey at California State University, Sacramento. The first Ethnic Studies class I took was an ETHN 14: Introduction to Asian American Studies course with Professor Wayne Maeda. ETHN 14 was part of my first year freshman learning community with the Educational Opportunity Program, and as I have had the time to reflect on my time as a student, I am glad I found myself in that learning community. From that very first Ethnic Studies course, I realized how much was missing from my K-12 education, and wondered why I was never taught about the history of my own community, the history of Filipino Americans and the ways we have contributed to shaping the land-scape of the United States. Taking Ethnic Studies courses allowed me to gain a critical lens and consciousness, centered around solidarity, community, and social change.

The one recollection I have of ever learning about Filipinos, or the Philippines, in high school is in one of my world history classes. I recall one paragraph. This one paragraph was dedicated to the Spanish-American war in the 1890s and the United States acquisition of the Philippines. In reality, this was the start of the Phil-ippines colonial rule under the United States, establishing a deep colonial influ-ence on the people of the Philippines, which is still felt today. That one paragraph was the only time I felt represented in the curriculum, not only in high school but in my whole K-12 educational experience. As I have gotten older and reflected on this experience, I have come to realize the disappointment that one paragraph actually represents, and have recognized that the one instance where I felt included was rooted in the colonial rule of the Philippines, my family's home country. I begin by sharing my K-12 experience to frame the impact that Ethnic Studies has had on me, and its importance in education and learning. This chapter reinforces the importance of storytelling, collecting oral histories, and looking to history to connect bridges to our personal and familial lived experiences.

Istorya: Storytelling and Family

From a young age, I have many memories of my mother telling me stories of her life in the Philippines, of the challenges and hardships that my maternal grandfather and grandmother faced raising thirteen children in the Northern Luzon province of Ilocos Sur. My grandparents endured challenging manual labor as farmers. They provided for their family through agricultural work, growing crops such as sugarcane, bitter melon or ampalaya, and rice.

Growing up, I listened to the stories from my mother time after time, although only passively. I initially viewed my mother's stories as just words, and did not recognize the true value and importance of everything she shared with me, until I began to take Ethnic Studies courses as an undergraduate student. It really was not until I took ETHN 11: Introduction to Ethnic Studies, where I began to see the true value of my mother's stories and their ties to our family's history. ETHN 11 with Dr. Gregory Mark placed a heavy emphasis on the importance of collecting oral histories and sharing our narratives. From there my interest grew and I found myself listening to my mother more intently and began to ask her questions on our family, their experiences and our history.

My mother, Adelaida Molina Masulit, migrated to the United States in 1973 at the age of twenty-one. This was the first time she rode an airplane. I often think of the emotions and amount of bravery this took for her to do. She was advised by her family to pack lightly, and at the time she was pregnant, with my older brother Rudy. With her she packed baby clothes, some clothing for herself, and an inabel blanket, which is a traditionally woven Ilocano blanket.

Like many Filipino immigrants before her, my mother came to the United States for more opportunities and a chance at a more prosperous life. The United States represented success and growth, and a means for her to also provide support for her family back home in the Philippines. According to my mother, she specifically immigrated to the United States to provide her children with the opportunity to be born U.S. citizens.

When my mother arrived she settled in Redwood City, joining the family of her husband. To our family, Spring and Charter street represent historical eras in our family history that will never be forgotten. Our Masulit households on Spring Street and Charter Street, served as home for many and was often the first stop for extended family members coming from the Philippines to establish a new chapter in the United States. If both houses can speak, they would share that they served as multigenerational homes, and helped to create the migration stories for many of our family. As historically true for many communities, immigrants often travel and settle in areas where they have existing relationships, where there are people and communities to greet them and offer them support and resources. For much of my family, that was Spring and Charter street in Redwood City, CA.

Before my mother's arrival to the United States, the Masulit side of our family had already migrated from the Philippines and found their way to the Bay Area.

This was the chapter of our family history that I did not hear often and have little recollection of, especially due to me losing my father at a young age. Through my sparked curiosity inspired by Ethnic Studies, I began to ask questions and sought to learn more about how the Masulits migrated to the United States. From what I have come to learn, the paternal side of my family, the Masulits, began their migration into the United States through Hawaii. In the early 1900s, Ilocanos began to be recruited to work as contract laborers in the sugar plantations of Hawaii. The migration of my Masulit family began with the eldest sons moving to Hawaii to work on the plantations, opening the pathway for our family's migration into the United States, and essentially the root of my mother's immigration story as well.

By having an understanding of Filipino American history and the deep historical ties the United States has within the Philippines, I have been able to learn and make connections on how my family's history directly ties in to the larger context of Filipino American history.

Glorya: From the Province to Hawaiian Sugar Plantations

The United States has more than 3.5 million people who identify as Filipino, making Filipinos the third largest immigrant population in the country (Ocampo, 2016). Filipino migration into the United States is deeply rooted in and is a cause of the long history of colonization of the Philippines. Spain held colonial rule over the Philippines for 300 years, beginning in the late 1500s. Spain's long presence in the Philippines has had long term influence on Filipinos culturally, providing historical reasoning to why over 80 percent of Filipinos are Roman Catholic. However, throughout the 1800s, Spain began to lose many of its colonies in Latin America. In the quest to become the strongest Western Empire, the United States went to war with Spain. As a result, the United States was able to purchase and obtain the Philippines, along with Puerto Rico and Guam, for $20 million (Ocampo, 2016).

Under the United States, the Philippines became a U.S. territory, allowing for Filipinos to be classified as U.S. Nationals, opening a pathway for migration into the United States. Their position as nationals meant that they were neither citizens or foreigners, but provided them with a classification that paved a way for Filipino immigration for thousands into Hawaii, California and Alaska to serve as contracted migrant agricultural labor. Filipino immigrants were not able to become naturalized citizens of the United States until 1946 (Roces, 2015).

With the Philippines becoming a territory of the United States, this opened the way for young Filipino men to be recruited as agricultural labor to the sugar plantations of Hawaii. These young men became *sakadas*, a term used for those who left the provinces of the Philippines to become contract laborers in the sugar plantations. This period of emigration from the Philippines into Hawaii, displays the ways Filipinos heavily relied on their kinship and networks, prior to English becoming a nationally mandated language in the Philippines there was no universal language connecting Filipinos. When migrating to Hawaii to work on the sugar plantations, Filipinos often found the company of others from their hometowns and provinces, as this provided a sense of community and ease of communication (Mabalon, 2013).

With the American colonial influences present in the Philippines, this resulted in major shifts for Filipinos, especially those living in the provincial areas of the country. These shifts pushed many Filipinos to seek opportunities to better their lives and the lives of their families. The Hawaiian Sugar Planters Association (HSPA) heavily recruited for Filipino contract laborers, first in the Visayas region of the Philippines, then shifting their recruitment focus to northern Luzon in the Ilocos region in the 1910s. The recruitment of Ilocanos by HSPA focused on recruiting single men, many of whom were illiterate, and from areas of the Ilocos region that were impoverished. Between 1909 and 1946, HSPA recruited over 126,831 Filipinos to emigrate and work as contract laborers in Hawaii's sugar plantations. Between 1906 and 1924 the provinces of Ilocos Norte and Ilocos Sur were estimated of having roughly 32,707 immigrants move to Hawaii to become contract laborers (Mabalon, 2013). A large majority of Filipinos migrating to Hawaii at this time were men, mostly due to gender-roles and expectations within families. It was common for families to utilize their resources to assist their sons to emigrate, while it was expected for Filipino women to have their primary goals be marriage and having a family. Many husbands and fathers would also leave for periods of time to work as contract laborers to provide support for their families back home in the Philippines. Aside from the active recruitment by HSPA, Filipinos became inspired by *sakadas* before them after seeing the money and goods that many of them were able to return home to the Philippines with. Hawaii was looked to as *glorya*, a land like heaven with opportunities for prosperity. For many Ilocanos migrating to be a contract laborer in the sugar plantations was a means of survival.

Once in Hawaii working in the sugar plantations, Filipinos experienced harsh working conditions and low pay wages, often ranging between $0.75 and $1.15. They would often work up to 10 hour days and 6 days out of the week. Their work days would begin at dawn, and would often only be provided with fifteen minute breaks for breakfast and thirty minute breaks for lunch. The labor was manually intense and backbreaking, having to cut and pile sugarcane bundles that would weigh up to seventy-five pounds. The work days would also include clearing weeds and irrigation canals and fertilizing the fields. If they were seen as killing time or not doing their work, the lunas, or bosses, would scold them and treat them unfairly (Kerkvliet, 2002).

Of the *sakadas* who emigrated to Hawaii to work in the sugar plantations, many of them would stay and establish lives in Hawaii; however, a percentage of them would also find themselves migrating to the west coast of the mainland United States. Of the 126,831 Filipinos who migrated to work as contract laborers in Hawaii from 1909 to 1946, about 16 percent of them went on to migrate to the west coast, including California (Mabalon, 2013). When Filipinos arrived in

San Francisco, they often were greeted by taxis and buses ready to take them to Stockton (Takaki, 1998). This generation of Filipino men who were contracted agricultural labor would become known as the *manong* generation, an Ilocano term used to display respect for male elders (Roces, 2015). Stockton became a central hub for Filipinos to work in agriculture. Once in Stockton, many Filipinos would find themselves in areas of employment such as domestic service, agriculture, or the fisherie in the Northwest and Alaska (Takaki, 1998).

Tungtong: Share Your Stories

The most important thing Ethnic Studies has taught me is the importance of storytelling. Ethnic Studies as an interdisciplinary academic discipline centers the experiences and histories of communities that academia has historically marginalized and omitted. Through Ethnic Studies I have been able to tie in pieces of my family history to that of the United States, affirming the contributions that we have made to the very foundation of the country. As many Ethnic Studies scholars will share, the field of Ethnic Studies is much deeper than a set of courses offered at a college or a course curriculum. It is a way of intentionally being inclusive and critical in our everyday lives. Through Ethnic Studies I began to see my family and community differently. I began to recognize them beyond just their relation to me. Ethnic Studies taught me to really humanize others and see the stories that we all have to share.

As I continue to learn and discover more details of my family's history, I reflect on the stories and their lived experiences, and how it is intertwined with Filipino American history. Ethnic Studies brings our stories to life and centers people. I am grateful to know the resiliency of my community and our history. We must continue to teach the importance of storytelling and sharing our narratives. As students and lifelong learners we have the ability to contribute and make an impact on our communities and are all a part of creating history.

References

Kerkvliet, M. (2002). *Unbending cane: Pablo Manlapit, a Filipino labor leader in Hawai'i. Office of Multicultural Student Services*. University of Hawai'i at Mānoa.

Mabalon, D. (2013). *Little Manila is in the heart: the making of the Filipina/o American community in Stockton, California* (pp. 25–60). Duke University Press.

Ocampo, A. (2016). *The Latinos of Asia: How Filipino Americans Break the Rules of Race*. Stanford University Press.

*Roces, M. (*2015). Filipina/o migration to the United States and the remaking of gender narratives, 1906–2010. *Gender and History, 27*(1), 190–206.

Takaki, R. (1998). *Strangers from a different shore: A history of Asian Americans*. Little, Brown.

ETHNIC STUDIES: AN INTRODUCTION

Fiji and Fijians in Sacramento

Mitieli Rokolacadamu Gonemaituba, Neha Chand, Darsha Naidu, Jenisha Lal, Jonathan Singh, Shayal Sharma, and Gregory Yee Mark

 ## Introduction and Background

(By Mitieli Rokolacadamu Gonemaituba)

"ETHN 14. Introduction to Asian American Studies" is a course taught at Sacramento State University that focuses on topics concerning various Asian Pacific American (APA) groups through a historical perspective. The instructor for the course is Dr. Gregory Yee Mark.

In the fall of 2016, Dr. Mark met and worked closely with two Fijian students, Jonathan Singh and Mitieli Rokolacadamu Gonemaituba, from his ETHN 14 class. They bonded over the topic of food. One day at lecture, Jonathan asked Dr. Mark about the best place for fried chicken in Sacramento. Dr. Mark responded by saying he'd better show him where, rather than just telling him about it. From there, the three would often meet up at restaurants recommended by Dr. Mark, and they developed a bonding. After the semester ended, the three kept in touch. Jonathan and Mitieli would visit Dr. Mark during his ETHN 14 lecture, or would meet him for lunch. It was during these times that the idea of writing something on the understudied community of Fijians in California arose. And Dr. Mark urged Mitieli and Jonathan to write something about their experiences of being a Fijian in California, and possibly publish it in the Ethnic Studies textbook for ninth graders. Dr. Mark explained to them that he understood that Fijians, like many other Pacific Islander groups, were understudied and that there are barely any academic/scholarly literature concerning the group. Dr. Mark was motivated to do this because he felt that all students, including Fijians, needed to be empowered and needed materials of their own in schools or classrooms. And he believed that through Ethnic Studies, this can be achieved.

After having discussed this idea with Jonathan and Mitieli, Dr. Mark came to notice a good number of Fijian students in his ETHN 14 class in the fall of 2017, and brought these new students into the project along with Mitieli and Jonathan. Then around the fall of 2017, a group of six of his Fijian students came together and wrote this chapter on the Fijian American perspective on different aspects of the Fijian community in the United States today. As part of the course, Dr. Mark assigns students to do research on one of the Asian American and Pacific Islander groups. The Fijian students were challenged by the general lack of research and information on Fiji and/or Fijians. One of the primary objectives of this chapter is to create more literature on this small ethnic group in the United States. This starts with the Fijian American students telling their own stories through their own voices.

The islands of Fiji are one of the well-known pacific nations in the South Pacific region. Located in a more accessible location, Fiji owns one of the most strategic locations in the area in terms of commerce and trade, falling on the line of one of the most important and advantageous trade routes of the world. The nation consists of over 300 islands, some of which are uninhabited. Two main islands are called Viti Levu and Vanua Levu. Suva, the capital of Fiji, is located on the eastern side of the Viti Levu island. The two main islands are home to a large number of the entire population of Fiji, which today can be estimated to be close to 1 million people. Suva, the capital, is one of the heavily populated cities in the entire country. It is the center of government and commercial activity. The major airport, Nadi International Airport, is located on the western side of Viti Levu, which serves to connect Fiji to the world and also bring large numbers of tourists who are attracted to Fiji's beautiful tropical climate and golden sandy beaches.

Naming Terms Used in Fiji

There are many terms of self-identification. Some of them are Fijian, Native Fijian, Indian Fijian, Indo-Fijian, and *iTaukei*. Recently, the Fijian government has made the move to use the term "Fijian" to include those of who are Fiji nationals or citizens. This has made it rather outmoded to use the term Indian Fijian and/or Indo-Fijian to identify Indians living in Fiji, who are descendants of the indentured laborers from India. However, with this move, there is still a need to have an identifying term for the native Fijians. The word used for this group is *iTaukei*, which loosely means "indigenous" in the native Fijian language. This chapter mostly uses the term "Native Fijians" to refer to the indigenous Fijians and the term "Indo-Fijians" to refer to Fijians of Indian ancestry, particularly descendants of the indentured laborers from India. The history of both these groups will be discussed in this chapter.

The First Fijians

The Native Fijians are considered to be descendants from one man, Lutunasobasoba. Lutunasobasoba and his family sailed the seas in search for new land to establish a new home. They came upon the shores of Fiji and made a home out of it. Their arrival on their new land was along the coastline of Viti Levu, known as Vuda Point. A timeline estimation of the first settler dates back to the 12th century.

After establishing a new home on the islands, Lutunasobasoba and his family (particularly his sons and family) spread out and made homes in other parts of the islands. This is how they populated the land and other islands in the region. Those early settlers broke off into different places and formed different villages and tribes and are still around today. The story of Lutunasobasoba is one that was passed down through the generations and through time and is still told today in families and perhaps in school too.

Religion

Today, the majority of native Fijians are Christians. The early exposure to Western Europeans was through Christian missionaries. Before the arrival of Christian missionaries, native Fijians had dark customs and practiced paganism and cannibalism. Eating the flesh of their enemies was done under the belief that it was the ultimate method to totally defeat their enemies. With the introduction of Christianity, the Native Fijian society saw the end of this dark era, and the end of cannibalism. Native Fijians today have made Christianity the center of what they do as individuals and as a group. Sundays are considered to be sacred days and are observed as sabbath in most places across the nation. With Indo-Fijians being the second largest population, there is a large number of people who practice Hinduism. Thus, the two most primary religions in Fiji are Christianity and Hinduism.

The Colonization of Fiji

Fiji was first introduced to Western Europeans through trade. With Fiji's vast natural resources and strategic location, channels of trade opened up from the late 1700s to the early 1800s. They were in business with many countries like Australia, New Zealand, the United States, China, and Great Britain. Around 1849, an American trading store that was stationed on one of the islands was looted, destroyed, and burned down by some of the natives. In reaction to this, the United States demanded reparations for these damages from Ratu Seru Cakobau, who had self-proclaimed himself to be *Tui Viti*, which translates to Chief of Fiji. This, however, stirred some conflict with other chiefs of other villages because Cakobau held no authority over them. Foreign powers were also skeptical of his chieftaincy , but that did not stop the United States from demanding compensations for damages to the store. This, in turn, placed Fiji, and especially Cakobau, in financial debt to the Americans.

To avoid further confrontation with the United States, Cakobau wrote to Queen Victoria offering to cede the islands of Fiji to Great Britain, in return for assuming the obligation of compensating the United States. After a second invitation to do so, Great Britain finally accepted, and on October 10, 1874, Fiji became a colony of Great Britain. Following this, Great Britain sent a government representative to govern the new colony. The representative was Sir Hercules Robinson, who became Fiji's first governor. He was later succeeded by Sir Arthur Gordon, who gave some limited authority to local Fiji chiefs to handle local affairs.

With Fiji being a colony of Great Britain, it opened up more economical, educational, and political opportunities for the islands. Now, Fiji's vast land resources and favorable climate gave way to the cultivation of several crops that were used for trade with other nations. Even though the islands were under the control and rule of Great Britain, land ownership was still controlled by Fijian natives. This made it difficult for the colony to expand economically because the natives were not welcoming to the idea of working hard labor on their own land. With labor needed to work the plantations, Great Britain recruited indentured laborers from India to become plantation workers.

Indians in Fiji

Between 1879 and 1920, Indians immigrated to Fiji as indentured laborers. Approximately 60,000 Indians worked on crop plantations, particularly sugarcane plantations, which generated Fiji's largest exported good. Upon arrival, their first contact with the native Fijians was not a pleasant one. There was a mutual attitude of disdain. Native Fijians saw the Indians as people who would potentially take their land away from them, and Indians were frightened at the sight of native Fijians, who were tall men with a fine physique that reminded the Indians of savage people in Indian mythology.

Indentured laborers were required to work for a certain period of time, depending on their contract agreement. When their contracts were up, some decided to go back to India and some stayed in Fiji. Most of these indentured laborers were recruited from a lower caste system in Indian society. The caste system was a class structure determined by birth and family. In other words, if your parents are poor, then you'd be poor too. Since most indentured laborers were from the poorest level of their caste system, going back to India meant going back to still being part of that same system, which did not appeal to them. Also, most of them barely had enough money to go back. Although most of them stayed behind, some still decided to go back to India. One of the motives to do so was because Indians did not want to die in a foreign land.

Indians have been in Fiji for more than 100 years. Despite being in a foreign land, they ensured that some of their cultural practices were not completely lost. Today, Indians in Fiji still practice their religions such as Hinduism and Islam. With a long-standing presence in Fiji, Indians become the second largest group in the entire Fijian population.

This chapter focuses on some specific aspects of Fijian culture, community, family, practices, and identity. The case studies are from first- and second-year Sacramento State students forming a diverse group of six individuals from the Fijian community. Some are individuals who were born in Fiji and moved to the United States, while some were born in the United States and have not been to Fiji. The group consists of both a Native Fijian and Indo-Fijian perspective, each discussing briefly a small aspect of their experiences as a Fijian.

This map of Fiji pinpoints locations where the families of the students are either from, or were born in.

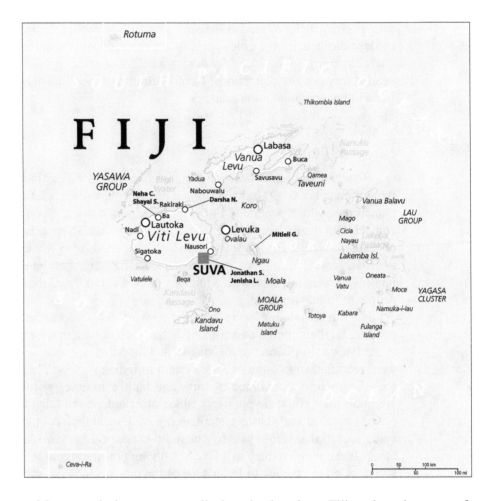

Most people have not actually heard a lot about Fiji, unless they are referring to its most famous product, Fiji Water. According to the 2010 U.S. Census, the population of Fijians living in the United States is around 32,000 and half of them are living in the state of California. The population of Fijians in the United States will continue to increase, and so will the demand for discussing the cultural heritage of Fijians not only within the communities they are in but also in most academic institutions.

Education and Discipline

(By Mitieli Rokolacadamu Gonemaituba)

I was born and raised in Fiji's capital city of *Suva*. Moving to the United States at age 15 in 2013 was a major change for me, especially the change in education. Most people would remember a time when they were both excited and scared to move from the eighth grade to the ninth. I felt the same way when I left high school to go to college. After graduating from Luther Burbank High School (LBHS) in Sacramento, California, I enrolled in Sacramento State (California State University, Sacramento [CSUS]). Now, I am a second-year student, pursuing a degree in construction management. It was in my first ever college semester in 2016 that I had my first Ethnic Studies class, ETHN 14. Introduction to Asian American Studies, where students would learn about basic aspects of the Asian American groups that are present in the United States today. Sitting in that class, students get to listen to Dr. Gregory Mark talk about Asian American history, and being mindful of the presence of some Pacific Islanders like myself in his class, he also included some information on Pacific Islanders in his curriculum. In this class, students get to learn about the many changes Asian and Pacific Islanders go through in American society. This played a part in my self-reflection on some changes I went through in the same society.

Mitieli Gonemaituba (right) and Veronica Bourke (left) after Mitieli's high school graduation from Luther Burbank High School, 2016, Sacramento, California.

Source: Kong Vang

One of the most significant changes that I was excited for was when I moved to the United States and entered high school. Everything was new, from the people to the class structure, to attitude and behavior, to fashion, and so on. Back in Fiji, the school system was structured differently and was closely similar to the British school systems. In colonial times, Fiji was colonized by the British. First

Mitieli Gonemaituba (center) and his friends, Martin Taylor (left) and Alfred Yaya (right). Stella Maris Primary School, Suva, Fiji, 2012.

Source: Mitieli Gonemaituba

to eighth grades were offered together in one school, usually called "primary school," and ninth to 12th grades in another, called "secondary school." I can still recall the time I had spent in school back in the islands, from kindergarten to ninth grade. School uniforms were a major part of it; it was the school's identity. Anyone could name the school a student went to simply by looking at the uniforms they wore. The strict rules as regards school uniforms instilled a strong sense of discipline in students. I remember wearing my white-and-gray Stella Maris Primary School uniform; our white shirt had to be tucked into our pants at all times, hair and nails had to be kept short and clean (girls had to braid their hair a certain style and were not allowed nail polish of any kind), only black sandals were allowed, and most importantly without exception, you could only come school wearing your uniform. Failing to do so would result in us being sent back home for the day. But that was not the same experience I had here in the United States. On my first day at Luther Burbank, I realized that I had never had to pick an outfit for school because with school uniforms, there were no choices. In addition to that, it was quite interesting to see some new styles that I had never seen in my life before, styles like "sagging," where a person's pants hung lower than their waistline. It was odd for me, but it was still interesting to see something new. Also, students had an extreme level of passion for their shoes. Brands like Nike were so adored and liked by my peers.

One of the changes that I experienced here in the United States, which I appreciated, was the fact that teachers were not allowed to physically hit the students as a form of punishment. In Fiji, there was little use for "detention," because when students did something wrong, they were just physically punished, like being hit on the hands with the teacher's yardstick. I remember a time in my second grade at Stella Maris where I was sent to the principal's office by my teacher, Ms. Williams, for quietly asking for my friend's eraser during a quiet writing time. When entering the principal's office, the first thing I saw was a belt hanging in the room, which he used to punish students who were called to his office, which is also what he used on me that unfortunate day. That kind of punishment in schools kept students on their best behavior, which is something I brought to the United States with me. During my time at Luther Burbank, I was never once written up for detention because I behaved well. I'd say it's because my time in Fiji really shaped me into a well-behaved student. I did what I was asked to do, turned in assignments on time, showed up early for school and class, and always tried to respect my teachers. It was really shocking to see how different that was during my time in high school. I saw students talk back to teachers, show up late for class, and saw students using their phones in class. Basically, I saw a lot of things that students did on a daily basis that would be highly prohibited in schools in Fiji. One of the things my friends do not understand is that the forms of discipline that was used in school was pretty much the same as the kind Fijian parents used at home. It is the norm for Fijian parents to be overly strict, and using physical discipline is not strange to nearly all Fijian children. Fijian parental skills may be harsh to some, but it is a way that Fijian parents ensure that their children are well behaved when they are not around, especially in school. A high priority for Fijian parents is their children's education, and molding them to be well behaved in school is a way to ensure their children's academic success. It sure has worked well for me. Being disciplined at home to behave well has made me into something of a good student, and that has pushed me to do good at school.

My experiences in Fijian schools are something I have in common with many parents of Fijian American students. In other words, if you have parents who were born and raised in Fiji, my experiences about school in the islands may be the similar to their own. Now, as I tell my friends stories of what it was like to go to school in Fiji, I enjoy seeing their faces express how much they would have disliked the experience that they would have gone through if they were me. Some of my Fijian American peers even changed how they felt about their parents' attitude toward their education. Some of them have come to understand that their parents are so strict on them with school, because the school system they went through back in Fiji was strict and challenging. Going through firm and strict discipline in school, parents of Fijian American students have implemented some of that discipline into their children's education. Even though they are from two different systems, I know some Fijian American students who say that their Fijian parents are strict about their education to the point where they should focus on nothing else but school. Perhaps, if they have gone through the same experience of school as their parents, they would understand why their parents feel that way. Looking back and remembering a day sitting in that ETHN 14 class, I learned that this experience of change that I went through is definitely not something that only I have gone through. Any person who moves somewhere new, particularly to a new country, will experience some form of change.

Our Indo-Fijian Roots

(By Neha Chand)

I am a graduate of LBHS, class of 2017 (one out of 14 high schools in the Sacramento City Unified School District). Currently, I am a first-year student at CSUS, and as for my major I am undecided. College is a time for self-exploration; therefore, at the beginning of the fall semester, I got the opportunity to take ETHN 14: Introduction to Asian American Studies. This Ethnic Studies course enabled me to explore college, because it strengthened skills such as critical thinking. Therefore, the course aided in going beyond course content, and it enabled the students to reflect on our personal connections to Asian Pacific Islander American history.

We learned about the narratives of the APA ethnic groups, and their experiences in America such as the creation of organizations, the labor-intensive occupations, and the strength to attain social and political rights in the United States. Relatively, in our Ethnic Studies course we were assigned to write a research paper on an APA ethnic group. We conducted research upon a factor we believed was important to an ethnic group we had selected. Some of the factors were in education, culture, and businesses, which reflected the sacrifices Asian Pacific Americans experienced to build a life in the United States. Through this assignment, I realized there is little to no research on Indo-Fijians. Therefore, the significance of this writing is to shed light upon the identity of the Indo-Fijians and their historical narrative in U.S. history.

During the late 1800s, the British colonizers wanted laborers that could work on the sugarcane plantations in Fiji. Therefore, the British recruited thousands of Indians that boarded the first ship that sailed to Fiji. The ship was called the Leonidas, which was a British-owned ship (V. Chand; D. Chand oral interview, January 4, 2018).

They were all told by the British that they would be paid a lot of money in Fiji. My great grandparents were among those on that ship. After the Leonidas departed India, the Indian passengers were told by the British sailors that the former are under the latter's control. In Fiji, the Indian workers worked in the hot sun as they tilled the land and planted sugarcane for a paltry pay. They were known as *Girmityas*, indentured laborers, and they had an agreement known as the *Girmit* (Pande, 2010, p. 58). The original 5-year agreement was extended for five more years. They were told they could return to India after the agreement ended (Pande, 2010, p. 58). However, the workers normally were unable to save enough money, and there was no means of transportation (D. Chand, oral interview, January 4, 2018).

The Indian workers were employed by the Colonial Sugar Refining Company (CSR) where they would plant and harvest sugarcane (V. Chand, oral interview, January 4, 2018). The company enjoyed a good profit and only a part of the share was given to the Indian workers (Pande,

Photo provided by Neha Chand

My parents and I going to a cultural gathering. My mom and I are wearing cultural clothes, October 2001, 24th Street, Florin Road.

2010, p. 58). For many, like my great-great-grandparents, it was difficult to rebuild their lives in a new country.

Indo-Fijians are of Indian ancestry but they were born in Fiji. The second and third generations (my great-grandparents and grandparents) were Indo-Fijians. My great-grandparents and grandparents adapted to the Fijian culture, while preserving their Indian heritage. Moreover, they helped their parents in sugar farming for the continuation of the business (V. Chand & D. Chand, oral interview, January 4, 2018).

I was born in Suva, Fiji. In 2000, there was a military coup in Fiji. The condition of the country was unstable due to racial tensions. Furthermore, for the safety and better opportunities such as in education and employment, my parents decided to move to the United States. It was difficult for my parents because they had to leave our family and begin a new life in the United States. My father told me they were homesick for about a year until they realized that this is it, "We are here for a brighter future and for me to have a better life" (V. Chand; D. Chand, oral interview, January 4, 2018).

Furthermore, I was 2 years old when I moved to the United States. Therefore, I adjusted to the American culture. Yet I grew up in a traditional home where we had a specific room that had statues of our deities. This room was a mini temple in our home where we could pray to our deities.

Moreover, my parents told me when they immigrated to California it was important that they found a Hindu temple, because in Fiji they went to temples. In order to continue our Indian culture in the United States, Hindu temples provide

Sri Siva Sumbramaniya Temple, Queens Road, Nadi, Fiji, 2001.

Source: Venay Chand

religious services for the Asian Indians, specifically the Indo-Fijian community. The services are organized by the Hindu temple founders and organizations. The religious programs, such as festivals, are held in the temples. For example, a main autumn celebration in the community is the 9-day festival to *Goddess Durga* known as *Navratri*. The statues of deities would be there to pray for prosperity. There would be Indian priests (*pandits*) or Indian teachers (*swamis*) who would narrate us the stories of our deities (V. Chand; D. Chand, oral interview, January 4, 2018). As a community, we would come together to celebrate this important religious holiday. Also, the temples helped my family develop networks in the Indo-Fijian community, because we did not have many close relatives living in Sacramento. This is how our community has strengthened and sustained our culture for future and younger generations in the United States.

To reflect on what it means to be a fifth-generation Indo-Fijian, who resides in the United States, brings a deeper meaning to my life. By going to temples, it allows me to understand rituals that our ancestors have passed down. An example of a ritual will be religious ceremonies where we offer fruits, sweets, flowers, and incense to the deities. Along with our ceremonies, we sing devotional songs as a way to show our gratitude to our deities. These religious practices create a strong sense of bonding with my culture. As I learn more about my origins it helps me connect to my family's history. When I have my own nuclear family in the future, I would like to go to the temples with them to learn more and embrace my beautiful culture.

Laxmi Narayan Mandir Temple, Elder Creek Road, Sacramento, California, 2018.
Source: Neha Chand

Through an Ethnic Studies course, I believe one will connect more to their ethnic identity by learning about historical narratives. The most important part is to see themselves being represented. One's representation can be seen by learning their ethnic group's history, as well as hearing other ethnic group's histories and seeing how they relate to one's family's experiences in the United States. Ultimately, all of our personal narratives would showcase how we are all apart of American history.

Arranged Marriages in the Indo-Fijian Community

Darsha Naidu

As a freshman at CSUS, I was granted with the opportunity to take an Ethnic Studies course titled ETHN 14. Introduction to Asian American Studies. I attended Monterey Trail High School in Elk Grove, which did not have an Ethnic Studies course, and I made use of the opportunity to take it in college. Even though this was a course requirement through the Full Circle Project, an organization that focuses on Asian American and Pacific Islanders achieving higher education, I found it to be a great course with a lot of fascinating topics. In this course, I learned about the history of different Asian American groups and the sacrifices made by them to make a living in the United States such as discrimination based on ethnicity. Being Asian American, my family can relate to the struggles of other Asian Americans. During this course, I found it interesting that there is little to no information published regarding Indo-Fijian heritage. This gave me the motivation to write about my family's history and background.

According to my parents, my maternal great-grandfather, Mr. Dhalbal Prakash, was born in one of the ships used to transport laborers from India to Fiji. Indian arranged marriages originated from the period when vedas, or large texts that contained sacred knowledge about the Indian teachings, rituals, and beliefs, were being chanted. During that time, nobody questioned the idea of arranged marriages. Since cultural rituals are still practiced, most arranged marriages happen based on how much money your family has or if your family is respectable in the eyes of the society, which is why the main purpose of arranged marriages was to keep the traditional and cultural beliefs alive while creating a family.

My great-grandfather's family stayed in Nasouri, Fiji, and had a huge influence on the village named Vuci since he was a prominent leader there. When migrating from India to Fiji, arranged marriages were one of the traditions still held by the Indians. The tradition of arranged marriages was adopted from old religious scriptures and continued to be practiced in the Indo-Fijian community. My great-grandfather wedded into an arranged marriage with my great grandmother, Chand Kaur, who was the daughter of another leader of a village in Nasouri. This arranged marriage took place when she was only 5 years old since getting married at an early age was then considered appropriate. When she turned 13, she was sent with her in-laws since it was believed she was mature enough to start having kids now. Thus, when my great-grandparents had an arranged marriage, all the rituals that were followed in India were followed in Fiji.

As times changed, some rituals were slowly being taken out of Indo-Fijian practice because the new generation of Indo-Fijians wanted more control of their lives and wanted to branch out of the traditional Indian practice. For example, one ritual practiced before an arranged marriage in Fiji was before getting betrothed, the bride and groom would exchange photos. If they approve each other, the groom side of the family was supposed to come visit the bride's family and tell her that she was reserved for that guy. However, in the United States, this ritual that is part of arranged marriages has died out. Most potential brides and grooms know a little about each other before getting married. Since the United States is a diverse place, most immigrant Indo-Fijian families encourage kids to socialize with other Indo-Fijians kids. Parents, in other words, start looking for suitable mates for their children at an early age. Indo-Fijian families want their children to befriend other Indo-Fijian children at Indian weddings and religious events. In arranged marriages, divorce tends to be rare. That's because both partners have respect for each other's traditions and families.

Looking at the Indo-Fijian community in the United States, my parents have taught me a lot about my culture and the traditions we follow. Even in the United States, I wear my traditional Indian clothes and jewelry to represent my Indo-Fijian roots. Both of my parents were born in Fiji, and in 1999, they immigrated to the United States. My mother was carrying me at the time and they wanted a better life for me, which is why they came to the United States. Growing up in a diverse area, my parents made sure that the Western culture didn't influence our family customs by teaching us about holy texts and religious songs where the concept of arranged marriages appeared from. Even though certain rituals of arranged marriages have changed over time, I hope to continue this tradition in the United States. Now, it is up to the future generation of Indo-Fijians to keep the tradition going. Having this community would help the younger and future generations learn about our family traditions. I hope that through the Ethnic Studies course, one can connect with their ethnic identity and learn about the struggles faced by many Asian American groups.

The Dance and Music of Fiji

(By Jenisha Lal)

All my life, I have always been asked, "How are you Indian but from Fiji? I thought that you were Indian from India. How did you end up in Fiji?" Answering repetitively a multitude of people throughout my childhood frustrated me. As a student from Florin High, one of the nine high schools in Elk Grove, I was exposed to many different cultures. However, it was not until I was in college in my first semester at CSUS that I realized I shared my frustrations with other students with similar backgrounds as mine. I took the Ethnic Studies course: Introduction to Asian American Studies (ETHN 14) and realized that there was a lot of things untold about Indo-Fijians and Native Fijians in mainstream literature. For most people, Fiji is a tropical getaway—a vacation from work and stress. While many indulge in the tropical energy that Fiji has to offer, many do not know the country's history or traditions.

Some traditions that are important in the Indo-Fijian culture are music and dance. Music and dance is said to be a universal language, that is, one does not need to understand another's language or customs to interact with it. It can be a very powerful unifying force. Through music and dance, Indians and Native Fijians were able to cross-culture and accept each other's culture, forming a new ethnicity of its own known as Indo-Fijians.

Coming from India

When the *Grimit* or *"Girmityas* (indentured Indian laborers) came from Lucknow, Uttar Pradesh, India, to the country of Fiji, they brought their music and dance along with them. The type of music that Indians brought with them was folk songs steeped in mythology. Indians also brought along some of their traditional dances styles to Fiji. Although many people consider Bollywood as a new phenomenon, they hardly realize it is the Indian film industry that is being dubbed so. Most of the dances in Bollywood have been inspired from classical Indian dance forms.

While in Fiji

Ever since Bollywood was introduced to the Native Fijians, it has influenced the society in terms of music and dance, making Bollywood a crucial aspect of Indo-Fijian culture. Over time, Indo-Fijians and Native Fijians cross-cultured for generations by sharing their traditions or styles with each other. For example, Native Fijian influences such as reggae style music and traditional dances have added to how Indians celebrate music and dance. This fusion, Indo-Fijian genre, was different compared to the genres attributed to Indians who were from India.

Examples of the "Fusion"

A bhajan, according to *The Garland Encyclopedia of World Music: South Asia: The Indian Subcontinent* (2000) by Alison Arnold and Bruno Nettl, is "an informal, loosely organized devotional music . . . probably one of the ubiquitous genres of Indian religious music." Indo-Fijians have carried bhajans with them to Fiji; it served as one of the best ways to express their devotion to God through music. However, in order to play this music certain instruments were needed. One particular instrument was the dholak, otherwise known as a "cylindrical drum," one of the major instruments used in Indian music, which is played by percussing the sides of the drum while in a sitting position. In addition to creating music, the dholak is also used as a metronome as it helps dancers to time their choreography. As the person creates the beats, the dancer would have to listen and recognize patterns and dance according to the beats.

Jus as the Indians introduced bhajans and dholaks, so too the Native Fijians introduced their music and traditional dances to the Indians as well. One Fijian dance in particular that is well known is the *meke*, which "is the traditional style of dance, which is a combination of dance and storytelling through song. Both men and women perform in the *Meke*, and the dance is viewed as a group collaboration in which men are expected to demonstrate strong, virile movements, whereas women are expected to be graceful and feminine." In addition to the music and dance, many Indo-Fijians adopted the afro hairstyle that was common among Native Fijians when they performed their traditional dances (M. Lal, oral interview, January 17, 2018).

Closer to Home

Sadly, not much is known about Indo-Fijians or Fijians' music and dances in the United States. However, Brigham Young University (BYU, Hawaii) has a Polynesian Cultural Center where many cultural dances and traditions of Fiji as well as many other islands are displayed. In fact, my father was offered admission to BYU and took a job as a part-time dancer and performed many Fijian dances with other students of Indo-Fijian or Fijian descent. But closer to home in California, there are annual Fiji Festivals that take place at Cosumnes River College in Sacramento. The lack of Indo-Fijian representation in extant literature has to be addressed so that more people would know about the rich and unique culture of Fiji. My Indo-Fijian friends and family have expressed their displeasure of having to constantly tell others about their background. We grew up learning very little about Fiji's history from textbooks; it was reduced to a footnote when there had been a whole population of Indo-Fijians that lived in America not knowing whether to identify ourselves as Indians or Pacific Islanders.

ETHN 14 is an important course because not everyone knows how important their culture or heritage is until they learn about their ancestors' struggles and their journey. The course is a stepping-stone toward addressing the lack of literature on Indo-Fijians and their heritage, and being born in Hayward, United States, for parents who were born and raised in Suva, Fiji, I have been lucky to have the opportunity to learn more about my Indo-Fijian culture through Ethnic Studies.

Fiji Food

(By Jonathan Singh)

Fijian food refers to the combined cuisine of Native Fijian and migrant Indian communities, each contributing a variety of foods with distinct flavors. During my childhood, the restaurants in the Sacramento area did not meet my requirements and therefore did not excite me. My mother's cooking would always cheer me up even when I was feeling down, as it was unique and delicious. She would always cook whenever she had free time, usually on the weekends. My favorite dish was lamb curry with cassava and dalo, and this was an interesting dish because it combined aspects from more than one cuisine. Growing in a family that not only uses food as a way to communicate but a reason for bringing people together, I was grateful for the life I was blessed with where food can be a catalyst for family emotions.

Being the first person in my family to attend college meant that not only did I successfully complete my high school stage senior year, but it was also a testament of the enormous support I had received from my loved ones. I graduated from Monterey Trail High School, which is in the Elk Grove Unified School District, in 2016 and then attended Sacramento State. I am currently a sophomore and, my ETHN 14: Introduction to Asian American Studies class really made me to be more intrigued about my heritage. Professor Mark created a space where you actually felt proud of knowing about your ancestry, and the class was designed to appreciate Asian Americans and Pacific Islanders and seeing my ethnicity discussed really made me feel special.

Class discussions were like a family discussion in a community of people who valued their ancestry and were curious to find out more about themselves. My Fijian heritage was something that honestly never piqued my interest prior to the class, as to me it seemed like the past was exactly that and I already knew who I was and what I was all about. Regardless of what I had thought, more information and discovery about my family's ethnicity made me to appreciate my life more.

I was born in 1997 in the island of Fiji, in the capital city known as Suva, where I lived with my mom, with our relatives living down the street; this close community created a strong bonding that was built upon family. With Fiji being a small nation, my mom and our relatives knew people that I had not even known existed; even when they had just met a person, they would somehow end up being part of the family. My family moved to the United States as a result of chain migration, following my first-generation relatives who had already been living there. I realized that food was the magic key to bring people together.

The celebrations that brought all of us together did not change even after my migration to the United States when I was 5 years old. It was quite a journey for me to travel to another country as a kid. I have to thank all my family members because it was a team effort driven by love to make sure everyone is together again. Not only did my palate for food increased culturally Influenced by my mom and step-dad,, but I was also able to see another point of view when visiting my dad's side of the family, which was Scottish and Irish. The way food was celebrated there was amazing and on a grander scale, with traditional American foods such as Thanksgiving turkey and macaroni casserole. Spices from different parts of the world, including oregano and cayenne pepper, would be variously mixed. To be

The removal of the banana leaves and tin foil (a substitute for coconut leaves), the final step in preparing *lovo*. Sacramento, California (2014).

completely honest, there were never really any Fijian restaurants in the city that could match my mother's cooking.

A thing that is characteristic of Fijian food is the traditional *lovo* (pronounced Low-vo), an underground oven setup where meat is cooked. A similar underground oven is also used for cooking in other communities; for example, in Hawaii it is called imu (pronounced E-moo), in Samoa it is called the *umu* (pronounced Ooh-moo), and the Maori call it the hangi (pronounced Han-gee), the Rotumans call it a *koua* (pronounced k-O-wa). No matter how it is called, it is an amazing way of cooking. In the islands of Fiji, meat is priced higher than that in the United States. Many Fijians in Sacramento like lamb, chicken, and pork and would purchase all from the local Fijian supermarket; my go-to place would be Fiji Mart down Del Paso Road, which is easier to access for purchase. Fiji's meat industry can be traced back to the colonization of Fiji by early Europeans around the 1860s. The settlement soon evolved into a society composed of New Zealand and Australia. New Zealand brought in a number of imports other than meat items, ranging from tea to chocolates as well. One can buy meat sourced from different places: one option is to purchase fresh lamb that was produced locally, usually from a farm that somebody who works at the store owns. The second option would be to purchase lamb imported from another country such as New Zealand. My mother uses a lot of spice in her cooking; when we were in Fiji these spices were imported from India. Spices add flavor to foods and I have tried my fair share of them thanks to my mother's amazing cooking skills. The *lovo* is also meant to make the meat more flavorful. Preparing and marinating the meat, followed by covering it with tin foil and banana leaves, makes the food twice as good, also ensuring a sense of cultural appreciation. Not only does *lovo* cooking impart a unique taste, but it also requires more than one person to help prepare the food, thus bringing more family members to work together. Banana leaves are used to cover the food as a final layer of protection against dirt; it also serves as an inner heating vent and imparts a unique smokehouse flavor. Digging the pit and setting it up takes the same amount of time as cooking the food and as such, a *lovo* is reserved for important events.

Food is the very idea that can bring people with their own individual lives and dilemmas together and let them have all their worries melt away for a brief moment. As the fire cooks the meal, the burning embers create everlasting bonds among the people.

Our Time is Now

(By Shayal Sharma)

I am a freshman at CSUS and I am majoring in health sciences. I graduated from LBHS in 2017. I am currently part of the Full Circle Project, which is a program at Sacramento State that increases the graduation rate for students from the Asian American and Pacific Islander community. It comes with several leadership opportunities, academic support, and all that good stuff. We are like our own little community within the school, and we had to take two classes in the fall semester of 2017 for that program, which fulfilled our General Education requirement. I was placed in a course about the history of Asian Pacific Americans taught by Professor Mark, through which I realized I'm part of something I am learning, which, indeed, sparked my interest.

Since I was fascinated with the material, it made me feel like I was finally included in a class curriculum, considering my family's previous generations lived during those old times. I instantly think of my parents when I hear the word "migration" because they migrated to America in 1991. My parents were one of those people searching for better opportunities and thus came to the land of freedom. They always emphasize on how they wanted a better future for us, their kids. The class was conducted by the Department of Ethnic Studies and my professor explained the significance of the Ethnic Studies movement, especially how it had played a major role in social justice within the community thus far. In the 1980s and 1990s, Fijian families left Fiji due to the British military taking over the government and built their lives here in the United States. In fact, my parents and my whole family fits into that category and they always reminisce about the times when they first came to the United States. The Ethnic Studies class taught by Professor Mark also expanded my knowledge of the past of what Asian Pacific Americans had to go through to get to where they are now. As a result, Fijians and people of different origins are living today in the United States and our voices need to be heard. Broadening the curriculum toward it is relevant more than ever because after everything that has happened in the past, education has led up to the point where we are today, including why we are here this very moment.

For my Ethnic Studies class, the assignment was to write a research paper about the significance of something that was a key contributor to a specific ethnic group, so I chose to write about my own people, Indo-Fijians. As I was writing my research paper about Indo-Fijians, I had questions about my own family roots and began to reflect on that. Who is an Indo-Fijian? It is a person who is of Indian descent, but born in Fiji. They can be referred to as Fijians or even Indo-Fijians as well. Why were there so many Indians in Fiji? There were thousands of Indians who left India for Fiji to work as indentured laborers. In fact, my great-grandparents, Rav Rattan and Chandmati Rattan, were indentured laborers who came on one of the ships to Fiji. They went to Fiji to work on sugarcane plantations. Then my grand-parents, Shanti Prasad and Dhayan Prasad, were born in 1929 and then later my parents, Shashi and Hirendra Sharma, were born in 1966.

Furthermore, my Ethnic Studies research paper concentrated on how the dom-inant group in the taxi industry in the early 2000s in Sacramento was mostly Fi-jians, meaning that it greatly contributed to the success of those families. I was a part of one of those families because my dad became a taxi driver in 2004, so I understand how it plays a key role in Fijian households sustaining a livelihood. My dad, Rakesh Sharma, claimed that 80% of the drivers in his company were Fijians. Based on my experiences, I made an inference that the taxi industry was the primary source of income for Fijian immigrants because it was not that easy getting a job being a minority and new to the country. My research paper was writ-ten from my dad's perspective because of his reasons of becoming an independent taxi driver, so he was my key informant. I learned how he survived in this country financially while being part of a minority group, which was by driving his taxi cab. He was an independent driver and told me that there were several of immigrants driving taxi to make a living during that period, especially people from Fiji.

Although, I had another key informant who is a current taxi driver, Mr. Ajit Chandra. In fact, my dad and he know each other through the taxi company. Mr. Ajit has been driving taxi for 12 years and is still working. I had an interview with him regarding how the taxi company served as a stable source of income and how it helped to provide for his family. He is an independent taxi driver just like my dad was, meaning that he decides his own hours so that it is up to him to decide a day's income. The taxi industry was, indeed, a contributor to his household, considering that he drives daily and as much as he possibly can. He kept talking about how the flexibility in work hours was a key factor and a major reason he chose that job. He has time to take care of his kids, such as dropping them off at school and cook-ing, or doing things around the house. He has had some good days and some bad depending on how much work he gets in a day. He picks his own hours, although high demand is what really controls his income. The industry has helped him and his family attain financial stability.

He said that if it wasn't for his job then he wouldn't not have known what to do to support his family. Money is needed to live a decent life in the United States. There were and are many immigrants in the same boat as him, such as my dad, who were employed by the taxi company to make a living to support their families. There were and are people of all colors who relied on the taxi industry for a steady source of income. A large number of families have been supported financially by the taxi company; I fall under that category.

He also confirmed that there are six taxi associations and as of now he claims that the taxi industry is culturally diverse. He also added that there are all types of people such as Indians, Fijians, Arabs, Pakistanis, Polynesians, Asians, and African Americans. For instance, the company he is working for is called "Island Star Cab Co." and the dominant group of employees in the company is Fijians. In fact, his uncle had come up with that name 20 years ago. He is from Fiji as well and he wanted to represent his pride, so that name seemed like the perfect fit to him. There are plenty of families that are being sustained with the help of the taxi company and even I am a part of such a family. It is important to realize that there is not too many of us, Fijians, but we still contribute to the community and want to be acknowledged.

Also, while working on my Ethnic Studies paper, it caught my attention that there was hardly any scholarly literature available on Fiji Indians. There was nothing about Fijians or Indians driving cabs, which is ironic because a majority of my dad's side of the family and friends drove taxi to earn a living to provide for their households. Even in the textbook that we had to read in class, there was just a section that mentioned something about Indians, but not much. After learning that we Fijians are understudied, I felt that it needs to change. We must broaden the curriculum for it to be inclusive of the APA community. When young students learn about their ethnicity and their heritage, it does have the ability to empower them to be the change they wish to see in the world.

Conclusion

To have Ethnic Studies a part of the curriculum has high significance because young students can learn things they never knew before about themselves and could feel included in American history. For instance, some students could finally relate to what is being taught and see people of their ethnicity getting some type of recognition. When you shed light upon some facts about being a minority, then it has the ability to affect social justice for all. Also, people should know their roots in general and be prideful of the same. Ethnic Studies can empower students to be the change and be inspired, which would definitely have a positive impact. People would start to question things like the continuity of race and racism. In addition, they would realize things they never knew before, which would lead to them learning more about their cultural identities.

Before we took the Ethnic Studies class, we had not really taken the fact of our ethnicities being understudied and poorly represented in literature, both textbooks and scholarly, personal, but now it is time for a change. We still are a part of this community and should be acknowledged. This chapter has the potential

Photo by Ann Thomas.

The group that wrote this chapter. From left to right (behind the flag).
Mitieli Gonemaituba, Jenisha Lal, Jonathan Singh, Darsha Naidu,
and Dr. Gregory Yee Mark. From left to right (in front of the flag).
Neha Chand and Shayal Sharma.

to have our voices heard. The significance and struggles of our ethnicities should
be included in history textbooks because we existed at any particular period. We
always get the short end of the stick, even in the schooling system, which is unfair.
There are more than just five races in the world and now is the time to broaden the
curriculum to create change. We always have to come together to fight for what we
believe in—in other words, form coalitions to push for change and if that is what
it takes then that is what we will do.

Minorities have voices that need to be heard because we are also the people
who build up this community. Being inspired by their past can also influence them
to become political activists, which can legally push to create change. We have all
been taught that everything that is written in black and white is the most important. We have the power to push for change because we are meant to evolve. This
chapter serves as a starting point for that endeavor to read about ethnic minorities
in our history books, which will have an impact on us as a whole. Ethnic Studies
as a discipline represents an opportunity to show the significance of social justice
and people of color, which would build a stronger community because it would be
more inclusive. We hope this chapter would lead to more research on Fijian ethnic
communities as regards health, education, employment, and so on.

Reflection Questions

1. What do these readings reveal about what it means to be a woman and woman of color? (Optional)

2. What are the similarities and differences between each of the readings? (Optional)

3. Some of the authors shared their early childhood memories related to womanhood. Do you have any early childhood memories that brought awareness about what it meant to be a woman or how women are viewed? Please offer a brief explanation using two examples to illustrate your point.

4. What are the social, political, and economic systems that frame the experience and identity of being a woman of color? (Optional)

5. In what ways did the readings extend or enrich your understanding regarding being a woman of color in the United States? Please offer a brief explanation using two examples to illustrate your point.

Identity and Institutions

Framing Questions

1. What do you think is the relationship between identity and institutions? (Optional)

2. In what ways, can you apply the theme of identity and institutions? What are the institutions that shape your identity?

3. Are the practices of institutions always visible when they shape our identity? If not, why would some practices be visible and others live out their existence in a covert manner?

4. In your own life, if you participate in more than one institution which institution impacts your life the most? Has this changed over time? (Optional)

Introduction

Brian Baker

This section includes selected readings that address themes and issues related to the relationship between *identity* and *institutions*. While this book itself has been divided into five sections, it is necessary to emphasize the fact that any discussion or understanding of *identity* and *institutions* in reality cannot and should not be viewed as being distinct from the "perspectives" and "history" sections. The readings so far should serve as a basis for understanding the processes and circumstances that influence how racial and ethnic groups come to define and understand their identities over time, where adaptions and changes are made through the process of "racial formation" as a strategy to either reflect or contradict the political, cultural, and social institutions of American society.

What is identity? Does the identity held by a racial-ethnic group remain the same over time or does it change? To what extent do larger social, political, and cultural circumstances foster a transformation in racial-ethnic identity? Identity has to do with processes and circumstances that are both internal and external to a specific group, and how a group will define itself on its own terms as well as how it is also defined by another group. A common theme of the readings in this section has to do with how identity as a process is connected to social institutions, such as law, politics, education, and even the media as popular and public culture. More importantly, many of the readings are rooted somewhere in a perspective relating to *institutional discrimination* as "the denial of opportunities and equal rights to individuals and groups that results from the normal operations of society."[1] In terms of the normal workings of society, racial and ethnic minorities as powerless groups exist in a variety of situations where the dominant society imposes its values and ideas in ways that have powerful and overwhelming effects on a group and how it manages to maintain its identity. At other times, given the structures of society, racial and ethnic minority groups pursue active strategies to assert or reclaim their identity as a process counter to assimilation.

This section begins with "Kill the Indian, Save the Child" by Debra Barker. The purpose of this article is to provide you with an awareness concerning the role of education in the cultural assimilation of American Indian children in the late 19th and early 20th centuries. The American government designed the *Indian boarding school* as an institution to inflict a program of forced assimilation on American Indian children. The fact that this educational program was founded on the ethnocentric philosophical principle *kill the Indian* is very telling due to the fact that Indian children were removed from their families and communities, and once under the control of the boarding school as a total institution, children were stripped of their racial-ethnic identities. In the process of learning how to read and write, Indian children were severely punished for doing anything associated with being Indian. Stories about violence and abuse experienced by American Indians are still remembered and told today, and Barker argues that the main purpose of the Indian boarding school as an institution had little to do with education and more to do with a program of *cultural genocide* implemented toward American Indians by the American government.

Julie López Figueroa examines the problem of American history as a master narrative that has functioned to omit the lived experiences of racial and ethnic minorities in "My Father's Labor." With a special focus on her father, Macedonio Figueroa, she presents an intimate and personal view of the "Bracero program" initiated by the American government that facilitated the movement of laborers from Mexico across the border to work in the United States beginning in the 1940s and ending in the 1960s. In terms of her own lived experience, she reflects on how she learned an American history in high school that only had a "minimal representation of Mexican or Mexican American people." A major problem of bias in the teaching of American history has been one where strategic and limited reference to Mexican Americans, Asian Americans, Africans Americans, and Native Americans were included to the extent that the master narrative was validated. Although she felt "alienated and villainized" it was her father who strategically planted the seeds necessary for an alternative view of history when he showed her his Bracero identification card. In 1954, at the age of 20, Macedonio Figueroa came to the United States as a Bracero, who eventually became a U.S. citizen in 1964. Her father's story "transformed and inspired" her, and she continued to grow this alternative view as a central component of undergraduate and graduate education. With his story, Macedonio Figueroa planted a seed the grew and expanded her worldview, and she continued to cultivate and nurture this perspective and she is now a professor of Latinx and Chicanx studies and Ethnic Studies.

In "Imaginary Indians" Brian Baker presents an overview of stereotypes as strategic inventions central to constructing and relegating American Indians to the status of *the other* in American society. The cultural inventions and ideas created in public and popular culture have been so powerful and effectively institutionalized that American Indians continue to experience what they view as obvious forms of institutional discrimination. Yet, given the workings of society's social institutions, which have normalized racism towards American Indians, Americans in general either refuse or possess the inability to acknowledge this fact. Baker discusses many aspects of popular and public culture, including the inventions of Indians as *children* who *roamed* over the land prone to being *wild* and *dancing* savages with an inherent ability to be *warriors.* All of these ideas have been effectively imposed over and associated with Indians, and given a complex system of institutionalized discrimination, not only have American Indians been relegated to the status of mascots in the world of American sports, the very racist notion of *redskin* has been nomalized as not being offensive.

Rita Cameron Wedding develops an approach for us to critically evaluate problems related to racialized discrimination at the individual and institutional levels in her article "Implicit Bias." She identifies such factors as colorblindness and microaggressions in addition to implicit bias as the "tools of modern racism" that function to "preserve and obscure racial inequalities." Unlike conventional definitions and approaches to systemic racism, Cameron Wedding highlights the "critical role of individual decision-makers" in sustaining "systemic racism." In extending her definition of systemic racism and developing her argument about the role of implicit bias, Cameron Wedding incorporates the importance of seeing and understanding the world through an "anti-racist" lens by referencing the work of Ibram X. Kendi, who argues that "anti-racist" rather than "not racist" is the opposite of "racist." To articulate the powerful and nuanced ways in which systemic racism works in the contemporary world, Cameron Wedding also draws from *The New Jim Crow* by Michelle Alexander. Central to Cameron Wedding's argument is the role "implicit bias" plays in systemic racism in the contemporary period. In general, people need to be aware of "attitudes or stereotypes that are outside our awareness and affect our understanding, our interactions, and our decisions." Within institutions such as the criminal justice or education, it is especially important that decision makers need to be aware of their implicit bias to change systemic racism.

This section on "Identity and Institutions" concludes with "And It's Time for Them to Come Down" by Rose Soza War Soldier. In terms of an American history that articulates a master narrative, figures like Father Junipero Serra and John Sutter are celebrated for their role in making California. Father Serra was the founder a network of missions established at 21 locations from San Diego to Sonoma with the purpose of converting Native people to Christianity. The mission system was a powerful institution tied to Spanish colonialism, having a negative impact on Native culture due to its oppressive nature, forcing Native people into slavery and prostitution. War Soldier points out that California Indians were seen as being "soulless" and were therefore in need of missionization. John Sutter was an entrepreneur who relied on Indian laborers to build Fort Sutter, which was completed in 1841. Sutter relied on slave labor and created a system dependent on the brutal treatment of Indian laborers, even forcing girls into prostitution. Following the gold rush, the foundation for a system of genocide supported by the state of California was in place, and many instances of genocide followed, especially around the time of the Gold Rush. Sutter and Serra are celebrated and memorialized throughout California in the form of statues, which are viewed as monuments to racism and genocide. Amid a period when larger symbols of racism are being called into question, War Soldier focuses her discussion on the removal of Serra and Sutter statues, which can be seen as a change or shift in the institutional landscape and master narrative of California history. War Soldier writes that "The physical manifestation of looming symbols of imperialism, genocide, and colonization is no longer being whole-heartedly embraced and celebrated."

All of the readings in this section are included to prompt students to critically examine the relationship between institutions and identity, and to understand how identity is a complex process that is central to race and ethnicity. Through time, and in various ways, racial-ethnic groups have had to struggle with identity especially in terms of powerful institutions which have attempted to alter or erase their identity, as in the case of the Indian boarding schools and cultural genocide, or within those institutions in which they are immersed where they either assert or alter some aspect of their identity. All of the readings in the section speak to the importance of identity, and at both the level of the individual and group, people attempt to protect or refashion their identities in terms of how they are immersed in the social, political, and cultural institutions of society.

Notes

[1] Quoted from *Racial and Ethnic Groups* (9th ed.), Richard T. Schaefer, page 77 (Pearson/Prentice Hall, 2004). See chapter titled "Discrimination" (pages 72–102).

[2] Michael Omi and Howard Winant, *Racial Formations in the United States*. New York: Routeledge. 1994.

Kill the Indian, Save the Child: Cultural Genocide and the Boarding School

Debra K. S. Barker

> *You, who are wise must know that different Nations have different Conceptions of things and you will therefore not take it amiss, if our Ideas of this kind of Education happen not to be the same as yours.*
>
> —Canassatego,
> Leader of the Six Nations,
> Lancaster, Pennsylvania, 1744

If you are familiar with the centrality of the oral tradition within American Indian cultures, you will understand how carefully we listen to the stories of our parents and relatives. As they tell us stories about their lives, they bequeath to us a living text of memory to help us structure our understanding of who we are and how we fit into the larger, more encompassing story of our tribe and culture. You will understand, also, that an integral part of the oral tradition is the voices of those offering testimony from their wisdom and experience.

The voices and testimony that follow speak to the family stories a good number of us have heard from our parents, grandparents, and elders; especially, they recall the story of their unwilling participation in the federal government's effort to re-educate on a massive scale thousands of American Indian children. Of course, education is valuable and empowering. Of course, education—in its most positive aspect—can afford all of us the skills and knowledge to help us realize whatever type of success we can imagine, whether we are talking about a conventional

Western education or an education grounded in traditional, tribal ways. The key is that the education be undertaken with respect for the dignity of the students and be designed to empower them, not to diminish them. The process of education that I will be discussing here is one that has emotionally and spiritually devastated generations of American Indian people, setting in motion a concatenation of repercussions, including cultural genocide and generations of family pain.

In recent years documentaries and studies on Indian history only briefly touch on the boarding school system, contextualizing it with a host of other oppressive measures taken by the federal government to destroy the cultures of the people who stood in the way of progress. With one exception, however, studies have relied less on the testimony of Indian witnesses than on the published research of white historians. Indian voices, for the most part, have gone unheard. Given the fact that in the last century Indian education became a national political issue, involving Congress, the War Department, and the Department of the Interior, I wanted to counterpoint Native voices with those of the politicians and policymakers whose philosophical positions and decisions so profoundly affected the lives of our ancestors.

Like so many other experiments and policies implemented by the federal government during the past few hundred years in its attempt to deal with "the Indian problem," the boarding school system ultimately did more harm than good. Understanding the point, Fuchs and Havighurst assert that this federal policy, "rooted in forced assimilation, paradoxically grounded in white humanitarianism . . . left a legacy of unpleasant memories that affect attitudes and policies today" (225). This legacy bequeathed more than simply "unpleasant memories" for generations to come, however. Although it appeared to be the solution the federal government had sought to the Indian problem, it became an instrument that emotionally scarred generations of innocent children, leaving them and their children, as well, victims of institutionalized cultural genocide.

If one were to ask those people who endured, fled, or simply survived boarding school about their memories of their teachers and their education, one might hear some surprising answers. John Lame Deer, a Lakota medicine man, relates in his 1972 autobiography that the Catholic mission boarding school he attended on the Rosebud reservation in South Dakota was run like a prison. My own Aunt Margaret, who attended the same school, loved the bread the students made in the bakery and enjoyed the Saturday night movies, especially *King Kong*. Feeling persecuted by the nuns, however, dreading their unceasing unkindness, she made a successful escape to Aunt Mary Cordier's house in St. Francis, never returning to earn her diploma. My mother, an alumna of 1952, also felt quite bitter about her experiences. She recalled constant hunger, incidents of physical abuse, and traumatic public humiliations for even minor infractions of rules. A particularly vivid memory she shared with me was that of one of the youngest girls at school being punished for wetting her bed. Determined to teach her a lesson, one of the nuns wrapped the child up in her wet sheets and threw her down the outdoor fire escape tunnel. Years later, my mother would still recall the child's terrified screams.

In her 1990 autobiography, *Lakota Woman,* Mary Crow Dog compares children who survived Indian boarding schools to "victims of Nazi concentration camps trying to tell average, middle-class Americans what their experience had been like" (28). As a child, I listened to my mother's stories of her own bleak, joyless childhood. Feeling helpless to comfort her, I could not even comprehend what it must have been like to be without one's family and utterly powerless in the hands of a group of people committed to not only controlling one completely, but also to erasing one's personal and tribal identity. Mary Crow Dog is indeed correct in her analogy.

Extermination by Civilization: Some American History

Indian education in America had been undertaken initially during the colonial period. One of the more successful efforts was that of the Society for Propagation of the Gospel in New England, a London organization which funded the establishment of an Indian college at Harvard during the 1650s. This group also underwrote the expense of books and of Bibles translated into Algonquian, as well as ministers and teachers to convert and educate the "heathen." Yet, as historian Christine Bolt points out, the Native-peoples "were able to educate the whites in the ways of the wilderness without making comparable demands on them and preferred the newcomers' material goods to their culture" (210). Later, in 1701, another English missionary organization, the Society for the Propagation of the Gospel in Foreign Parts, established 170 missions in the colonies (210), inciting a tide of missionization and education that gained momentum as the numbers of Euramericans grew and encroached relentlessly upon Indian land. Even as early as 1744, however, tribal leaders recognized that the curricula and objectives of a Euramerican education were irrelevant to the Indian graduates returning home. Furthermore, colonial educational practices compromised graduates' chances of even surviving in their native environment. Respectfully declining the Euramericans' request to inculcate any more of their young people, the sachems of the Iroquois Confederacy explained:

> *Several of our young people were formerly brought up at the colleges of the Northern Provinces; they were instructed in all your science; but when they came back to us, they were bad runners; ignorant of every means of living in the woods; unable to bear either cold or hunger; knew neither how to build a cabin, take a deer, or kill an enemy; spoke our language imperfectly; were therefore neither fit for hunters, warriors, or counselors; they were totally good for nothing. We are, however, not the less obliged by your kind offer, though we decline accepting it; and to show our grateful sense of it, if the gentlemen of Virginia will send us a dozen of their sons, we will take great care of their education, instruct them in all we know, and make men of them. (Qtd. in Franklin 98)*

Bolt supports the chiefs' objections and suggests yet another reason why a Euramerican education afforded Indians little benefit in the white world: "Patronized and coerced, required to undertake irksome and sometimes unintelligible tasks and finally offered no secure place in the white world if they wanted, the lot of the small number of educated Indians was an unenviable one" (211).

The federal government and the American public as a whole registered ambivalence when it came to solutions to the Indian problem. In 1792, Benjamin Lincoln, politician and former Revolutionary War general, expressed his hope that Indians would be treated fairly and humanely. Nevertheless, he called for a plan to defoliate the land, thus starving out the "beasts of the forest upon which the uncivilized principally depend for support" (qtd. in Pearce 68). The Trail of Tears, which followed as a result of President Andrew Jackson's deliberate enforcement of the unconstitutional Indian Removal Act of 1830, evoked sympathy among many of those who learned of the death march that claimed thousands of Indian lives as they walked the thousand miles between their homes in the Southeast and Oklahoma. Ironically, the tribes immediately involved, the Five Civilized Tribes, were friendly and "civilized" by Euramerican standards. The Cherokee, for instance, had established their own schools for their children and were printing books and a newspaper in their own language. According to Fuchs and Havighurst, the Choctaw, another of the "Civilized" tribes, had established "a comprehensive school system of their own with twelve schoolhouses and non-Indian teachers, supported by tribal, missionary, and federal funds" (223).

Yet another factor that inflamed public sentiment regarding "the Indian problem" was the phenomenal popularity of the captivity narrative. This was a genre of popular literature which disseminated to the general public the melodramatic image of the Indian as "the consummate villain, the beast who hatcheted fathers, smashed the skulls of infants, and carried off mothers to make them into squaws" (Pearce 58). In accepting this representation, people easily viewed Native people as sub-human and, therefore, undeserving of the same sympathy they might extend to people of their own race. Politicians and philanthropic organizations devoted to the cause of saving this inevitably "vanishing" people would finally conclude that Indians must either conform entirely to the values, religious beliefs, and vocations of white Americans or they would become extinct. As David Adams points out, "The option to maintain a separate cultural identity simply did not exist" (36). Henry Price, the Commissioner of Indian Affairs in 1881, established the position of the federal government in no uncertain terms:

> There is no one who has been a close observer of Indian history and the effect of contact of Indians with civilization, who is not well satisfied that one of two things must eventually take place, to wit, either civilization or extermination of the Indian. Savage and civilized life cannot live and prosper on the same ground. (Qtd. in David Adams 1–2)

In the wake of post-Civil War westward expansion, the growth of the railroad, and Manifest Destiny—the credo buoying up pioneers and entrepreneurs westward in quest of gold and land—the Indian problem became a national issue. Clearly, philanthropists working in behalf of Indian interests would not tolerate all-out extermination; as historian Robert M. Utley points out, "public sentiment overwhelmingly favored destruction by civilization rather than by killing" (35).

A federally controlled policy of civilization through education and aggressive missionization appeared to be the most promising avenue of endeavor. After all, according to one Indian agent's report to Congress, the Brule Sioux, my ancestors, had shown potential to be civilized. Pointing out that, although in the past they had been "splendid animals, having but few human hopes, and much more of the animal than intellectual in their composition," they had begun to live in log cabins (qtd. in David Adams 40). What modern people might not realize, however, was that the Brule Sioux—like other tribes—were given no other choice. The federal government had ordered them to surrender themselves so they could be assigned to reservations.

Indian agents noted in their reports to Congress, however, the apparent futility of civilizing Native children who continued to live within families that persisted in practicing their traditional religion and language. Thomas Morgan, Commissioner of Indian Affairs from 1889 to 1893, warned that if Native children were allowed to grow up within their parents' homes, they would become corrupted by "fathers who are degraded and mothers who are debased." Rather than embrace white Christian values, Indian children would inevitably come to "love the unlovely and to rejoice in the unclean." In Morgan's view, the only way children could "escape the awful doom" of savagery was "for the strong arm of the Nation to reach out, take them in their infancy and place them in its fostering schools . . ." (qtd. in Prucha, *Americanizing the American Indian* 243).

The education of thousands of Indian children became not only a monumental undertaking, but an expensive one, as well. A solution to the problem was offered by Captain Richard Pratt, a former overseer of the Ft. Marion Indian prisoner-of-war camp in Florida and self-styled expert on rehabilitating Indians. His solution was to convert abandoned military forts into boarding schools and then implement an educational program based on a military model. Like others who felt they had special insight into Indian cultures, he thought that Indian people valued neither punctuality nor respect for government authority, clearly hallmarks of "civilized" behavior. The structure and discipline of military training seemed to be the answer to the problem, provided that schools could work with pupils young enough to be successfully indoctrinated.

His first project, the Carlisle Indian School, was established in 1878 in Carlisle, Pennsylvania, and would provide the model upon which federal and mission boarding schools, as well as reservation day schools, based their programs. By 1902, there were ninety reservation boarding schools in existence (David Adams 65), all essentially operating with the ideology espoused by Richard Pratt in an 1881 letter to Senator Henry Dawes. Acknowledging the price the Indian child would have to pay in order to gain the privilege of assimilating into mainstream American life, the Indian would be forced to

> *lose his identity as such, to give up his tribal relations and to be made to feel that he is an American citizen. If I am correct in this supposition, then the sooner all tribal relations are broken up; the sooner the Indian loses all his Indian ways, even his language, the better it will be for him and for the government. . . . (Pratt 266)*

In an address to a Baptist convention in 1883, Pratt elaborated upon the philosophy of education that guided his work with Indian children: "In Indian civilization I am a Baptist, because I believe in immersing the Indians in our civilization and when we get them under holding them there until they are thoroughly soaked" (Pratt 335).

Even as the ideological groundwork was laid for the detribalization of indigenous nations, no one thought to consult Indian people about the prospect of their cultures being eradicated. In fact, policymakers could not understand why Indians were not eager to embrace "civilization." Bolt suggests the paternalistic ethnocentrism that prompted white policymakers to view their culture as clearly superior to any other, observing that whites quite naturally viewed their "home environment" to be more wholesome than those of African Americans and Indians. Because their "home environment" was "held by whites to be the cause of the 'inferiority' of the two races, educators assumed that they would gratefully abandon their values and institutions when prompted to do so by their 'superiors'" (217). Unfortunately, the time soon came when many parents were given no choices regarding their children's education or even their religious training.

Having no ready pupils for his experiment, Pratt embarked on a recruiting mission that took him to my family's reservation in South Dakota, where he persuaded reluctant parents to hand their children over into his care. Pratt, whom historian Robert M. Utley deems wrongheaded but well-meaning, at least gave Indian parents the choice of rejecting his offer. From 1879 to 1918, the Carlisle Industrial School represented a successful model of Indian education that other schools in the United States and Canada would emulate. According to Utley, "During his twenty-four-year tenure the school educated, in all, 4,903 Indian boys and girls from seventy-seven tribes" (xiii).

What made possible the realization of the Carlisle school, as well as that of other federal boarding schools, reservation day schools, and mission schools, was the intrinsic nature of the reservation system itself. Advocates such as Francis Walker, Commissioner of Indian Affairs in 1872, argued that policymakers needed to be hardheaded when it came to "the treatment of savages by a civilized power." As Walker observed, reservations were necessary to bring "the wild beasts [the Indians] to the condition of supplicants for charity" (qtd. in Thomas 60–61). Assigned to reservations, designated wards of the government, and forced into complete economic dependency, Indians were at the mercy of government attempts to control and coerce them into compliancy. Having conquered them militarily, the federal government could then undertake a well-planned campaign to exterminate Indian cultures, resulting in "devastating cultural implications" for the human beings involved (Utley xvii).

In the years to come, Indian agents, serving on reservations as representatives of the federal government, condoned any means necessary to fill boarding schools, lending new significance to the term, "compulsory education." In fact, Congress enacted legislation in 1892 formally empowering government officials to use force when Native parents balked at the prospect of their children being taken from them, herded onto trains, and transported hundreds of miles away to boarding schools. David Adams notes that not until 1904 were officials required to obtain parental consent to remove their children to non-reservation boarding schools (89).

To enforce compliance with the new compulsory attendance law, Indian agents used whatever means necessary. For example, at the Yankton Agency in South Dakota, the home reservation of my great-grandfather, John Cordier, agents withheld rations to reluctant parents (David Adams 202). Consequently, children at the Pine Ridge agency knew that if they played truant, their parents might starve. J. B. Harrison, of the Indian Rights Association, reported: "When a child was absent from school without a good reason, the rations of the whole family were cut off til he returned" (qtd. in David Adams 203).

During the autumn, agents often supervised what were essentially kidnapping raids. Agency police were ordered to hunt down and seize bodily children who were-hiding or had been hidden by their parents. Fletcher J. Cowart, agent of the Mescolero Agency in New Mexico, described in his annual report for 1886 the cries and "lamentations" of Indian mothers and the stark terror of small, uncomprehending children about to be taken away by impatient strangers, perhaps never seeing their parents again (199). After witnessing such a particularly wrenching scene, one agent understated a dimension of Indian culture that he had observed, noting in his annual report to the Commissioner of Indian Affairs, "I have been impressed with the great fondness Indians have for their children. This may be one cause why they do not like to part from them" (qtd. in David Adams 205). A remarkably empathetic agent, W. D. C. Gibson, reported in 1887,

> *It is really a pitiful sight to witness their distress and sorrow at times when they come to talk about the children and ask how many 'moons' before they come home, while their appearance indicates that they had passed a restless night, or perhaps not slept any. (163)*

In comparison with the tone and tenor of other agents' reports, this agent appears to be one of the few who viewed Indians as human beings, rather than as obstinate and godless savages.

One of the most dramatic accounts of parents' resisting the kidnapping of their children comes from an annual report filed by an agent at the Yakima agency. In his 1885 report, Agent R. H. Milroy explained that he was forced to arrest and lock up Cotiahan, a Yakima tribal leader who refused to reveal where he had hidden his child. Making an example of him to the other band members, Milroy chained the father's leg and "put him to sawing wood, and told him if he refused to work, he would be tied to a tree and whipped" (200).

Had the children and parents been able to foresee the humiliation, anguish, and deprivation that constituted their children's "education" in these boarding schools, they might have resisted the agents' overtures even more aggressively than they did. As he was being led onto the train bound for Carlisle, Luther Standing Bear recalls thinking at the time that he was being taken away to be killed. "I could think of no reason why white people wanted Indian boys and girls except to kill them, and not having the remotest idea of what a school was, I thought we were going East to die," he writes (*Land of the Spotted Eagle* 230–31).

Barbed Wire and the Bible

In one sense those children would "die," passing from one life to another: stripped naked of the clothes their mothers had made for them, renamed with the names of American Civil War heroes and famous Indian fighters, and re-educated to adopt the "civilized" values of the race that had conquered them. In a quite literal sense, however, hundreds of children died. Neglect, hunger, disease, homesickness—even suicide—left the testimony of acres of little tombstones at boarding schools all over the United States. Luther Standing Bear tells us that "In the graveyard at Carlisle most of the graves are those of little ones" (*Land of the Spotted Eagle* 234). Chief Standing Bear goes on to say that by the third year Carlisle Indian School was in operation, almost one-half of the Plains children had died. Sadly, anxious parents back home might never be notified that their children were ill, much less dead and buried. Too often, rather than deal with the questions and tears of bereft parents, Indian agents would leave telegrams and letters to gather dust on their desks (*My People, the Sioux* 162–63). Ojibwa scholar Basil Johnston recalls a particularly virulent epidemic at his boarding school that claimed "between thirty to fifty boys at a time: chicken pox, measles and mumps . . ." (82). Not surprisingly, John Cook, Indian agent at the Rosebud reservation, warned that given "the large percentage of deaths among the scholars" at Carlisle, parents would not allow their children to be taken away (*Annual Report* 1881, 52).

When military and prison systems induct a new member into their respective institutions, their first step is to dismantle the individual's identity. Boarding school inductions followed similar lines. When Basil Johnston first met his new classmates at Peter Claver's Residential School, he was struck by the fact that they all had been shaven bald. In a 1900 article she published in *The Atlantic Monthly,* Dakota writer Zitkala-Ša (Gertrude Bonnin) describes being dragged screaming into a chair, where she was tied and her hair cut. (A shocked student once asked me,

"Did they do the same thing to white girls who went away to school?") Zitkala-Ša explained to her readers that in Dakota culture, to have one's hair cut meant two things, both momentous. Either one had been publicly exposed as a coward or one was in the throes of grief at the loss of a dear one. Along with the haircut, the children were then subjected to a further humiliation—delousing—a practice that persisted until the 1960s, according to Mary Crow Dog. An alumna of my mother's school, who attended in the late 1960s, Crow Dog reports in the chapter of her autobiography entitled "Civilize Them with a Stick" that the nuns would "dump the children into tubs of alcohol, a sort of rubbing alcohol, 'to get the germs off' " (35).

Stripped of their clothes, which were usually burned, children were issued uniforms that distinguished them as inmates, so to speak. In the last century, girls were given dresses which were close-fitting and to Zitkala-Ša's thinking, immodest. Boys were issued little military uniforms, which they later learned to sew for themselves and their classmates. Betty Eadie writes in her 1992 memoir that after the haircut and delousing, girls were issued "two dresses each, one color for one week, the other for the following week. These uniforms would help identify runaways" (7).

Just as children were stripped of all outward marks of identity, they were threatened, bullied, and beaten to conform to their teachers' expectations of what constituted civilized behavior. When Congress considered enacting legislation banning corporal punishment in boarding schools, Captain Richard Pratt was incensed, insisting that such a ban "would mean the end of Indian schools" (qtd. in Hyde, *A Sioux Chronicle* 57). Children received a spectrum of punishments for speaking their own language, for instance. Marcella La Beau remembers that children caught speaking Lakota would have their mouths washed out with soap before they were punished (qtd. in Josephy 436). A Klamath man recalls that older boys were forced to walk around a tree stump for an hour, carrying a fence rail on their backs (David Adams 125). One of the most dramatic incidents of punishment is recounted by a Blackfoot student, Lone Wolf, who witnessed the event. Angered at hearing a boy speaking his Native language, a white supervisor threw the boy across a room, breaking his collarbone (qtd. in Josephy 435).

Because the constitutional right of freedom of religion was denied to Indians, Indian children were forced to practice the religion of whatever Christian denomination prevailed at their school. Children were also punished for not worshipping with the zeal the teachers demanded of them. Mary Crow Dog's grandmother told her a story that happened when she was very young and caught by the nuns playing jacks instead of praying. As a punishment, she was locked in a tiny cell in an attic, in the dark, and fed only bread and water for a week (Crow Dog 32). Betty Eadie recalls, "My sister Thelma was often beaten by [the nuns] with a little hose and was then forced to thank the Sister who had done it or be beaten again" (9).

Unable to bear the regimentation, spoiled food, bleak living conditions, and utter lack of emotional support, many children ran away. Consequently, one agent at Cheyenne and Arapaho Agency felt compelled to place bars on the dormitory windows and padlock the doors to prevent children from escaping (David Adams 127). Even in this century, according to Betty Eadie, children were locked in their rooms at night (8). Punishment for running away was usually severe. As Mary Crow Dog explains, her grandmother and her fellow inmates were made examples to other children after they were found and returned to school: "The nuns stripped them naked and whipped them. They used a horse buggy whip on my grandmother. Then she was put back into the attic—for two weeks" (32). One particularly incensed school principal hunted down a group of escaped Ute students, drove them back at gunpoint "like wolves," then threatened to hang them (David Adams 219). Luckily, my Aunt Margaret was never caught. Just last summer, while we were at Rosebud, she pointed out to me the route she took to escape what had become an intensely miserable period of her life.

As I look at old photographs of my mother and Aunt Margaret's school grounds, as well as those of other schools, I am struck by two images that recur with frequency: the barbed wire fences and the rows of little children behind those fences, identically dressed, staring warily into the camera. From all the accounts I have read and heard, from the 1880s to the 1960s, the typical boarding school operated on a daily basis like a military prison for children. Basil Johnston and his classmates objected to the absolute lack of privacy, of having every hour of day scheduled: "The boys resented the never ending surveillance that began in the morning and ended only late at night, after they had all fallen asleep; a surveillance that went on day after day, week after week, month after month, year after year" (137). My mother recalls having only two hours of free time a week outdoors—on Sunday afternoon. She said that boys and girls could mingle and talk on the grounds, but everyone had to remain standing for that time; no one was allowed to sit on the ground, unless the person had a telephone book to sit on. (My mother would later laugh about the irrationality of this stipulation: "Where on earth were we going to get telephone books?") Apparently, the nuns were concerned that students might engage in sexual activity on the school grounds in full sight of everyone. "They treated us like we were savages," my mother said.

Children awoke each morning to reveille and fell asleep to taps. Medicine man John Lame Deer remembers falling in for roll call four times each day. He recalls, "We had to stand at attention, or march in step" (25). His grandson Archie Lame Deer, who is my mother's age and perhaps a classmate of hers at St. Francis, tells us that a priest would order the boys to march around the playground holding sticks as if they were rifles. "If we'd had blond hair and blue eyes," he jokes, "you might have taken us for Hitler youth in Nazi Germany" (49).

Even girls were not exempt from the military regimentation. In her book *Oglala Women,* Marla N. Powers presents testimony from a woman who attended Rapid City Indian School, recounting the bugles and bells that dictated when they awakened, ate, worked, had inspections, and slept. The girls marched, too: "We fell into formations. We had officers for each company . . . a captain and a major. . . . We knew every drill there was to be known, right flank, left flank, forward march, and double time" (111). Thomson Highway adds that he knew of girls getting their heads shaved for "minor infractions" of rules (*War against the Indians*).

The education and training most children received was equally regimented, culturally irrelevant, and ultimately a waste of time, according to a number of disillusioned graduates. Understanding nothing about Indian people, teachers assumed that the children were unfeeling and impervious to humiliation. Charles Eastman, who earned his M.D. at Boston College, writes in his autobiography *From the Deep Woods to Civilization* of the humiliation of class recitation at Dr. Alfred Riggs Santee Training School: "For a whole week we youthful warriors were held up and harassed with words of three letters . . . rat, cat, and so forth . . . until not a semblance of our native dignity and self-respect was left" (46). To make the learning process even more fraught with anxiety, students reciting their lessons were asked to do so "taking the position of a soldier at attention" (Pratt 244).

Christine Bolt notes that in both white and Indian cultures children learned by memorization. However, the rote learning by which Indian children were inculcated with the religion and values of the dominant culture must have been not only tortuous, but bewildering as well. Bolt explains,

> *The Indian mission children were asked to memorize hymns and passages from Scripture which they frequently did not understand and which contradicted all their own learned traditions. Incomprehension was compounded by the fact that pupils of every degree of attainment were at first taught together. . . . (213)*

The ninth-grade students at Pierre Indian School in South Dakota must certainly have puzzled over the usefulness and relevance of *Julius Caesar* and *Lady of the Lake* to the lives they would lead as they adapted to their dramatically changing world. Indeed, how could Shakespeare help a Cheyenne person negotiate the cultural transition from tribal values to those of the American West? No doubt Paiute children in Nevada prior to 1931 were equally mystified by the following lines they were forced to memorize and recite:

> *What do we plant*
> *When we plant the tree?*
> *We plant the ship*
> *That sails the sea. . . . (Qtd. in Szasz 33)*

My aunt Margaret never did have an occasion to use the Latin she was taught after she learned to speak English, although she did point out that Mass and prayers were in Latin, hence the necessity of the hours spent memorizing all those Latin verb conjugations. Studying secretarial skills as a part of her curriculum, my mother at least received an education that would theoretically prepare her to survive and earn economic independence in the white world.

Going on to earn an Associate's Degree from Haskell Institute, a former boarding school which is today a university, my mother managed to surpass the expectations non-Indian teachers and administrators usually had of Indian students. From the inception of the boarding school idea, however, federal officials generally held very low expectations of what Indian students might achieve professionally after they completed school. Secretary of the Interior Henry Teller had articulated a philosophy of education that had been adopted not only by Richard Pratt at Carlisle, but also by boarding schools everywhere up until the middle of this century. Within the curriculum of these schools, Teller declared, "more attention should be paid to teaching them to labor than to read" (qtd. in Prucha, *American Indian Policy* 271).

Students were expected to become laborers or domestic servants. In fact, policymakers envisioned Native people leaving their reservations to join the ranks of what was viewed at that time as a permanent underclass in white society. Captain Pratt's vision was that eventually tribal people would be swallowed up into the melting pot of immigrants that had become mainstream Euramerican culture. What he probably did not foresee, however, was that his philosophy would defeat the aspirations of some Indian people to use their education to secure more fulfilling professions than those in manual labor or domestic service.

Chief Standing Bear's situation is a case in point. Like so many others at the mercy of a paternalistic boarding school, he had little say in determining his own future. Standing Bear had wanted to spend his entire day in the classroom getting an education, rather than devote half of it working in the tinshop learning a profession that would be useless back at Rosebud. Eventually, after pointing out that the government was supplying his reservation with an abundance of tinware, he asked Captain Pratt if he could learn carpentry instead. Pratt refused his request. Standing Bear writes, "What worried me was the thought that I might not be able to work at the trade after I returned home. But Captain Pratt could not understand why I wanted to make a change, and so the matter was dropped" (*My People, the Sioux* 176). In this century, white educators' expectations of their Indian students clearly have not changed. In his 1992 autobiography, *The Gift of Power,* medicine man Archie Lame Deer states that his boarding school teachers held the opinion that "we Indians were only good at menial jobs. They did not prepare us to become teachers, lawyers, or doctors" (49).

According to the testimony of Native people and historians, boarding school students were essentially trained, then treated as indentured servants, not as scholars—a fact that students' parents were unaware of. Making the best of a difficult situation, parents such as those of Luther Standing Bear and Stay at Home Spotted Tail hoped that their sons' white education would afford them both professions and the knowledge they would need to protect and defend both personal and tribal interests. Unfortunately, this was not the case for Chief Spotted Tail's son. Visiting his son at Carlisle in 1880, Spotted Tail talked with the Lakota boys from Rosebud, learning that they were all generally "miserable and homesick" (Hyde 322). However, when he discovered that his son was working at harness making, rather than learning to read, write, and speak English, "the thunder began to roll," George Hyde explains, noting that ordinarily Spotted Tail's son would be back home at Rosebud, "training to become a chief," not a farmhand (322).

Although the students were there ostensibly to earn an education, child labor was vitally important to support the expense of maintaining the boarding school. Indeed, one-half of the pupils' day was devoted to the maintenance and upkeep of their prison, including farming, cooking, sewing their own uniforms, and making their own shoes. In his memoir, *Battlefield and Classroom,* Richard Pratt explains that even children too young to be put to work had to ". . . witness the productions of the older ones in harness making, tin ware, boots and shoes, clothing, blacksmith and wagon making . . ." (259). The prized jobs at his school were those in the kitchen, recalls Basil Johnston, because there students could eat the leftover food from their teachers' plates and at least satisfy their incessant hunger (49). Johnston's recollection of hunger echoes the testimony of students over a range of residential institutions. Not until the publication of the Meriam Report in 1928 and the subsequent investigations of the Red Cross was it widely known that children had to survive on "a diet that was the equivalent of slow starvation" (Szasz 19). The Meriam Report criticized the boarding school system on another charge, as well—the failure to demonstrate the practices they taught. Girls in home economics classes were lectured on the elements of proper nutrition and meal planning; yet, the schools themselves rarely provided milk, fruit, or vegetables in the children's diets (351).

A cruel irony, of course, was that graduates returning to the reservation might not find an opportunity to use the education or vocational training they received in these institutions. Robert Utley points out that "with the spoils system ascendant, the few government jobs available rarely went to Indians, and few Carlisle graduates found any occupation to utilize their newly learned talents" (xvi). As in the case of Standing Bear, who found no use for his training as a tinsmith, other students, such as those trained as hatmakers and tailors, found few opportunities to become independent and self-supporting once they returned home.

On the other hand, Indian graduates were not always successful in finding a place in the white world, either. My grandfather, Levi Prue, who graduated from Haskell Institute with a degree in accounting, could find only occasional, short-term employment at home—or within a Bureau of Indian Affairs office or other Indian agencies. After finding that white employers in Omaha were not anxious to hire an educated Indian, my grandfather, who loved to read and disliked the mind-numbing tedium of sheer manual labor, went to work in a cold storage company, then a sheet metal plant, before finally trading in his dreams for a bottle. On the advice of Uncle Moses Red Owl, who feared that she would not find a BIA (Bureau of Indian Affairs) job on the reservation, my mother decided not to return to Rosebud to look for work. Instead, she moved to a succession of white towns looking for some kind of meaningful employment. Unfortunately, she never had the opportunity to exercise her college degree or her shorthand skills (taking dictation at 120 words a minute). During the 1950s, racism against Indians had not abated much since my grandfather's day, so my mother also resigned herself to factory work.

At least my mother and grandfather did not have to face the type of racial discrimination that prevented them from securing a residence in the white world. In *My People, the Sioux,* Luther Standing Bear writes of his discouragement at facing racial discrimination in Philadelphia, where he wanted to work as a clerk in Wanamaker's Store. He explains, "I was to prove to all people that the Indians could learn and work as well as the white people . . ." (179). Unfortunately, he was denied the opportunity to prove his equality—white landlords refused to rent a room to him. Chief Standing Bear explains, "When I would find something that seemed suitable, and the people discovered my nationality, they would look at me in a surprised sort of way, and say that they had no place for an Indian boy" (189).

Sadly, many graduates returned to the reservation finding they did not belong there, either. A white education was an acquisition of dubious value for young people returning home expecting to reintegrate into their communities, earn a living, and move on with their lives. As Robert Utley points out, "The result was that they either existed in a shadow world neither Indian nor white, with acceptance denied by both worlds, or they cast off the veneer of Carlisle and again became Indians" (xvi). Commenting upon this predicament from a Native perspective, John Lame Deer writes, "When we enter the school, we at least know that we are Indians. We come out half red and half white, not knowing what we are" (27). For Sun Elk, a Taos Pueblo graduate, his homecoming would be a heartbreaking one. Soon after his arrival, tribal elders came to his parents' home, and, completely ignoring him, made the following pronouncement to his father:

> Your son who calls himself Rafael has lived with the white men. He has been far away. . . . He has not . . . learned the things that Indian boys should learn. He has no hair. . . . He cannot even speak our language. He is not one of us. (Qtd. in Josephy 436)

Alienated from home and family, culturally as well as emotionally, some Indian people have struggled with their ambivalence about claiming a relation to the people of whom they had been taught to be ashamed. Inculcated with white values and taught the Euramerican version of American history, Pequot minister William Apess, for instance, before he went on to work as an Indian rights activist, grew up "terrified" of Indians. LaVonne Brown Ruoff explains that "whites had filled him with stereotypical stories about Indian cruelty but never told him how cruelly they treated Indians" (1781). Albert White Hat, now a professor at Sinte Gléska University and spiritual leader at Rosebud, recalls having grown so alienated from his cultural roots that when he and his friends would watch western movies, "we cheered for the cavalry" (Beasley 41).

The emotional cost of the boarding school experience upon generations of Native families has been incalculable. When I was a child I would watch my mother brood for hours, chain smoking over memories that intruded insistently upon the present. Passed around from relative to relative, from orphanage to boarding school, she—like so many other Indian children—had to bear the consequences of her parents' shattered lives. Her life story and those of other boarding school survivors remind me of Basil Johnston's description of the youngest children at his boarding school, "the babies":

> *They were a sad lot, this little crowd of babies; they seldom laughed or smiled and often cried and whimpered during the day and at night. . . . [T]hey were hunched in their wretchedness and misery in a corner of the recreation hall, their outsized boots dangling several inches above the asphalt floor. And though Paul Migwanabe and Joe Thompson and other carvers made toys for them, the babies didn't play with their cars and boats; they just held on to them, hugged them and took them to bed at night, for that was all they had in the world when the lights went out, and they dared not let it go. (60)*

Given such testimony, we must ask: What was to be the destiny of children like these? What were the experiences of children who grew up never feeling the nurturing of parents, who emerged from an institution without knowing how to function within a family, without possessing a sense of belonging to a particular group, of sharing a particular history, or of feeling pride in their ancestors? Whom were these individuals allowed to feel proud of? The Pilgrims? Christopher Columbus? These are the queries of the academic researcher, of course. Yet, they are also questions posed with bitterness by those who recognize that their own cultural heroes and tribal identities have been erased out of history by the Colonizers. We have been spiritually dispossessed with that erasure, bereft of our language and our pride in being Indian, diminished by the loss of the cultural knowledge that constitutes the psychic infrastructure of a people. My ancestors made this point more emphatically: A people without a history is like wind across the buffalo grass. A history, after all, is a narrative, a story. And the boarding school robbed generations of Indian children of the stories of their families and tribes, stories that would have otherwise empowered them with knowledge, wisdom, survival skills, and a spiritual foundation.

Aside from being an instrument of cultural genocide, another insidious effect of the boarding school system has been its effectiveness in eroding the foundation of tribal culture, the family. Since the inception of the boarding school system in the last century up to the present, Indian families all over the United States have struggled and are still struggling with healing the pain of generations of family dysfunction. The documentaries, *The War Against the Indians* and *The Native Americans,* both present testimony from Native people explaining that the years of institutionalizing did not foster in children the nurturing skills they would need to be parents. One of the producers of another well-known documentary on boarding schools, *In the White Man's Image,* Matthew "Sitting Bear" Jones, explains how the boarding schools have perpetuated generations of dysfunction within families: "They didn't teach us to be parents at the schools and we didn't have parents to teach us to be parents. When we had children we didn't know how to raise them" ("Boarding Schools" B2).

My approach to the subject of the boarding school system, as I have noted, grows out of my desire that the voices of adult children survivors be heard, and that the audiences which listen will understand how this important dimension of Indian history fits into the larger context of factors that have played a role in the attempted cultural genocide of the first Americans. For Indian audiences, I hope that this testimony will bring the kind of healing shock I experienced after reading an interview with Carol Anne Heart Looking Horse in Sandy Johnson's *The Book of Elders*. Her story and those of others have helped me to construct the narrative of my family, as I hope they will for other people.

In her interview, Looking Horse discusses the "historical grief" we bear and its relation to not only the attempted eradication of our culture, but also the trauma our parents experienced as they were forced through this process. As tribal nations regain control over the education of their own children, she observes, Indian teachers have been able to teach our young people about the relationship between this history and our parents' personal experience. In doing so, we are able to help young people to make strides in recovering their culture, learning a history of America that does not demonize their ancestors, and regaining pride in tribal heritage.

An important key to this recovery lies in the tribal college. In sites such as Sinte Gleśka University on the Rosebud reservation, for instance, students have the opportunity to learn from Indian professors and to complete a core curriculum of Lakota studies that includes language, history, and traditional knowledge. At the same time, students can remain in proximity to their families and communities, sustaining the family bonds that have been so cherished within traditional families. A major challenge that tribal colleges all over the United States face, however, is financial. As always, the destinies of Native people have been subject to the seemingly capricious decisions of the federal government. For instance, although Congress had at one time authorized financial support of amounts up to $6,000 for each student attending college, the Reagan administration made cuts in allocations. By 1989 a student might receive only $1,900 of the funds Congress had originally allocated (Wright and Tierney 17). Even now, Congress continues to slash appropriations once promised to Indian tribes—funds which would enable Native people to pursue their dreams of economic independence and self-determination. Thankfully, a handful of tribal communities—not all— are experiencing an economic and cultural renaissance, due to gaming revenues that enable tribes to build new schools and hire qualified teachers to help bring the next generation proudly into the coming century. And, they will be proud, for they will have the choices our parents and grandparents were denied: to walk in either world, in the tracks and in the image not of the Colonizers, but of the ancestors.

Works Cited

Adams, David Wallace. *The Federal Indian Boarding School: A Study of Environment and Response, 1879–1918.* Diss. Indiana University, 1975.

Adams, Evelyn C. *American Indian Education, Government Schools and Economic Progress.* New York: King's Crown Press, 1941.

Annual Report of the Secretary of the Interior. Washington: GPO, 1879–1895.

Beasley, Conger, Jr. "The Return of the Lakota: An Indian People Thrive 500 Years After Columbus." *The Environmental Magazine* Sept.–Oct. 1992: 381.

"Boarding Schools Likened to Concentration Camps." *Indian Country Today (Lakota Times)* 5 Oct. 1994: B2.

Bolt, Christine. *American Indian Policy and American Reform: Case Studies of the Campaign to Assimilate the American Indians.* London: Allen & Unwin, 1987.

Cowart, Fletcher J. "Reports of Agents in New Mexico." Secretary of the Interior. *Annual Report of the Secretary of the Interior.* Washington: GPO, 1886.

Crow Dog, Mary, and Richard Erdoes. *Lakota Woman.* New York: Harper Perennial, 1990.

Eadie, Betty J. *Embraced by the Light.* New York: Bantam Books, 1992.

Eastman, Charles. *From the Deep Woods to Civilization: Chapters in the Autobiography of an Indian.* 1916. Lincoln: U of Nebraska P, 1977.

Franklin, Benjamin. "Remarks Concerning the Savages of North America." *The Writings of Benjamin Franklin.* Ed. Albert Henry Smyth. Vol. 10. New York: Macmillan, 1907. 10 vols.

Fuchs, Estelle, and Robert J. Havighurst. *To Live on This Earth: American Indian Education.* New York: Doubleday, 1972.

Gibson, W. D. C. "Reports of Agents in Nevada." Secretary of the Interior. *Annual Report of the Secretary of the Interior.* Washington: GPO, 1887.

Hyde, George E. *A Sioux Chronicle.* Norman: U of Oklahoma P, 1956.

———. *Spotted Tail's Folk: A History of the Brule Sioux.* Norman: U of Oklahoma P, 1961.

In the White Man's Image. Prod. Christine Lesiak and Matthew Jones. Video-cassette. PBS Video. 1991.

Indian Removal Act of 1830. 28 May 1830, c. 148, 4 stat. 411.

Johnson, Sandy. *The Book of Elders: The Life Stories of Great American Indians as Told to Sandy Johnson.* San Francisco: Harper Collins, 1994.

Johnston, Basil H. *Indian School Days.* Norman: U of Oklahoma P, 1988.

Josephy, Alvin M. *500 Nations: An Illustrated History of North American Indians.* New York: Alfred A. Knopf, 1994.

King Kong. Dir. Ernest B. Schoedsack. Perf. Fay Wray, Bruce Cabot, Robert Armstrong. Universal, 1933.

Lame Deer, Archie, and Richard Erdoes. *The Gift of Power: The Life and Teachings of a Lakota Medicine Man.* Santa Fe: Bear & Company, 1992.

Lame Deer, John (Fire), and Richard Erdoes. *Lame Deer, Seeker of Visions.* New York: Pocket Books, 1972.

Meriam, Lewis, et al. *The Problem of Indian Administration.* 1928. Introd. Frank C. Miller. New York: Johnson Reprint Corporation, 1971.

Milroy, R. H. "Reports of Agents in Washington Territory." Secretary of the Interior. *Annual Report of the Secretary of the Interior.* Washington: GPO, 1885.

The Native Americans. Narr. Joy Harjo. 3 episodes. TBS Productions. 1992.

Pearce, Roy Harvey. *The Savages of America: A Study of the Indian and the Idea of Civilization.* Baltimore: Johns Hopkins UP, 1953.

Powers, Marla N. *Oglala Women: Myth, Ritual, and Reality.* Chicago: U of Chicago P, 1986.

Pratt, Richard Henry. *Battlefield and Classroom: Four Decades with the American Indian, 1867–1904.* Ed. Robert M. Utley. Lincoln: U of Nebraska P, 1964.

Prucha, Francis Paul. *American Indian Policy in Crisis: Christian Reformers and the Indian, 1865–1900.* Norman: U of Oklahoma P, 1976.

———, ed. *Americanizing the American Indians: Writings by the "Friends of the Indian," 1800–1900.* Cambridge: Harvard UP, 1973.

Ruoff, A. LaVonne Brown. "William Apess." *The Health Anthology of American Literature.* Ed. Paul Lauter. Vol. 1, 2nd ed. Lexington, MA: D. C. Heath, 1994. 1780–81.

Standing Bear, Luther. *Land of the Spotted Eagle.* Lincoln: U of Nebraska P, 1933.

———. *My People, the Sioux.* Lincoln: U of Nebraska P, 1975.

Szasz, Margaret Connell. *Education and the American Indian: The Road to Self-Determination Since 1928.* 2nd ed. Albuquerque: U of New Mexico P, 1974.

Thomas, Robert K. "On an Indian Reservation: How Colonialism Works." *The Way: An Anthology of American Indian Literature.* Eds. Shirley Hill Witt and Stan Steiner. New York: Alfred A. Knopf, 1972. 60–68.

Utley, Robert M. Introduction. *Battlefield and Classroom: Four Decades with the American Indian, 1867–1904.* Ed. Robert M. Utley. Lincoln: U of Nebraska P, 1964. ix–xix.

The War against the Indians. Narr. Harry Rasky. Canada Broadcasting Corporation. 1992.

Witt, Shirley Hill, and Stan Steiner, eds. *The Way: An Anthology of American Indian Literature.* New York: Alfred A. Knopf, 1972.

Wright, Bobby, and William G. Tierney. "American Indians in Higher Education." *Change*. March–April 1991: 11–18.

Zitkala-´Sa. (Gertrude Bonnin). "The School Days of an Indian Girl." *Atlantic Monthly* Feb. 1900: 185–94. Rpt. in *American Indian Stories*. Washington: Hayworth Publishing House, 1921. 52–56.

ETHNIC STUDIES: AN INTRODUCTION

My Father's Labor: An Unknown, but Valued History

Julie López Figueroa and Macedonio Figueroa

 ## Important Words and Concepts in This Chapter

There are several important words and concepts throughout the upcoming chapter. The words appear several times in different places in order to help you remember the words and understand the chapter. The words are defined several times.

- Right before the chapter begins
- In text boxes throughout the chapter
- In red and boldfaced within the chapter
- In a glossary in expanded form at the end of the units

Some of the words also appear in other chapters. Talk about the words with other students, teachers, friends, and family members before you read, while reading the chapter, and after you have read the chapter.

Historiography

1. The writing of history, especially the writing of history based on the critical examination of sources, the selection of particulars from the authentic materials, and the synthesis of particulars into a narrative that will stand the test of critical methods.
2. The principles, theory, and history of historical writing (e.g., a course in *historiography*).

Assimilation

Assimilation is the process by which a minority individual or group takes on the characteristics of the majority and attempts to be accepted as part of the majority group.

Bracero

A guest worker initiative that spanned the years 1942–1964. Millions of Mexican agricultural workers crossed the border under the program to work in more than half of the states in America.

Oral History

Oral history refers both to a method of recording and preserving oral testimony and to the product of that process. It begins with an audio or video recording of a first-person account made by an interviewer with an interviewee (also referred to as narrator), both of whom have the conscious intention of creating a permanent record to contribute to an understanding of the past.

Family History

A record of incidents and occurrences important to our immediate families or ancestry.

Segregation

The separation or isolation of a race, class, or ethnic group by enforced or voluntary residence in a restricted area, by barriers to social integration, by separate educational facilities, or by other discriminatory means.

Research Question

The primary question guiding someone's research. The research question is usually large enough to have several subquestions within it.

Colonization

Political control of one nation over another that is institutionalized in direct political administration by the colonial power, control of all economic relationships, and a systematic attempt to transform the culture of the subject nation. It usually involves extensive immigration from the colonial power into the colony and the immigrants taking on roles as landowners, business people, and professionals. Colonialism is a form of imperialism.

Although I graduated from high school in 1987, I can easily remember taking high- school history courses. Memorizing history for the sole purpose of passing exams and in preparation to meet college requirements describes me as a learner in high school. Influencing this approach was the minimal representation of Mexican or Mexican American people in history textbooks that conveyed the silent, but firm message that anything of historical significance was already documented. Although my parents always taught me to be proud of my Mexican heritage, my history books in high school hardly recognized the presence or contribution of someone that looked like me. Parallel to this experience and outside of school, I loved listening to my family history for hours on end and enjoyed visiting local historical sites as well as museums. Needless to say, who I was as a learner inside and outside the classroom could not be more different.

This chapter explains how learning of my father's history in California impacted my outlook on history as well as opened my mind up to think about education so differently. To this point, learning of my father's history was one of the reasons I became a college professor in Ethnic Studies. In the end, this chapter urges you, the students, to become scholars and contributors to building a more inclusive and personal connection to history in collaboration with the teachers.

How Does One Learn History?

Traditionally, history seems to be taught as a series of indisputable facts. In this way, history seems inaccessible and at times inflexible to modern revisions or making personal connections. In truth, there is tremendous room to re-interpret history through what is called **historiography** (Dray, 1971). **Historiography** is a method used to study how history is gathered and studied, written, and shared. Thinking back to my ninth grade, I remember looking at and memorizing continents, countries,

Dr. Julie López Figueroa

Photo by Arya Allender West

and states that comprised the United States. Although I appreciated learning about these faraway places, these places were so far removed from my daily reality that I had no choice but to memorize versus learn. At the end of each year, I felt like a consumer of history rather than learner of history. I was a learner of history when I could relate to and respond to the history.

I understood history played an invaluable role in understanding my life, especially when I thought about my upbringing. To provide some contexts, I share some of my background. I was raised in predominantly African American and Mexican American neighborhoods in San Jose, California. I attended an elementary school that was taught by teachers of color. My parents attended an American Indian Education Center to participate in different workshops. While my father did the cooking at home, my mom attended workshops to learn nutritious recipes, given what local food was available. My father learned how to develop creative art lessons to facilitate learning for my sister, brothers, and myself. Needless to say, lessons on slavery and American Indians marked moments of my being fully engaged with the readings and lectures because I wanted to understand my community members. To learn about myself in the ninth grade, the only lessons offered focused on the California Missions, the Mexican American War, and the Louisiana Purchase. These lessons seemed to underscore the theme of **assimilation**. Whether it was the Irish, Italians, or Mexicans discussed in Social Studies, history sent the strong message that finding a home and succeeding in the United States meant assimilating. One assimilates to blend in so that differences no longer exist. For me, blending in meant losing the ability to speak with my parents. As someone who grew up bilingual, I could not accept that losing Spanish would make my life better if I could no longer communicate with my family and friends who loved me. Living as a bilingual person in California where most of its cities are named in Spanish, completely agreeing with these messages on **assimilation** made little sense to me.

My Father's History: Developing a Sense of Place

As a young person in high school, I felt both alienated and villainized in the U.S. history lessons and textbooks. On the one hand, I could not personally connect to this history and on the other, it appeared to only represent folks that looked like me as the "Mexican Problem." Feeling demoralized and frustrated by these "facts," I remember going to my dad and asking him why he had decided to come to the United States. Like most other immigrants, he said, "Coming to the United States meant my children would have access to great educational opportunities." While my father's intention was both noble and admirable, this statement did very little to help me diffuse my feelings of frustration with the history I was learning in school.

I told him it was painful to learn history the way it was being taught in school. In response, my father told me he wanted to show me something. He returned to the kitchen and placed a small metal box on the table. Because I never saw that box before, my curiosity was definitely high. He pulled out a paper card and handed it to me. I took the card and noticed the front cover of the card had English and Spanish words on the outside.

Once I finished carefully reading the words on the front of the card, I opened the card to discover my father's picture inside. Instantly, I knew it was some kind of identification card. Eagerly I explored the card again when my father's voice in the background came into focus. My father explained that card was his **Bracero** identification card. He explained that the U.S. Department of Labor contracted Mexican labors to address the labor shortage that resulted when a significant number of U.S. citizens were off fighting in World War II. After he spoke those words, I looked up at him with new eyes and a new sense of understanding about myself in relation to history. I wanted to find out everything there was on the **Bracero** program, such as where Braceros were employed, how much they were paid, and where they lived and worked. I also wondered how my dad survived in the Southern states given that Jim Crow laws had been in full swing in the United States. Ultimately, I wanted to know why and how my father became a Bracero above all else. Unfortunately, my father's history exceeds the number of pages allotted for this discussion, but I will share the following brief history to offer some insight.

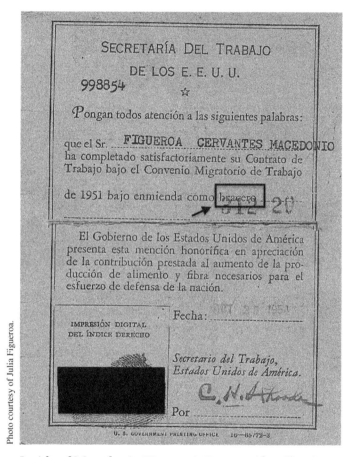

Photo courtesy of Julia Figueroa.

Inside of Macedonio Figueroa's Bracero identification card.

Macedonio Figueroa

My father was born in Jiquilpán, Michoacán in 1934. He worked in agriculture from the time he was 8 to 15 years old. In fact, when he was 11 years old he migrated to the United States to pick cotton in Texas. Years later, in 1954, at the age of 20, my father chose to become a Bracero as a way to move beyond the limited employment opportunities available for someone who grew up working in the farming and ranching industries and had no formal schooling. One year later, my father was relocated to Michigan where he picked beets and cucumbers. Then in 1959, my father came to California where he worked in Oxnard to harvest lemons, lettuce, and strawberries. In 1961, my father worked for an Italian farmer and owner named Mario Lazzarini in Pescadero, California. Pescadero is a coastal town located off Highway 1 between Santa Cruz and Half Moon Bay, California. Although Michoacán was a coastal state, my father worked so hard from a young age that he had no free time to visit the ocean in Mexico. Needless to say, my father felt overwhelmed by seeing the ocean for the first time. The sounds, movement, and vastness of the ocean became my father's refuge at the end the day. On a side note, he loved the ocean so much that growing up we spent every third weekend by the ocean.

Much later in 2004, while on one of those trips to the ocean, my father casually pointed to Mr. Lazzarini's farm. His former work site to this day continues to be located directly across the Pigeon Point Lighthouse on Highway 1. Interestingly enough, my father visited the Lazzarini farm with my older sister, Marina, in 2014 only to learn that Mr. Lazzarini grandson now owns the business and property. My father was welcomed like a long-lost family member. The grandson wanted to know everything he could about his grandfather and my father was kind enough to oblige. Working in Pescadero was an amazing experience for my father not just because of the ocean but also because Mr. Lazzarini sponsored my father's ability to apply to become a U.S. resident, which opened up the pathway for my father becoming a U.S. Citizen by 1964 just as the Bracero Program was terminated.

Backside of Macedonio Figueroa's Bracero identification card.

My father said he worked alongside African Americans, some poor Whites, Filipinos, and Chinese aside from other Braceros.

Listening to this **family history** compelled me to jump up from the kitchen table, eagerly search for the U.S. map my parents kept and return to the table. I unfolded the map and began to circle all the places my father had worked as a Bracero. Knowing that my father along with other contracted Mexican laborers contributed toward stabilizing the economy during World War II gave me such immense pride. The geography lesson that was playing itself out as my father shared his labor history across the Southwest, Midwest, and some Southern states gave me a sense of belonging.

My father encountered different landscapes, but also confronted a variety of political views, unexpected warm welcomes, and learned about other people's histories that he would have not otherwise learned if he had never left Mexico. He also learned about discrimination as he worked in many different states. One of the earliest forms of discrimination my father faced was in Texas. Although my father did not speak English, other Mexican Americans would interpret signs for my father indicating they were not welcomed into certain establishments because they were Mexican. My father said it was not unusual to find public signs that stated "No Mexican or Dogs Allowed" hanging in windows of stores, restaurants, barbershops, or bars. The more my father traveled across the United States, the more he realized every single racial/ethnic group had its turn at being discriminated against.

While these men were so different from him, it was when working alongside them that he could see how much they have in common. Regardless of how they came into doing agricultural work, my father understood they were all working hard to improve their lives in spite of limited opportunities for advancement. Working in the Southern states, my father quickly grasped the public sentiment toward non-Whites, but in particular African Americans. Although my father witnessed how easily some of his non-African American coworkers would give in to public sentiment that African Americans were indeed more inferior, he consciously avoided the divide-and-conquer mentality. My father was not going to entertain the idea that he was somehow better than African Americans given his experiences facing racial discrimination.

The more I sat looking at the circled locations on the U.S. map, the more I began to see these circled locations as historical sites I would hope to visit someday. I considered these historical sites because my father contributed to the well-being of the United States. These historical sites served as anchor points and reminded me that in truth, history is much more multicultural than what is taught in a typical history course. I imagine it took a lot of courage for him to leave Mexico and come to an unfamiliar country without his family or knowing how to speak English. I cannot imagine what my father must have lived through, or the strength it took to survive the humiliation he most likely confronted as a Bracero in the United States. The circled places on the map gave me a sense of belonging and instantly made me confident and allowed me to let go of the imposed stigma I felt through the traditional teachings of history about Mexican and Mexican American people.

Transformed and Inspired by My Father's History

As an undergraduate, I declared Chicana/o Studies as one of my two majors at the University of California, Davis. To fulfill major course requirements, I enrolled in a Mexican American history course and a course on Pre-Columbian History of Mexico taught by a well-known historian and scholar, Dr. Vicki Ruiz. Because Dr. Ruiz created assignments that brokered opportunities to locate our family history within U.S. history, I could take my father's labor history and relate it to what we were reading in my college textbooks. While I was emotionally pained to learn about how slavery, conquest, and **colonization** shaped the identity of Mexican and Mexican Americans, I also felt empowered by understanding how certain cultural foods and traditions have survived over 500 years. I was excited to formally learn a bit more about the positive contribution of Braceros during World War II, and thrilled to know we have color television today because of the Mexican inventor Guillermo González Camarena. The oral history my father shared about being a Bracero ignited a passion for learning and a desire to expand my knowledge. Truthfully, I was surprised by my renewed enthusiasm for history. However, my response made sense according to Grebler, Moore, and Guzman (1970) who studied the impact of family **oral history** on Mexican American students. They found that when students learned about their **family histories** and how their families strived for excellence, students used their family history as a source of inspiration to work though challenges with greater optimism. Understanding how one's family survived, lived through hardships, and succeeded opened the door to imagining what is possible in one's life regardless of the unknown.

My father's history inspired me to imagine how I could serve the world or at least provide another perspective on the world. The answer came to me while taking a Mexican American history course with Dr. Ruiz's class. I read an article by Gonzalez (1985) in which he discussed the **segregation** experience of Mexican American children. This article, in part, responded to my curiosity as to why so few Mexican Americans graduated from high school. In fact, I remained dissatisfied with much of the literature that blamed Mexican American culture or how the use of eugenics identified Mexican Americans as being genetically less intelligent to explain high dropout rates from school. At the same time, the literature offered no explanation as to why some Mexican Americans academically performed well without assimilating. My father's labor history along with the educational history of Mexican Americans influenced my decisions on how to use my education as a form of service, but also helped me understand how to apply history in my work.

References

Dray, W. H. (1971). On the nature and role of narrative in historiography. *History and Theory, 10*(2), 153–171.

Gonzalez, G. G. (1985). Segregation of Mexican children in a southern California city: The legacy of expansionism and the American southwest. *The Western Historical Quarterly, 16*(1), 55–76.

Grebler, L., Moore, J. W., & Guzman, R. C. (1970). *The Mexican-American people*. Free Press.

ETHNIC STUDIES: AN INTRODUCTION

"Imaginary Indians" Are Not Real

Brian Baker

 Important Words and Concepts in This Chapter

There are several important words and concepts throughout the upcoming chapter. The words appear several times in different places in order to help you remember the words and understand the chapter. The words are defined several times.

- Right before the chapter begins
- In text boxes throughout the chapter
- In red and boldfaced within the chapter
- In a glossary in expanded form at the end of the units

Some of the words also appear in other chapters. Talk about the words with other students, teachers, friends, and family members before you read, while reading the chapter, and after you have read the chapter.

Imaginary Indians

A concept used to emphasize the stereotypes and images related to and associated with Native Americans that appear in popular culture, especially through the mass media or typified by team names and mascots used in sports.

Prejudice

To make a judgment about an individual or group of individuals on the basis of their social, physical, or cultural characteristics. Such judgments are usually negative, but prejudice can also be exercised to give undue favor and advantage to members of particular groups. Prejudice is often seen as the attitudinal component of discrimination.

Institutional Discrimination

Policies, rules, and practices created and followed by companies, agencies, and other government or nongovernment organizations favorable to a dominant group and unfavorable to another group that have existed for a long time, and that get repeated over and over.

California Racial Mascot Act Discrimination

Section 221.3 of this California law stipulates,

1. Beginning January 1, 2017, all public schools are prohibited from using the term Redskins for school or athletic team names, mascots, or nicknames.

Through this enactment of this law, California became the first state in the United States to ban the use of "Redskins" in public schools.

Indigenous

Those people whose family and ethnic group inhabiting a land before it was taken over (colonized) by another nation. Indigenous can also mean not only the first people on a land, but also still alive and (possibly) still inhabiting some part of that land to which that person's ancestors inhabited.

Bureau of Indian Affairs

Interior Department agency that serves as the principal link between federally recognized Native American populations (officially *American Indian tribes*) and the U.S. government.

Introduction

In this chapter, we explore expressions of **imaginary Indians**.[1] The expressions addressed have to do with ideas and images that are associated with and attributed to American Indians. The ideas and images related to **imaginary Indians** exist in popular culture in both an historical and contemporary context. For example, in terms of history, it was common for Americans to describe American Indians as *savages*. In the contemporary period, when we get into the idea of American Indians being used as mascots or names in sports, they are being imagined as *warriors*. For example, in high school or at colleges and universities in the United States, even including professional sports teams, fans attending games will engage in certain behaviors or practices such as the *tomahawk chop*. These examples illustrate the point that people act on ideas and behaviors in terms of how they *imagine* American Indians. This is what I call **imaginary Indians**, as people in general already have a set of ideas and images in their heads that they associate with and attribute to American Indians.

In this discussion of **imaginary Indians**, I also introduce other important social science concepts such as **prejudice** and **institutional discrimination**, and how they are interrelated. I then introduce the problem of how *imaginary Indians* as a set of ideas that characterizes Americans Indians as *the other*. After a brief discussion of these concepts, we explore some themes and examples of *imaginary Indians* rooted in history, where the ideas and images are related to the inequality and injustice experienced by American Indians. Toward the end of this chapter, we explore contemporary examples of *imaginary Indians* as in the case of *mascots*. I conclude with a short discussion of the "California Racial Mascot Act" passed in 2015 as it relates to *redskins* and Indian mascots. Although it can be shown that *redskin* is a word and idea rooted in racism, some Americans continue in their efforts to normalize and validate the "r word" as socially and politically acceptable.

Prejudice, Institutional Discrimination, and "the Other"

It is the set of ideas and stereotypes that exist in popular culture that create *imaginary Indians*. They are not real and exist in the imaginations of people. While *imaginary Indians* are not real, they influenced the daily lives of American Indians in history and continue to do so in the twenty-first century. Social scientists who investigate racial and ethnic relations have often related the inequality and injustice experienced by racial and ethnic minority groups as an outcome of **prejudice** and *institutional discrimination*. These two are very basic and important concepts, and they are connected to each other.

First, *prejudice* refers to preconceived ideas and notions held by people toward other groups.[2] The forms of *prejudice* in general that are of most concern relate to race, ethnicity, gender, or ability. Often these ideas exist in popular culture, and it is possible for someone to already form an opinion about another group without having any direct knowledge or personal experience. For example, someone just posted pictures of t-shirts on my Facebook page. The t-shirts reflect the *alcoholic* aspect of *imaginary Indians:* one t-shirt stated *My Indian Name is "Drinks Like a Fish"* and another noted *My Indian Name is "Crawling Drunk."* Thus, prejudice relates to the ideas and images, especially those that are negative and harmful to the group who is the target or subject of the prejudice.

Second, **discrimination** refers to situations when people act on prejudice, where they treat members of one group differently than members of another group (Aguiree & Turner, 2004, p. 6).[3] Generally, **discrimination** is an action related to *prejudice*. While the t-shirts mentioned in the previous paragraph reflect an idea or image of *American Indians are alcoholics* the fact that the t-shirts were made and produced in large numbers to be sold in stores, that this is a form of **discrimination** related to race. To deny someone, a job based on their race, that is discrimination. Both of these examples are actions are forms to *racial discrimination.*

A larger and more complex form of **discrimination** is **institutional discrimination**, which occurs when society as a whole works to the advantage of some groups (*more powerful groups*) and to the disadvantage of other groups (*less powerful*) who are denied access to valued resources.[4] While there are many examples of laws passed by the U.S. government that limited the lived experiences of various **racial and ethnic groups**, an excellent example of *institutional discrimination* that occurred in the United States was the Jim Crow era of the American South. During that time, the idea of *separate but equal* defined the time period. Comparatively, the resources and opportunities available to Blacks were fewer and less valuable when compared to the resources and opportunities for Whites. The way society was structured worked to the disadvantage of African Americans, and the laws and norms of that time period operated in ways that normalized the everyday forms of inequality and injustice they experienced.

In recent years, scholars in the field of Ethnic Studies have used **the other** as a way to understand the experiences of racial and ethnic minorities in American society. In general, by using the term *minority groups*, we are referring to groups that are less powerful when compared to the *majority group* (Aguiree & Turner, 2004, p. 4).[5] Overall, historically and currently, racial and ethnic minority groups have been less powerful groups in society. In describing his own experience as a Mexican American individual, Arturo Madrid wrote about experiencing life as **the other** in American society.[6] A minority group is relegated to the status of *the other* when it is set apart from and distinguished by the majority as being different. In addition, and this is very important, the racial and cultural differences being highlighted as different are also assumed to be inferior. Madrid shares important aspects of his biography in a time period before colleges and universities included larger numbers of racial and ethnic minorities as students. Given the time period when he was a university student, fellow students assumed he was a groundskeeper because there were not many Mexican American students on campus. Because the groundskeepers on campus tended to be Mexican Americans, students assumed that he was also a groundskeeper. Due to his racial-ethnic background, Arturo Madrid was socially isolated from the predominately White student population. Because the number of Mexican American students at the university was very low, he had a difficult time relating or being connected to an institution that did not value his **racial-ethnic identity**.

Historically, prejudice and discrimination affected the lives of American Indians, as law and policy emphasized their status as **the other**. I discuss some ways in which American Indians were imagined as *the other*. In doing so, I make a connection between historical images and ideas to a contemporary form of **imaginary**

Indians. In discussing *Indians as mascots*, I place an emphasis on *redskins*. Although this is a term rooted in racism toward American Indians historically, its use in the contemporary period is an example of **institutional discrimination**. I close by presenting a short discussion of the **California Racial Mascot Act**, passed in 2015. With this law, California became the first state to outlaw *redskin* as a team name or mascot in public schools, and therefore, addressed the problem of **institutional discrimination**.

Roaming on the Land

Although it is possible to challenge dominant ideas related to *imaginary Indians*, it is difficult to change them after they have become deeply embedded in American popular culture. Basically, stereotypes related to *imaginary Indians* have been around for a couple of centuries or more. I remember a camping trip to Sequoia/Kings Canyon National Park in California. On this trip, and in the redwood forest, and based on my identity as American Indian, I experienced *institutional discrimination* in the twenty-first century. Traveling with a group of friends in late spring, we saw and participated in many activities that the national park had to offer, such as hiking, camping, and swimming. As American Indians (**Chippewa, Wintun, Abenaki**), we experienced something so powerful and striking that it stood out from everything else we experienced. We encountered something so simple and created by Americans and imposed over the landscape: words on a sign that communicated ideas related to *imaginary Indians.*

In the park, we went on the trail to Moro Rock. At the summit, we were struck by the view of the Great Western Divide, it was truly spectacular. We talked about the beauty of the landscape and admired it, and like many tourists, we took pictures to memorialize our adventure. It was after this that we noticed a sign designed for tourists. Created by the National Park Service, the sign outlined two brief histories of Moro Rock, one having to do with its geological history and the other having to do with the human history of the area. It was the official human history inscribed on the sign that shocked us. The human history of the area began with this *imaginary Indian* declaration: *Indians roamed here for several thousand years.* What? Who? Were they lost? Were they just ignorant savages who did not know where they were for thousands of years? As American Indians who happen to be teachers and professors, we were especially aware of the power of the misconception being communicated. First, and especially important, the word *Indians* is a term that erases the *Monache* from this specific place altogether. The *Monache* are the people **indigenous** to this area, not *Indians*. Because the *Monache* are not included in this official version of history, they are removed from it.

A second problem with this sign has to do with the idea of the *roaming* or *wandering Indian*, an important characteristic or quality of *imaginary Indians* created during Manifest Destiny. The idea of Indians *roaming* over the land is especially important and powerful: it validated the idea that Indians did not settle on the land because they simply roamed over it. In the colonial process, White American law-makers and officials working in the **Bureau of Indian Affairs** exploited *roam* and *wander* in reference to American Indians in order to justify how the United States would deal with they viewed as the "Indian problem." Eventually, it became necessary to constrain the *roaming Indians* and to limit their human existence on the land by drawing reservation boundaries around them in order to enclose and isolate them from American society. Once relegated to an isolated and inhumane existence on reservations where it was not possible to support their families, the *roaming Indian* no longer existed as an obstacle to Americans who were provided with the opportunity to settle the land when American Indians were confined to reservations.

It was here, at this public place, that we experienced **institutionalized racism** toward us as **Chippewa, Wintun, and Abenaki peoples**. To include the idea that *Indians roamed here for thousands of years* in this history is a powerful action related to the invention of *imaginary Indians*. But, this seemingly innocent inscription was followed by yet another *imaginary Indian* invention: *Neither sign nor record indicates that they considered Moro Rock a special place*. What? Were those Indians blind too? Did they roam around Moro Rock for thousands of years and not realize that it was there? At the same time, the National Park Service has preserved a village site in this area, which is evidence that memorializes their residence. In addition, because this is evidence about residence, this also indicates that they did consider the area to be a special place because this was their homeland. The fact that the *Monache* did not feel a need to post a sign nor leave a record on Moro Rock is only evidence that they had a different cultural understanding and awareness of the world.

In a very simple yet powerful way, the National Park Service inscription to Moro Rock reinforces dominant ideas and stereotypes about American Indians. Before leaving this place, and in front of the sign that represented **imaginary Indians** and **institutional discrimination**, as **indigenous** peoples we mimicked the idea of *roaming Indians* unaware of their surroundings. We took pictures to memorialize our own Indian ignorance.

> . . . **they did consider the area to be a special place because this was their homeland.**

 ## Being Like Children

The Americans created many strategic images pertaining to American Indians to fuel the colonial machine driven by them across the land, and like bumps and potholes in the road, Americans understood that they had an never ending Indian problem. From the 1800s and well into the mid-1900s, the fact that Americans viewed American Indians as *a problem* is important. To describe or view American Indians as *a problem* reflects their negative bias toward them, viewing American Indian as *the other*.

Indigenous People Highlighted in This Chapter

1. Chippewa
2. Abenaki
3. Wintun
4. Monache
5. Cherokee
6. Lakota
7. Illini
8. Cheyenne
9. Muskogee
10. Miwok

In the United States, Indigenous people are sometimes called Native Americans or American Indians. When discussing Native Americans, it is more clear to use the name of the specific indigenous group.

Because Americans viewed and understood them as *blood-thirsty savages* who were prone to *laziness*, Americans viewed them as being incapable of looking out for their own interests and needs. In fact, in the early nineteenth century, American political officials increasingly described Indians as *children*, sometimes even referring to them as *red children*. This idea, that *Indians are like children*, is embedded in the 1831 ruling made by the U.S. Supreme Court in the *Cherokee*

© Transcendental Graphics/Contributor/Getty

Courtesy of Brian Baker.

The two pictures here portray American Indians in "imaginary" ways by exaggerating stereotypes. The picture on the left shows an image of Uncle Sam spoon-feeding an American Indian presumable because they are not able to take care of themselves. Bottle photo is from the collection of Dr. Brian Baker.

Nation v. Georgia. This case is important because it established the legal precedent that the United States is like a "guardian" who cares for the **Cherokee Nation** as the "ward" of the U.S. government. Basically, this case is premised on the idea that American Indians are like *children*. Citizens of the Cherokee Nation who were bilingual (*who spoke English and Cherokee*), who were well educated and literate (*they published newspapers in the Cherokee language and had public schools*), and who were business owners were relegated to the status of being *wards* of the government because they were considered to be like *children*. Through its self-appointed position of *guardian* looking out for the *wards* under its care, the American government created the idea of the *Great Father* doing good things when caring for the *red children* who, due to their own cultural inferiority, required constant American paternalistic guidance.

Near the latter part of the 1800s, indigenous peoples who at one time possessed the ability and means to sustain their own livelihoods were now blamed for the fact that they could not even feed or clothe themselves. While they continued to possess a sense of being **indigenous** to the land, Americans began to understand the *red children* as indigents on the land. Therefore, it became necessary for the *Great Father* to feed them. In a picture taken on the Pine Ridge Indian Reservation in 1891, a photographer captured a number of **Lakota people** standing in line on *ration day*. Instead of paying attention to the political and cultural circumstances associated with their geographic isolation or American racism toward Indians as the more relevant factors which prevented the Lakota in the photograph from making a living on their own terms, the accepted stereotype of the time viewed them as *lazy*. Because the **Lakota** were *lazy* and like *children*, they were responsible for their own poverty and starvation, and Americans had to feed them.

Popular culture accepted this view of American Indians, and this stereotype was captured in an ad for *Boston Baked Beans* in the early twentieth century. In this ad, we are confronted by a carefully designed Uncle Sam as a good guy spoon-feeding an Indian. The ad identifies the Indian pictured as being Sitting Bull, a famous and well-known Lakota leader who left his mark on American history. While Sitting Bull is a real person in history, Uncle Sam is a fictional character connected to American patriotism. In the ad, Sitting Bull is short and is wrapped in blanket, and his appearance is *savage* and *animal* like. The fact that Uncle Sam is much taller and is holding the spoon for a much shorter Sitting Bull invokes the basic idea of a parent spoon-feeding a young child. In this image, a strong and powerful leader like Sitting Bull in Native American history was portrayed akin to *red children* incapable of feeding himself.

> In terms of racism toward American Indians, *redskins* as a racially offensive term played a part in the history of violence and injustice experienced by American Indians.

Indians as Redskins, Warriors, and Mascots

During a time period when Americans imposed many constraints over Indians that prevented them from practicing their religions and speaking their languages, Americans became increasingly fascinated with *imaginary Indians*. For instance, during a time period when American Indian children were sent to Indian Boarding Schools run by the American government, where they were severely punished when they spoke their languages or practiced their religions, Americans began to *play Indian*. For example, fraternal organizations were founded by nonnative people, such as the *Order of Redmen*, and sports teams took on names associated with *imaginary Indians* as in *chiefs* or *warriors*, and they also created **Indian mascots**. It is important to point out that in a time period when there was extreme racism toward American Indians and they were set apart from society as *the other*, at a time when Indian children were brutalized for *being Indian*, non-Indians began to act as *imaginary Indians*. Today, *Chief Wahoo* of the Cleveland Indians and the *Washington Redskins* are examples of *institutional discrimination* in the contemporary period. The fact that Americans regarded and viewed Indians as *wahoos* and *redskins* affected the lives of American Indians.

> **In Kelseyville, California, the local high school changed the name of its mascot from *Indians* to the *Knights* in 2008.**

As a mascot or team name, the *imaginary Indian* in the world of sports has become an acceptable and common aspect of popular culture. Indian mascots are one of the most visible ways *imaginary Indians* exist in popular culture today. In this imaginary world, Indians are viewed as *fierce heathen warriors* inherently prone to being *cold blooded* and *cunning* in their ability to *fight* and *kill*. In recent decades and throughout the country, there have been a number of heated debates in sports at high schools, colleges, and universities, as well as professional sports related to Indian mascots. In Kelseyville, California, the local high school changed the name of its mascot from *Indians* to the *Knights* in 2008. The *imaginary Indian* at Kelseyville High School had nothing to do with the local **indigenous people** or history of the area. This *imaginary Indian* was successfully challenged by the local California Indian tribe, the *Habematolel Pomo of Upper Lake*.[7] At the University of Illinois, Chamagne-Urbana, *Chief Illiniwek* as the mascot had been a source of debate and controversy for decades. The name of the sports teams at UICU is the *Fighting Illini*, but the image itself has nothing to do with the history and culture of **Illini Indians**. While the UICU retained its team name, the mascot, *Chief Illiniwek*, was retired in 2007 and is no longer the official mascot of the university.[8]

The most obvious example of *institutional discrimination* has to do with the *Washington Redskins*. In terms of racism toward American Indians, *redskins* as a racially offensive term played a part in the history of violence and injustice experienced by American Indians. In 2013, Dallas Goldtooth (*Lakota*) posted a picture of an 1863 newspaper clipping from *The Daily Republican* on his Facebook page. This newspaper article from Minnesota shows us the racism toward American Indians in the nineteenth century by showing us that American citizens could receive a bounty for American Indian scalps: the article announced that the "reward for dead Indians has been increased to $200 for every red-skin sent to Purgatory."[9] In posting a picture of the article from 1863, Goldtooth wrote,

> *It was only 5 generations ago that a white man could get money for one of my grandfather's scalps.*

> *At the time . . . it was Redskin that was used to describe us.*

> *So those who fail to understand the significance of this whole debate, think deeper about the word legacy. Is the legacy of racism, death, and plunder worth keeping?*

It is important to point out this is only one example of *redskin* in American history, where Indian scalps were sold like fur pelts for cash. This happened in many parts of the United States in the 1700s and 1800s. The reality here is that *redskin* is a demeaning word directly tied to racism and the extermination of American Indians. For example, the State of California paid $1,100,000 to militia groups who attacked and killed California Indians in 1852. Here, *redskin* is associated with the *bounty* that settlers and Americans received for the scalps of American Indians they killed, and these occurred in times where there was no warfare between Americans and American Indians.[10]

Many American Indians have questions about the team name of the *Washington Redskins*, and view it is an example of *institutional discrimination*. In 1992, Suzan Shown Harjo (*Cheyenne/Muskogee*) filed a case with U.S. Patent and Trademark Office challenging the *Washington Redskins*. The strategy here was that, if the *Washington Redskins* lost its protected trademark, the owners of the team would then change the name of the Washington team. While Harjo almost won, the ruling was overturned and the case was refiled by Amanda Blackhorse in 2014. The case was decided in favor of Blackhorse on the grounds that *redskins* is a word that is disparaging (*offensive*) to American Indians. The case is still not completely settled, and the owner of the *Washington Redskins* continues to assert that the team name "honors" American Indians.

The California Racial Mascot Act

On October 11, 2015, Governor Jerry Brown signed into law **The California Racial Mascots Act (CRMA)**.[11] By doing so, California became the first state to ban the use *redskins* as a team name and/or mascot. The legislation clearly prohibits the use of "racially derogatory or discriminatory school or athletic team names" in California public schools.[12] A deadline of January 1, 2017 was established for schools to decide on a new mascot and they would also be provided with some financial assistance in doing so, as there will be a number of financial costs to schools to comply with the law (*logos on gymnasium floors, etc.*). This law affects four schools in California: Gustine High School, Calaveras High School, Chowchilla Union High School, and Tulare High School.

After the Governor Brown signed CRMA into law, one American Indian teenager from Jackson, California, Dahkota Kicking Bear Brown (*Miwok*), who was involved in this legislative initiative stated:

> I hope everyone can move forward positively and select a new mascot, inclusive of all students to represent their campus community.[13]

In fact, one California high school pursued this course of action in 2011. While this was before the actual law was signed into law, a discussion about *redskins* had already been happening in Colusa, California. Despite strong emotions and nostalgic connections to the *redskin's* mascot which had been an important part of the school's history and identity, members of the community and high school did the right thing. They opted to implement a change in their school as an institution in order to embrace a more positive and inclusive future. In changing their name and their identity from the *Redskins* to the *Redhawks*, Assistant Principal Mike West made the following point:

> Give them their identity and let them run with it . . . Let them go forward and develop new traditions for their mascot.[14]

Conclusion

Unfortunately, **prejudice** and **institutional discrimination** have shaped the lives and experiences of racial and ethnic minority groups for quite some time. Although it is possible to challenge the *imaginary Indian* invented by Americans, it is extremely difficult to change those ideas as they have become so deeply embedded in American culture. Especially in the world of sports where Indians are made into mascots, these **imaginary Indians** have become effectively institutionalized. *Imaginary Indian* ideas remain visible in the world of sports, where Indians are reduced to mascots and team names. But, with respect to *redskins* as an obvious and negative aspect of the *imaginary Indian*, there seems to be some seeds for positive change. California law now requires public schools in the state to discontinue using *redskin* because it is a racially offensive term. When we look at American society and culture over time, we can identify changes in race and ethnic relations between an historical period (as in the 1850s, for example) and the contemporary period. By doing so, we understand how law has been an effective part of social change.

References

Aguiree, A., Jr., & Turner, J. (2004). Ethnicity and ethnic relations. In A. Aguire & J. Turner (Eds.), *American ethnicity: The dynamics and consequences of discrimination* (4th ed., pp. 1–24). McGraw Hill.

Baker, B. (2007). Imaginary Indians: Invoking invented ideas in popular and public culture. In J. L. Figueroa, B. Mosupyoe, & B. Baker (Eds.), *Introduction to Ethnic Studies* (pp. 261–275). Kendall-Hunt.

Lindsey, B. (2015). *Murder state: California's native American genocide, 1846–1873.* University of Nebraska Press.

Madrid, A. (1997). Being "the other": Ethnic identity in a changing society. In J. Henslin (Ed.), *Down to earth sociology* (pp. 505–511). The Free Press.

Notes

[1] See Baker (2007).

[2] See Aguiree and Turner (2004).

[3] See Footnote 2, p. 6.

[4] See Footnote 2, p. 10.

[5] See Footnote 2, p. 4.

[6] Madrid (1997).

[7] See www.upperlakepomo.com/.

[8] See *In Whose Honor?* New Day Films (1997). While this documentary is very effective in highlighting the problem of *Chief Illinwek*, it is outdated in the sense that it was released before the mascot was officially retired. For additional information, see *Chief Illiniwek: Beloved by Students, (Still) Banned by the University.* Article available online, Indian Country Today Media Network: *http://indiancountrytodaymedianetwork.com/2013/04/29/chief-illiniwek-beloved-students-still-banned-university-149098.*

[9] http://indiancountrytodaymedianetwork.com/2013/11/13/dakota-man-exposes-vile-history-redskins-facebook-152241

[10] For an historical analysis of violence toward native people in California, see Lindsey (2015).

[11] On October 11, 2015, Governor Jerry Brown signed into law *The California Racial Mascots Act* (Assembly Bill No. 30). Introduced by Assemblyman Luis Alejo, this law prohibits public schools in California from using the term *redskins* beginning January 1, 2017. California became the first state to acknowledge *redskin* as a racial slur toward Native Americans. Visit the California State Legislature website at https://leginfo.legislature.ca.gov/faces/billNavClient.xhtml?bill_id=201520160AB30 for more information.

[12] https://leginfo.legislature.ca.gov/faces/billNavClient.xhtml?bill_id=201520160AB30

[13] http://edsource.org/2015/california-is-first-in-the-nation-to-ban-redskins-school-mascot/88948

[14] Colusa prepares to say good-bye to redskins.

Implicit Bias: Individual and Systemic Racism

Rita Cameron Wedding

Racism has not ended; it has just been concealed by the tools of modern racism such as implicit bias, stereotypes, color blindness, microaggressions, and language. These tools of modern racism work in tandem to preserve and obscure racial inequalities. The explicit laws of exclusion, and discriminatory practices in housing, school segregation, and access to public accommodations such swimming pools and transportation were outlawed only to be replaced by laws that can reproduce covert and systemic forms of racism that preserve the same racial arrangements as those that existed prior to the passing of the 1964 Civil Rights Act.

Systemic racism is defined as the integration of patterns, procedures, practices, and policies operating within institutions in ways that intentionally or unintentionally, consistently penalize, and (disenfranchise or put at a disadvantage), people who are members of non-White racial/ethnic groups.[1] Though many people denounce the existence of systemic racism in 2020, the American Medical Association declared racism, in its systemic, cultural, interpersonal, and other forms, as a serious threat to public health.[2] Systemic racism cannot be viewed as one event; it's accumulative, as the impact of any type of discrimination places individuals at risk, and more vulnerable to subsequent forms of discrimination.

This chapter will discuss how bias and racism inform individual decision making and as a result contributes to systemic racism. This is accomplished by obscuring racial strategies that are alternatives to explicit racism and overt discrimination, such as implicit bias, color blindness, stereotyping, and microaggressions, which ensure the entitlements of whiteness are not lost.

Most definitions of systemic racism do not address the critical role of individual decision makers, whether an elected official, law enforcement, or bystanders in the park, in preserving systemic racism. Everyone, regardless of where they sit on the decision-making continuum, will make decisions informed by their own biases or racism to keep systemic racism intact. Thus, the relationship between individual racism and bias normalizes the outcomes of systemic racism and must be addressed.

Fighting against systemic racism

Systemic racism works effectively in maintaining the racial hierarchy because it is designed to obscure any outcomes based on bias, and not facts. Few people will admit they made a decision that is racist or because they *don't like Black people*. To the contrary, racist decisions must appear to have no bearing on race whatsoever in order to obtain the consensus of well-meaning people and stakeholders responsible for constructing policies, procedures, and business norms in public and private sectors, including law enforcement, education, and employment.

As long as people don't examine racially disparate outcomes through a racial lens; as long as outcomes in social institutions don't reveal a racial correlation such as pre–civil rights era racism for example, lynching, cross-burning, or the use of racial slurs; and as long as it's not their intention to be racist, they think they are not racist. This is a falsehood because we know that anyone who supports, or advocates for racist policies through their actions, inactions or expresses a racist idea, even if we do so in the commission of our jobs, is complicit in systemic racism.

Ibram X. Kendi provides the following explanation of racist actions.

- Racist: One who is supporting a racist policy through their actions or inactions or expressing a racist idea.
- Antiracist: One who is supporting an anti-racist policy through their actions or expressing an antiracist idea.

Kendi further explains,

The opposite of 'racist' isn't 'not racist.' It is 'anti-racist'. What's the difference? One endorses either the idea of a racial hierarchy as racist, or racial equality as an antiracist. One either believes problems are rooted in groups of people, as a racist, or locates the roots of problems in power and policies as an antiracist. One either allows racial inequities to persevere, as a racist, or confronts racial inequities, as an antiracist. There is no in-between safe space of 'not racist'. The claim of 'not racist' neutrality is a mask for racism.[3]

The criminal justice system built in a post-slavery period is perhaps the most pernicious of all racial projects. Though disparities in disproportionate plea bargaining, sentencing, sentencing guidelines, and convictions based on race are well documented, racial strategies can mask the racial dimensions and cause the racial outcomes to be attributed to the race of the individuals involved, not the consequences of racism.

In her book *The New Jim Crow*, Michelle Alexander likens the criminal justice system to the conditions of the Jim Crow Era because it similarly denies basic civil rights to African Americans who are convicted felons. According to Alexander, merely reducing sentence length by itself does not disturb the basic architecture of the New Jim Crow. "So long as large numbers of African Americans continue to be arrested and labeled criminals, they will continue to be relegated to a permanent second-class status upon their release, no matter how much (or how little) time they spend behind bars. The system of mass incarceration is based on the prison label, not prison tine.[4]

Further, Michelle Alexander states:

> *The racial dimension of mass incarceration was its most striking feature. No other country in the world imprisons so many of its racial or ethnic minorities. The United States imprisoned a larger percentage of its black population than South Africa did during the height of apartheid. In Washington D.C., our nation's capital, it is estimated that three out of four young black men (and nearly all those in the poorest neighborhoods) can expect to serve time in prison.[5]*

The criminal justice system is one of the most efficient, successful, and immoral racial projects of all.

As a society, many well-meaning people can overlook the racial dimensions of the criminal justice system because of implicit bias, stereotypes, and color blindness—all carried out through individual decision making, but collectively supporting systemic racism.

If the Civil Rights Act made good on its promise to end discrimination based on race, color, religion, sex and national origin, the social capital that accrues to whiteness would have been erased and White men and White women would no longer be able to maintain racial dominance.

What is unconscious or implicit Bias?

Unconscious bias, also known as *implicit bias*, refers to attitudes or stereotypes that are outside our awareness and affect our understanding, our interactions, and our decisions. Researchers have found that we all harbor unconscious associations—both positive and negative—about other people based on characteristics such as race, ethnicity, gender, age, social class, and appearance. Implicit bias is not just about having a bad attitude towards a particular group. Research has shown that when our brains experience fear, threat, or anxiety our brains activate. "If scientists could scan our brains when we see spiders or snakes, they would see that the area of our brains that focuses on fear, threat, anxiety and distrust is triggered or, as neuroscientists say, 'activated.'"[6]

In other words, our implicit biases shape not only how we think about a group but can result in a persistent unconscious association between Black people and corresponding stereotypes. Because the stereotypes that associate Black people with crime become inextricably linked in our minds, it is not surprising that in one study, 60 percent of viewers who watched a crime story with no picture of the perpetrator falsely recalled seeing one, and of those, 70 percent believed the perpetrator was African American. When we think about crime, we "see Black," even when it's not present, at all."[7]

An essential function of racial stereotypes is to prime the minds of people with information, mostly misinformation, which suggests all Black people are criminals, and dangerous. This makes the public more likely to overlook racist political projects and easier to perceive their guilt and to justify longer prison terms. From 1993 to 2009 more people were incarcerated for drug crimes than violent crimes [Kendi 42]. White people are more likely than Black and Latinx people to sell drugs, though racial groups use drugs at similar rates. However, Black people are far more likely than Whites to be jailed for drug offenses and remain in prison for the same length of time as violent White criminals [Kendi 42].

Racial stereotypes are also used to justify political projects such as the "War on Drugs." In June 1971, President Nixon declared a "War on Drugs." He dramatically increased the size and presence of federal drug control agencies and pushed through measures such as mandatory sentencing and "no-knock" warrants. A top Nixon aide, John Ehrlichman, later admitted,

You want to know what this was really all about. The Nixon campaign in 1968, and the Nixon White House after that, had two enemies: the antiwar left and black people. You understand what I'm saying. We knew we couldn't make it illegal to be either against the war or black, but by getting the public to associate the hippies with marijuana and blacks with heroin, and then criminalizing both heavily, we could disrupt those communities. We could arrest their leaders, raid their homes, break up their meetings, and vilify them night after night on the evening news. Did we know we were lying about the drugs? Of course, we did.[Legalize it All, How to Win the War on Drugs, Harper's Magazine, 2016]

Nixon temporarily placed marijuana in Schedule I, the most restrictive category of drugs. The War on Drugs was essentially a war on Black people driven by stereotypes and racism. The War on drugs began at a time when illegal drug use was on the decline causing arrests and convictions for drug offenses to skyrocket, especially among people of color.[8]

Racial disparities, for example, crack vs. cocaine, were embedded in sentencing of drug crimes. At one time the sentencing ratio was 100:1, in other words 100 times more cocaine was needed than crack, to trigger the same sentence. This was a racial and class dimension as crack was more likely to be used by Black people and poor Whites because it was cheaper. Thus, the racial impact for what is essentially the use of the same substance did grave harm to Black people.

In 1985 a media campaign saturated the public airways with images of Black "crack whores," "crack dealers," and "crack babies." These images seemed to confirm the worst negative racial stereotypes about inner city Black people.[9] Stereotypes about Blacks makes them look like criminals, so it makes it easier to convict them, give them longer sentences, and even surveil in all public spaces because they look suspicious. Later, the Obama administration reduced the disparities to 18:1, but that did little to reduce the harm already done.

According to Michelle Alexander,

> . . . as many as 80% of young African American men now have criminal records and are thus subject to legalized discrimination, e.g., the New Jim Crow, for the rest of their lives. These young men are part of a growing under-caste, permanently locked up, and locked out of mainstream society.[10] [M. Alexander, The New Jim Crow, p. 7]

When we consider the effects of systemic racism, we not only have to consider the lifelong impact on these men, but also their families.

The "War on Drugs" based on stereotypes and lies about the Black community was a very effective racial project that preserved the value of whiteness at the expense of Black individuals and families, a cost that is still being paid. The racial elements of the criminal justice system last well beyond incarceration. It has been estimated that 1 of every 13 Black people have lost their right to vote due to a felony conviction.[11] Additionally, they face the inability to acquire federal student loans, public housing, and face lifelong discrimination in employment. *Research shows that on average, Black male offenders received federal sentences that were approximately 20 percent longer that White male offenders for the same crime.*[12]

On January 1, 2018, California's The Fair Chance Act, became a law that generally prohibits employers with five or more employees from asking about conviction history before making a job offer. This type of law is also known as a "Ban the Box" law. Though this law is designed as a remedy, it is not a reparation that can fix the harms already done.

Color blindness, racism, and implicit bias masked how the war on drugs was a war on Black people? Another well-known racial strategy that is still used today is color blindness. The rules of color blindness are as all-encompassing as the stereotypes they protect. The rules of color blindness are, "we shouldn't talk about race, we shouldn't think about race because race doesn't matter." Color blindness can effectively shut down the public discourse on race, or any critical thinking about race because it silences the public discussions about racial injustice. The penalty for violating the tenets of a color-blind society labeled anyone who talked about race as "the racist in the room."[13] The post–civil rights strategy of color blindness was designed by conservatives not to end racism, but to preserve existing racial hierarchies by obscuring the racial dimensions of projects such as the criminal justice system. Individual decision makers who pretend not to notice race are complicit in leaving systemic racism *unchallenged*.

Lastly, one of the most thorough racial projects, the school-to-prison pipeline, relies on implicit bias, racial stereotypes, and color blindness embedded within multiple public sectors from law enforcement to education, ensuring that racial inequalities continue.

The school-to-prison pipeline is how our educational systems act as pathways for Brown and Black children to end up in the juvenile justice system with little effort. The disproportionate disciplinary and special education outcomes for students of color create a two-track system: the "disciplinary track" and "special education track." Both tracks make it more likely that students of color will be displaced out of school and into the juvenile justice system.[14]

Across the country, school officials have given armed police unfettered access to arrest, frisk, and remove children from classrooms across the country. Many schools across the country use school resource officers to manage school related problems that were in the past the responsibility of teachers. As a result, the vast number of referrals of children to law enforcement come from schools.

This is because no one is immune from implicit bias. Implicit biases of all school decision makers, school resource officers, teachers or administrators can result in disparate outcomes. Perhaps, we can glean some valuable insight from a Yale University preschool study in which teachers were outfitted with eye scan technology and told to observe the most challenging behaviors of girls and boys in their preschool classes. The study revealed that when looking for challenging behaviors (though there were none in the study), the teachers gazed longer at the Black children, particularly the Black boys. A lesson that can be learned from this study is how implicit biases can mistakenly tell us where to focus our attention and from whom we should expect to "find the problem" (www.npr.org/sections/ed/2016/09/28/495488716/bias-isnt-just-a-police-problem-its-a-preschool-problemcitation).

Racism, color blindness, and implicit bias work together resulting in the differential application and enforcement of policies and laws

In 2014, at the request of the U.S. Department of Justice, I was asked to provide training to a large urban juvenile court in Tennessee that was under review for potential civil rights violations against African American children. The city is almost evenly represented by Black and White children, but the day we went to the detention center, every single child in detention that day was Black. The first questions we asked the judges were, "Where are the White kids and do you have a separate juvenile hall for White kids? For me, its defied logic that not a single White child was in detention, yet it was seemingly normal for them to only lock up Black children.

As we sought to understand how Black children exclusively ended up in juvenile hall, we looked at the charges for which children were most likely placed in detention; they were not violent crimes, but discretionary offenses that could be handled without arrests since White children broke the same laws without being arrested. Two of the offenses that resulted in the arrest of a disproportionate number of African American children were indecent exposure and inciting a riot. These laws boiled down to sagging pants (indecent exposure) and watching a fight (inciting a riot). It appeared, at least on that day, White children were unlikely to be cited for these typical adolescent indiscretions. Once a child is detained for reasons of bias rather than justice, they have been thrust into the school-to-prison pipeline.

Decision Maker's Implicit Bias Supports Systemic Racism

In this same juvenile hall, after the implicit bias training, the juvenile court judge said to me, ". . . if I find out who's discriminating in my court they will be fired." What he didn't seem to understand is that everyone, regardless of their race, or their position, for example, judges, probation or police officers, groundskeepers, and cooks, can and do have biases that become the basis of their decision making.

In a California juvenile detention center, one probation supervisor stated that even when they use structured (objective) decision-making tools to control for bias in decision making, bias can still occur. The probation supervisor said that supervisors had the authority to override the outcomes of the structure decision-making tool. Upon review, they learned that in most cases the overrides (decisions to keep a child in the juvenile hall) involved "big, Black boys." This is yet another example of how decision maker bias, and not facts, can contribute to systemic racism.

Such disparities in decision making are found across the country. Here is an excerpt of an e-mail I received from a judge in Michigan: ". . . every time I visit a prison or a juvenile detention facility I am struck by the numbers, the obscenely disproportionate number of Black inmates that we have here in Michigan." Similarly, in Texas, a high school administrator expressed his frustration that ". . . so many who come as students leave as felons."

In schools, decision maker bias at every decision-point can coalesce to normalize the arrest, removal, or suspension, of even a kindergartener for having a tantrum. Black girls are five times more likely to be suspended than White girls; twice as likely to be suspended than White boys, and nearly three times as likely to be referred to the juvenile justice system. Black girls are also 20 percent more likely to be charged with a crime than White girls, and one study found that prosecutors dismissed only 30 percent of cases against African American girls, while dismissing 70 percent of cases against White girls.[15]

From slavery to today, our country has utilized sophisticated racial strategies, and constructed elaborate racial projects for the sole purpose of preserving a racial hierarchy.

But in the words of Dr. Ibram Kendi, ". . . if we truly believe that all humans are equal, then disparity in condition can only be the result of systemic discrimination."

 ## Notes

[1] Shirley Better, "Institutional Racism: A Primer on Theory & Strategies for Social Change", p. 11.

[2] www.ama-assn.org/delivering-care/health-equity/ama-racism-threat-public-health

[3] Dr. Ibram Kendi, *How to be an Antiracist*, p. 15.

[4] Michelle Alexander, *The New Jim Crow*, p. 14.

[5] Michelle Alexander, *The New Jim Crow*, pp. 6–7.

[6] *An overview of Implicit Bias by the Equal Justice Society.*

[7] www.alternet.org/2014/05/white-people-commit-most-heinous-crimes-so-why-america-terrified-black-men

[8] Michelle Alexander, *The New Jim Crow*, p. 6.

[9] Michelle Alexander, *The New Jim Crow*.

[10] Michelle Alexander, *The New Jim Crow*, p. 7.

[11] Reuters Graphics, Travis Hartman, Samual Hart, Jonnelle Marte, Howard Snyder, July 14, 2020, The Race Gap – United States Sentencing Commission.

[12] Reuters Graphics, Travis Hartman, Samual Hart, Jonnelle Marte, Howard Snyder, July 14, 2020, The Race Gap – The Sentencing Project .

[13] Lani Guinier, Gerald Torres, 2002 "The Minor's Canary", p. 56.

[14] *Cobb, 2009 in Implicit Bias in Child Welfare, Education, and Mental Health Systems.*

[15] Equal Justice Initiative 2017.

"And it's time for them to come down": History, Memory, and Decentering Settler Colonialism

Rose Soza War Soldier

In the aftermath of cell phone video footage documenting the killing of George Floyd in Minneapolis, Minnesota on May 25, 2020, national conversations questioned the purpose and intent behind memorials, monuments, and statues. The graphic video shocked many viewers across the United States, and the world, into discussion and action. Indeed, Floyd's murder served as a tipping point for many aligning with the Black Lives Matter movement and other social and political organizations. A hot summer began filled with hundreds of public marches, protests, and occupations across the country along with voracious consumption of books primarily about race, race relations, and anti-racism, all during a national health emergency and global pandemic.

On Saturday afternoon June 20, 2020, a group of Angelinos expressed their frustration with a summer of social and political unrest by pulling down the statue of Junípero Serra in Serra Park on Olvera Street in Downtown Los Angeles. As the toppled statue, lay dripping in red paint, and bound with rope, questions emerged. Who was Junípero Serra, what was his legacy, and how did this act fit with the larger series of events unfolding across a smoldering nation? Serra, the founder of nine of California's twenty-one missions, has been the subject of controversy for decades. In video footage captured by local media one can hear the surrounding crowd shouting, "bring it down."[1] Alexandro José Gradilla, associate professor of Chicano studies at CSU Fullerton, noted that this part of the city is no stranger to violence and controversy. According to him, "so much racial violence has occurred there. There was a massacre of Chinese workers. There was a massacre of African Americans, so that site has had a lot of historic violence. The fact that the Natives are trying to restore something by tearing that statue down, I think is quite significant and in a big picture way, quite healing,"[2] In subsequent days and weeks, additional statues and monuments were defaced, removed, or relocated to storage throughout California and the country. Citizens and public officials seized the moment to engage in public debate about what statues, monuments, and memorials symbolized. Some argued Serra statues commemorated the Spanish heritage of what is now known as the State of California and any criticism of him represented an anti-Latino position. In contrast, many California Indians and their non-Native allies pointed out that missions served as sites of violence, pain, grief, and death. Their grief galvanized them to action. Further, Serra statues symbolize an enduring nostalgia for a peaceful past that did not exist and effectively erased Native histories, voices, experiences, and memories.

While much of the national unrest focused on Confederate memorials, in California targets for removal included Christopher Columbus, Junípero Serra, and John Sutter. In some instances, the state or private institutions, like the Catholic Church and Sutter Hospital, chose to proactively remove their public displays. Yet in other cases, individual or community force brought them down. The removal of these idols represents the culmination of a decades-long push by Natives and some non-Native alliances. However, many non-Natives publicly expressed grievance and argued the 2020 removals represented revisionist history. Indeed, revisionist history began with building these memorials, monuments, and statues as symbols supporting a specific historical narrative.

Carved in stone, cast in bronze, monuments, memorials, statues, and plaques, play a role in the way regional, state, and national memory functions. In part, history investigates the way memory forms, persuades, and maintains knowledge and exalts certain individuals or commemorates events. Public memorials, monuments, and statues often serve as ideological tools of white supremacy and suppression.[3] These symbols and stories are often both the products of and perpetuators of a one-dimensional past. The construction is purposefully designed to last generations and instill respect and idolatry of events and individuals classified as heroes. Authority is implied in these public displays of memory and its implied permanence generally goes unquestioned while imparting a sense of pride and empathy about these individuals and their stories. However, if you remove scheduled maintenance, these sturdy, unquestioned items may become worn, crumble, and fade. They are not permanent, they are maintained.

Historian Ibram X. Kendi discusses the role denial has played in U.S. history and maintenance of a specific historical narrative. He comments, "But what's also part of America is denying all of what is part of America. Actually, this denial is the essential part of America. Denial is the heartbeat of America."[4] While Kendi's argument refers to the attack on the U.S. Capitol on January 6, 2021, he contextualizes history and asserts a need for an urgently truthful discussion about ethnic and race relations. He calls for direct discussion. How can we resolve current social and political problems, such as racism, anti-Indianism, sexism, economic inequality, and more, if we ignore or deny history and this legacy that directly ties to contemporary issues and events?

In response to this question, a common refrain and part of public lexicon is that slavery is the original sin of the United States of America and race (and racism) derived from it. Certainly, slavery had a role. However, I respectfully ask readers to also consider the role of imperialism and genocide of Native peoples and lands as part of the triumvirate upon which the colonies and country were built.[5] As a professor in my graduate program, Dr. Matthew C. Whitaker, regularly commented, this is not about what he termed, "oppression Olympics," wherein one engages in comparative analysis to prove which population had worse treatment; rather, it is about a more complete understanding of history and recognizing the way race, racialization, and racism operated and continues to operate.

The United States as a nation was born out of genocide and imperialism with acquisition of Native lands a unifying goal of settler-colonial violence. Well before the founding of the country, Pope Alexander VI issued a Papal Bull in 1493 that played a key role in the Catholic Church justifying its theft of Native lands based on religious difference, not phenotype or race. Early writings from Europeans clearly illustrate the dehumanization of Natives. The concept of viewing Natives as "soulless" and requiring "saving" is inherently paternalistic, condescending, ethnocentric, and disregards Indigenous cultural practices. Eventually race, racialization, and racial hierarchy would reinscribe upon religious differences.[6] As a result, a uniquely American construct of race emerged to justify theft of land and perceived inferiority in comparison to perceived white supremacy. The Supreme Court codified the "Doctrine of Discovery," in 1823 Johnson v. McIntosh decision which stripped Native rights to their lands and is still cited as legal precedent.[7] As recently as 2005, Justice Ruth Bader Ginsburg cited the "Doctrine of Discovery" in her 8 v. 1 legal opinion of *Sherrill v. Oneida Indian Nation*.

Therefore, discussions about race in the United States inherently require the inclusion of Native peoples and Native histories. Specific to Indigenous peoples, Dakota historian Waziyatawin details the need for truth-telling, which includes using accurate words to describe events and policies, because, "if the settler society denies the injustices of the past and present, then the impetus to maintain the status quo is strong; there is no recognized need for change."[8] Likewise, historian William Bauer, Jr., Wailacki and Concow, describes narrative and historiography, "The 'California Story' rationalized Settler colonialism, exculpated white Americans for nineteenth and twentieth-century violence, and erased Indigenous People from historical and contemporary scene."[9] Furthermore, historian Roxanne Dunbar-Ortiz asserts, "The history of the United States is a history of settler colonialism-the founding of a state based on the ideology of white supremacy, the widespread practice of African slavery, and a policy of genocide and land theft."[10] These three scholars explicitly explain the ways in which the commonly held historical narrative overlooks inclusion of Native histories. Therefore, the removal of monuments and statues, particularly of specific individuals, whether the Confederacy or colonial California, represents a more accurate historical narrative. Absence of historical context, maintaining Serra and Sutter statues, is a decision to celebrate imperialism, colonization, and genocide. Monument removal forces the public to grapple with one-dimensional imagery by interacting with and reflecting on the historical motivations for such iconography.

Reflect on your own educational experience. What did you learn about Native peoples and their names, histories, stories, and lands? Have you encountered a statue of a Native person? In comparison, particularly if you were raised in California and attended school in the state, are you familiar with the names John Sutter or Junípero Serra? Where did you learn their names? What stories do you associate with them? Have you encountered anything named after them? Perhaps a school, road, hospital, or did you ever think about how the San Diego Padres or San Francisco 49ers got named? California Indian protests against Serra and Sutter statues represent a decades long push against the celebration of imperialism, colonization, and genocide. In short, Serra and Sutter are not our heroes; and it is important to point out, some of their contemporaries also viewed them, or the institutions they led, as cruel and inhumane. In describing testimonies from religious officials and European travelers, Ohlone-Costanoan Esselen/Chumash scholar Deborah Miranda noted, "These people saw through the eyes of their time and what they saw disturbed them deeply."[11]

As products of a state-sponsored educational system, familiarity with Serra and Sutter is near universal among many California students. However, some experience a sense of dissonance when learning accurate history about Serra or Sutter. This experience clearly demonstrates the political nature of history and its significance in storytelling. The contemporary presence of Natives sometimes causes dissonance, recently illustrated with CNN's Election Day Poll of Arizona voters and its November 3, 2020, on air graphic which listed: White, Latino, Black, Asian, and "Something Else."[12] In a state where nearly 30 percent of land is tribal land and Native voters played a key swing vote in the presidential election, an on-air graphic erased Natives' existence, and their political role. CNN later apologized for its casual dismissal of Natives residing in Arizona, but the occurrence demonstrates how a corporate colonial-state views Natives.

California began the process of reflecting and acknowledging its educational shortcomings and dissonance by forming a Truth and Reconciliation Council. On June 18, 2019, Governor Gavin Newsom issued an executive order establishing the Council in part because "the state of California and California Native Americans have never jointly formally examined or documented their relationship for the express purpose of acknowledging and accounting for historical wrongs committed by the state of California toward California Native Americans."[13] The state history is rooted in violence. The first civilian governor of California, Peter Burnett, asserted in his first state address, "That a war of extermination will continue to be waged between the races until the Indian race becomes extinct must be expected.

While we cannot anticipate this result but with painful regret, the inevitable destiny of the race is beyond the power or wisdom of man to avert."[14] Born in Tennessee to a slave-owning family, Burnett brought his racist ideologies from not only his home state but also from his experience in Missouri and Oregon, where he supported legislation to ban all Blacks from the state. If Governor Newsom and those on the Council recognize that the Council itself is merely a beginning, then it has potential. It remains to be seen how the state will move forward in addressing history and reconciling the violent past on which the state is built. As historians Damon Akins and William Bauer note, "Despite the long and rich history of Indigenous people in California, historians, anthropologists, and everyday people disconnected California Indian history from California history."[15]

Ethnic Studies emerged in part to address the lack of faculty and accurate histories, stories, voices centering BIPOC (Black, Indigenous, People of Color) experiences. Groups pushed for the exclusion of false narratives that tended to glorify and aggrandize individuals since these symbols became shorthand for celebration and passive acceptance. Nick Estes, Lower Brule Sioux, asserts, "Settler narratives use a linear conception of time to distance themselves from the horrific crimes against Indigenous peoples and the land," for example the celebration of imperialism, colonization, and genocide by individuals like Serra and Sutter. In contrast, Estes notes, "There is no separation between past and present, meaning that an alternative future is also determined by our understanding of our past. Our history is the future."[16] Therefore, the battle over history and symbols is certainly about the past, but most importantly is also futuristic because it relates to a time wherein colonizers are not celebrated—it centers a Native future.

Long before the removal of statues of Serra and Sutter during 2020, both figures received public criticism and concerted efforts to challenge their status as worthy of celebration. The quincentennial of Columbus's arrival in 1992 certainly generated public protest, and in 2006, scholar Jack Forbes lobbied the Davis City Council to rename "Sutter Place." He proposed "Risling Court," to honor David Risling, Hupa, a cofounder of Native American Studies at UC Davis. The City Council unanimously supported renaming it.[17] Sutter's Fort, named for its founder John Sutter, located in Sacramento and part of the State Historic Parks system, experienced petty vandalism, and protest. The Fort and surrounding settlement, built by California Indian slave labor, served as the entry point for many traveling to the area prior to statehood and certainly after discovery of gold at Sutter's Mill near current-day Coloma. As a result, Sutter is considered one of the foreign founders of the area, and his son ultimately sold large parcels of land upon which the city of Sacramento was built.[18] The Park staff acknowledges the site as a place of violence and pain. On its website Fort staff note, "Like a number of historic sites in California, Sutter's Fort has nominally shared the complex, and often disturbing nineteenth century history of California with its often deadly consequences for California Native Americans. The failure to fully incorporate that history in the park's interpretation programs has led to an unbalanced perspective about John

Sutter and his legacy, along with that of other settlers. The near-exclusion of California Native Americans' lived experiences in this story also has led to a failure to acknowledge how this historic site represents a painful reminder of that history to their descendants."[19] As a result, the site is in the process of evaluating the interpretation of Sutter's Fort.

Perhaps less visible to a non-Native public, it is important to note that calls for statue removals occurred well before the twenty-first century, but the 2020 summer's political environment created unprecedented receptive listening and action. For example, in 2018, the San Francisco Arts Commission voted to send into storage the two-ton "Early Days" statue standing at Civic Center Plaza. It depicted a fallen American Indian, dressed in Plains style, not accurate to the geographical region, cowering at the feet of a Catholic missionary who points to heaven, while a Spanish cowboy raises his hand in victory. It had stood since 1894 with calls for its removal occurring at least since the 1990s, if not much earlier.[20]

The contestation surrounding Serra occurred for decades.[21] In years past, Serra statues throughout the state had red paint thrown onto them, were knocked over, heads decapitated, or words sprayed onto them. Since 1934 the Diocese of Monterey compiled records in support of the canonization of Serra and Fr. Noel Moholy of San Francisco began lobbying for Serra sainthood in 1958. Pope John Paul II eventually beatified Serra in 1988 and Pope Francis declared Serra a Saint in 2015, which was met with numerous protests, many led by California Indians.[22] Indeed, Pope Francis recognized the Church's violent and criminal past. In 2015, when visiting Bolivia, he acknowledged, "many grave sins were committed against the Native people of America in the name of God." He continued, "I humbly ask forgiveness, not only for the offense of the Church herself, but also for crimes committed against the Native peoples during the so-called conquest of America."[23]

The twenty-one missions in California have long been places of pain and grief, but to some California Indian practitioners of the Catholic faith they may represent a place of comfort. Andrew Galvan, Ohlone curator for Mission Delores, and who supported and participated in Serra sainthood ceremony maintains, "The missions were an unmitigated disaster for the Indians of California," and continues, "There's no denying that."[24] Tongva, Kelly Caballero, describes when at Mission San Gabriel, "It feels heavy. It's thick. It's a thick air that I breathe when I'm there. But you can't deny history, and you just have to accept it, and educate people on the reality of what the missions did."[25] Her statement illustrates the complicated and nuanced relationship California Indians have with the colonial-state and its colonial legacy.

Consequently, it should not be surprising that Native groups like the State-wide Coalition Against Racist Symbols, and others, worked to "de-Serra" and "de-Sutter" cities throughout the state with several statues' removals in 2020. On the evening of Juneteenth, June 19, 2020, protesters gathered at Golden Gate Park in San Francisco and joined together to topple statues of Serra, Francis Scott Key, who composed The Star-Spangled Banner, and President Ulysses Grant. In the aftermath, the city ordered their removal and that they be sent to storage. Commissioned in 1906 and completed in bronze by 1907, the Serra statue had stood for over a century. In response to the toppling, San Francisco Mayor London Breed noted the cost of cleanup, and also commented, "I have asked the Arts Commission, the Human Rights Commission, and the Recreation and Parks Department to work with the community to evaluate our public art and its intersection with our country's racist history."[26] She also ordered a Columbus statue to be sent to a storage facility.

In contrast to these individual and community led removals, the city of Ventura issued a joint statement from its Mayor, a Chumash cultural leader, and a Priest from San Buenaventura Mission Church to announce the removal of 9-foot-tall bronze Serra statue in front of Ventura City Hall in anticipation of public protest calling for its removal.[27] Dedicated in 1936 as a product of President Roosevelt's Federal Art Project under the auspices of the New Deal. The original stone version stood outside of Ventura City Hall until it was replaced in 1989 with a bronze version. Ultimately during a July evening, it was removed and sent to storage in 2020.[28]

In the state Capitol of Sacramento, Columbus, Serra, and Sutter statues disappeared, in some instances through voluntary means. An 8-foot-tall Sutter statue stood outside Sutter Medical Center, located at the northeast corner of 28th and L streets. It had been donated by the United Swiss Lodge of California in 1987 and had stood for the past thirty-two years. The hospital ordered its removal to storage in June, a week after employees found it covered with red paint.[29] Jesus Tarango, tribal chairperson of the Wilton Rancheria, the only federally recognized tribal Nation in Sacramento county, commented, "We hope that this removal will finally open a path to a truthful and exact history of atrocities that took place against our people at the hands of John Sutter and others, and that our history will be taught in schools to not only our native students, but to the masses. We cannot expect true change or atonement without an honest portrayal of history."[30] During July at Capitol Park, a Serra statue was toppled and ultimately sent to storage. Funded by the Native Sons of the Golden West and the California State Legislature, the 8-foot-tall statue had stood there since 1967.[31] Finally, the Capitol building staff ordered the removal and possible return of a four-ton marble and granite statue of Queen Isabella of Spain and Christopher Columbus which stood at the center of the state rotunda since 1883. It had been gifted to the state by Darius Ogden Mills, a banker who made his wealth during the California Gold Rush.[32]

In the aftermath of the Serra statue being toppled on the 4th of July on Capitol grounds, the first California Indian elected to Legislature, Assembly Member James C. Ramos, Serrano/Cahuilla, (D-Highland) introduced legislation AB 338 in January 2021 to formally replace it. Cosponsored by six Northern California tribes, the bill would remove the 1965 state statutory requirement that a Serra statue stand on Capitol grounds. Instead, a replacement monument with input from local tribal Nations would be designed for Capitol grounds and the new Capitol

Annex would include a hearing room painted with a mural dedicated to California Indians.[33] Because the Serra statue creation and placement occurred through state legislation and a $30,000 investment from the state general fund, it would take additional state legislation to formally replace it, though without similar state funding. In August 2021, Ramos's legislation passed with a bipartisan vote of 28 to 2 and went to Governor Gavin Newsom for his signature.[34] On California Native American Day, Governor Newsom signed AB 338 into law.[35]

The physical manifestation of looming symbols of imperialism, genocide, and colonization is no longer being whole-heartedly embraced and celebrated. Out of those statues and monuments removed, it is important to note that many are relatively new and placed within roughly the last 30 to 50 years in a state that is over 170 years old. As a result, how are these statues more reflective of the time in which they were built and what does it mean that contemporaries of Serra and Sutter experienced no compulsion to build monuments to them? Further, the removal raises questions about whose voices and memories are remembered or suppressed in history. Some critics argue that removal represents "cancel culture" wherein political correctness runs amok. However, many of these critics dismiss the full history of these individuals and the institutions they led. In addition, the dissonance some critics experience undoubtedly occurs because they are asked to decenter settler-colonialism and center California Indian voices and experiences. As a result, their complaints appear to be more about grievance than historical accuracy.

History is a site of power and politics. Part of its power is the ability of history and those who write it to erase and rationalize past actions of peoples or the state. Thus, mainstream society accepted distorted stories as universal truths while eliminating Native histories or reducing them to caricatures.

The creation of many of these statues, like most monuments to the Confederacy, occurred long after the lives of the individuals they depict. It is reasonable to ask, Why do these supporters have a vested interested in maintaining this historical narrative? They seek a romanticized revival of the past in which they may justify violence and rationalize theft of Native lands. Indeed, Catholic Archbishop Salvatore Cordileone responded to removal of Serra statues at Golden Gate Park and Mission San Rafael by holding exorcisms to combat the "evil," of those who toppled them.[36] Removing statues does not translate into these individuals being lost to history. Instead, it is about eliminating their public exaltation, placing them into historical context, and recognizing revisionist history occurred with the building of these statues and monuments to perceived heroes. Further, removal or placing statues and monuments in historical contextualization is the first step, but there needs to be responsible reflection about the next step. Morning Star Gali, Ajumawi band of the Pit River Tribe, campaigned to remove several statues and describes them as, "monuments to racism. These are monuments to genocide. And it's time for them to come down."[37] The future is Indigenous.

Notes

[1] "Junipero Serra Statue in LA Comes Down," accessed January 12, 2021, www.youtube.com/watch?v=JZHFjoof2ag.

[2] Jessica De Nova, "OC scholars say removal of Father Junipero Serra statues could start healing process for oppressed communities," *ABC 7 News*, June 24, 2020, https://abc7.com/father-junipero-serra-statue-history/6263102/.

[3] For more information about historiography and symbols see: James J. Rawls, "The California Mission as Symbol and Myth," *California History, 71*, no. 3 (1992): 342–361; Ibram X. Kendi, "Mascots, Myths, Monuments, and Memory," accessed January 13, 2021, https://www.youtube.com/watch?v=87Ph9AqDQf0; Erika Doss, *Memorial Mania: Public Feeling in America*. Chicago: University of Chicago Press, 2010; Robyn Autry, "Elastic Monumentality? The Stone Mountain Confederate Memorial and Counterpublic Historical Space," *Social Identities, 25*, no. 2 (2019): 169–185.

[4] Ibram X. Kendi, "Denial is the Heartbeat of America," *The Atlantic*, January 11, 2021, www.theatlantic.com/ideas/archive/2021/01/denial-heartbeat-america/617631/.

[5] Dina Gilio-Whitaker, "Unpacking the Invisible Knapsack of Settler Privilege," accessed January 13, 2021, www.beaconbroadside.com/broadside/2018/11/unpacking-the-invisible-knapsack-of-settler-privilege.htmls.

[6] Ronald Takaki, "The Tempest in the Wilderness: The Racialization of Savagery," *The Journal of American History, 79*, no. 3 (1992): 892–912.

[7] Walter R. Echo-Hawk, *In the courts of the conqueror: The ten worst Indian law cases ever decided*. Golden, CO: Fulcrum Publishing, 2012.

[8] Waziyatawin, *What does justice look like? The struggle for liberation in Dakota homeland*. St. Paul, MN: Living Justice Press, 2008, 83

[9] William J. Bauer, *California through Native Eyes Reclaiming History*. Seattle: University of Washington Press, 2016, 5.

[10] Roxanne Dunbar-Ortiz, *An Indigenous peoples' history of the United States*. ReVisioning American History. Boston: Random House, 2014, 2.

[11] "Toppling mission monuments and mythologies conference," accessed January 13, 2021, www.youtube.com/watch?v=OeWBCtxw4W8&list=PLlP0zEksDMkNv25GqI2KPhMfvidO_S6G3&index=2.

[12] Laura Zornosa, "It appears CNN deemed Native Americans 'something else' sparking a backlash," *The Los Angeles Times*, November 5, 2020, www.latimes.com/entertainment-arts/tv/story/2020-11-05/it-looks-like-cnn-called-native-americans-something-else-theyre-not-happy.

[13] See "Executive order N-15-19" California Office of the Tribal Advisor, accessed January 15, 2021, https://tribalaffairs.ca.gov/.

[14] Peter Burnett, "State of the state address," The Governors' Gallery, accessed January 13, 2021, https://governors.library.ca.gov/addresses/s_01-Burnett2.html.

[15] Damon B. Akins & William J. Bauer. *We are the land: A history of native California*. Berkeley: University of California Press, 2021, 2.

[16] Nick Estes, *Our history is the future: Standing Rock versus the Dakota access pipeline, and the long tradition of Indigenous resistance*. New York: Verso Press, 2019, 14.

[17] "Minutes of the meeting of the Davis City Council January 10, 2006," City of Davis, accessed January 20, 2021, http://documents.cityofdavis.org/Media/Default/Documents/PDF/CityCouncil/CouncilMeetings/Minutes/Archive/Minutes-2006-01-10-City-Council-Meeting.pdf.

[18] Albert L. Hurtado, *John Sutter: A life on the North American frontier* Norman: University of Oklahoma Press, 2006.

[19] "History of Sutter's Fort State Historic Park," accessed January 20, 2021, www.parks.ca.gov/?page_id=21507.

[20] Daniela Blei, "San Francisco's 'Early Days' statue is gone. Now comes the work of activating real history," *The Smithsonian Magazine*, October 4, 2018, www.smithsonianmag.com/smithsonian-institution/san-francisco-early-days-statue-gone-now-comes-work-activating-real-history-180970462/.

[21] Rupert Costo & Jeannette Henry Costo, *The missions of California: A legacy of genocide*. San Francisco: The Indian Historian Press, 1987.

[22] For information about California Indian positionality regarding the mission system, see: *News from Native California* 28, no. 2 (Winter 2014/2015); Deborah Miranda, *Bad Indians: A tribal memoir*. Berkeley: Heyday Press, 2013.

[23] Jim Yardley & William Newman, "In Bolivia, Pope Francis Apologizes for Church's 'Grave Sins.'" *The New York Times*, July 10, 2015, www.nytimes.com/2015/07/10/world/americas/pope-francis-bolivia-catholic-church-apology.html.

[24] Erin Blakemore, "Why are Native American groups protesting Catholicism's newest saint," *The Smithsonian Magazine*, September 25, 2015, www.smithsonianmag.com/history/why-are-native-groups-protesting-catholicisms-newest-saint-180956721/.

[25] "Lost LA: Borderlands," accessed January 20, 2021, www.pbs.org/video/borderlands-pixo98/.

[26] Nico Savidge, et al, "Statues of Junipero Serra, Ulysses S. Grant toppled at Golden Gate Park," *The Mercury News*, June 20, 2020, www.mercurynews.com/2020/06/20/junipero-serra-statue-toppled-at-golden-gate-park/.

[27] Kimberly Rivers, "Time to remove Serra statue," *VC Reporter*, June 18, 2020, https://vcreporter.com/2020/06/time-to-remove-serra-statue-chumash-church-and-city-agree/.

[28] Historic Preservation Committee, City of Ventura, accessed January 22, 2021, www.cityofventura.ca.gov/DocumentCenter/View/22039/2020-07-01_Item-1_PROJ-14599.

[29] Vincent Moleski, "Protesters march, rip down Serra Statue in Capitol Park," *The Sacramento Bee*, July 5, 2020, www.sacbee.com/news/local/article244012732.html.

[30] Lance Armstrong, "Community responds to removal of John Sutter Statue, Valley Community Newspapers, July 3, 2020, www.valcomnews.com/community-responds-to-removal-of-john-sutter-statue/.

[31] "Father Serra Statue in Capitol Park," Sacramento Room Digital Collections, accessed January 22, 2021, https://sacroom.contentdm.oclc.org/digital/collection/p15248coll1/id/2137/.

[32] "Crews Remove California State Capitol Christopher Columbus Statue," CBS 13, accessed January 22, 2021, https://sacramento.cbslocal.com/2020/07/07/california-state-capitol-christopher-columbus-statue-removed/.

[33] "Ramos Introduces Bill to Replace Toppled Serra Statue at Capitol," Press Release, accessed February 12, 2021, https://a40.asmdc.org/press-releases/20210128-ramos-introduces-bill-replace-toppled-serra-statue-capitol. The original tribal Nation co-sponsors include: Wilton Rancheria, Buena Vista Rancheria of Me-Wuk Indians, Chicken Ranch Rancheria of Me-Wuk Indians, Ione Band of Miwok Indians, Shingle Springs Band of Miwok Indians and the Tuolumne Band of Me-Wuk Indians.

[34] "Ramos Measure to Add Native American Monument to Capitol Park were Serra statue Once Stood Will go to Governor," Press Release, accessed September 4, 2021, https://a40.asmdc.org/press-releases/20210823-ramos-measure-add-native-american-monument-capitol-park-where-serra-statue.

[35] Kim Bojorquez, "Gavin Newsom signs law to replace Sacramento Junipero Serra statue with monument for tribes," *The Sacramento Bee*, September 24, 2021, www.sacbee.com/news/california/article254079163.html.

[36] Michael Cabanatuan, "S.F. Archbishop holds exorcism at San Rafael Church where Junipero Serra statue was vandalized," *San Francisco Chronicle*, October 17, 2020, www.sfchronicle.com/bayarea/article/S-F-archbishop-holds-exorcism-at-San-Rafael-15655608.php.

[37] Carly Severn, "How do we Heal?" KQED, July 7, 2020, www.kqed.org/news/11826151/how-do-we-heal-toppling-the-myth-of-junipero-serra.

Reflection Questions

1. How can we use some of the concepts to evaluate the perspectives we hold to be true? (Optional)

2. What aspects of the readings do you agree or disagree with and why?

3. Reflecting on the readings, what are the perspectives that dominate and define our life in the United States? (Optional)

4. What are the solutions and challenges we can draw from the readings to positively influence our quality of life?

5. Which perspectives do you hold on to and which have you let go of at this point in your life? What process or guidelines did you apply to negotiate your perspectives? Do you think these readings can enrich this process?

Response and Responsibility

Framing Questions

1. What are some dominant themes that lead you either to believe race relations may or may not change? Please provide some examples as to why you think change will or will not happen.

2. Given the previous readings, why do you think this section is called "Response and Responsibility"? (Optional)

3. How would you define the term *response* given the previous readings and comparing that with your own experience? What inspires you to respond to a situation versus not responding at all? (Optional)

4. How would you define the term *responsibility* given the previous readings and comparing them with your own experience? What inspires you to take responsibility and when are you not inspired to take responsibility? Please offer a brief explanation using two examples to illustrate your point.

ETHNIC STUDIES: AN INTRODUCTION

Introduction

Eric Vega and Julie López Figueroa

Ethnic Studies concerns itself with both abstract ideas and social justice. It presents historical and sociological information regarding race, ethnicity, gender and class. At the same time Ethnic Studies also discusses strategies for confronting unequal social relations in our community and nation. These discussions and dialogs offer us a chance to think critically about how others have confronted questions of power and privilege. This is both tricky and complex because the subject matter of inequality is not purely abstract or academic.

The specific struggles of women and people of color for liberation and respect are in themselves political controversies. Simply raising the issue of race or ethnicity is for many people an unsettling political terrain. But this is exactly the world of ideas and social struggle that informs this book. Both parts are integral to Ethnic Studies research and both parts continue to reanimate our lectures and study. In other words, this book is not just a data dump of terms and abstract ideas to memorize for the teacher. That is because the subject consistently breaks the bounds of objective analysis. The data and terms raise uncomfortable questions regarding response and responsibility.

A few years ago our Department of Ethnic Studies received racially motivated death threats. The caller felt deeply threatened by the intersection of people of color analyzing questions of race and ethnicity. This immersion in political controversy is not likely to be found in the Geology or Math departments. That is not to suggest Ethnic Studies has the "truth" or even complete answers to the difficult questions that surround us. It is more true to say our readings and our study are precisely about going deeper and learning how we can use language and ideas to inform our strategies for making the world a better place. As an example, this book asks the reader to move away from shallow or simplistic responses to racism. In our classes it is not enough to observe that the Ku Klux Klan makes you feel bad or sad. It is more important to ask questions regarding the historical and ideological context for white supremacist organizations. How do you respond to hate organizations when they work to insert themselves into popular consciousness? When you move beyond their cartoon like imagery, to what extent are their ideas accepted? These are difficult questions rooted in both theory and practice.

On the theoretical side, there are many explanations for the recurring controversies and issues connected to racial and ethnic relations. One way of approaching this topic is to examine identity. Who are we? Do we socially construct ourselves? What is the history of identity and what is its connection to the order of the nation? Historically, in the social sciences, intellectuals have formulated classic questions to help us examine popular ideas regarding identity. People like Freud, Marx and Nietzche have argued that we must examine the subconscious, money relations or the will to power if we want to honestly examine how people see themselves and relate to others. Ethnic Studies continues this tradition of observation and questioning. It asks the following kinds of questions. How have racial and ethnic groups been silenced or marginalized? What is the relationship of identity to power? In what ways do we have a fixed identity? What are the consequences of a constructed identity? As we work our way through these complex questions we rely on basic terms and theories. Stereotypes, ethnocentrism, assimilation and theories of prejudice and discrimination are the building blocks for examining questions related to racial and ethnic identity. But again it is critical to acknowledge that these words and ideas arise out of the struggles of historically subjugated peoples. That is not to suggest that social struggles are limited to problems associated with oppression and victimization. It is instead to say that our ideas about ourselves and about the world around us are fundamentally connected to the actual struggles of people. This means that an accurate description of the ethnic experience in this country must include an examination of social movements, political demands, styles of organizing, legal information and strategies that people of color have used historically to achieve their objectives.

This section of the book offers examples of how scholars, activists and communities have responded to the challenge of identify and power relations. Overt, popularly supported violence, segregation and discrimination are an important part of this nation's history of race relations. Subsequent attempts at comity have resulted in important legislative and judicial reforms that we think of as civil rights. But how much has changed? Has the werewolf face of white supremacy been replaced with a smiley face that disguises deeper problems? The 1954 Supreme Court decision, *Brown v Board of Education of Topeka Kansas* has often been touted as the turning point in U.S. race relations. The popular opinion holds that the post-Brown era is all about tolerance, institutional neutrality and desegregation. Professor Scott provides a critical assessment of this view. As a matter of history, racial and ethnic minorities have placed great emphasis on education as a cornerstone for upward mobility and equal treatment. Despite tremendous opposition they voiced support for civil rights laws and integration of the public school system. But the resources and political will to see educational opportunity become a reality has not occurred over the last fifty years. Instead resegregation and mass incarceration are increasingly the norm. Professor Scott examines this lack of progress and the absence of a mass movement demanding racial justice in schools. He concludes his article by analyzing strategies and viewpoints that focus on educating African American children.

Emerging out of the Black Power Movement, Pan African Studies has grown over the last forty years to create a body of knowledge that reflects the experience of the African diaspora. In *A Voyage of Discovery: Sacramento and the Politics of Ordinary Black People*, Professor Covin describes the evolution of Black Studies and its connection to the Sacramento community. Issues of identity and power are not simply the story of politicians and elites. As discussed in this article, Pan African Studies must also be the history of how working class people have negotiated with power in their everyday lives to create political space and unity.

Response and resistance to forms of abusive power do not follow a straight line. Sometimes it involves negotiation at other times it involves open challenges and disruptions to the prevailing order. As an example, over a long period of time many people negotiated their way through slavery but ultimately it was not reformed but abolished. Today an emerging political movement is beginning to challenge assumptions regarding the inhumane treatment of undocumented workers in this country. In her article, *Arizona: Ground Zero for the War on Immigrants and Latinos(as)* Professor Ramirez discusses the recent history of punitive anti-immigrant laws passed in the state of Arizona. These laws, including efforts to restrict Ethnic Studies courses have generated a swift and enduring movement of activists willing to challenge traditional law enforcement perspectives on immigration. To date, an energetic Latino(a) based civil rights movement has successfully used marches, political rallies and boycotts to challenge racial profiling and institutionalized discrimination. This article asks us to think about "illegality" as a framing device for popularly supported inequality. The powerful chapter by Tim Fong titled "Asian American and Pacific Islanders Harmed by Trump COVID-19 Blame Campaign" examines the historical realities of racism against Asian American and Pacific Islander (AAPI) communities. To contest the treatment of AAPI communities, Fong invites readers to know they can exchange feeling powerless to becoming empowered by getting involved in movements that seek to counter anti-Asian hate.

The chapter by Annalise Harlow—"We can't just stand aside now": Oakland's Fortune Cookie Factory Stands with Black Lives Matter—showcases how one Oakland Chinatown community local business owner, Alicia Wong, of Fortune Cookie Factory becomes an ally to the Black Lives Matter movement. Wong's decision to create a cookie as a public symbol of solidarity was more than ideology. Manifesting this solidarity required buying new tools and investing in a special electric cutter to produce these BLM cookies. Producing these cookies for public viewing and consumption contested the misconstrued belief that Asian American community is politically passive.

The final chapter, "The 65th Street Corridor Community Collaborative Project: A Lesson in Community Service," in this section looks at how the Ethnic Studies

Department at Sacramento State has worked with Will C. Wood Middle School and Hiram Johnson High School to address issues raised by the parents and students in those communities. Operating by one of Ethnic Studies principles to serve the community, this chapter highlights some strong lessons learned about how to broker, foster, and sustain a university–school partnership. Centering community voices enabled the 65th Project to effectively offer tutoring/mentoring assistance, and college preparation for students through Student Bridge Program and for parents by way of the Parent Bridge Program, and finally there is a leadership component for the university students seeking to serve in the designated communities. Relying on a team of CSUS faculty and students and rooted in theories of community psychology, this project continues to provide tutor/mentor assistance, college preparation, and leadership training and parent partnership programs.

Challenging the Dilemma of *Brown v. Topeka Board of Education*: And the Rush Toward Resegregation

Otis L. Scott

 ## Introduction

It has been more than six years since this nation took a brief time out to reflect on the significance of the 1954 landmark Supreme Court decision, <u>Brown vs. Topeka Board of Education</u>. Across the nation countless events were staged in commemoration of the path breaking Court decision. Most of these events hailed the significant role <u>Brown</u> played in dismantling the walls of *de jure* Jim Crow segregation enclosing public schools in southern and border states of this nation. Not nearly enough attention was given to the fact of public school regegregation occurring in the post <u>Brown</u> era.

This article is a general examination of the pre- and post-<u>Brown</u> eras with critical attention given to the extent to which the Court decision addressed the dreams of proponents of public school desegregation. I contend that the effects of <u>Brown</u> must be understood within a heuristic model that demands we critically examine the responses of American society – especially its formal governing institutions – and secondly, its citizenry, to policies and practices of desegregation. In raising these concerns I also raise up the need for a critical examination of the concept of integration which has, and to a diminishing extent today, still serves as the norm driving the discourse around public school desegregation. The core of my discussion turns on the phenomena of public school resegregation which has rendered hollow the promises of the Warren Court's ruling in this important case.

Contributed by Otis L. Scott. © Kendall Hunt Publishing Company

Historical Context

The United States prior to the Brown v. Board decision of 1954 was for all intents and purposes an apartheid society. Policies and practices separating African Americans from white Americans was a defining feature of this nation beginning in the seventeenth century. Segregation practices long existing by habits of custom and heart were engrained into the nation's social formations and subsequently canonized in local, state and national laws.

Given this fact of history the United States was created with what the historian W.E.B. DuBois called the color line (DuBois 1903). The line has divided Black and whites into two distinct societies; separate and unequal. The metaphorical line is as much an issue today as it was at the dawn of the 20th century following the 1896 Supreme Court decision in Plessy v. Ferguson. This decision established in legal concrete, that the races – particularly African descended people and white people – were to be kept separate in public spaces, thus limiting social contact. This decision also had negative implications for other people racialized as a *minority* in the United States. Again, following habits of heart and mind in matters of race long in force in this nation, Plessy articulated this nation's policy on race. Namely, the separation of African people from white people was right, just and proper in order to maintain domestic tranquility and most importantly, white supremacy.

There were few spaces in public life in the United States where the operation of what became known as the "Jim Crow" doctrine of racial separation was more pronounced and more destructive than in public education. And so where were the practices of the pronouncement more destructive than when used to deny African American children living in border and southern states a quality education and the life enhancing opportunities expected from receiving a quality education.

Jim Crow's Children

This nation's dereliction in providing any form of a meaningful education for African Americans long predates the 1896 Plessy decision. The Virginia legislature as early as 1680 passed a law prohibiting Africans from gathering together for any reason. Doing so was punishable by "Twenty Lashes on the Bare Back well laid on" (Irons 2002).

The intent of such severe legislation was to discourage slaves from forming their own schools and from meeting to conjure up plans to overthrow their masters. If Africans in colonial America received any form of education it was one heavily doused with biblical teachings counseling the virtues of obedience, supplication, faith in the deliverance of God and the benevolence of white people. Throughout the antebellum south any efforts at providing a quality education (primarily teaching literacy skills) for African men, women and children were typically clandestine. Such efforts were almost always illegal. Slave owners feared that any form of literacy would lead to insurrection. One defender of this position asked in 1895, "Is there any great moral reason why we should incur the tremendous risk of having our wives and children slaughtered in consequence of our slaves being taught to read incendiary publications?" (Irons 2002).

The first institutionalized efforts to educate African Americans were made after the Civil War by the Reconstruction Congress. There is clear evidence that African Americans took advantage of the opportunity to learn to read and write (Bullock 1967). If one reviews the policy positions taken by African Americans elected and appointed to office during the brief period of Reconstruction (1865-1876), it will be revealed the extent to which newly freed African Americans expressed an unflagging desire for an education for both adults and especially for children. Reconstruction efforts were brought to a screeching halt after 1876 by virtue of the grand betrayal brokered between the political forces supporting the Republican, Rutherford B. Hayes and those supporting Democrat, Samuel B. Tilden. After receiving sufficient electoral votes to be declared president of the United States in 1877, Hayes, honoring his promises to Southern politicos, began dismantling the fledgling and fragile political – legal infrastructure crafted by African Americans and their white allies for including freed men and "free men" into the civic culture of this nation. In effect, Hayes sabotaged efforts by African Americans to become citizens by re-creating the ante bellum conditions for racists in both the north and the south to again get the upper hand in determining the racial etiquette of the south and the nation as a whole. For African Americans this meant a return to the abject status of racial pariah. This status was assured by the by the 1896 Supreme Court ruling in <u>Plessy v. Ferguson.</u>

 ## <u>Plessy</u> as Prologue for <u>Brown</u>

Typical of the educational environment for African Americans living in the post <u>Plessy</u> south is described by James T. Patterson (2001),

Schools for black people were especially bad-indeed primitive . . . .

Sunflower County, Mississippi, a cotton plantation region, had no high schools for Blacks. In the elementary grades of the county's

Black schools, many of the teachers worked primarily as cooks or domestics on the plantations. Most had no more than a fourth grade education (10).

Continuing, he notes that,

In the 1948–49 school year, the average investment per pupil in Atlanta public school facilities was $228.05 for Blacks and $570.00 for whites. In 1949-50 there was an average of 36.2 Black children per classroom, compared to an average of 22.6 among whites (11).

By the early 1950s just as in the preceding decades after the civil war, racial segregation was the hallmark of American apartheid. Public schools in the south and border states were the parade ground where Jim Crow marched and drummed out his message of separation, inequality and inferiority. Schools for African American children were the by products of systematic and institutionalized racism.

Chinks in the armor of Jim Crow began to appear in the decades of the 1940s primarily due to the activism of the National Association for the Advancement of Colored People (NAACP). The NAACP had won some important cases before the U.S. Supreme Court in controversies involving all white primary elections (*Smith v. Allwright* 1944) and segregated law schools (*Sweatt v. Painter,* 1950). The belated initiatives by presidents Franklin D. Roosevelt to open the nation's war industries to African American workers and Harry Truman's Executive Order (E.O. 9981, July 26, 1948) desegregating the armed forces as the decade of the 1940s closed, at least gave notice that the Executive Branch was willing to address America's race dilemma.

The Brown Case

When the 1950s began Linda Brown had just turned six years old. In some respects she typified the thousands of African American children attending segregated public schools. She lived within walking distance, or a short car ride, of a white school in or near her Topeka, Kansas neighborhood. In Linda's case there was a bit of an irony. She lived in an integrated neighborhood and regularly played with white school children. On occasion her white playmates even stayed overnight in her parent's home. Yet, she could not attend the white elementary school just a few blocks from her house. Instead she had to rise early each school morning, walk through a dangerous train switch yard, which was usually a hang out place for some of the town's derelicts and transients, catch a bus which took her to an all Black elementary school some two miles from her house.

Fed up with the color line and the indignities of public school segregation, Oliver Brown, Linda's father, challenged Topeka, Kansas' Jim Crow school system. The challenge came after his being refused to register his daughter in the white school near his house. Typically a mild mannered man – not having a record of activism –Oliver Brown sought out the assistance of the local branch of the NAACP headed by McKinley Burnett (Kluger 1976). Burnett is often times acknowledged as the understated and real hero of the Brown saga. It was he who developed the strategy, organized parents, pulled together the resources necessary to challenge the Topeka School Board's segregation policies (Irons 2002). It was McKinley Burnett who convinced the national NAACP to take on the Topeka case as part of a growing number of school segregation cases the national office was seriously considering.

The Brown case was initially heard before the District Court for the District of Kansas on February 28th, 1951. Robert L. Carter, an able and respected attorney with the NAACP Legal and Defense Fund argued for an injunction forbidding Topeka's public schools from segregating African American elementary school children from white children. By all accounts Carter's presentation was masterfully structured and convincingly presented to the District judges. Indeed, the judges of the District Court were moved to register their empathy for African American children deprived of the higher quality education typically provided to white children. On this point the Court noted, "Segregation of white and colored children in public schools has a detrimental effect on colored children" (Kluger 2002). But the judges refused to issue an injunction, resting their decision instead on the fact that the provisions of the 1896 <u>Plessy</u> decision which decreed that public schools were to be "separate but equal" was still the law of the land.

On October first of the same year, the Brown case was joined with other law suits from South Carolina, Delaware, Virginia, and the District of Columbia challenging public school segregation. While the end results of the Brown case are well-known and certainly represent a sea change in the application of the 14th amendment's equal protection clause to African American children, it was not the first challenge to segregated public schools. In 1849 a similar challenge in the Sarah Roberts case (<u>Roberts v. City of Boston</u>) was filed in Boston, Massachusetts. In 1947, seven years before the Brown decision, The California State Supreme Court declared that the segregated public school system in Orange County, in southern California, was discriminatory towards Mexican American elementary school children (<u>Mendez v. Westminster School District</u>). In Kansas between 1881 and 1949 some eleven cases were filed challenging segregated schools. At the time Brown was argued before the U.S. Supreme Court, the racially segregated public school system was the norm in a good part of the nation. It was legally sanctioned or permitted in twenty four states.

The legal strategy leading to the cases comprising <u>Brown</u> deserves more attention than is the subject of this article. It is important to point out that the assault against public school segregation was well-strategized in advance by some of the best legal minds – Black and white – associated with the NAACP. The plans were underway earnestly in the 1930s with legal challenges being considered against segregation in graduate and professional schools, voting rights and housing (Greenberg 1994).

The chief architect of the desegregation strategy was Charles Hamilton Houston, who was the dean of the Howard University Law School while he was also taking the lead in orchestrating a response to public school segregation. The core of the strategy was its focus on graduate and professional education institutions rather than elementary education. Houston's thinking was that by drawing on the "equal" provisions of <u>Plessy</u> and forcing states to build professional and graduate schools *equal* in all aspects to the white graduate and professional schools, he would overwhelm their ability to support two separate systems of graduate and professional education. Using this strategy he won a landmark decision in 1936 when the Maryland Supreme Court ordered the University of Maryland's law school to admit Donald Murray, a Black student, rather than send him to an out of state law school. (<u>Murray v. Maryland</u>). He won a similar case before the U.S. Supreme Court in 1938 (<u>Missouri ex rel Gaines v. Canada</u>). The Supreme Court in this case found that the University of Missouri, though it did create a separate law school for Black students, the facility-in a building shared with a hotel and a movie theatre-provided a "privilege . . . for white students" which it did not provide for Black students.

In 1939 Houston's prize student, Thurgood Marshall, took over as the chief counsel for the NAACP and established the NAACP Legal Defense and Education Fund. By the late 1940s Marshall was of a mind that the "validity" of the segregation statutes which the NAACP had left unchallenged with its "equalization" strategy was insufficient as a strategy for dismantling segregation laws. At the time the elementary school cases were accepted by the NAACP, the organization's strategy was focused on proving that public school segregation imposed restrictions on African American school children which denied them equal protection of the laws as prescribed by the 14th amendment to the U.S. Constitution. Interestingly, Marshall and his brilliant team of colleagues drew from the research studies by social and behavioral scientists in making their case. In particular the doll studies by Professors Kenneth Clark and his wife, Mamie, were instrumental. Using black and white dolls the Clark's demonstrated that the behaviors of African American children choosing white dolls in a testing situation, and attributing to the dolls positive characteristics, displayed the extent to which segregation had diminished the children's sense of identity and self esteem. Their studies, while controversial, were sufficient to convincing the Justices of the destructive effects racial segregation can have on children.

Significance of Brown

To assert that the unanimous decision rendered by the Court on May 17, 1954 was of landmark proportions is now well-supported. Given its message and the times, the ruling was tantamount to the earth tilting a few degrees off its normal axis. The Court's pronouncement that "separate educational facilities are inherently unequal," and thus constituting a denial of the equal protection clause of the 14th amendment, was for its day a profound rebuke of the long standing provisions of the 1896 Plessy decision. In effect the Court said that African American children deserved to receive an opportunity for an education which constitutionally should be on par with that provided to most white children living in the South.

Because of many questions and uncertainties as how to implement the provisions of the decision, the Supreme Court delivered a Brown II decision a year later. This decision did not provide necessary direction to southern school boards or establish the standards they were to follow in desegregating their public schools. Instead, the Court established the vague principle that desegregation should proceed "with all deliberate speed." This limp edict allowed southern states, their school boards and their public officials – elected and appointed – an escape route from implementing fourteenth amendment provisions of the first Brown decision.

Limitations of Brown II

Brown II was a failure. It failed to give sufficient guidance and direction to the federal courts in desegregation cases. As such, it did not hold states or courts accountable for implementing 14th amendment protections for African American public school children in the south. Thus, only the most courageous judges would venture on their own and rule in the favor of fourteenth amendment protections for African American school children. Brown II was also a failure in that it succumbed to the deeply entrenched belief of white supremacy and separation of the races subscribed to by the great majority of white southerners and no few northerners. The Warren Court, notwithstanding its unanimous decision in Brown I, was not about the business of transforming southern racial values and practices. It had spoken loudly in extending the 14th amendment a new to African American children, but it was not about to take on – head to head – the ideology of white supremacy. The court had gone as far as it cared on the issue of state sponsored school desegregation.

And because of this the "with all deliberate speed" clause allowed southern politicians, policy makers of various stripes and the ordinary white citizens to dodge school desegregation. As noted above, the Supreme Court should have stepped in and ordered compliance with its ruling. It took no such action. As a result racial segregation in southern school districts changed very little between 1955 and 1964 (Patterson 2001). Regarding the glacial movement of desegregation in the south, James T. Patterson notes, "By early 1964, only 1.2 percent of black children in the eleven southern states attended school with whites" (Patterson, 2001). Similarly, northern schools were virtually untouched by desegregation until the mid 1970s. The major point here is that the adherents of Brown were unable to muster the political or moral might necessary to transforming the decision into a national social/political strategy. The object of which would have been to desegregate this nation's public schools.

The fact that this was not done is more of a comment on the unwillingness of this nation's leadership communities to advance desegregation than it is a negative comment on the failings of the U.S. Supreme Court. It is more a critical comment on the lack of a national will; a will undergirded by the moral premise that it is fundamentally wrong, intolerable and unacceptable for any of this nation's children to have to attend schools – especially those segregated by race – where they will predictably receive an inferior education. An education which will also predictably, close doors of opportunity in their faces.

While there were many millions of Americans of all ethnicities and social economic classes in agreement that African American children and children of color should have an opportunity for a quality education, there was never a national consensus of commitment to bringing about the radical changes in how this nation conducted the business of public school education. To wit, there was never a national will to make Brown other than the symbolization of an education norm. That this is the case is disturbingly illustrated by the strident and racist oppositional voices generated by both Brown decisions.

Resistance to the Brown Decisions

To state that the Supreme Court's desegregation decision caused severe undulations in the social, political and legal fabric of the south is to speak to the obvious. This was not a decision that most southerners were expecting although for decades there were growing signs of African American impatience with Jim Crow.

In the main, resistance to the Brown decisions was the order of the day in the south. While there was some reluctant compliance in states, e.g., Arkansas and Tennessee, in the main, resistance was fierce and unrelenting. Typically such resistance took three forms: litigation, privatization and terror. Most southern states challenged desegregation orders through the courts; thus, dragging out implementation. Privatization of public schools was a second form of resistance. White parents, with the aid of school officials and politicians, formed private academies and other institutions, often times using public funds as a way of evading desegregation. The third form of resistance was well known: the use of terror. White segregationists formed hate groups like White Citizen's Councils which became vehicles for transporting hate speech and acts of terrorism against African Americans and anyone else, or anything, presumed to be a threat to segregation.

The most effective assault against the idealistic, albeit vague, mandates of the Supreme Court was launched by presidents Richard Nixon, Ronald Reagan and the two presidents Bush. All four presidents were hostile to desegregation and especially when the federal courts ordered bussing to implement desegregation. Nixon, sought to change what he and his administration believed was an overly active federal judiciary (with particular criticism aimed at the decisions by the Warren Court). Attempting to mitigate this activism he began appointing conservative judges to the federal judiciary and to the Supreme Court. Appointees to the federal judiciary in the decades of the 70s and 80s were made by presidents committed to shaping a more conservative federal judiciary with judges having no zeal for enforcing civil rights laws. It is perversely ironical to note that during this era of redemption, President Ronald Reagan, with inarguably mean spirited intentions, nominated Clarence Thomas, no ally of civil rights activists and the second African American to serve on the U.S. Supreme Court, to replace Thurgood Marshall.

In a series of Supreme Court decisions beginning in 1974 and extending into the mid nineties, the conservative voices on the Court and elsewhere in the federal judiciary essentially rendered a moribund Brown, dead. Examples of key decisions during this period were Milliken v Bradley (1974); Board of Education of Oklahoma City v. Dowell (1991); Freeman v. Pitts (1992); Missouri v. Jenkins (1995).

In Milliken, a Detroit, Michigan case, the Court made Brown all but irrelevant for most northern cities by not approving desegregation plans combining city and suburban schools. In the Board of Education of Oklahoma City v. Dowell the Court ruled that school districts could be released from desegregation orders if they created "unitary" – meaning racially mixed – schools. In the Freeman case the Court provided that a school district could dismantle its desegregation plans without having to desegregate its faculty or provide students equal access to its programs. In <u>Missouri v. Jenkins</u>, the Court prohibited efforts to attract white suburban and private school students voluntarily into city schools by using strong academic programs. Adding an additional nail in the coffin of school and parent-based initiatives to achieve racial balance in public schools, the Supreme Court in 2007 ruled in two cases: <u>Parents Involved in Community Schools v. Seattle School District, No.1</u> and <u>Crystal Meredith v. Jefferson County Board of Education</u>, that attempts to mitigate segregation by using race based formulas to create more classroom diversity were unconstitutional.

Today for all intents and purposes the idealistic provisions of <u>Brown</u> are memories of a failed future. This is because of the factors previously mentioned: a combination of a weak commitment by policy makers at all levels to enforce desegregation; a Supreme Court's unwillingness to pursue enforcement of its mandates; an intense backlash by both southerners and northerners against court ordered desegregation; no national will to undo segregated schools; the general inability of the African American civil rights community and allies to mount an effective response to the loop hole language in the "with all deliberate speed" clause.

Post <u>Brown</u> and Public School Resegregation

In a 2009 report, "Reviving the Goal of an Integrated Society: A 21st Century Challenge," authored by Gary Orfield, we are given a fresh and disturbing look at the consequences of no meaningful implementation and enforcement of the 1954 Court decision. A telling conclusion of Orfield's study is that this nation's public schools are predominately racially segregated – separate and unequal. The nation has rushed back to the past.

Several scholarly retrospectives of the decades since <u>Brown</u>, (Frankenberg and Lee, 2002; Orwell and Eaton, 1996; Dawkins and Braddock 1994), have noted that since the mid 1980s African American and Latino students have become increasingly more segregated in public schools. Again, the significant problematic here is – not that increasing racial isolation is underway – to be sure this is a concern – but the fact that the schools attended by African American and Latino students are more closely associated with "low parental involvement, lack of resources, less experienced and credentialed teachers, and higher teacher turnover all of which in combination exacerbate educational incquality for mostly minority students" (Frankenberg and Lee 2002; Kozol 2005; Darling-Hammond 2010).

Contemporary racial segregation results from a complicated web of economic, political, social and legal issues not directly related the past *de jure* race based proscriptions separating social and education interaction. A post civil rights economy from which white Americans benefitted allowing them upward mobility out of central cities to suburbs and exurbs where their children attended quality schools, to a large extent has accounted for today's school segregation. But this factor alone cannot be left unexamined. We also must understand, as previously argued, this nation has never made a serious and sustained commitment to providing a quality education to Black and Brown children. And for that matter, poor white children suffer similarly from inferior education opportunities. Resulting from this are the millions of children left behind in squalid teaching and learning environments.

The trend toward resegregation is occurring in every region of the U.S. Indeed, more Black students attended segregated school at the beginning of the 21st century than the decade after <u>Brown.</u> Linda Darling-Hammond informs us that by the year 2000, 72 percent of Black students attend predominantly minority schools. This compares to 68 percent in 1980. (Darling-Hammond 2010) In the Northeast nearly four of five Black students attend schools where they and other students of color are the majority of the school population.

Nearly half of Black students in the Northeast and the Midwest attend schools defined as intensely segregated. In these schools 90–100 percent of their students are people of color. One in six Black students attend schools defined as hyper segregated – that is – nearly 100 percent of their peers are students of color.

The fact that public school resegregation is occurring is a cause for attention by public policy makers, community leaders, parents and others professing a belief in values and practices of multicultural and diversity teaching-learning practices. For there is something to be said for schooling which brings students from diverse racial, ethnic, religious, economic backgrounds together in a classroom. One could persuasively argue that doing so prepares them for optimally functioning in a diverse nation and global community. Such learning occasions can be a humanizing experience for all-including teachers and administrators.

As normatively optimistic and desirable as public school desegregation and a quality education are, it is trumped by what I consider to be the most significant threat to African American students posed by public school resegregation. Compelling studies inform us of abiding features of segregated and hyper segregated attended by Black students. About 50 percent of these students attend schools where 75 percent of the students are impoverished. By way of contrast, only five percent of white students attend similar schools. In schools where poverty is extreme–meaning – schools where 90–100 percent of students are poor, 80 percent of these students are Black and Latino (Orfield and Lee 2005).

An increased number of African Americans are themselves impoverished and attending schools where they are joined by an increasing number of Black, Latino, and to a lesser extent, Asian and White students. In too many urban areas of the U.S. poor Black students are 70–100 percent of all poor students of color. Their education experiences tend to be circumscribed by a series of institutionalized limitations and deficiencies.

We are informed by researchers (Orfield and Lee 2005; Hochschild, 1984; Darling-Hammond 2010) that academic achievement is in many instances related to poverty. Schools attended by Black students tend to be plagued by fewer qualified/ credentialed teachers and administrators, fewer instructional resources and materials, low performance on standardized tests, fewer AP and college preparation courses, high exposure to gangs, violence and crime.

These schools are described as "dropout factories" (NY Times, May 2009). It is true that not all schools attended by poor students of color are composites of the litany of dysfunction previously described. There are examples of schooling where teachers and administrators, parents, community members, and students are crafting and experiencing first rate public school educations. These schools should be celebrated and supported (Ogletree 2004). But these exemplars are a typical – not the rule. Too many African American students are attending segregated public schools where their education experiences are preparing them for a 21st century caste existence similar to that visited upon previous generation of the children of Jim Crow.

What Is to Be Done?

The reality of social formation in this nation is that its history of discrimination, the *minoritizing* and marginalizing of cultural groups is deeply institutionalized in the social formation of this nation. We cannot escape who we are. No matter the feel good fluffy escapist attempts by popular culture outlets to portray contemporary America society as post racial. The color line remains as a defining feature of who we are. Yet, as a nation we remain hopelessly deluded, believing that the race based sins of the past are in the past.

This is clearly evident when one looks at the state of public school education for African American children. These are children attending urban schools where they are not being prepared to take advantage of opportunities for social, economic, and education mobility. The central education issue for the African American community is not one framed by *who the child sits next to in a classroom, but whether or not the child is receiving a quality education at the school she/he is attending.* The compelling social/education/political challenge for the African American community is not desegregation, but access to *quality education.* There is compelling and disturbing evidence that African Americans in too many of this nation's urban public schools are being drastically shortchanged by poor quality education.

Responding to the Challenge

The question at this point then becomes how does one respond to the fact that the promises of <u>Brown</u> have not been realized. The question becomes paramount especially being that the nation has clearly lost its interest in public school desegregation as a desired public policy outcome. In the main, I believe the responses should be framed, or at least influenced, by what have been the responses to efforts to effect public school desegregation. Indeed, there are salient lessons to be learned from this history. For example, one of the important lessons learned from <u>Brown</u> is that, at least for the foreseeable future, there is neither the national will nor leadership to reshape public schools around policies and practices of racial desegregation. That is, there exists no national discourse focused on reshaping schools around resource allocation practices designed to insure that all children have an opportunity to receive a high quality education experience. Another clearly delivered lesson from <u>Brown</u> is that the parents of children attending quality public schools in suburbs and exurbs are adamantly against any desegregation schemes which take their children from neighborhood schools. Parents are also only tepid to any in-bussing efforts bringing urban children into suburban schools and neighborhoods. Still another lesson learned and which must be heeded is that the African American civil rights and the progressive elements of the nation's education communities have been unable to develop the strategies needed to excite and sustain the interest of a nation in the benefits of a high quality public school education for all children.

Given these and other lessons gained from the post-<u>Brown</u> era and the predictable lack of appetite for more substantive approaches to institutional change in this nation, this writer is not surprised that the typical small "l" liberal approaches to addressing the shortcomings of the nation's response to public school desegregation. Contemporarily the strategies offered and righteously defended include the following in various iterations:

- Mounting a national campaign to educate Americans regarding the inequalities of education provided to urban dwelling African Americans and other people of color and the dire implications of this.
- Energizing civil rights organizations to take more aggressive lobbying tactics on behalf of access to quality education for all public school students.
- Filing law suits on behalf of aggrieved students of color.
- Energizing and holding public policy makers accountable for passing legislation designed to close education gaps and holding school officials accountable for implementing the expectations.

These strategies are in and of themselves reasonable. They lay claims on this nation's advocacy organizations, policy making and education leadership to do the right thing on behalf of public school children. Indeed, noble intentions. But, unfortunately, these pronouncements fail to take into account the history of responses this nation has made to the social justice claims by people of color. If the past is prologue, one cannot simply put blind faith in the likelihood that these approaches- even if adopted – would have the desired effect. The strategies place too much stock in normalistic and gradualistic approaches to social change. Such approaches have historically inadequately met the social objectives of people of color. These approaches too often rest on the presumptive belief that decision making processes are basically fair, equally accessible to prince and pauper alike, and are fundamentally committed to the concept and practices of a quality education for all children. The evidence supporting these beliefs is tragically thin.

Given the gravity of the challenges facing African American children and given the responses by this nation to desegregation efforts along with the lessons learned from <u>Brown,</u> it is time for African Americans to give serious attention to other strategies. The social and cultural costs for not doing so are too horrifying to disregard. Simply stated, consider the life chances for a young person graduating from high school today without the critical thinking skills, numeracy skills, reading skills and experiences with information technology. Consider the life chances of young Black males and females who have dropped out of school before graduating.

I am recommending that African American parents, community members and leaders develop education strategies based on a fundamental proposition emanating from the social history of African descended people in this nation. The proposition is this. African Americans, and any allies gained along the way, must first and foremost take the responsibility for educating African American children. The proposition is neither defeatist (likely to be alleged) nor cynical. Its truth is based in the truth of the social experiences of African Americans. This truth demonstrates that there have been only two instances in nearly four centuries of the African presence in this part of the diaspora where the federal government has willfully committed resources to educate African people.

The first was during the Reconstruction Era after the Civil War with the formation of the Freedmen's Bureau. According to historian, John Hope Franklin, the Bureau's most significant impact was providing education opportunities for newly freed slaves. The Bureau established and helped to administer an array of educational institutions from day schools to colleges (1966). The second instance of a federal commitment to addressing and repairing social damage done to African Americans due to institutionalized and individual discrimination was during the administration of President Lyndon B. Johnson. The Johnson administration's advocacy of civil rights and equal opportunity legislation set the tone for improvements in education programs benefiting African American and poor children and for opening access to colleges and universities. Unfortunately, both periods were short-lived and existed within the maelstrom of challenge and resistance, especially from white southerners.

Specific Prescriptions

Against this backdrop and given what we know about the nation's responses to the concept and practice of descgregation and given the grave consequences now facing African American students in too many inner city schools, I strongly recommend two other courses of action. Both can be undertaken simultaneously.

First, African American must reorganize institutional resources, e.g., families, churches, civic and social organizations, etc., around another fundamental proposition. Namely, educating children is the primary responsibility of African Americans. Any one wishing to assist in this effort should be considered, but the primary responsibility rests with African Americans. Institutionalizing this proposition can take several delivery forms, among these are:

- Private schools-secular or sectarian
- Charter schools
- Gendered schools-all male or all female
- Charter magnet schools

These institutions would be open to all students, but the emphasis would be on providing African American students a high quality culturally relevant education experience. The considerable wealth (more than 800 billion dollars in annual spending power) and talent from such sectors in the African American community such as: education, business, entertainment, churches, professional athletics and ordinary citizens must be marshaled and focused on providing education alternatives to African Americans. The ability to do this exists. The will to do so must be cultivated, bolstered and sustained. In short, African Americans must themselves take on this imperative project.

This is a much needed and long overdue approach to addressing the fact that this nation has not taken the education interests of African American and most children of color seriously. Again, this step towards education independence and self-reliance is dictated by the African American's social history. As pointed out above, this history is replete with incidences of betrayal and subterfuge by the institutions charged with protecting the rights of African Americans (Bell 2002). It seems foolhardy, and in fact, is culturally suicidal, to continue to depend on extant institutions of education to prepare African American children to compete on equal footing with others in this nation. Lessons from African American history speak to the need for a drastically different education paradigm. The stakes for not doing so are much too high. A people simply cannot advance socially, economically, politically or culturally, if their children and subsequently, their adults, are miseducated at worst, and poorly educated at best.

Secondly, most segregated public schools attended by Black students are institutions of education malpractice. These are not redeeming, freeing institutions committed to preparing students for the challenges of making a living in an increasingly interconnected world of work. Students have little or no transferable skills, experiences or knowledge bases which can be used in either the legitimate domestic or international marketplaces. Deprived of a quality education, Black students are not able to compete with better educated students for access to colleges and universities, vocational training or workforce employment in other than dead end entry level low wage jobs. Tragically, students fitting this profile live lives that are swift, brutish and short; too many of them are destined to fill jails, prisons and cemeteries.

And because the stakes are so terribly high, public policy makers, parents, community members, the faith community and all other civic, social organizations must be held accountable. The Black community – its leadership and parents must take the lead in the response. This tragic situation threatens to continue creating and institutionalizing a caste of people having nothing to contribute to the progress of Black people or anyone else. They will constitute what the historian Carter G. Woodson forewarned as a casualties of a destructive education system, a new category of slaves (Woodson 1990).

To the point. Time has long past for Black leadership to do the organizing, discovery work and litigation necessary for pressing class action law suits on behalf of Black students receiving low quality public school education. This situation must be as aggressively pursued as was the strategy developed and implemented by Charles Hamilton Houston and those brave men and women who joined him in the decades long struggle against *de jure* public school segregation.

The schools attended by Black students are supported by tax dollars. Those tax dollars are used by public officials–both elected and appointed – to craft and serve up teaching and learning experiences known and proven to be inferior to the quality of education provided to students attending more affluent schools. It is known and documented that Black, Latino and poor white students, if they do graduate from high school, have received an education that is – with few exceptions – inferior to that received by their counterparts graduating from better supported and resourced school systems. The differential education experience ill prepares Black students to compete on par with students having a stronger public school learning experience (Kozol 2005).

I do not argue here that all public school students must have the *same* public school learning experience. I do argue that all public school students must have an opportunity to receive a *quality* education. Absent the element of *quality*, Black students are denied opportunities to compete for access higher education and training, rewarding workforce employment and in short, lose out on opportunities to fully develop their human potential.

Herein rests the basis for class action law suits. The core argument rests on the proposition that a low quality education, fueled and supported by public tax dollars, effectively deprives Black students of the provisions of the equal protection clause of the 14th amendment of the U.S. Constitution. The class action suits should allege that local, state and national systems of public supported education, using tax dollars, plan and implement curricula, hire teachers, administrators and others, intimately involved in the delivery of an inferior education experience for students.

The critically important organizing and research strategies needed as a prerequisite to launching the litigation urged here are outside the scope of this discussion. I recommend that the seed can be planted by parents, community leaders, lawyers and others committed to striking out on a more aggressive path to resolve, what I consider the paramount civil rights issue of this day. Namely, providing a high quality education to Black children and by extension to all children. I am not arguing against the reformist approaches previously noted in this discussion. They are also necessary. But they have their limitations. They don't fundamentally restructure how public education is delivered in this nation. Successful class action suits will have that affect. Tax dollars will have to be used in ways assuring that a quality education for all students is the objective and desired outcome.

It seems foolhardy and indeed, culturally destructive, to continue depending on the extant education processes to educate Black students. At the risk of overusing a clichè, a paradigm shift is in order. The stakes for not doing so are much too high. For the last three decades we have borne witness to the destruction of miseducated and poorly educated Black youth. A people cannot advance socially, politically, economically or culturally, if their children are poorly educated-giving rise to a poorly educated, vulnerable and otherwise subjugated generation of adults.

There is a long enduring historical lesson which bears serious and steadfast attention. History is not kind to a people who deliver up their children to a society's institutions of education when these institutions, like the others comprising the social order, have been implicated in the historical oppression of the people.

Selected Sources

1. Bullock, H. (1967). A History of Negro Education in the South. Cambridge, Massachusetts: Harvard University Press.
2. Bell, D. (2004). Silent Covenants. New York, New York: Oxford University Press.
3. Darling-Hammond, L. (2010). The Flat World and Education. New York, New York: Teacher's College Press.
4. Dawkins, M.P. and Braddock, J.H. (1994). *The continuing significance of de-segregation: School racial composition and African American inclusion in American society.* Journal of Negro Education. 63(3), 394–405.
5. DuBois,W. E.B.(1953). The Souls of Black Folk. New York, New York: Blue Heron.
6. Frankenberg, E. and Lee, C. (2002). Race in American Public Schools: Rapidly Resegregating School Districts. Cambridge, Massachusetts: The Civil Rights Project Harvard University.
7. Franklin, J.H. (1966). From Slavery to Freedom. New York, New York: Vintage Books.
8. Greenberg, J. (1994). Crusaders in the Courts: How a Dedicated Band of Lawyers Fought for the Civil Rights Revolution. New York, New York: Basic Books.
9. Hochschild, J. (1984). The New American Dilemma: Liberal Democracy and School Desegregation. New Haven, Connecticut: Yale University.
10. Irons, P. (2002). Jim Crow's Children. New York, New York: Penguin Books.
11. Kluger, R. (1976). Simple Justice: The History of Brown v. Board of Education and Black Americans' Struggle for Equality. New York, New York: Alfred P. Knopf.
12. Kozol, J. (2005). The Shame of a Nation. New York: Crown.
13. Orfield, G. and Eaton, S. (1996). Dismantling Desegregation: The Quiet Reversal of Brown v. Board of Education. New York, New York: The New Press.
14. Orfield, G. and Lee, C. (2005). Why Segregation Matters: Poverty and Educational Inequality. Cambridge, MA.: The Civil Rights Project.
15. Patterson, J. (2001). Brown v. Board of Education: A Civil Rights Milestone and its Troubled Legacy. New York, New York: Oxford University Press.
16. Woodson, C.G.(1990). The Miseducation of the Negro. Nashville, TN.: Winston-Derek.

A Voyage of Discovery: Sacramento and the Politics of Ordinary Black People

David Covin

Good Afternoon,

Thank you for the introduction.

I am honored and humbled to be invited to speak at the 40th Anniversary of Ethnic Studies at Sacramento State University. It is a singular honor to be invited to speak at the university where I taught for 35 years, to be invited by my home department, and my home program of Pan African Studies within that department, to be invited by my colleagues. This honor is enhanced by the distinction of the department. This Ethnic Studies department is one of the most outstanding in the country. An indicator of that reality is that one of its past chairs, Dr. Otis Scott, is the only person ever elected to two consecutive terms as President of the National Association of Ethnic Studies. Another indicator is the distinction of each of the separate programs which constitute it: Asian-American Studies, Latino/Chicano Studies, Native American Studies, and Pan African Studies. My program, Pan African Studies, as currently constituted, is one of the strongest in the country. It has a sterling legacy of teachers, scholars, activists, and mentors. As a continuation of that legacy, its current composition, consisting of nationally and internationally renowned faculty members, places it in the first rank in the United States, and in the world.

Sac State's Ethnic Studies Department has a quadruple legacy of scholarship, teaching, activism, and mentoring. It is built – and operates – to serve students and to serve the community. There is no *link* between the department and the community. There is a *commonality*. That is represented, for example, by Cooper-Woodson College – which unites students, faculty, and community residents in a mentoring and support system. In the whole country there is no counterpart.

To be chosen to speak by such an illustrious group of colleagues is, indeed, a humbling honor.

This afternoon I'm going to talk about a Voyage of Discovery that has taken place over the past 40 years. It is the voyage of my discipline, Pan African Studies. By extension, it represents the voyage made by every aspect of the Ethnic Studies department. My focus is specifically on Pan African Studies. In the course of the discussion I will use one of my books as an illustration of how a particular work contributes to the voyage.

Pan African Studies, as the field is named on this campus, and Black Studies, as it is more widely known, elsewhere is also designated as Africana Studies, Africology, Afro-American Studies, and various and sundry other appellations.

By whatever name, 40 years ago, it was virtually non-existent as an academic discipline. Beginning at San Francisco State, in 1966, the first Black Studies departments and programs were established. In 1968 and 1969 there was an explosion in their number following the assassination of Dr. Martin Luther King, Jr. The program here began as part of the broader program of Ethnic Studies, in the academic year, 1969-70. The Black Studies programs and departments established in those early years were not academic disciplines. They were part of a social movement – the Black Movement, more popularly known as the Black Power Movement.

They were not academic disciplines because there were no academic Black Studies departments or programs to produce the scholars who would populate them. If we look at the early incumbents of Black Studies positions on this campus, for example, we find Dr. William Gibson, who was a historian; Dr. Maxwell Owusu, who was an anthropologist; Dr. Addison Somerville, who was a Psychologist; Jesse McClure, who had an MSW; Dr. Fannie Canson, who was an Educational administrator; Mugo-Mugo Gatheru, who was an author and a historian; Gabriel Bannerman-Richter, who was an English teacher and writer; Dr. Allan Gordon, who was an Art Historian. Not one of them was the product of a Black Studies Department. In the cohort I came in with in 1970, there were two of us who were political scientists, an artist, a dramatist, a fine arts graduate who was a poet, and a social worker. No graduates of Black Studies departments. There weren't any.

Black Studies, as an academic discipline, had to be created. The job of early Black Studies departments was to do precisely that: *Create* Black Studies.

It did not have to be done out of whole-cloth because there was a rich tradition of Black scholarship which could be drawn on. But that tradition was academically diffuse. There was the incomparable and path-breaking work of Dr. W.E.B. Du-Bois, the historical work of Dr. Carter G. Woodson, and Dr. John Hope Franklin. There were the pioneering studies of John Henrick Clark, C.L.R. James. There was Dr. Anna Julia Cooper, the Harlem Renaissance writers, scholars, artists, musicians. There was the Negritude movement. The work of sociologists like Dr. C. Eric Lincoln and anthropologists like Dr. Sinclair Drake. The political scientist, Dr. Ralph Bunche. Dancer/scholars like Katherine Dunham. There was a rich history of scholarly investigation and artistic creativity. But there was no academic discipline devoted, particularly, to mining and developing that treasure trove.

The people I've mentioned were stars – luminaries – but there were very few foot-soldiers dedicated to this work. Most Black people who had come to maturity before the 1950s, were not high-school graduates. Those who were hired to teach Black Studies in the 1960s and 70s had to figure out the parameters, the dimensions, of this new field. That work was both driven and complicated by the reality that the field had emerged out of a social movement.

One of the constants of the human condition is that if you get two people together, they will disagree with each other – on just about anything. Add to that people who are fired up about a social movement – extremely opinionated – and others steeped in the tradition of objective academic rigor, and you have a very explosive mix indeed. Figuring out what this new discipline was going to be – the very first step in creating Black Studies – was no walk down a garden path.

Combined with this was the condition that a lot of these new faculty members were practicing "learning as you go." They hadn't read Ida B. Wells, Mary McCleod Bethune, David Diop, Paul Lawrence Dunbar, Phyllis Wheatley, Marcus Garvey. These people weren't covered in any classes taught in the colleges and universities they'd attended. The new teachers had to learn them on their own. And for several years that's what most Black Studies consisted of - drawing on the rich seed-bed of scholarship and artistic accomplishment that earlier generations of Black people had produced – but which had enjoyed a very narrow audience, accomplishment that was almost entirely excluded from traditional academia.

How do all these disparate people, doing their own basic learning, in the throes of a social movement, figure out what their discipline is going to be? They were learning almost everything as they went along. I'll use what happened here to illustrate some of what that means.

Does Black Studies (Afro-American Studies) – as many people thought, believed, and argued – mean the study of Black people in the United States? Here – on this campus – almost half the people teaching Black Studies were from Africa: Maxwell Owusu, Mugo-Mugo Gatheru, Gabriel Bannerman-Richter, John Shoka. It didn't make sense for Black Studies to be restricted to the United States. As people educated themselves they increasingly became exposed to the African *diaspora* – a term many had never even heard before they began their careers as Black Studies professors. The African *diaspora* – Black people in the United States, but also in the Caribbean, Central America, South America, even Canada for heaven's sake – for starters. How does one convey that the field encompasses all these African peoples? On this campus, the faculty said, Let's make it clear, explicit, that Black Studies means the study of African people – *wherever they are*. Let's call ourselves Pan African Studies. They changed the program's name from Black Studies to Pan African Studies. Its mission – was to join with others – across the world – to create an academic discipline of a new type.

Let me lay out what that means. Despite the remarkable work done by pioneering Black scholars and artists, by comparison with other works produced, those by or about people of African descent were negligible. In the discipline I was trained in, political science, for example, in the two major journals of the discipline, from 1886–1990, a period of 104 years, a total of 6,157 articles were published. Fifty-four of those were focused on Black politics. 6,103 were not. Of the 54 articles on Black politics – 17 were really not on Black politics at all, but were about slavery, the politics of slavery. In reality, then, only 37 articles focused on Black politics after the Civil War. Approximately one-half of one percent of all the articles. That's what I mean by negligible. 99.5 percent of the articles were not about Black politics. Plainly and simply, that means for most people who wanted to study Black politics, there was nothing to study.

The task that fell to these new scholars was – creating a literature, a subject matter, a body of knowledge for their discipline – even as they were trying to figure out its parameters.

How did they do?

We'll use Pan African Studies at Sac State as an indicator. CSU Sacramento is not a Research I institution. That means its primary mission, the mission of its faculty, is not research, but teaching. Community service is also a major responsibility of this university – a responsibility greatly heightened for Pan African Studies. In California, research is primarily the mission of the UC system. It is funded to support research. The workload of its faculty is based around research. That is not true here. Research in the CSU system, has to be torn out of faculty members' hides.

Given all that, how did the Pan African Studies faculty – who were not paid to do original research, to produce subject matter – but to disseminate it – how did they do?

Faculty members associated with Pan African Studies at Sac State since its inception have written 64 books, almost 700 articles, book chapters, book reviews, and short stories. They have produced major works of art – which have been hung, played, and performed in galleries, theaters, and concert halls all over the world. They have been consultants on projects of every kind all over the planet. They have produced films, CDs, radio and television programs. They have produced web-sites and blogs. They have created and edited journals. They have appeared in radio, television, newspaper, journal, and magazine interviews. They have had articles, even books, written about *them*.

Now, let us compare their production of Black articles over 40 years, to that of another academic discipline, political science, for the whole country: over 104 years. All of Political Science over 104 years: 37 articles. Pan African Studies at Sac State over 40 years: 700.

This is one program, in a non-Research I institution. Can you imagine the total amount of work produced by Black Studies scholars in colleges and universities of every description, including Research I institutions, throughout this region, throughout this state, throughout this country, and throughout the world over these

40 years? It is . . . staggering. It is an academic achievement of colossal magnitude. And it is recognized . . . by almost no one. That is why this anniversary needs to be celebrated and broadcast – to every village and hamlet.

This discipline has been sailing on an unprecedented Voyage of Discovery.

I'm going to use my book, *Black Politics After the Civil Rights Movement: Sacramento, 1970–2000,* as an illustration of the kinds of places this voyage has taken us, the kind of discovery such research produces. By the way, that title is the publisher's title. I call the book, *The Politics of Ordinary Black People.*

It took me 40 years to write it. So you can see I was not working on a publish or perish schedule. I would have perished.

The objective of academic research is to produce new knowledge, at the very least, to produce promising and likely speculations. Most of us produce the latter: promising and likely speculations.

I liken the conduct of original research to taking voyages of discovery. Their objectives are the same. What is "original" research but going somewhere no one's ever been? If somebody's already been there, it's not original.

Christopher Columbus undertook voyages of discovery. But he wasn't looking for someplace new. He was looking for some place old – the Indies, the Orient, the East. He was looking for a new "passage" to the Indies. That's what he was trying to discover. He didn't "discover" the new passage. He didn't know there was a whole hemisphere between Europe and the East. Going for the East – he ended up in the West.

That's what doing original research is like. You don't know where you're going. You often end up at a different place than you thought you would. You are often surprised, and often don't know where you are once you've arrived. You may even think you're some place you're not. Columbus thought he was in the Indies. He ended up somewhere he didn't even know existed.

That's original research. Every time you begin it, you are entering the unknown.

In the 40 years since the advent of Black Studies, Black Political scientists have produced a tremendous amount of research. Bearing witness to their productivity is that unlike the U.S.A., the American Political Science Association, the APSA, has had three Black presidents during that period, one of them a woman (the three followed by some forty-five years the Presidency of Ralph Bunche in 1954). Presidents of the APSA are elected on the basis of their leading role in the discipline. So the three Black presidents speak to the quality of Black scholarship over the past four decades. Political Science, nevertheless, remains a backwards discipline on questions of race, despite the prodigious output of Black scholars, because white scholars and *all* non-Black scholars produce articles on Black politics at about the same rate they always have.

Despite the many discoveries of my colleagues in the field of Black politics, there were a number of unanswered or even unaddressed questions I wanted to explore. That's why I did the research that produced this book.

Most political studies deal with officeholders, appointed officials, bureaucracies, organizations, social movements, individual actors – variations across class, gender, age, race, public opinion, as well as connections among these variables – at the local, state, national, and international levels. I wanted to understand how ordinary Black people – who held no political office – fit into that complex aggregation of structures, activities, and orientations.

One of the salient findings of most of the major studies was that the Black politics of the 30 years between 1970 and 2000, usually referred to in the literature as the Post-Civil Rights Era, had not been worthy successors of the Civil Rights and Black Power epoch. Black politics had become increasingly dysfunctional. Some scholars also identified a declining significance of race, identified in politics, as deracialization.

Some preliminary studies I had done raised questions about these findings. While it was incontestable – as other studies showed that after the late 1970s the Civil Rights and Black Power Movements had ended, it was equally incontestable that ferocious opposition to those gains persisted. Yet my work showed, and no serious work really contradicted it, that the gains of the Civil Rights and Black Power movements continued, and in most instances had been enhanced. How could that be, I wondered, if Black politics had become increasingly dysfunctional.

I used Sacramento as a universe to explore these questions. A 2002 edition of *Time* magazine unintentionally validated the academic viability of the project by identifying Sacramento as the city most representative of the diversity of the national population.

Focusing on Sacramento I was able to look in much more detail at Black organizations, residential patterns, social networking, social movements, officeholders, political campaigns, and three critical elements derived from social movement research: social spaces, social narrative, and social memory, than I would have been able to do looking at the country at large, or even at a very big city.

I was also able to identify national Black political efforts which were present in Sacramento, such as the War on Poverty, the Harold Washington Mayoral campaign, the Jesse Jackson Presidential campaigns, and the Million Man March. In them I could examine the relationships between national and even international political efforts and local ones.

I divided the analysis by decades, in order both to make it manageable and to enable the identification of changes, trends, and continuities over time.

Let me highlight some of my principal findings:

1. The emergence of a significant Black middle class in Sacramento, beginning in the mid 1960's, and increasing rapidly in each subsequent decade.
2. A fluid Black population, with births, deaths, and people moving in and out of the area.

3. A tendency of Black people to identify certain governmental programs, governmental offices, and geographical areas as "theirs" regardless of demographic characteristics.
4. A tendency of other population groups to acquiesce to such Black claims.
5. Affronts to Black people served as powerful incentives for mobilizing Black people, with the police department most frequently the source of the affronts.
6. A high level of organization among the Black population, characterized over time by a significant decrease in the number of working class organizations and an almost geometric expansion in the number of mixed and middle-class organizations.
7. An almost total absence of organization of the Black underclass, except the Nation of Islam, and a very small number of secular organizations during the 90s.
8. A consistent increase in the total number of Black organizations and in the number of organizations intentionally founded to be specifically Black, despite widely disseminated notions of a declining significance of race.
9. No support for the proposition that for Black people, between 1970 and 2000, there was a decline in the significance of race. If anything, the data showed an *increase* in the significance of race.
10. A general and consistent lack of political involvement by Black churches throughout the whole period.
11. The Nation of Islam bucked the trend of Black religious detachment from politics from 1984 on.
12. The cathartic and empowering effect of the appeal for Black Unity.

I'll talk about a few of these findings to illustrate their explanatory power.

The tendency of Black people to identify certain social spaces as their own, and to take them over, is related to Black use of social narratives and social memory. Black people, more than any other similarly oppressed or exploited group, were empowered and mobilized by the Civil Rights and Black Power Movements. As a result, the War on Poverty, closely connected to those movements, was claimed by Black people when it came to Sacramento. For the most part, they captured it, though most poor people in Sacramento were not Black, they were white. Yet in every target area where there was a significant Black population, Black people ended up running the poverty organization whether the majority or plurality was white or Latino, because in no case was the majority or plurality Black. This is one instance of the tendency of Black people to identify certain social spaces as their own and take them over.

Another avenue that opened up such possibilities for Black people arose when the Sacramento City Council went to a district system of election, Black activists worked hard to develop two Black-influence districts. Each of those 2 districts, council district 2 and council district 5, had white super majorities. Yet Black people, using Black narrative to dominate political spaces, claimed those districts as their own and twice elected Black people in district 2, and once got a Black person appointed. In district 5 they elected 1 Black person, got another appointed, and later elected a Black person to consecutive terms. Still later, in District 8, where the plurality population was white, but in which Black people had mobilized to have boundaries drawn to make it a Black influence district, Black people elected a councilman to two consecutive terms, and when he died, elected his wife to the seat. In every single one of these electoral instances, white, Latino, and Asian populations deferred to Black assertions.

The significance of the cathartic and empowering impact of the appeal to Black Unity was revealed in the distinction between organizing and mobilizing.

There is a persistent, perpetual, and relentless appeal for Black Unity that emerges from African peoples. It is an appeal which makes no rational sense. Within the United States the Black population is too large, too dispersed, too varied, too complex, and too conflicted for Black Unity to have any possibility of being realized organizationally. Yet the appeal to Black Unity has a powerful effect as a mobilizing tool.

Black people in the aggregate crave racial unity. That's why metaphors such as house slaves, field slaves, uncle Toms, Aunt Gemimas, oreos, and handkerchief heads are so effective. That's why Clarence Thomas, Wardell Connerly, and Condoleeza Rice are such anathemas. They accent disunity, the fractured condition of the Black population.

The irony is that contested figures such as Shelby Steele and Alan Keyes accurately reflect the reality that the Black population is not monolithic. Most Black people wish it were, because they believe – if it were, they would be much more effective in achieving their collective aspirations. This is all wishful thinking, but it is powerful wishful thinking with profound implications for Black political life. It "keeps hope alive" – and raises the prospect of realizing *The Impossible Dream.*" The appeal to Black Unity can *mobilize* the Black underclass without the need to *organize* it. Whereas only the underclass has shown the ability *to organize* itself, it rarely does, and then – except for religious purposes and gangs – only for short periods of time. Appeals to Black unity, however, issued by the Black working class and the Black middle class can and do effectively *mobilize* the Black underclass.

Which brings me to . . . Barak Hussein Obama. He is . . . the manifestation . . . of the impossible dream. How did he occur? To answer that question, one must first understand the role of the Black electorate in the Presidential election – particularly in the Democratic primaries. That means not concentrating on polling numbers, the party platform, who Ted and Caroline Kennedy endorsed, what Pfloufe's and Axelrod's strategies were. It doesn't even mean examining the effects of the Congressional Black Caucus. It means scrutinizing the deep work of ordinary Black people. The census is misleading. In the election of Harold Washington in Chicago, the Jesse Jackson Presidential campaigns, Obama's primary victories on Super Tuesday – deep Black organizational work and appeals to Black unity resulted in Black mobilizations which by all conventional measures, were impossible, because they actually seemed – to increase the size of the Black population.

How did the realization of *the impossible dream*, the election of Barak Hussein Obama to the presidency of the United States of America, occur?

A rigorous analysis of the political work of ordinary Black people in Sacramento over a thirty-year period provides critical clues for us. How did Robbie Robertson, elected in a Sacramento City Council district with an overwhelming white majority, occur?

How did Dan Thompson, elected in a Sacramento City Council district with an overwhelming white majority, occur?

How did Grantland Johnson, a product of this program at Sac State, elected in a Sacramento City Council district with an overwhelming white majority, occur?

How did Lauren Hammond, also a product of this program, elected in a Sacramento City Council district with an overwhelming white majority – for four consecutive terms, occur?

How did Sam Pannell, elected to the Sacramento City Council from a white plurality district for two consecutive terms, occur?

How did Bonnie Pannell, elected in the same City Council district for three consecutive terms, occur?

How did Grantland Johnson, elected to the County Board of Supervisors in a district with not only a white super majority, but with a Black population as a negligible minority, occur?

What this study shows is an extraordinary, day-to-day organizational life of ordinary Black people – organizing and mobilizing at a far greater intensity than any other population group, and across a broader spectrum of political issues, creating a dense and networked organizational infrastructure, which is effective at seizing and dominating public spaces and selected social narratives. It shows a driven, emergent Black middle class; cross-class, cross-gender, cross-sectional, cross-national mobilizations in an effort to achieve the chimera of Black Unity. All this comes from a demeaned part of the population, woefully bereft of material resources, and tremendously outnumbered – who, against all odds, assert claims to office, create a narrative to give their claims authenticity, and hyper-mobilize in a transcendent search for unity.

This study shows us that ordinary Black people do what other ordinary people do: They participate in their children's school and after school activities. They are in the PTO, or PTA, as the case might be. They coach little league, are soccer moms, referee Pop Warner football leagues. They join professional associations, hold offices in labor unions, join environmental organizations, women's organizations, and volunteer in raising funds for cancer survivors. They populate recreational leagues for softball, basketball, bowling and golf. They join the VFW and the American Legion. They are active participants in the Democratic and Republican parties. They do what everybody else does. And then – they create – in addition, a wholly alternative world. Of women's and men's organizations, health organizations, educational organizations, professional organizations, civil rights organizations, PACs, voter registration efforts, health advocacies, legal ventures, political education webs, blogs, newsletters, magazines, whole cultural venues – all of which are Black. They invest themselves – fully – in two entirely different worlds.

I mentioned the APSA. There is also the National Conference of Black Political Scientists. Black political scientists belong to, and are active in both. There is the American Sociological Association. There is also the Association of Black Sociologists. There is the American Medical Association. There is also the National Medical Association (which is Black). There is the American Bar Association. There is also the National Bar Association (which is Black). In every arena of life in this country – black people are engaged in the dominant organizations and in counterpart organizations which are Black. They also engage in Black organizations for which there are no dominant counterparts. This research shows that these tendencies have not stopped. They have not diminished. On the contrary, they increased – dramatically – between 1970 and 2000. This is an extraordinary expenditure of effort – of resources, both human and material – that goes far beyond the norm. It speaks to a felt need, because if people didn't feel an urgency for such exertions – a need for them – they certainly wouldn't engage in them.

Sometimes . . . it works. Not only in this city, and this county. But in the person of the President of the United States of America – becoming the living embodiment of *the impossible dream.*

This is where we need the microscope – a kind of biological chemistry, if you will. We can't get at the root of the mysteries abiding in the continual realization of *impossible dreams* by looking only at the big people. We have to look at the little people. And to do that we have to approach research questions from outside the dominant paradigm. We must rely less, as it were, on our understandings of musculature, and develop our understandings of chemical interactions. We must have a reliable vision of the micro as well as the macro. That's how we can produce – in this arena – new knowledge, or at the very least, promising and likely speculations.

We cannot begin to understand these phenomena without the very specific scholarship Pan African Studies brings to the table.

These – are the Voyages of Discovery – on which our scholars and our students – set sail.

Arizona: Ground Zero for the War on Immigrants and Latinos(as)

Elvia Ramirez

Introduction

Few issues today elicit as much controversy and debate as undocumented immigration. Recent immigration laws passed by the Arizona legislature – most notably SB 1070 – have catapulted immigration issues to the national spotlight. Claiming that the federal government has failed to uphold its responsibility of securing our national borders (particularly the one shared with Mexico), politicians in Arizona have passed a series of laws targeting undocumented immigrants. In this article, I review the politics of immigration as they have unfolded in the state of Arizona. Based on an analysis of newspaper articles and social science research, I examine the debate surrounding the passage of SB 1070, one of the most punitive anti-immigrant laws ever passed by any state legislature in recent U.S. history. First, I explain what SB 1070 is and discuss why it generated much controversy and debate. I then document resistance strategies employed by opponents of SB 1070, followed by a review of subsequent bills introduced by Arizona politicians that target immigrants and their children, immigrant teachers, and Ethnic Studies programs. I conclude with an analysis of factors explaining the current anti-immigrant and anti-Latino(a) climate present in the state of Arizona.

What Is SB 1070?

On April 23, 2010, Governor Jan Brewer from Arizona signed the Support Our Law Enforcement and Safe Neighborhoods Act – also known as SB 1070 – into law.

Contributed by Elvia Ramirez. © Kendall Hunt Publishing Company

Introduced by Republican state Senator Russell Pierce and drafted by the private prison industry (which would stand to benefit financially from the imprisonment of immigrants), SB 1070 seeks to criminalize undocumented immigrants by defining their presence in the U.S. as "trespassing." Under federal law, unlawful presence is considered a civil infraction (rather than a crime) and can result in deportation (Guskin & Wilson, 2007). Under SB 1070, however, it would be a state crime to be in the country illegally, and immigrants would be forced to carry proper immigration paperwork at all times (Garcia & Chandler, 2010; Rentería, 2010). Failing to carry papers would be considered a misdemeanor, punishable by up to six months of jail and a $2,500 fine before deportation (Riccardi, 2010a). This law would thus make Arizona the first state in the nation to criminalize undocumented immigrants (Rentería, 2010). Furthermore, under SB 1070, police officers would be required to question someone's immigration status if they had "reasonable suspicion" that person was undocumented. Police officers would thus be required to function as immigration agents and arrest anyone who could not produce documents proving their legal status (Garcia & Chandler, 2010). SB 1070 would also make seeking work illegal for day laborers, and would make transporting and employing undocumented immigrants a crime (Garcia & Chandler, 2010; Riccardi, 2010a). The law was set to take effect on July 29, 2010.

SB 1070 and the Institutionalization of Racial Profiling

The signing of SB 1070 into law generated a flurry of criticism and reaction throughout the country. Immigrant rights activists, civil rights leaders, politicians, religious leaders, and ordinary citizens interpreted SB 1070 as a racist attempt by the Arizona legislature to terrorize immigrant communities and institutionalize racial profiling. In particular, many felt the law's provision that police officers question individuals suspected of being undocumented would lead to the unfair targeting of Mexicans/Latinos(as). As Alfredo Gutierrez, a Mexican American former state senator from Arizona, observed, "'Reasonable suspicion' in Arizona isn't going to be someone who looks like a Canadian, whatever a Canadian looks like, it's going to be someone who looks like my family" (as cited in Hing, 2010a, para. 4). Indeed, though the overwhelming majority of Mexicans in this country are U.S. citizens or legal immigrants, "Mexicanness" is often a basis for suspecting "illegality" under immigration law, and Mexicans/Latinos(as) who speak Spanish and have brown skin color are generally subjected to greater levels of surveillance and harassment by immigration enforcement personnel (Johnson, 2000; Romero, 2006). Civil rights leaders thus feared that Latinos(as) who are U.S. citizens or legal residents would also be negatively impacted by this law. Alessandra Soler Meetze, president of the ACLU of Arizona, for example, commented, "A lot of U.S. citizens are going to be swept up in the application of this law for something as simple as having an accent and leaving their wallet at home" (as cited in Riccardi, 2010a, p. 2). Interestingly, law enforcement agencies were not entirely supportive of SB 1070 either, particularly because they feared it would lead to racial profiling and loss of the public's trust (Riccardi, 2010a; Wood, 2010a). In short, many felt SB 1070 would promote racial profiling by subjecting people of color, particularly Latinos(as), to increased surveillance and harassment by law enforcement agencies.

The fears of racial profiling articulated by critics of SB 1070 are certainly not unfounded. Research finds that police officers *do* engage in racial profiling when they are entrusted with immigration enforcement duties. Since 1995, Section 287(g) of the Immigration and Nationality Act (INA) has allowed Immigration and Customs Enforcement (ICE) to enter into partnership agreements with local law enforcement agencies that grant a limited set of immigration enforcement powers to police officers. (The use of police officers as immigration agents is thus not unprecedented; in fact, the 287(g) program served as an inspiration for the architects of SB 1070). A study by the U.S. Inspector General evaluating the 287(g) program found that police officers participating in this program receive an inadequate amount of training and supervision by ICE and often engage in racial profiling (Immigration Policy Center, 2010). Many other studies have reached similar conclusions. A report by the ACLU of Georgia, for example, argues that police officers deputized as immigration agents through the 287(g) program in Gwinnet County, Georgia engaged in racial profiling insofar as they "disproportionately target[ed] people of color for pretextual stops, investigations, and enforcement" (ACLU of Georgia, 2010, p. 5). The report notes that although racial profiling was a problem in Gwinnet County before the implementation of the 287(g) program, racial profiling only got worse after the county participated in the program, with Latinos(as) suffering the brunt of law enforcement harassment.

Perhaps the most egregious case of racial profiling and harassment of Latinos(as) by local police deputized as immigration agents under the 287(g) program is that of the notorious Sheriff from Maricopa County in Arizona, Joe Arpaio. Joe Arpaio led the largest 287(g) operation in the country, essentially turning his police department into a de facto immigration-enforcement agency (Immigration Policy Center, 2010; Sterling, 2010). An overzealous, xenophobic anti-immigrant crusader, Arpaio would have his deputies raid Latino(a) neighborhoods and workplaces in search of undocumented immigrants (Sterling, 2010). Moreover, under his supervision, prisoners were housed in tent cities under the blazing Arizona desert sun, made to wear pink underwear, were served spoiled food, and were reportedly physically assaulted as well (Hing, 2010c). Given his abuses of power, the Obama administration revoked his 287(g) agreement in 2009, though this has not stopped Arpaio from continuing his immigration sweeps in predominantly Latino(a) neighborhoods. Arpaio has also been under federal civil rights investigation into whether his department systematically violated the rights of Latinos(as) and engaged in racial profiling while enforcing federal immigration laws (Riccardi, 2010b). Recently, he was sued by the U.S. Justice Department for refusing to cooperate with this federal civil rights investigation (Medrano, 2010a).

The case of Joe Arpaio clearly illustrates the potential for racial profiling and other abuses when local police are granted immigration enforcement duties. In fact, this is a major reason that civil rights groups and activists have called for the repeal of 287(g) programs. According to the Immigration Policy Center, 287(g) programs are also problematic because they result in mistakes by police officers. For example, in 2007, Pedro Guzman, a Latino male who is a U.S. citizen and is developmentally disabled, was wrongly identified as an undocumented immigrant by local police participating in a 287(g) program. Guzman was then transferred to an ICE detention center and deported to Mexico (Immigration Policy Center, 2010). Clearly, even when police officers are trained in immigration law, they engage in racial profiling and make costly mistakes as a result. Significantly, the potential for racial profiling is even greater under SB 1070 than under the 287(g) program, given that SB 1070 does not provide for the training of police officers in immigration law.

Shortly after being introduced, SB 1070 was amended to bar police officers from using race/ethnicity as grounds for questioning individuals – a move interpreted by critics as a mere "cosmetic" change that made SB 1070 "minimally less racist" (Hing, 2010b). Opponents of SB 1070 thus continued to mobilize against the measure.

Resistance Strategies

Opponents of SB 1070 challenged the measure in three major ways, including: (1) organizing marches and protests; (2) calling for boycotts of Arizona; and (3) filing lawsuits challenging the constitutionality of the measure. For example, on May 1, 2010, as part of the yearly worldwide march commemorating International Workers' Day, thousands of people marched in San Francisco's Mission District to denounce SB 1070 and to demand immigration reform (Berton, 2010). Many also gathered that same day in downtown Sacramento to press for similar demands. Furthermore, in mid May of 2010, immigrant rights activists gathered at Sun Life Stadium in South Florida to protest before the game between the Arizona Diamondbacks and the Florida Marlins (Chardy, 2010). Also, up to 200,000 people took to the streets in Phoenix, Arizona in June 2010, in what was the second largest march in Arizona's history (Fernandez, 2010b). Marches and protests were also held in many other parts of the country.

The second major strategy used by opponents of SB 1070 was the use of the boycott. This strategy had been effectively used in the 1990's against Arizona when politicians there had voted against a holiday honoring Dr. Martin Luther King Jr.'s birthday (Wood, 2010b). Many critics of SB 1070 hoped that a boycott of Arizona would constitute a "wake-up" call to citizens of Arizona and would dissuade other states from enacting similar legislation (Wood, 2010b). California Senate leader Darrel Steinberg, for example, petitioned Governor Arnold Schwarzenegger "to 'deliver an unequivocal message' of disgust by tearing up the state's contracts with Arizona businesses and government agencies" (Theriault, 2010, para. 1). Many cities throughout the country, including Sacramento, thus approved boycotts of Arizona. Furthermore, several civil rights groups and unions, such as the Service Employees International Union, the National Council of La Raza, Asian American Justice Center, and League of United Latin American Citizens, announced travel boycotts of Arizona. Academic organizations, such as the American Educational Research Association (AERA), American Anthropological Association (AAA), Mujeres Activas en Letras y Cambio Social (MALCS), and the Southwestern Anthropological Association, also announced they would not be holding their annual meetings in Arizona.

Musicians and other celebrities also joined in on the boycott of Arizona. Led by Zack Rocha from Rage Against the Machine, a coalition of artists formed a group called "The Sound Strike" in order to raise awareness about SB 1070. These artists promised to skip Arizona on concert tours until SB 1070 was repealed (Michaels, 2010). "Fans of our music, our stories, our films and our words can be pulled over and harassed every day because they are brown or black, or for the way they speak, or for the music they listen to," explained Zack de la Rocha (as cited in Michaels, 2010, para. 3). Zack de la Rocha also expressed fears that other states in the nation would follow Arizona's lead, a pattern portending disastrous consequences for immigrants and people of color. "If other states follow the direction of Arizona," de la Rocha remarked, "we could be headed towards a pre-Civil Rights era reality" (as cited in Michaels, 2010, para. 7).

Other musicians and celebrities also joined the effort. Eugene Rodriguez from the U.S.-based group Los Cenzontles, for example, wrote a *corrido* (a popular ballad) titled "State of Shame" denouncing SB 1070 (Frontera Norte Sur, 2010). Furthermore, in Mexico City, a concert starring Latin American musical groups Jaguares, Maldita Vecindad, and Molotov was held to publicly protest the passage of SB 1070. Sports teams also joined in on the protest against SB 1070. Arizona's professional basketball team, the Phoenix Suns, for example, wore jerseys that said "Los Suns" in order to express solidarity with Latinos(as) and others opposing SB 1070 (Lewis, 2010).

The third major strategy used by opponents of SB 1070 was filing lawsuits challenging the constitutionality of the measure. Some of the groups filing lawsuits include the American Civil Liberties Union (ACLU), Mexican American Legal Defense and Education Fund (MALDEF), and the National Association for the Advancement of Colored People (NAACP). These groups labeled SB 1070 as "extreme" because it "invites the racial profiling of people of color, violates the First Amendment and interferes with federal law" (Chardy, 2010, para. 10). A Phoenix police officer, Officer Martin Escobar, also filed a lawsuit against the measure, arguing that it would force him to violate Latinos(as)' civil rights and would subject him to disciplinary action if he failed to enforce the law and legal action if he did (Duda, 2010). On July 6, 2010, the U.S. Department of Justice also filed a lawsuit against the bill because it felt the measure intruded into areas (immigration and border security) of authority reserved only for the federal government (Richey, 2010).

Current Status of SB 1070

Just hours before it was to go into effect, a federal judge halted the implementation of most of SB 1070's provisions. U.S District Judge Susan Bolton issued a temporary injunction against the most controversial elements of the bill, including the requirement that police officers check a person's immigration status while enforcing other laws, the requirement that immigrants carry their paperwork at all times, and the provision that made it unlawful for undocumented immigrants to seek employment in public places. The judge also blocked police officers from making warrantless arrests of suspected undocumented immigrants. Provisions of the law that did go into effect included the law's prohibition on stopping a motor vehicle to pick up day laborers, knowingly employing undocumented workers, and a provision striking down sanctuary city policies (Cattan, 2010). Attorneys for Governor Jan Brewer immediately appealed the decision. On April 11, 2011, the Ninth Circuit Court of Appeals in San Francisco, California, struck down Governor Brewer's appeal and upheld Judge Susan Bolton's ban on the most controversial sections of SB 1070 (Riccardi, 2011). It is possible the case may now go before the Supreme Court.

The Saga Continues

The fact that most of SB 1070 has been declared illegal by U.S. District Judge Susan Bolton and the Ninth Circuit Court of Appeals has not deterred politicians in Arizona and elsewhere from pursuing laws similar to SB 1070 as well as other measures that are even more anti-immigrant and patently unconstitutional. According to a report released by Immigration Works USA, more than twenty-five states may try to pass laws similar to SB 1070 when their state legislatures convene in 2011 (Goodwin, 2010). There is indeed strong support for this measure throughout the country, with polls showing a 60 percent voter approval rating for the measure (Carcamo, 2010). SB 1070 may also come to California, the state with the largest share of immigrants. In November 2010, the California secretary of state's office authorized a signature drive by a tea party activist to put a similar law as Arizona's before California voters. If it gathers enough signatures, the proposal, dubbed "Support Federal Immigration Law Act," will go before California voters during the 2012 election cycle (Lagos, 2010). If this measure were to go before California voters, there is a strong possibility it would be approved. A poll conducted by USC/Los Angeles Times in May 2010 found that half of California voters approve of Arizona's immigration measure, though support for this measure is divided along racial/ethnic, age, and party lines: Whites, older voters, males, and Republicans are largely in favor of it, while most Latinos (71%) and Asians (57%) oppose it (Wu, 2010). All the contentious and bitter politics associated with the immigration controversy in Arizona may thus come to (or, more accurately stated, *return* to) California in the near future.

Politicians in Arizona, led by Russell Pearce, have also challenged birthright citizenship for the U.S.-born children of undocumented immigrants. Anti-immigrant advocates like to refer to these children as "anchor babies," suggesting that undocumented immigrant parents use their U.S.-born children to establish themselves in this country (Guskin & Wilson, 2007). Yet, as Guskin & Wilson (2007) note, having a U.S.-born child does not provide a path for legalization for undocumented immigrants nor does it protect them from deportation. Nonetheless, Arizona Republicans were pushing for bills (SB 1308 and SB 1309) that would have eliminated the right of U.S.-born children of undocumented immigrants to automatically become U.S. citizens. Legislators in at least a dozen other states agreed to push for similar legislation (Vock, 2010).

As critics note, the push to deny citizenship for the U.S.-born children of undocumented immigrants is patently unconstitutional. The Supreme Court has previously ruled, in the 1898 case of *United States v. Wong*, that children born in the U.S. are automatically U.S. citizens, regardless of their parents' immigration status (Hing, 2011b). Critics thus interpret the push to end birthright citizenship as mere spectacle. "This is political theater, not a serious effort to create a legal test. . . . It strikes me as unwise, un-American, and unconstitutional" commented Gabriel J. Chin, a law professor at the University of Arizona (as cited in Lacey, 2011a, p. 2). Such a proposal also represents a huge step back in regards to civil rights for immigrants and people of color. As Karen Narasaki from the Asian American Justice Center insightfully observes, proponents of this measure "would drag us back to a time when minorities were not considered equal to whites nor worthy of being citizens . . . While their language is more carefully chosen than that used a century ago, their motives are no less clear" (as cited in Hing, 2011a, para. 12).

Arizona politicians also introduced a measure (SB 1405) that would have forced hospitals to check a person's immigration status before rendering non-emergency medical care (Hing, 2011b). This measure would have thus forced medical professionals to function as immigration agents – a move medical professionals and many others critiqued for endangering the lives of immigrants and their children, as well as placing the public's health at risk (since immigrants with contagious diseases would fear seeking medical help).

Senator Russell Pearce also introduced SB 1611, an "omnibus bill" that is even more punitive towards immigrants than SB 1070. This measure would: (a) bar children from K-12 schools if they cannot produce a U.S.-issued birth certificate or naturalization document; (b) prohibit undocumented immigrants from attending community colleges and universities in Arizona; (c) cut off undocumented immigrants from emergency medical care; (d) require individuals filing for a marriage license to show their immigration papers; (e) require individuals buying or operating a vehicle to show proof of legal residence; and (f) require businesses to use E-verify, the federal immigration database (Hing, 2011b). Like previous bills, this measure included provisions that are unconstitutional. For example, it goes against legal precedent established by the 1982 Supreme Court case of *Plyler v. Doe*, which established children's rights to K-12 public education regardless of their parents' immigration status.

In mid-March 2011, the Arizona Senate voted down all these anti-immigrant bills (i.e. SB 1308, SB 1309, SB 1405, SB 1611). It also rejected SB 1407, a bill which would have required schools to gather information about the immigration status of their students (Hing, 2011c). The Senate's repudiation of these bills was reportedly the result of pressure from the business community, which was concerned about the "unintended consequences" of such anti-immigrant legislation. In a letter addressed to Senator Pearce and signed by the Greater Phoenix Chamber of Commerce and sixty CEO's from Arizona-based businesses, business leaders articulated concerns about the impact of boycotts on Arizona businesses (Hing, 2011c). "It is an undeniable fact that each of our companies and our employees were impacted by the boycotts and the coincident negative image," wrote the business leaders (as cited in Hing, 2011c, para. 16). Immigrant rights activists rejoiced over the Senate's rejection of these bills. "These are major wins for the fight for a better Arizona," remarked Jennifer Allen, executive director of Border Action Network (Hing, 2011, para. 8). It is likely, however, that the Senate's vote represents a mere temporary break in anti-immigrant bashing rather than a fundamental shift in Arizona's stance on immigration. These anti-immigrant measures may in fact resurface later in the Arizona legislature or as ballot propositions (Barr, 2011).

Arizona's Attack on Ethnic Studies and Immigrant Teachers

In addition to passing a suite of anti-immigrant measures, politicians in Arizona have attacked Ethnic Studies programs and immigrant teachers. Less than three weeks after signing SB 1070 into law, Governor Jan Brewer approved House Bill 2281, a measure targeting Ethnic Studies courses in public (K-12) schools. The brainchild of Tom Horne, then-superintendent of public instruction, HB 2281 bans courses that "promote resentment toward one race; that are designed for students of one race; that promote ethnic solidarity 'instead of treating students as individuals'; or that encourage 'the overthrow of the United States government" (Richardson, 2010, para. 2). School districts that do not comply with the law stand to lose ten percent of state funding (Llanos, 2010). The law was set to go into effect December 31, 2010.

HB 2281 was aimed specifically at the Tucson Unified School District's Mexican American Studies program, which, according to Tom Horne, was promoting "ethnic chauvinism" (Reyes, 2010; Richardson, 2010). TUSD's program reportedly first came to Horne's attention in April 2006 when Dolores Huerta, co-founder of the United Farm Workers (UFW) and a prominent civil rights activist and leader, told students at a high school there that "Republicans hate Latinos" (Richardson, 2010). Horne (a Republican) subsequently sent his top aide,

Margaret Garcia-Dugan, to speak to students and offer an alternative (i.e., Republican) perspective, but students walked out during her speech (Grado, 2010). Horne has also been critical of the program's curriculum, particularly its use of the books *Occupied America* by Rodolfo Acuña and *Pedagogy of the Oppressed* by Paolo Freire. According to Horne, these books are "inappropriate" because they teach Latino students that they are "mistreated" (Lacey 2011b).

The passage of SB 2281 unleashed a firestorm of controversy, criticism, and debate (though not nearly as much as did SB 1070). Human rights experts from the United Nations condemned the measure for violating Arizona's obligation to promote a culture and climate that is respectful of diversity (Richardson, 2010). Critics also noted that HB 2281 stifles free speech, perpetuates the exclusion of people of color from the curriculum, and whitewashes (and thus distorts) history. David Rodriguez, a professor of Chicano(a) Studies at California State University, Northridge, for example, remarked, "This law stifles free speech, it stifles critical information and the expression of a community that has experienced discrimination of all sorts" (as cited in Llanos, 2010, para. 11). Similarly, Myla Vicenti Carpio, an Assistant Professor of American Indian Studies at the University of Arizona, stated, "This is another way of silencing others' history . . . For them to say we don't want Ethnic Studies, it means that these specific histories aren't important and that they are threatening this narrative that America is great and doesn't do anything wrong" (as cited in Fernandez, 2010a, para. 14).

On his last day as the state superintendent of public instruction, and before assuming his new position as the state's Attorney General, Tom Horne declared that TUSD's Mexican American Studies program was in violation of all four provisions of HB 2281. However, the district's other Ethnic Studies programs (e.g. Native American Studies, Asian American Studies, and African American Studies) were not deemed to be in violation of HB 2281 and could thus continue (Lacey, 2011b). Thus, only the district's Chicano(a) Studies program was ordered shut down – a decision interpreted by critics as a clear sign that Arizona's bigotry and racism is fixated on Mexicans/Latinos(as) (Tobar, 2011). Teachers from the Tucson Unified School District have filed a lawsuit in federal court challenging the legality of HB 2281 (Lacey, 2011b). The teachers' lawyer, Richard M. Martinez, says the challenge will argue that HB 2281 violates the First and Fourteenth Amendments of the U.S. Constitution because it targets just one district (TUSD) and one group of people (Mexican Americans) (Zehr, 2010).

State officials in Arizona have also launched attacks against immigrant teachers. A few months after SB 1070 and HB 2281 were signed into law, Arizona's Department of Education implemented a policy barring teachers with "accents" from teaching English-language learner classes. Like other anti-immigrant measures, this policy had a disproportionate impact on Latinos(as). During the 1990s, Arizona had hired hundreds of teachers whose native language was Spanish to teach in bilingual education programs (Jordan, 2010). In 2000, however, Arizona voters approved a ballot measure banning bilingual education, and these teachers were subsequently switched to English-language courses. The racist and nativist climate in Arizona has undoubtedly emboldened state education officials to also target these immigrant teachers (Jordan, 2010).

How Arizona Became Ground Zero for the War on Immigrants and Latinos(as)

How did Arizona become ground zero for the war on immigrants and Latinos(as)? In other words, why is Arizona the epicenter of the nation's contemporary anti-immigrant and anti-Latino(a) backlash? According to some immigration experts, the immigration controversy in Arizona has its roots in immigration enforcement policies enacted in the 1990s by then-President Bill Clinton. During this period, California was experiencing an intense wave of anti-immigrant xenophobia, much like Arizona is experiencing today. For example, in 1994, California voters (most of whom were white) approved Proposition 187, an initiative that would have restricted the rights of undocumented immigrants to access education and non-emergency healthcare (Reese & Ramirez, 2002). As a way of shielding himself from the anti-immigrant backlash emerging principally in California, Clinton began spending an unprecedented amount of money on border enforcement – especially on those segments of the border (e.g., El Paso, TX and San Diego, CA) most used by undocumented immigrants coming in from Mexico (Cornelius, 2005). The policies he enacted to fortify the border included Operation Hold the Line in El Paso, Texas (1993), Operation Gatekeeper in San Diego, CA (1994), Operation Safeguard in Arizona (1995), and Operation Rio Grande in southeast Texas (1997) (Cornelius, 2005). According to Douglass Massey, a professor of sociology and public affairs at Princeton University, these border enforcement operations had the effect of diverting immigration flows "through the Sonoran desert into Arizona, which until then, had been a quiet backwater both with respect to border crossings and immigration settlement" (as cited in Wood, 2010c, para. 4). The Tucson sector is now the leading corridor for undocumented entry, making the state of Arizona the main gateway for undocumented immigrants coming in through Mexico (Cornelius, 2005). The flow of undocumented immigrants into Arizona has been unsettling for many in the state, particularly for the older, conservative white population, which is often hostile to immigrants and fearful of increasing diversity and multiculturalism.

Other researchers point to the long history of conservative politics in Arizona. For example, Jack Pitney, a political scientist at Claremont McKenna College, notes that Arizona is, after all, the home of U.S. Senator Barry Goldwater (i.e., "Mr. Conservative"), a politician often credited for reviving conservative politics during the 1960s (Wood, 2010c). Concomitantly, Pitney notes that "Arizona has always had a contrarian, cantankerous streak," which he attributes to older whites' fears of changing demographics in the state of Arizona – particularly the increasing presence of Latinos(as) (Wood, 2010c, para. 10). Furthermore, Amy Goodman notes that Arizona was the only Western state that seceded from the U.S. and joined the Confederacy during the Civil War; a century later, it also opposed the recognition of a Martin Luther King Jr. federal holiday (Goodman, 2010). Conservative, anti-immigrant, and racist politics are thus long established traditions in Arizona.

Still other scholars, such as Deborah Kang, a postdoctoral fellow at UC Berkeley, notes that the current focus on Arizona is myopic, reflecting an ignorance of history. Kang states, "What always surprises me about these debates is how quickly we forget . . . Some in the media have reported that SB 1070 marks a new high-water mark for anti-Mexican sentiment in the United States and a new precedent in the history of American immigration law" (as cited in Wood, 2010c, para. 12). Yet, Mexican immigrants, she notes, have been repeatedly scapegoated for this nation's economic troubles. For example, during the 1920s, 1930s, and 1950s, Mexicans (including undocumented immigrants, legal residents, and U.S. citizens) were forcibly deported from the U.S. in deportation campaigns – all in the midst of a national economic downturn (Wood, 2010c). Indeed, when times get tough, politicians strategically direct people's anger towards immigrants (and other disenfranchised populations) and away from politicians and employers (Reese & Ramirez, 2002). The current economic crisis in this country thus makes the conditions ripe for nativism and racism. Unfortunately, immigrants and the Latino(a) community have become the convenient scapegoats for our society's current social and economic ills.

Conclusion

This chapter examined the politics of immigration in Arizona and critically reviewed the series of laws being passed by the Arizona legislature targeting immigrants and the larger Latino(a) community. Reputedly distressed over the federal government's 'unwillingness' to secure our national borders, politicians in Arizona passed SB 1070 and introduced other bills aimed at deterring undocumented immigrants from entering and settling in the state of Arizona. Although these anti-immigrant bills have been popular with the larger (particularly older, conservative White) public in Arizona and throughout the country, they do nothing to address the root causes of migration and are thus ineffective in stemming the flow of undocumented immigrants into the country. Instead, these policies only perpetuate racial profiling and lead to the political, economic, and social disenfranchisement of the immigrant community in general, and of the Mexican/Latino(a) community in particular. Politicians in Arizona have also launched attacks on Ethnic Studies programs, particularly Chicano(a) Studies, and on immigrant teachers. As social justice advocates note, HB 2281, along with SB 1070, threatens to transform Arizona into a "new South" – that is, a state notorious for its institutionalized discrimination against racial/ethnic minorities (Medrano, 2010b).

Civil rights leaders and immigrant rights activists have vehemently critiqued the racist policies being proposed and enacted in Arizona and have effectively mounted resistance to these measures via marches and protests, boycotts, and lawsuits. These resistance strategies have been largely successful; most of SB 1070 has been declared illegal by the courts, and politicians in Arizona have abandoned (at least for now) other draconian anti-immigrant measures (e.g., SB 1308 and SB 1309). The struggle for immigrant and human rights is far from over, however. Many other states are proposing similar anti-immigrant legislation as Arizona, and it is possible that Arizona's attack on Ethnic Studies programs may also spill over into other states. It is thus critical that we all become engaged in the struggle for social justice and help challenge the repressive and intolerant climate that exists in Arizona and in many other parts of the country. *La lucha sigue!*

References

American Civil Liberties Union (ACLU) of Georgia (2010, March). The persistence of racial profiling in Gwinnett: Time for accountability, transparency, and an end to 287(g). Retrieved from http://www.acluga.org

Barr, A. (2011, March 18). Ariz. rejects immigration crackdowns. *Politico*. Retrieved from http://www.politico.com

Berton, J. (2010, May 2). Thousands protest new Arizona law. *San Francisco Chronicle*, pp. C1.

Carcamo, C. (2010, June 2). Poll: Californians narrowly support immigration law. *Orange County Register*, pp. A.

Cattan, N. (2010, July 29). Arizona immigration law 2010: As SB 1070 takes effect, Mexicans say 'Adios, Arizona'; Arizona immigration law targeting immigrants has already encouraged Mexicans to begin returning home, even as a U.S. judge halted key portions of SB 1070 from taking effect. The Mexico government is boosting legal services in Arizona, and shelters in Sonora state are preparing for an influx. *Christian Science Monitor*. Retrieved from http://www.csmonitor.com

Chardy, A. (2010, May 18). Arizona immigration law protested at Florida Marlins game. *Miami Herald,* pp. B3.

Cornelius, W. (2005). Controlling 'unwanted' immigration: Lessons from the United States, 1993–2004. *Journal of Ethnic and Migration Studies, 31*(4), 775–794.

Duda, J. (2010, August 13). Arizona and Maricopa county election officials investigate Arpaio TV ads. *Arizona Capitol Times*. Retrieved from http://azcapitoltimes.com

Fernandez, V. (2010a, May 28). Arizona's ban on Ethnic Studies worries more than Latinos. *La Prensa – San Diego*. Retrieved from http://www.laprensa-sandiego.org

Fernandez, V. (2010b, June 4). Thousands protest SB 1070 in Phoenix rally. *La Prensa - San Diego*. Retrieved from http://www.laprensa-sandiego.org

Frontera Norte-Sur (2010, May 21). The Arizona prairie fire spreads. *La Prensa – San Diego*. Retrieved from http://www.laprensa-sandiego.org

Garcia, A., & Chandler, B. (2010, May 20). Has Arizona replaced Mississippi as the most racist state? *Jackson Advocate*, pp. 4A.

Goodman, A. (2010, April 29). Arizona's immigration law: An open invitation to racial profiling. *The Oregonian*. Retrieved from http://www.oregonlive.com

Goodwin, L. (2010, October 28). Report: 25 states considering Arizona-style immigration laws. *Yahoo! News*. Retrieved from http://news.yahoo.com

Grado, G. (2010, November 15). Culture war brewing over Ethnic Studies in Tucson schools. *Arizona Capitol Times*. Retrieved from http://azcapitoltimes.com

Guskin, J., & Wilson, D. L. (2007). *The politics of immigration: Questions and answers*. New York: Monthly Review Press.

Hing, J. (2010a, April 23). Arizona legalizes racial profiling with SB 1070, says advocates. *Colorlines: News for action*. Retrieved from http://colorlines.com

Hing, J. (2010b, April 30). AZ tweaks SB 1070, now minimally less racist, still just as dangerous. *Colorlines: News for action*. Retrieved from http://colorlines.com

Hing, J. (2010c, September 23). Joe Arpaio accused of misusing $80 million in taxpayer funds. *Colorlines: News for action*. Retrieved from http://colorlines.com

Hing, J. (2011a, January 5). Lawmakers in 14 states coordinate birthright citizenship attack. *Colorlines: News for action*. Retrieved from http://colorlines.com

Hing, J. (2011b, February 23). Arizona's suite of new anti-immigrant bills moves to Senate. *Colorlines: News for action*. Retrieved from http://colorlines.com

Hing, J. (2011c, March 18). Arizona may finally be ready to 'take a time out' on immigrant bashing." *Colorlines: News for action*. Retrieved from http://colorlines.com

Immigration Policy Center (2010, April 2). Local enforcement of immigration laws through the 287(g) program: Time, money, and resources don't add up to community safety. Retrieved from http://www.immigrationpolicy.org

Johnson, K. (2000). The case against race profiling in immigration enforcement. *Washington University Law Quarterly*, 78(3), 676–736.

Jordan, M. (2010, April 30). Arizona grades teachers on fluency. *Wall Street Journal*. Retrieved From http://online.wsj.com

Lacey, M. (2011a, January 4). Birthright citizenship looms as next immigration battle. *New York Times*. Retrieved from http://www.nytimes.com

Lacey, M. (2011b, January 8). Citing 'brainwashing,' Arizona declares a Latino class illegal. *New York Times*, pp. A1.

Lagos, M. (2010, November 24). State Ok's anti-illegals ballot initiative petition. *San Francisco Chronicle*, pp. C4.

Lewis, C. (2010, May 13). Arizona bans Ethnic Studies in schools; Debate over Latino influence heightened. *National Post*, pp. A13.

Llanos, C. (2010, May 12). Arizona Ethnic Studies ban condemned. *Pasadena Star – News*. Retrieved from http://www.pasadenastarnews.com

Medrano, L. (2010a, September 2). Joe Arpaio: Why is Obama administration suing an outspoken Arizona sheriff?; The Justice Department said Thursday that Sheriff Joe Arpaio of Arizona's Maricopa County is not cooperating in an investigation into whether his department has used racial profiling in sweeps to catch illegal immigrants. *Christian Science Monitor*. Retrieved from http://www.csmonitor.com

Medrano, L. (2010b, December 31). Ethnic Studies classes illegal in Arizona public schools as of Jan. 1; Much of the controversial Arizona immigration law remains tied up in court, but a law banning Ethnic Studies in Arizona is set to take effect Saturday. A Tucson school district vows to fight it. *Christian Science Monitor*. Retrieved from http://www.csmonitor.com

Michaels, S. (2010, May 27). Rage Against the Machine leads Arizona boycott. *Guardian Unlimited*. Retrieved from http://www.guardian.co.uk

Morning Star (2010, July 8). World – Obama sues over Arizona's racist law.

Reese, E. & Ramirez, E. (2002). The new ethnic politics of welfare: Struggles over legal immigrants' rights to welfare in California. *Journal of Poverty, 6(3)*, 29–62.

Rentería, M. (2010, July 15). A look at the SB 1070 law. *San Antonio Express-News*, pp. 16CX.

Reyes, R. A. (2010, June 3). The other Arizona battle: A new law makes Ethnic Studies classes illegal; Since when is it bad to learn about different cultures? *Christian Science Monitor*. Retrieved from http://www.csmonitor.com

Riccardi, N. (2010a, April 13). Arizona passes strict illegal immigration act. *Los Angeles Times*. Retrieved from http://articles.latimes.com

Riccardi, N. (2010b, September 18). Internal memo accuses Arpaio's office of misdeeds; The sheriff's No. 2 man allegedly headed improper inquiries and surveillance. *Los Angeles Times*. Retrieved from http://articles.latimes.com

Riccardi, N. (2011, April 12). Court upholds ban on Arizona immigration law. *Los Angeles Times*. Retrieved from http://articles.latimes.com

Richardson, V. (2010, May 13). Arizona governor now targeting Ethnic Studies; law infuriates liberals again. *Washington Times,* pp. A1.

Richey, W. (2010, July 29). SB 1070: appeal seeks to reinstate all parts of Arizona law; The toughest provisions of SB 1070, the Arizona law about illegal immigration, were blocked Wednesday by a judge. Arizona Gov. Jan Brewer said

Thursday she is appealing the decision. *Christian Science Monitor*. Retrieved from http://www.csmonitor.com

Romero, M. (2006). Racial profiling and immigration law enforcement: Rounding up of usual suspects in the Latino community. *Critical Sociology, 32*(2–3), 447–473.

Sterling, T. G. (2010). *Illegal: Life and death in Arizona's immigration war zone.* Guilford, CT: Lyons Press.

Theriault, D. C. (2010, April 28). California Senate leader: Tear up contracts with Arizona over immigration law. *Contra Costa Times*. Retrieved from http://www.contracostatimes.com

Tobar, H. (2011, January 14). Offended at being dragged into Arizona controversy; Ethnic Studies foes cite professors' Mexican American history book. *Los Angeles Times*. Retrieved from http://articles.latimes.com

Vock, D. C. (2010, December 20). Arizona lawmakers fight 'birthright citizenship.' *Sacramento Bee*, pp. A1, A13.

Wood, D. B. (2010a, April 26). Arizona immigration law puts police in 'impossible situation'; A new Arizona anti-illegal immigration law asks police to perform tasks that are often contradictory, critics say – enforcing immigration law and criminal law. *Christian Science Monitor*. Retrieved from http://www.csmonitor.com

Wood, D. B. (2010b, April 28). Arizona immigration law: California leads call for boycotts; the new Arizona immigration law spurred California officials to call for boycotts of its eastern neighbor, and the effects to image and industry could be both symbolic and substantial. *Christian Science Monitor*. Retrieved from http://www.csmonitor.com

Wood, D. B. (2010c, August 3). How Arizona became ground zero for immigration reform; Arizona didn't turn into a pressure cooker for immigration reform overnight, historians say. *Christian Science Monitor*. Retrieved from http://www.csmonitor.com

Wu, Suzanne (2010, June 1). Immigration law divides California voters. *USC College News*. Retrieved from http://dornsife.usc.edu

Zehr, M. A. (2010, September 22). Tucson students aren't deterred by Ethnic Studies controversy. *Education Week*. Retrieved from http://www.edweek.org

Asian American and Pacific Islanders Harmed by Trump COVID-19 Blame Campaign

Timothy P. Fong, PhD

Professor of Ethnic Studies
California State University, Sacramento

My ethnicity is not a virus. We knew it was going to happen. Donald Trump kicked off his presidential reelection campaign in June 2020 with rallies in Tulsa, Oklahoma, and Phoenix, Arizona, using the racially charge term "Kung Flu" to stir up his supporters. This was a calculated effort to use racism to blame others and divert from his failed leadership with the COVID-19 pandemic. We expected an escalation of this type of rhetoric from Trump and his enablers that began with tweets referring to COVID-19 in March 2020 as the "Chinese Virus" and the "Wuhan Virus." The use of these terms sparked an immediate response from Asian American civil rights organizations and congressional representatives demanding an end to the use of such labeling.

Trump's tactics had immediate consequences not just for Chinese Americans, but by association, all Asian American and Pacific Islander (AAPI) communities. The STOP AAPI Hate Reporting Center received 3795 hate-related incidents between March 19, 2020 and February 29, 2021 (Jcung et al., 2021a). STOP AAPI Hate acknowledged the number of incidents reported represent merely a fraction of the number of hate incidents that actually occurred during this time period. The number of reported incidents came with the increase of Trump campaign ads specifically blaming China for the global pandemic.

Viruses spread quickly. Hate and racism spreads just as fast and can get out of control if left untreated. On March 21, 2021, eight people were shot and killed at

Atlanta-area spa businesses, six of whom were Asian women. An official spokesperson for the county sheriff's office investigating the case downplayed any possible racial motivation, and added insult to this deadly crime by describing the suspect as merely having "a really bad day." It was later discovered the spokesperson promoted t-shirts that labeled the coronavirus an "IMPORTED VIRUS FROM CHY-NA" (Kornfield & Knowles, 2021). STOP AAPI Hate released another report shortly after the Atlanta shootings citing the number of hate incidents dramatically rose from 3,795 to 6,603 just in March 2021 (Jeung et al., 2021b).

Hate and violence against AAPIs is not new. The most obvious macro-level historical periods of antagonism were around the 1882 Chinese Exclusion Act that was not repealed until 1943 to the internment of Japanese Americans during WWII (1942–1945). Other periods were around the 1982 murder of Vincent Chin in Detroit, Michigan. Detroit was the center of anti-Asian hostility because Japanese automotive imports were blamed for the decline of the big three auto companies (Ford, General Motors, and Chrysler). The two men who killed Chin worked in the auto industry and blamed Chin for their own and the nation's economic woes. It did not matter that Chin was Chinese American and not Japanese. The Vincent Chin case was significant because it led to national protests and the first federal civil rights trial for an Asian American (Zia, 2010).

Balbir Singh Sodhi, a Sikh American gas station owner in in Mesa, Arizona, was murdered in a hate crime after September 11, 2001 terrorist attacks carried out by Islamic militants associated with the extremist group al-Qaeda. Sodhi, who had a beard and wore turban in accordance with his Sikh faith, was profiled as an Arab Muslim. The assailant who boasted after his arrest, "I'm a patriot. I stand for America all the way," was found guilty of first-degree murder of Balbir Singh Sodhi (SALDEF, 2011). Since 2011 hate crimes against Sikh Americans have continued. On April 15, 2021, a shooter killed eight people, including four Sikhs at a FedEx facility in Indianapolis, Indiana. Police authorities said the perpetrator visited white supremacist websites before the attack (Andrea & Contreras, 2021). In 2012, another white supremacist killed six people at a Sikh temple in Oak Creek, Wisconsin (The Sikh Coalition, 2012).

There is a long and ugly history of racism against AAPI communities. Stereotypes of being "perpetual foreigners" to now the "Chinese Virus" scapegoat AAPIs as "the other." The latest version of this has manifested into increased hate and violence. This does not impact just one group, but all AAPI groups. A Pew Research Center survey conducted just after the shootings in Atlanta found 81 percent of Asian American adults said violence against them is increasing, compared to just 56 percent of all U.S. adults who said the same. When asked the reason why violence has increased, 20 percent used two words: Donald Trump (Ruiz et al., 2021).

Anti-Asian discrimination has led to increases in anxiety, depressive symptoms, and sleep problems among those who are targeted. The recent STOP AAPI Hate Mental Health Report concluded victims of anti-Asian hate perceived danger and had feelings of helplessness which negatively impacted their mental health and social connections. However, about 28 percent of victims of anti-Asian hate reported their racial trauma was relieved after reporting to STOP AAPI Hate. This suggests that reporting is an important strategy for victims to cope with hate incidents. Sharing stories about one's own experience relieves the sense of isolation and the burden of facing racial discrimination alone (Saw et al., 2021c). This relates to another survey of victims of anti-Asian hate conducted by Sherry Wang, PhD, an associate professor of counseling psychology at Santa Clara University. Wang found those who faced anti-Asian hate incidents reported very low levels of bystander intervention to thwart harassment or help after the incident (Abrams, 2021).

In light of heightened tensions and awareness of anti-Asian hate, what can we do? We can start by signing up for bystander intervention and de-escalation training to support AAPI communities. In response to the rise in anti-Asian and xenophobic harassment, Hollaback! joined with Asian Americans Advancing Justice to provide basic, but highly effective, one-hour, interactive training for participants to learn the positive impact of bystander intervention on individuals and communities. All trainings are conducted online and are easily accessible.

We can learn about and support other anti-racist and social justice movements such as Black Lives Matter. The Asian American civil rights movement would not be what it is but for the Black liberation and civil rights movements that preceded and grew alongside us. We have a moral imperative to join in demands for justice. Just as we must fight and seek accountability for the racist actions and hate crimes against AAPIs around the COVID-19 pandemic, so too must we be willing to confront racism in all forms throughout our society, including in our own communities. We see COVID-19 exposing the deep inequality in our society. There are disproportionate infection and death rates among Black, Brown, Pacific Islander, and Native people. There are dangerous working conditions for immigrants who are also essential workers, especially immigrants and those who are undocumented.

We can raise our voices, we can vote, and we did vote. Nationally, around 4 million AAPI voted in the 2020 presidential election. This was massive increase from just under 2.8 million who voted in the 2016 election, and some of the biggest increases came in critical swing states (Reimann, 2021). A CNN exit poll found 61 percent of AAPI voters supported Joe Biden compared to 34 percent who supported President Donald Trump (CNN, 2020).

There is now a new administration in the White House that is not using anti-Asian rhetoric and President Biden signed into law anti-hate crime legislation in response to the surge of attacks on Asian Americans during the COVID-19 pandemic. The legislation, introduced by Rep. Grace Meng, D-N.Y., and Sen. Mazie Hirono, D-Hawaii, aims to make the reporting of hate crimes more accessible at the local and state levels. This is achieved by (1) boosting public outreach and ensuring reporting resources are available online in multiple languages, (2) directs the Department of Justice to designate a point person to expedite the review of hate crimes related to COVID-19, and (3) authorizes grants to state and local governments to conduct crime-reduction programs to prevent and respond to hate crimes (Edmondson & Tankersley, 2021).

There are several moments in our nation's history and in our individual lifetimes that charts the course for our collective futures. We see one of those moments is right now. The heightened attention on anti-Asian attacks has renewed the call for more Asian American Studies courses and programs in colleges, universities, and increasingly in high schools. We must all realize that racist and volatile rhetoric can quickly become normalized unless we understand why it emerges, take assertive steps stop it, and change the trajectory of history.

References

Abrams, Z. (2021, July). The mental health impact of anti-Asian racism. *American Psychological Association Monitor on Psychology, 52*(5). www.apa.org/monitor/2021/07/impact-anti-asian-racism

Andrea, L., & Contreras, N. (2021, April 20). "Turn the power strip off": FedEx shooter viewed white supremacist websites, IMPD says. *Indianapolis Star*. www.indystar.com/story/news/local/indianapolis/2021/04/20/fedex-shooting-brandon-hole-viewed-white-supremacist-sites/7302207002/

CNN Politics. (2020). Exit poll. www.cnn.com/election/2020/exit-polls/president/national-results

Edmondson, C., & Tankersley, J. (2021, May 20). Biden signs bill addressing hate crimes against Asian-Americans. *New York Times*. www.nytimes.com/2021/05/20/us/politics/biden-asian-hate-crimes-bill.html

Jeung, R., Yellow Horse, A. J., Popovic, T., & Lim, R. (2021a, March). STOP AAPI Hate 2020–2021 National Report. https://stopaapihate.org/wp-content/uploads/2021/05/Stop-AAPI-Hate-Report-National-210316.pdf

Jeung. R., Yellow Horse, A. J., & Cayanan, C. (2021b, May). STOP AAPI Hate 2020–2021 National Report. https://stopaapihate.org/wp-content/uploads/2021/05/Stop-AAPI-Hate-Report-National-210506.pdf

Kornfield, M., & Knowles, H. (2021, May 18). Captain who said spa shootings suspect had "bad day" no longer a spokesman on case, official says. *Washington Post*. www.washingtonpost.com/nation/2021/03/17/jay-baker-bad-day/

Reimann, N. (2021, April 21). Asian-American voter turnout soared over 45% in 2020 election, study finds—and that's probably an undercount. *Forbes*. www.forbes.com/sites/nicholasreimann/2021/04/21/asian-american-voter-turnout-soared-over-45-in-2020-election-study-finds-and-thats-probably-an-undercount/?sh=7c9ea92439ea

Ruiz, N., Edwards, K., & Lopez, M. (2021, April 21). *One-third of Asian Americans fear threats, physical attacks and most say violence against them is rising*. Pew Research Center. www.pewresearch.org/fact-tank/2021/04/21/one-third-of-asian-americans-fear-threats-physical-attacks-and-most-say-violence-against-them-is-rising/

SALDEF. (2011). The first 9/11 backlash fatality: The murder of Balbir Singh Sodhi. https://saldef.org/balbir-singh-sodhi/

Saw, A., Yellow Horse, A. J., & Jeung, R. (2021c, May). STOP AAPI hate mental health report. https://stopaapihate.org/wp-content/uploads/2021/05/Stop-AA-PI-Hate-Mental-Health-Report-210527.pdf

The Sikh Coalition. (2012, August 5). Sikh Coalition responds to tragic shooting in Wisconsin. www.sikhcoalition.org/blog/2012/sikh-coalition-responds-to-tragic-shooting-in-wisconsin/

Zia, H. (2010). Detroit Blues: "Because you motherfuckers." In J. Yu-wen, S. Wu, & T. Chen (Eds.), *Asian American studies now*. Rutgers University Press.

ETHNIC IDENTITIES RECONCILIATION VOICE MATTERS
INCLUSION EMPOWERMENT & DECOLONIZATION
STRUGGLE SOVEREIGNTY SOCIAL JUSTICE HOPE
ETHNIC STUDIES: AN INTRODUCTION

"We can't just stand aside now": Oakland's Fortune Cookie Factory Stands with Black Lives Matter

Annalise Harlow[1]

Undergraduate Student
California State University, Sacramento

Grief struck every corner of the globe in 2020 as COVID-19 made a home for itself in communities of all backgrounds. In the United States, grief-struck in many forms. In only the very beginning hours of the summer, COVID-19 was drowned out by the anger and pain that our nation felt for the death of George Floyd and the unjust death of Breonna Taylor. As people from all communities, races, and ages joined together in protest of police brutality and in support of Black Lives Matter, more questions arose about what is the role of allies. For many spaces in the Asian American community, supporting Black Lives Matter meant confronting anti-blackness in their own community and evaluating what cross-racial allyship could be.

In a new initiative launched by the Oakland Asian Cultural Center (OACC) called "Open E.A.R.S. for Change," anti-racism and social justice are at the center of the initiative. In this three-phase program series, "Open E.A.R.S. for Change" seeks to "highlight local stories of cross-cultural solidarity" and with "E.A.R.S." standing for "engage, activate, rise-up, series," that is exactly what is accomplished in their first podcast episode.

Episode one of the "Open E.A.R.S. for Change" initiative, titled "Let's Talk Oakland," discusses what anti-racism looks like in the Oakland Chinatown community. In this discussion, local business owner Alicia Wong of Fortune Cookie

Factory joins OACC's Akemi Chan-Imai, OCA-East Bay's Jessica Li, and Good Good Eatz's Trinh Banh to explain how her family's business has become an ally to the Black Lives Matter movement and the Black community. A family business, Oakland Chinatown's Fortune Cookie Factory has had its doors open since 1957, spanning three generations. In "Let's Talk Oakland," Alicia Wong steps up to discuss how her family uses their cookies as a "way to convey ideas." As a younger member of the Fortune Cookie Factory, Wong describes how her parents "generally give [her] a lot of room to make cookies" and that is exactly what we see reflected in a number of popular cookies from the Fortune Cookie Factory. The Fortune Cookie Factory, popular for its ability to create cookies with themes and even a special cookie for Pride month, felt that with the voice of Black Lives Matter so present and with their own desire to support Black Lives Matter, it was only right to create a cookie expressing their support. Creating this special cookie proved to be a learning curve as Wong discusses how they "had to figure out a way to put the BLM logo directly on the cookie … and wanted [people] to look at it and see what [the purpose] was." Buying new tools and investing in a special electric cutter to get the job done, a beautiful fortune cookie, adorned in Black Lives Matter's signature colors of black and gold was created.

Originally hesitant toward the idea of such an emotional and politically charged message, Wong's parents were unsure of whether or not a cookie supporting Black Lives Matter was a good idea and if it would result in a backlash toward

Source: © Oakland Fortune Factory; panda mural by Steven Anderson Art

their business. Wong understood their fear, but also that they needed to take action to support Black Lives Matter, even if that meant releasing the cookies without their knowledge. For Wong, releasing a cookie in support of Black Lives Matter meant tossing aside a politically passive sentiment all too common in the Asian American community. Wong's release of the Black Lives Matter cookie asserted that as

Source: © Oakland Fortune Factory

Asian Americans and as an Asian American-owned business "we can't just stand aside now."

The impact of the BLM cookie was overwhelmingly positive. From phone calls to even a handwritten letter, the overwhelmingly positive and gracious response to the Black Lives Matter cookie is what eased the hesitancy and the fear that Wong's parents initially felt. For Wong's parents and even herself, they had no idea that a cookie could affect an individual so deeply.

The fact that the impact was so meaningful is what helped to change the way that Wong and her parents viewed their role as allies in the Black Lives Matter movement. Through her parents' experience with the Black Lives Matter cookie, Wong realized that getting involved and showing them that they have the power to "do something positive" can "change the minds of older generations who are kind of stuck on the fence and not wanting to get involved" in political issues.

For the older generations of the Asian American community, political allyship and participation can be frightening. Oftentimes, Asian Americans are overlooked as they are too often swept under the "Model Minority" rug and not expected to have a voice in political matters. This idea of the "Model Minority" has not only curbed political participation but has long stirred feelings of anti-Blackness within the Asian American community. Jessica Li of the OCA-East Bay Chapter recognizes the anti-blackness sentiment that resides in conversations of the Asian American community and asks Good Good Eatz's Trinh Banh, "How we might be able to shift the perceptions of individuals who haven't bought into the culture of anti-blackness?" And how within our own [Asian American] communities we can show solidarity with Black lives. Banh enthusiastically agrees with much of what Wong expressed earlier which is that through action we can change minds. As seen with the Fortune Cookie Factory, Banh describes such acts of solidarity as a way for older generations to form "a positive relationship [and experiences] with someone of another culture" and therefore "reinforce our humanity." Even if these experiences are just the beginning of the greater conversations, Banh believes that by putting forth action and allowing the results to speak for themselves, older generations of Asian Americans can put together the tough conversations about race and the solidarity that those conversations demand.

With her parents' full support now, Wong and her family decided to take it one step further and donate the proceeds from their Black Lives Matter cookies to organizations that support Black lives. This process, as with each cookie that was crafted, was done meticulously and with solidarity in mind. As a small business, Wong and her family recognized their financial limitations and so as a solution, they followed a two-part criterion that ensured that the organizations that they donated to were financially transparent and that at least 60 percent of their donations went directly to supporting Black lives. Eventually landing on two organizations that met their criterion, the proceeds from their Black Lives Matter cookies were donated to the NAACP and the Innocence Project.

From the idea of using fortune cookies to "convey a message," the Fortune Cookie Factory found a way to harness the power of cross-racial solidarity and create something uniquely powerful. In wake of the racially charged rhetoric

Source: © Oakland Fortune Factory

surrounding the COVID-19 pandemic and the spike in anti-Asian hate crimes in Oakland and across the country, cross-racial solidarity is needed now more than ever.

The Fortune Cookie Factory's rally of support for Black Lives Matter is one example of how communities strengthen one another while simultaneously strengthening themselves. The issue of racism does not belong to a single individual or to a single community, but it is an issue for all people in every community. Arising from a deeply unsettling year filled with grief and anger, a message printed on a cookie proved to have the power to bridge inaction and fear into action and solidarity between two communities who can only be more powerful together. The Fortune Cookie Factory reminds us that while we find much joy in coming together, we have only taken the first few steps toward the larger issue. Racism, related to Black or Asian lives, is far from gone and it is critical that moving forward from this trying year that we continue all efforts to strengthen solidarity between racial and ethnic communities.

 Note

[1] Annalise Harlow is an undergraduate student pursuing a bachelor's degree in sociology and a minor in Asian American studies at California State University—Sacramento.

The 65th Street Corridor Community Collaborative Project: A Lesson in Community Service

Gregory Yee Mark, Julie López Figueroa, Christopher Shimizu, Jasmine Duong, and Jazmine Sanchez

I have had tutors in my classes since my first year at Johnson, so 6 years at Johnson and now 10 years at Will C. Wood. I taught Special Ed. History and some Language Arts at Johnson serving about 80 special ed. students per year. I've been teaching Gen. Ed. History and Language Arts at Will C. Wood for 10 years at about 150 students per year, so rough calculations, close to 2000 students have had the opportunity to have a 65th Street Corridor tutor in my classes. In addition, 65th has hosted the Will C. Wood Book Club for 9 years for a field trip… Those student field trips represent another 300 students! Isn't it crazy to think how many students between Will C. Wood and Hiram Johnson have had the opportunity to work closely with a tutor from 65th—to hear the story of a tutor's journey that led to college, to establish a relationship with a mentor and to create memorable experiences—and that is only the # of students who have passed through 1 teacher's class. Think how many more students in other teachers' classes there have been.

At Will C. Wood I had a young tutor who spoke very passionately to my students about her journey to college—how she always wanted to go to college but as a child of migrant workers, her attendance was sometimes spotty and how she always felt dismissed by her high school counselor. It wasn't until she had an English teacher help her fill out a college application that she came to attend Sac. State. You know her; of course; Griselda Casillas! Griselda stayed with me that year and later became the coordinator of 65th for WCW. She finished her Master's in Psychology and continued her partnership with 65th, presenting several

Contributed by Jasmine Duong. © Kendall Hunt Publishing Company.

65th Street Corridor Community Collaborative Project logo.
Source: Aury Gutierrez-Zavala and Lucy Tran-Ruelas.

times at the Book Club field trip for Esperanza Rising! I recently saw Griselda and she told me this story: She is now working at American River College as a part-time counselor and had a meeting with an American River student, a girl named Samantha. When Samantha walked into Griselda's office she looked right at Griselda and said, "I know you! You used to be a tutor in Mrs. Ledbetter's History class! I remember you telling us about how you got to college!"

You see, Dr. Mark—the 65th project you created years ago doesn't just affect the students in my classes, but sometimes affects the lives of the tutors even more, in life changing ways. It has been my privilege to be associated with 65th for such a long time. It has given me the chance to see my middle schoolers grow up to become college students and I don't think a teacher could ask for any better reward than that one.

Thanks again for all you do.

Respectfully yours,
Deborah Ledbetter

The 65th Street Corridor Community Collaborative Project (65th Street Corridor) has been an integral component of the Sacramento State Ethnic Studies (ES) Department as the department's community service branch. In fall 2001, Dr. Gregory Yee Mark founded the 65th Street Corridor Project upon the original principle that Ethnic Studies should be rooted in service to the community and community-based research. In 2021, it celebrated its 20th year of service.

The Beginning ... as Remembered by Gregory Yee Mark

The beginning for me started with my friend, Maurice Williams coming to see me at the January 9, 1969 *Asian Experience in America: Yellow Identity*

Symposium. He said to me, "We met last night, we're going out, are you with us?" In other words, the previous night the Black Student Union (BSU) met and decided that they were going out on strike because the UC Berkeley administration would not approve Black Studies courses. Would the Asian American students go out on strike with the Black students? A week later, on the Berkeley campus, the Third World Liberation Front (TWLF) was established; it was a coalition comprised primarily of Black, Asian American, Chicano, and Native American students, supported by some faculty and staff.

The TWLF Strike started on January 19, 1969. I went "On Strike" due to four founding principles.

1. United States history had to be reinterpreted and retold to include people of color.
2. Ethnic Studies should explore and educate people about their racial and ethnic identities.
3. Ethnic Studies should fight for social change to create a more just society.
4. Ethnic Studies should be an integral part of the community and therefore should be directly involved with community service and community-based research.

The Fight for Ethnic Studies

Sacramento State was highly impacted by the two Third World Liberation Front Strikes at San Francisco State College (now University) and University of California, Berkeley. As a result, in 1970, Sac State created the Center for Ethnic Studies which later evolved into the Department of Ethnic Studies (ES). Professor Wayne Maeda, the original Asian American Studies faculty member who taught for 43 years, recalled in 2011 that

> *Beginning an Ethnic Studies program, hiring faculty, developing curriculum and the general demand for fundamental change at the campus level was made infinitely less confrontational by enormous sacrifices of students and faculty at both SF State and UC Berkeley. Moreover, they provided us models for classes, curriculum, and they even came to Sac State to provide guidance and inspiration to us. Thus, we were able to institute the first Asian American course in the fall 1970, which was team-taught.*

Service to the Community

Fifty-two years ago, the previously mentioned four founding principles laid the foundation for the new academic discipline, Ethnic Studies. The student strikes at San Francisco State and the UC Berkeley were new, unique, revolutionary, and creative. Much of the impetus was the idealism of the 1960s forged through the Civil Rights, Anti-War, and Farmworkers' movements. These movements, coupled with a generation of students of color, helped push the door slightly open to create a more relevant education, and a culture of community service.

The 65th Street Corridor Community Collaboration Project

(By Gregory Yee Mark)

In fall 2001, in the spirit that led to the early development of Ethnic Studies, interested faculty at Sacramento State developed three general community service project goals for the 65th Street Corridor Project. They were (1) to bridge university resources and community needs; (2) to serve underrepresented and disadvantaged groups; and (3) to address emerging community issues such as racial and ethnic identity for the community's youth, and to improve intra- and intergroup relations.

Given available University resources and students' schedules, I felt the best high impact project should be with neighboring "in need" schools. I met with three Sacramento City Unified School District high school principals, and I decided on Hiram Johnson High School (referred to as Hiram Johnson or HJHS or HJ). In initial meetings with Hiram Johnson administrators and a few teachers, most of the ES faculty were present, and, as a result, it fostered a deeper sense of department solidarity, purpose, and support for the partnership. The vision of service was never meant to be random shot in the dark but a systematic comprehensive Ethnic Studies Department taking a strong leadership role to mobilize the 65th Street Corridor community. In this way, the university itself becomes a more viable part of this community and consequently a stronger anchor in the Sacramento region.

Hiram Johnson High School

My name is Michael Washington, a social science teacher at Hiram Johnson for the past 16 years. Hiram Johnson is located in South Sacramento and is represented by a very dynamic population that has its challenges but also it many strengths. One of our great campus and community attributes is our cultural diversity. When our school district made Ethnic Studies a graduation requirement nearly three years ago, we saw this as an opportunity to connect our students' backgrounds, past, present, and future experiences with everyday curriculum in Ethnic Studies. The course was constructed with help by the CSUS Ethnic Studies Department and uses its major concepts for the one semester course for 9th grade students. It was a no brainer when the opportunity arose for Hiram Johnson to partner with the Ethnic Studies department once again this past school year.

—Michael Washington

In November 2001, Sac State ES faculty interested in developing the community service project met with the HJHS principal Andre Duyon and discussed possible collaborative projects. The staff developed a 9th grade Ethnic Studies course.

Manisha Sims, teacher at Hiram Johnson High School, in her Ethnic Studies course.

Source: © Manisha Sims, 2021.

Part of Duyon's rationale was if 9th graders were to learn more about their own selves, their community histories, and about their fellow students, then the high school would benefit from having them for the next four years as more motivated and higher achieving students.

A pivotal part of the project's success was high school students taking an Ethnic Studies course with university Ethnic Studies students working with them who knew the material, and would have insight into what high schoolers would benefit the most from curriculum development and later providing tutorial services. Principal Duyon assigned a young teacher, James Fabionar, who had graduated from Hiram Johnson High School and was an Asian American studies major at the University of California, San Diego. James accepted the assignment, and by spring 2002, he worked with 12 Sac State Ethnic Studies students to create the course curriculum, which was implemented in fall 2002.

Expanding the Project and Creating Partnerships

In our partnership with Hiram Johnson, Principal Duyon introduced the 65th Street Corridor staff to the Health Start Program (today known as the Wellness Program). In spring 2002, Healthy Start was planning to do a community survey. During that spring semester, the Ethnic Studies 194 class, "Research in Ethnic Studies," utilized their knowledge learned in conducting the Healthy Start survey. That day, the team (of which Sac State students were 60%) completed 359 in person surveys in eight different languages. The main survey findings of what they thought were community social problems fell into two primary categories: (1) drinking/drugs and (2) fighting/violence. In addition, the Sac State ES194 students conducted focus groups with locals, and the findings were similar to the survey results.

After the first semester of the HJHS Ethnic Studies class, the principal identified an important student need. To improve academic performance, the principal proposed to me a tutoring/mentoring program for his students. Hence, in spring 2002, the 65th Street Corridor Project began a Hiram Johnson tutoring/mentoring program in math, science, English, and Ethnic Studies classes. From fall 2002 to spring 2018, over 12,000 Hiram Johnson students were tutored and mentored by 1100 65th Street Corridor Tutor/Mentors.

Through these expansions, the efficacy of the 65th Street Corridor Project was improving, and we could turn our attention to creating a full "corridor" by looking towards the middle school system.

Will C. Wood Middle School

In 2002, Jim Wong, the Will C. Wood Middle School principal, proposed expanding the 65th Street Corridor Tutoring/Mentoring project to his school. Between 2002 and 2021, approximately 12,000 WCW students have been tutored/mentored (2002–2018). In addition, 820 Sac State students have participated in the WCW 65th Street Corridor projects.

In addition, the following year Mr. Wong proposed a "conference/field trip" (2003) to Sac State for Will C. Wood parents, many of whom were recent immigrants with little western education. Many of these parents were Southeast Asians from the mountains of Laos, Vietnam, Thailand, and Cambodia, and had never set foot on a university campus. The conference and field trip(s) to Sac State gave these and other parents an introduction to an institution of higher learning and they were encouraged to view college as a viable future pathway for their children.

Professional Development

Since its inception, the project has stressed professional development. Primarily, Ethnic Studies faculty members and 65th Street Corridor student staff were encouraged to present about the collaborative partnership at major regional, national, and international conferences. When possible, at these meetings, faculty attended training workshops and conducted them as well. From 2016 to the present, project faculty have conducted nine Ethnic Studies curriculum development workshops of which most have focused upon the Sacramento City Unified School District and neighboring district teachers.

Between the years 2002 and 2019, faculty and students presented at 25 conferences ranging from Sac State's annual multicultural conferences to Hong Kong

(2013, Asia-Pacific Regional Conference on Service-Learning Hong Kong), to Taiwan (2015, Asia-Pacific Regional Conference on Service-Learning in Taipei's, Fu Jen University), to the East coast cities such as New York (2002, NCORE) Miami (2010, NCORE), and, of course, Hawai'i (2014 & 2022, International Education Conference).

Additional benefits for the Ethnic Studies department itself have been strengthening faculty and student morale and accelerating the team-building process.

Students

In order to maximize Sac State student growth and leadership, it was imperative to build community among ourselves as colleagues, and also build community where professors empower and provide ES students with professional development opportunities. The 65th Street Corridor Project Ethnic Studies faculty consciously worked towards creating a partnership with students that placed value on their work and contributions. Simultaneously, the faculty made concerted efforts to nurture student growth, especially their leadership skills. Here are some things previous staff members have to say about working with the project.

> The greatest impact the 65th Street Corridor Project has had on me has definitely been my personal growth and professional development. I had the best support and guidance from the 65th Street Corridor faculty, which encouraged me to pursue higher education and I was able to, be accepted into the master's program in counseling at Sacramento State. I also had the wonderful opportunity to present at the National Association for Ethnic Studies Conference in New Orleans (2013) and the 4th Asia-Pacific Regional Conference on Service-Learning in Hong Kong (2015). It was life changing and it helped me view the world with different lenses, those of colorful, meaningful, and creative experiences that have helped shape who I am.
>
> —Aury G. Gutierrez-Zavala

> Being a part of the 65th Street Project's community mobilization efforts have definitely provided me with professional development, personal growth, and leadership skills, which I continue to utilize in my career as a multicultural counselor, advocate, and educator for first-generation and underserved/under-represented students at UC Davis.
>
> —Aury G. Gutierrez-Zavala

Developing Leadership

The leadership program focuses on assisting first-generation college students, many of whom come from low-income families, with their campus experience during their first two years. A faculty member teaches a course designed for migrant students new to university life, form, and functions, and focuses on assisting students with making a successful transition to the university (Kim-Ju, 2011). Another faculty member offers community project opportunities such as those that will be discussed later, and for the highly self-motivated students, they have the opportunity to move on to leadership positions such as coordinators in the 65th Street Corridor Projects. These student staffers lead orientations and training sessions, hold reflection sessions for student volunteers, manage on-site supervision, and make presentations at professional conferences.

The Present

The 65th Street Corridor Project initiated the original Tutoring/Mentoring Project at HJHS, WCW and at for three years at Nicholas Elementary School. During its 16 years of operation (2002–2018), over 19,000 public school students and 1300 Sac State students participated in this project.

Currently, the 65th Street Corridor Community Collaborative Project operates four programs. At Will C. Wood there are three projects: The Ethnic Studies History Project, Will C. Wood Field Trips (2), and the 8th Grade Ethnic Studies course. At Hiram Johnson High School, the primary project is the Ethnic Studies Tutoring/Mentorship Program. In 2022, a new school site will begin to implement 65th Street Corridor Projects.

Ethnic Studies History Project

(By Gregory Yee Mark, Jasmine Duong, and Jazmine Sanchez)

I am Jasmine Duong, another coordinator for the ESHP. I joined the 65th project in fall 2020 because I wanted to gain experience with speaking to middle school students. The goal and narrative of the project spoke to my own interests. More specifically, I wanted to share my own experience with pursuing higher education as a first generation Asian American and my backstory as the child of Vietnamese refugees. I noticed students who were of similar ethnic backgrounds were more interested in my story. I mentioned the reasons why my parents pushed me to pursue higher education, such as having a comfortable life in the long term, as well as finding an occupation that made me feel fulfilled.

Being a presenter for WCW students was quite a fulfilling experience. Each time I presented, I was reminded of the reason why I chose to pursue higher education. All the hardships and experiences I had within academia was discussed throughout the presentations. Rather than ignoring the results of my mistakes, I emphasized the importance of learning from them. I feel that the project reaffirmed my passion for learning, as well as working with K through 12 students. Ultimately, my goal was to have the students understand that higher education is accessible and an exciting journey to pursue."

—Jasmine Duong

I am Jazmine Sanchez, and I have been a coordinator for the ESHP since fall 2020. I joined the 65th Street Corridor because I wanted to gain experience with public speaking and was excited about the opportunity for professional development. As a part of 65th Street Corridor, I oversaw the training and participated in the Ethnic Studies History Project at Will C. Wood Middle School. Being closer in age to the students allowed the students to feel more connected to the content. I told the students about my journey to college and being a first gen student, and the struggles I faced.

One of my main roles in the project was collecting data from each class. The data includes rating the presenter, feedback about the project, and the race/ ethnicity of the child taking the survey. We also learned that the presentations were highly praised by the students and the kids really felt a connection with our presenters."

—Jazmine Sanchez

The Ethnic Studies History Project started in 2016. It is a biannual program for students at Will C. Wood Middle School to encourage them to attend university by celebrating the diversity of the Sac State campus. During 50-minute periods, one or two Sac State students give presentations on their families and ethnic histories, while tying in their own journey towards higher education. The purpose of the project is twofold: firstly, to create connections with students coming from diverse backgrounds and introduce them to the concept of ethnicity and Ethnic Studies, and secondly, to encourage them to pursue higher education, which has statistically seen less admissions from students who identify as racial or ethnic minorities.

Each semester since its inception, presentations have been made to 10 to 15 classes, in which there are about 30 students in each class. For the spring semester of 2021, presentations were given to 360 7th and 8th graders at Will C. Wood. The response from the middle schoolers, teachers, faculty, and Sac State volunteers have been overwhelmingly positive every semester.

Student Staff

When middle school students were invited to hone in on their family history through The Ethnic Studies History Project, students became historians rediscovering, reconnect, and reorienting themselves with the way the experience their elders, what it meant for their families to secure a better life as a form of education. From a student perspective, this was also an invaluable learning to have Sac State student come into their classroom and share their journey into higher education as well as their family backgrounds. Being engaged and engaging this experience, overall, opened the doors to be more hopeful about the future.

WCW Teacher Testimony

The opportunity to pause and think is very powerful. Being able to reflect allows for students to be present in the moment. For example, I witnessed a student thinking calculating the number of years it would take for her to complete college beyond completing middle school. This project may never fully understand how many lives they've changed for future generations to come. We will always be thankful. The investment of time in youth always pays off.

Middle School Student

#1 testimony: Grateful is the word that best describes feeling connected to the project. Listening to a presenter who shared my enthusiasm for art was great! Graduating and applying to Sac State is my goal.

Middle School Student

#2 testimony: Having the presenter clearly explain the pathway to college was incredibly helpful. With this information, I realize college is a realistic option for me. With the discussion on financial aid, I realize that it would be affordable too! It was a great experience to be given this information.

Middle School Student

#3 testimony: It was great to hear from the presenter that you don't have to rich to go to college, you just need a plan. Knowing I can still be successful even though I'm low-income was a relief. I realize anything is truly possible if you remain hopeful and ask questions along the way. I liked how both presenters had nothing like me, yet were able to pursue and succeed in college.

Will C. Wood Field Trips

(By Julie López Figueroa)

In the past, 65th Street Corridor also supported two annual Will C. Wood field trips, namely, the Parent/Student field trip and Book Club field trips. The field trips were anchored in the idea of promoting college awareness and readiness.

The field trips at Will C. Wood were first initiated by Principal Jim Wong in 2004. Given his tremendous respect for the families and students he served, I was invited as the Field Trip Coordinator and I was joined by a couple of 65th Street Corridor student staff to attend a couple of monthly parent meetings. A diverse group of parents from different cultural, linguistic, and racial backgrounds were gathered in one room. With the support of Sac State and Will C. Wood translators and translation devices, we hosted on average 100 parents in different rooms in the University Union. We invited our University President, the Dean of the College of Social Sciences, and the Chair of the Ethnic Studies Department to welcome Parents to the campus and to the day. The presence and visibility of the administration signaled to Parents they were valued and important to our university. For many parents, attending the Parent Fieldtrip would be the first time on a university campus.

Will C. Wood Book Club Field Trip.
Source: © Aury Gutierrez-Zavala.

When Ms. Ledbetter, a teacher that served as the faculty advisor for the Book Club, reached out to see if we could consider hosting the Book Club on campus, Dr. Mark and I were eager to say yes. Over the last ten years, the Book Club Field Trip rotates in its themes. These field trips are also about reinforcing a college going culture. Again, we rely on the 65th Street Corridor Staff, tutor/mentor, and Sacramento State students.

Our capacity to exceed parents' expectations happened not just because of the activities, but also because we partnered with different units on campus that shared our vision. At the University level, we are thankful to to Office of the President, Student Affairs, and the College of Social Sciences and Interdisciplinary Studies. We are so thankful to our campus family located in Admissions and Outreach, College Assistance Migrant Program (CAMP), Cooper Woodson, Educational Opportunity Program (EOP), Financial Aid, Housing Office, University Library, *Sac State's Parents* & Families Program, and The Well. Aside from the various offices on campus, we were always so grateful to the 65th Street Corridor student staff and the 65th Street Corridor Student Tutor/Mentors. I want to especially thank the sisters of Sigma Pi Alpha, Inc. who made the 65th Street Corridor their philanthropy. Beyond this sorority, there were also other student organizations that generously sent their members to volunteer for our field trips.

We have proudly served Will C. Wood through fieldtrips for 17 years and will continue to do so to the best of our abilities. The 65th Street Corridor Project fulfills one of the tenets of Ethnic Studies, which is practicing cultural humility and working in partnership with community to lift up the community.

(By Gregory Yee Mark)

The Tutoring/Mentoring Project utilizes CSUS Ethnic Studies student majors, who tutor and mentor Hiram Johnson students enrolled in the school's Ethnic Studies classes. In October 2016, Governor Jerry Brown signed AB 2016 which required California high schools to offer Ethnic Studies curriculum. At Hiram Johnson High School this led directly to the school's implementation of Ethnic Studies courses. Due to the long-standing collaboration between the high school and the 65th Street Corridor Project, Michael Washington, an Ethnic Studies teacher at Hiram Johnson, requested a tutoring/mentoring project which has led to Sac State ES majors contributing to strengthen the high school's ES classes.

In the shortened spring 2020 semester, 14 of the 39 enrolled Ethnic Studies majors from ES 195A, "Ethnic Studies Field Work," took part in the tutoring program. Besides making a significant difference to the high school students, this project provides a good vehicle to further institutionalize service to the community into the Ethnic Studies university curriculum.

Student staff

As a tutor, it was great experience and challenging experience to supplement the teacher's lessons by translating material as a college student to high school students, especially around the topic of Ethnic Studies. Teaching something you learned to someone else requires a skill level that what I was not use to as a college student. Working with the students, though, inspired me to become an Ethnic Studies teacher at the K-12 grade.

High School Teacher

When tutors introduced themselves, shared their background and explained why Hiram Johnson was their school of choice, students were open and receptive. The tutors were always supportive and open shared advice with the goal of inspiring 14- to 15-year-old teenagers. While Hiram Johnsons students can be very skeptical of folks with genuine intentions, they immediately responded to the Sac State Tutors. Asking for help and support with their classwork was not an issue. Having tutors in the room to support student learning was really powerful for our students. The impact of this engagement between Sac State tutors and our students led to improvements of grades this semester in Ethnic Studies.

Will C. Wood 8th Grade Ethnic Studies Course 2020-2021

(By Gregory Yee Mark and Christopher Shimizu)

The newest initiated project is the 8th Grade Ethnic Studies course at Will C. Wood Middle School. Tuan Duong, the principal of Will C. Wood, introduced

Michelle Romero-Jimenez to the 65th Street Corridor Project. She had proposed the new ES course due to her observations and interactions with her students, who wanted to learn more about themselves and their classmates' diverse cultures and histories.

The project is one of the first Ethnic Studies programs at the middle school level in the country. It started in fall 2020 and was received positively by the students and Ms. Jimenez. The first class of 24 students had an ethnographic breakdown of nine Hispanic/Latino students, ten Asian students, two Native Hawaiian/Pacific Islander students, one White student, and two students that identified with more than one race.

This new ES course has brought an important element to the University's Ethnic Studies *Corridor Vision*. This 65th Street Corridor partnership starts with the Department of Ethnic Studies majors, who will tutor/mentor high school students. At the same time, the Sac State students get the practical experience and provide service to the community. In turn, the high school students will present their term papers to WCW students with emphasis on the 8th grade ES class. Then the 8th graders will do presentations at their feeder elementary schools. Thus, the vision of a pathway goes both ways along the corridor where all can learn from each other.

Strengthening the Vision

On February 7, 2020, a meeting was held to mobilize the three neighboring education tiers. This included Ethnic Studies faculty and 65th Street Corridor student staff. Hiram Johnson High School representatives were administration including the school's principal, and the high school's Ethnic Studies faculty. Will C. Wood cosponsored the meeting led by the school's principal and two teachers.

A major outcome was for the 65th Street Corridor partners to continue to work in unison, to communicate, to be transparent, and to strengthen a seamless journey for all students up and down the corridor.

This pathway starts at the university and goes five miles south to the heart of Little Saigon at 65th and Stockton Blvd. Just like the journey to learn about our own histories, to fight for social justice for all, to be proud of our racial/ethnic identities, and to provide for service wherever it is needed: there will be potholes, red lights, yellow lights, green lights, right turns, and left turns but we will go straight ahead one block at a time, creating a corridor that starts with us and ends with the generations that will follow.

Concluding Remarks

Student Staff

Because the 65th Street Corridor is deeply rooted in community mobilization and civic engagement, it is poised to help make a significant impact in the lives of underserved and underrepresented students, currently, and for future generations.

Historically, many Ethnic Studies programs were developed because of student and community involvement and participation. Scholars have pointed out the historical divergence of faculty, students, and community, and the intent is to bridge that gap by engaging in community service that requires the support of all three components.

Despite the COVID-19 outbreak, the 65th Street Corridor Community Collaborative Project has actually expanded and flourished with two new programs that fit well with the project's vision. For the past 52 years, Ethnic Studies has been largely centered in higher education, and fairly recently in high schools. With the 65th Street Corridor Project's pioneering work at the middle school level, we are building a model for what Ethnic Studies curriculum and community outreach can look like. This, coupled with Will C. Wood's yearlong 8th grade Ethnic Studies course, can provide by example of what can be done with a truly collaborative partnership between a major university and neighboring public schools.

The Sacramento State Ethnic Studies model of education and community mobilization has been successful, and it has demonstrated how to be inclusive of student participation, serving the needs of ethnic communities and organizing them to address pressing social issues. This model brings Ethnic Studies back to its roots of student and community involvement.

One of the best gifts this program offers has to be when students serve as role models by publicly speaking about their personal life journeys. When students speak about their histories, struggles and show their vulnerability, that grabbed every 9th grade students' full attention. There is so much more we hope to do with this partnership with Sac State. We are so compelled to extend the program on our campus but the entire 65th Street Corridor community. We are excited about this program for our students and South Sacramento.

—Hiram Johnson High School Teacher

Reflection Questions

1. In your view, how much do context and politics define the human condition? (Optional)

2. To what degree do you believe these readings demonstrate a response and/or responsibility? (Optional)

3. Of the readings in this section, was there one reading in particular that you believed to be most effective in demonstrating response and responsibility given your own background? Please identify the reading and provide a brief explanation for your selection.

4. What are your personal examples that illustrate your own response and responsibility? (Optional)

5. Given the readings, what kind of person does it take to be responsive and responsible when it comes to creating positive race relations? Please offer a brief explanation using two examples to illustrate your point.

CPSIA information can be obtained
at www.ICGtesting.com
Printed in the USA
BVHW020757071222
653601BV00001B/1

9 781792 458385